POLLUTION AND CRISIS IN
GREEK TRAGEDY

Pollution is ubiquitous in Greek tragedy: matricidal Orestes seeks purification at Apollo's shrine in Delphi; carrion from Polyneices' unburied corpse fills the altars of Thebes; delirious Phaedra suffers from a 'pollution of the mind'. This book undertakes the first detailed analysis of the important role that pollution and its counterparts – purity and purification – play in tragedy. It argues that pollution is central in the negotiation of tragic crises, fulfilling a diverse array of functions by virtue of its qualities and associations, from making sense of adversity to configuring civic identity in the encounter of self and other. While primarily a literary study providing close readings of several key plays, the book also provides important new perspectives on pollution. It will appeal to a broad range of scholars and students, not only in Classics and literary studies, but also in the study of religions and anthropology.

FABIAN MEINEL is an affiliated researcher at the Centre Paul-Albert Février, Aix-en-Provence (Université d'Aix-Marseille, CNRS, TDMAM-UMR 7297).

POLLUTION AND CRISIS IN GREEK TRAGEDY

FABIAN MEINEL

Centre Paul-Albert Février, Aix-en-Provence
(Université d'Aix-Marseille, CNRS, TDMAM-UMR 7297)

CAMBRIDGE
UNIVERSITY PRESS

University Printing House, Cambridge CB2 8BS, United Kingdom

Cambridge University Press is part of the University of Cambridge.

It furthers the University's mission by disseminating knowledge in the pursuit of education, learning and research at the highest international levels of excellence.

www.cambridge.org
Information on this title: www.cambridge.org/9781107044463

© Fabian Meinel 2015

This publication is in copyright. Subject to statutory exception and to the provisions of relevant collective licensing agreements, no reproduction of any part may take place without the written permission of Cambridge University Press.

First published 2015

Printed in the United States of America by Sheridan Books, Inc.

A catalogue record for this publication is available from the British Library

Library of Congress Cataloguing in Publication data
Meinel, Fabian, 1982– author.
Pollution and Crisis in Greek Tragedy / Fabian Meinel; Centre Paul-Albert Février, Aix-en-Provence.
pages cm
Includes bibliographical references and index.
ISBN 978-1-107-04446-3
1. Greek drama (Tragedy) 2. Pollution – Religious aspects. I. Title.
PA3131.M395   2015
882'.0109 – dc23   2014037958

ISBN 978-1-107-04446-3 Hardback

Cambridge University Press has no responsibility for the persistence or accuracy of URLs for external or third-party internet websites referred to in this publication, and does not guarantee that any content on such websites is, or will remain, accurate or appropriate.

To my family,
   the recently deceased and the newly born

> ... on the sand,
> Half sunk, a shattered visage lies, whose frown,
> And wrinkled lip, and sneer of cold command,
> Tell that its sculptor well those passions read
> Which yet survive, stamped on these lifeless things ...
> (Percy Shelley, *Ozymandias*)

Contents

Preface and acknowledgements	*page* ix
Note on the text and translations	xi
Abbreviations	xii

	Introduction	1
	Plays with pollution	1
	Backdrops	3
	Tragedy and crisis	6
	Pollution, crisis, tragedy	8
	Texts and contexts	13
	The plot	15
1	Pollution, interpretation and understanding	18
	Euripides' *Hippolytus*	21
	A journey inwards: Sophocles' *Oedipus tyrannus*	46
2	Pollution and the stability of civic space	74
	Law and stability and ancient Greece	76
	Pollution and civic stability	82
	Sophocles' *Antigone*	84
3	Evaluation and stability in Aeschylus' *Oresteia*	114
	Part I: evaluation, justice, pollution	117
	Part II: stability and justice	127
	Appendix: pollution, purification and release	135
	Excursus: rereading the *Oresteia*: Euripides' *Iphigenia among the Taurians*	140
	Release and purification in *Iphigenia among the Taurians* and the *Oresteia*	147
	Pollution, purification and release	153
	Metatheatre, rewriting and the question of release	161

4	Pollution, purity and civic identity	172
	Purity, space and civic identity	175
	Ethnic purity and identity	182
	Aeschylus' *Suppliants*	186
	Sophoclean variations: excursus to Colonus	205
	Euripides' *Ion*	212
	Envoi	244

Bibliography 247
Index locorum 268
General index 273

Preface and acknowledgements

Pollution has a way of sticking with you. It's certainly exciting in view of the subject matters that usually come with it. Ancient Greece is no exception. We enter a strangely beguiling world here, far removed from the 'noble simplicity and quiet grandeur' Winckelmann once found embodied in Greek sculpture. Instead of solemn white marble, we encounter the gaudy universe of murder and violence, sex and death, blood and demons. Instead of mighty Laocoön, a muted sigh of fortitude on his lips as he suffers intolerable pain, we encounter Theophrastus' endearingly eccentric 'Superstitious Man', who will not go near a woman in childbirth, for fear of pollution.

Greek tragedy's pollution has, in my case, proved particularly adhesive. To be sure, tragedy is often 'grand', though never 'simple'; the pollution we encounter in it adds, if you will, that touch of the exotic and eccentric. Not that this is in general something to be smiled at. Tragic pollution is often frightening and disturbing. Polluted Oedipus brings the plague to Thebes and 'woes beyond reckoning'; Polyneices' disintegrating corpse spreads pollution, and with it an atmosphere that even for the armchair academic, safe and sound in his cosy lair, feels suffocating. It's oddly fascinating, all the more attractive for its uncanniness.

The strange fascination of (tragic) pollution certainly goes some way towards explaining the origins of this book (though you will find that it has very little to do with 'feelings' and 'atmospheres'). Its existence, however, is owed to the powers, not of horror, but of inspired teaching, sage guidance and friendship. This book is the revised version of a PhD dissertation submitted at Freie Universität Berlin. First thanks accordingly go to my 'Doktormutter' Renate Schlesier. Her support in every endeavour and perspicuous academic advice are one thing; quite another the model she has provided as the forever caring, rigorous, untiring and formidably learned poet-scholar that she is.

Others have directly contributed. I had the great pleasure to work with Albert Henrichs during a year as a Visiting Fellow at Harvard University. His enthusiasm was truly contagious; I never left any of our extended lunch (or dinner) reunions without having discovered afresh the beauty of tragedy. Robin Osborne has been extremely generous in sharing his insights on a variety of matters and read various parts of the manuscript; his own work has been an inspiration in the depth and breadth of its inquiry. Bernd Seidensticker, the second examiner of the dissertation, read, and commented on, the manuscript with great care and to my profit; so did the anonymous readers for Cambridge University Press, who suggested valuable improvements. It goes without saying that I take full responsibility for remaining mistakes and idiosyncrasies of interpretation.

Less direct, though no less important, has been the influence of a number of teachers during formative years at Gymnasium Fridericianum Erlangen; and thereafter at Corpus Christi College, Cambridge, where I benefited from the wisdom and support of several individuals. In particular I would like to extend heartfelt thanks to Barrie Fleet, who has lastingly deepened my love of the classical languages (and of sparkling wine); Neil Hopkinson, whose supervisions in the Clock Tower of Trinity – fireplace, sherry and all – will not be forgotten; and Christopher Kelly, for his unflagging support and friendship.

Cambridge University Press' Michael Sharp, Gillian Dadd and Jodie Hodgson have been a pleasure to work with and I thank all three for masterfully guiding me through the process of turning a PhD manuscript into a book. My copy-editor Nigel Hope deserves a similar eulogy: his expert proficiency has continually amazed me and saved me from a number of minor and major embarrassments. I should like to take the opportunity also to thank the German Academic Exchange Service (DAAD) for their contribution to my stay at Harvard; and the Fondation Hardt in Vandœuvres/Geneva for a research scholarship: the weeks there were unforgettable and I would like to thank Monica and Heidi for their hospitality and Alcione, Anna, Antonio, Bob, Christiane, Marella, Marilena, Margherita and Wytse for their company.

My final nod is to friends and family. Nicolas Wiater has been an important source of wisdom; Anja, Codruţa, Simon and Torsten important sources of (in)sanity. Nick Dodd has not only been a best pal, but also a diligent reader of the entire typescript. My family deserves the concluding note. Their love and support are beyond words. With the greatest humility, therefore: thank you.

Note on the text and translations

In the case of citations from tragedy, the Greek text usually follows the editions in the Oxford Classical Texts series. Translations of tragic passages are mostly my own, often following existing translations and in particular the Loeb translations of Alan Sommerstein (Aeschylus), Hugh Lloyd-Jones (Sophocles) and David Kovacs (Euripides). Other translations I have consulted include the *Oresteia* translations of Christopher Collard (Oxford, 2002) and Alan Shapiro and Peter Burian (New York and Oxford, 2003) as well as the translations offered in the Aris & Phillips Classical Texts series (especially in the case of Euripides).

Abbreviations

For ancient authors and their works the abbreviations in H. G. Liddell, R. Scott and H. S. Jones, *Greek—English Lexicon with a revised supplement*, 9th edn (Oxford, 1996) have been followed. In a number of cases, however, the abbreviations adopted here diverge. Thus, for Demosthenes I use Dem. (rather than D.); for Euripides Eur. (rather than E.); and for Thucydides Thuc. (rather than Th.). For the plays of Aeschylus' *Oresteia* I have adopted *Ag.* (for *Agamemnon*), *Choe.* (for *Choephori*) and *Eum.* (for *Eumenides*).

Abbreviations of periodicals are those recommended in *L'Année philologique*.

Otherwise the following may be noted:

FGrHist	F. Jacoby, *Die Fragmente der griechischen Historiker* (Berlin, 1923–58)
Kahn	C. H. Kahn, *The art and thought of Heraclitus. An edition of the fragments with translation and commentary* (Cambridge, 1979)
LSCG	F. Sokolowski, *Lois sacrées des cités grecques* (Paris 1969)
LSJ	H. G. Liddell, R. Scottand H. S. Jones, *Greek—English Lexicon with a revised supplement*, 9th edn (Oxford, 1996)
LSS	F. Sokolowski, *Lois sacrées des cités grecques. Supplement* (Paris, 1962)
ML	R. Meiggs and D. M. Lewis, *A selection of Greek historical inscriptions to the end of the fifth century* BC (Oxford, 1969)
MW	R. Merkelbach, M. L. West, *Hesiodi Theogonia; Opera et Dies; Scutum*, 3rd edn (Oxford, 1990)
PMG	D. L. Page, *Poetae melici Graeci* (Oxford, 1962)
RO	P. J. Rhodes and R. Osborne, *Greek historical inscriptions 404–323* BC (Oxford, 2003)

SEG	*Supplementum epigraphicum graecum* (1923–)
Smyth	H. W. Smyth, *Greek grammar*, rev. by G. M. Messing, Cambridge, MA. (1980)
SM	B. Snell and H. Maehler, *Pindarus. Carmina cum fragmentis*, 2 vols., 8th edn (Leipzig, 1987–9)
TrGF	B. Snell, R. Kannicht and S. Radt, *Tragicorum graecorum fragmenta* (Göttingen, 1971–)
West	M. L. West, *Delectus ex iambis et elegis Graecis* (Oxford, 1980)
Σ	Scholion

Introduction

Plays with pollution

For structural anthropologists, who after neurotics are those most obsessed with purity and impurity, pollution may have to do with 'matter out of place'.[1] In the Athenian tragedies of the fifth century BC, staged each year within the framework of the City Dionysia and in a theatre purified for these purposes by city officials called *peristiarchoi*,[2] pollution is anything but 'out of place'. In Greek tragedy, pollution is ubiquitous and central. Even the most casual reader of tragedy – or theatregoer – will readily remember, perhaps with a sense of unease, some of the plays' haunting images: the spectacularly visual blood and gore of Aeschylus' *Oresteia*, with its blood-dripping, polluted protagonists, from Agamemnon, sacrificer of his daughter, to Clytemnestra, husband-slayer, to Orestes, the matricide pursued by Erinyes (so horrid in the original performance that, as legend has it, terrified women miscarried in the theatre)[3] and seeking refuge and purification at Apollo's shrine in Delphi; the plague of Sophocles' *Oedipus tyrannus* and its apparent cause, wretched Oedipus, 'pollution of the land', murderer of his father and bedfellow of his mother; or the pollution exuding from Polyneices' corpse in *Antigone*. Hardly less prominent is pollution in some of the most beloved of Euripides' plays, from *Medea* and *Heracles*, with their child-slaying protagonists, to *Hippolytus*, in which we encounter, besides well-known types of murder- and death-pollution, the curious notion of a mind (Phaedra's) 'polluted' as the result of errant erotic desire. Notions of purity and attempts at purification are paramount, too. Indeed,

---

[1] Douglas (1966) 35 speaks of dirt as matter out of place (following Lord Chesterfield's dictum); this definition of dirt is central to her understanding of pollution.
[2] On these *peristiarchoi*, see Σ Aeschin. 1.23; *Suda* s.v. καθάρσιον; Pollux 8.104; see also Cole (2004) 48.
[3] So the *Life of Aeschylus* tells us: see Page's OCT of Aeschylus, 332.10–13.

the concepts of pollution and purity are absent only from [Aeschylus']
Prometheus and Sophocles' *Philoctetes*.[4]

The ubiquity of pollution (but also of purity and purification) is a distinctive feature of tragedy. No other genre, neither in the fifth century nor before, displays a similar obsession with this thematic nexus. Should this baffle us and make us wonder why? One is tempted to answer, flatly, in the negative. Tragedy, after all, regularly deals in murder and death, and pollution is closely connected with both: the prominence of pollution in tragedy, we may conclude, is simply the result of its preferred subject matter.[5] And yet: it may well be that the ubiquity of pollution in tragedy has much to do with the ubiquity of murder and death in tragedy. But is there perhaps more to it than simply being the by-product of the preferred subject matter?

We may proceed from this avowal of wonder and curiosity by doing a bit of matter-of-fact history. It has often been noted that Homer is silent on murder- and death-pollution.[6] Even though the idea of pollution, to us, as children of the Enlightenment, would seem to represent something very ancient, a sign perhaps of 'primitive thought', historical evidence suggests that pollution became a real issue only after Homer (assuming the traditional dating of Homer to the eighth century BC). The first recorded purification from murder-pollution occurs in the *Aethiopis* of Arctinus of Miletus, dating roughly from the middle of the seventh century BC.[7] Incidentally, lustral basins begin to appear in the archaeological record around the same time, marking an important step in the organisation of civic space.[8] The first written laws likewise date from this period, around 650 BC.[9]

One way to interpret this evidence would be to postulate that the increasing importance of pollution, suggested *ex negativo* by the increasing

---

[4] In all but these two plays as well as Sophocles' *Ajax*, the presence of the concepts of pollution and purity is reflected in the presence of μια- and καθαρ-words. In Sophocles' *Ajax*, the protagonist speaks, more vaguely, of λύματα, which require ἁγνίζειν (λύμαθ' ἁγνίσας ἐμά, 655). On this purification and its overtones of Orphic-Eleusinian eschatology, see Krummen (1998) 301–16.

[5] This is the conclusion reached by Parker (1983) 16 in the case of tragic murder-pollution.

[6] Dodds (1951) 35–50 (part of the chapter in which Dodds formulates his famous view of the development from a 'shame culture' to a 'guilt culture'); Moulinier (1952) 58–61; Lloyd-Jones (1983²) 70–8; Parker (1983) 66–70, 130–43; Hoessly (2001) 56–81; Osborne (2011) 167–8; Eck (2012) 89–129. Already the scholiast on Homer *Il.* 11.690 remarked that there was no murder-purification in Homer. Parker (1983) 66–70 warns against overemphasising the gulf between Homer and later attitudes to death-pollution. Eck (2012) 106–29 suggests that the notion of pollution resulting from killing (in battle) is not entirely absent from Homer.

[7] Proclus' summary informs us that the *Aethiopis* involves Achilles being purified by Odysseus for the murder of Thersites: see T. W. Allen, *Homeri Opera Vol. V*, Oxford 1912, 105–6.

[8] Cole (1988) 162.   [9] Gagarin (2008) 39; see also Osborne (2011) 170.

importance of purification, has to do with the rise of the *polis*; that pollution, like law, is somehow important to the developing city-state; that pollution, perhaps, negotiates the kind of questions which arise in a community as social organisation advances. An insight of this sort is an incitement to further reflection. Pollution as a 'medium for the negotiation of questions important to the community' sounds very much like tragedy itself and the sorts of interests tragedy is often said to have. We may infer that the ubiquity of pollution in tragedy is perhaps not a by-product of tragedy's subject matter but the index of its aptness in the negotiation of the kind of concerns tragedy has.

The present study suggests that this is indeed the case. Taking this position as a starting point, it then considers whether pollution (and the ritual nexus of which it forms part) may not have a pointed function in tragedy as a kind of murmuring undercurrent or, rather, a compositional reference point. The result you hold in your hands: an account, by no means comprehensive but, I hope, informative and suggestive, of the kind of functions pollution and its ritual counterparts may have as 'murmuring undercurrent' or compositional reference point in the tragic plays staged in the theatre of Dionysus in fifth-century BC Athens. It argues that the ensemble of pollution, purity and purification (and in particular pollution) constitutes a convenient tool in the negotiation of tragic crises.

Backdrops

One may be sure that the importance of pollution in tragedy is not the arcane knowledge of the initiated few. To take but one notable example, the teaser on the paperback edition of Robert Parker's magisterial and widely read account of pollution and purification in early Greek religion promptly draws attention to it: 'Anyone who has sampled even a few of the most commonly read Greek texts will have encountered pollution. The pollution of bloodshed is a frequent theme of tragedy: Orestes is driven mad; Oedipus brings plague upon all Thebes.'[10]

It is curious, therefore, that no study exists exploring the above questions. Aristotle's influential theory of tragic catharsis, it seems, has drawn attention away from the tragedies themselves (and I should say straight away that this book is not concerned with Aristotle). In comparison with the extensive body of literature on what is but a single sentence in the *Poetics*

---

[10] Parker (1983).

4 Introduction

(1449b24–8),[11] treatments of the role of pollution, purity and purification in the actual plays are practically non-existent.

Certainly, there are exceptions. The *Oresteia* in particular has invited comment, traditionally to the effect that the trilogy moves from (rigid) ritual to law, homing in on the last play, the *Eumenides*, in which complex purifications from pollution turn out to be insufficient for the matricide Orestes and are supplanted (or supplemented) by legal procedure.[12] Other plays, too, have prompted the occasional foray, within wider discussions, into matters of pollution, purity and purification. Aeschylus' *Suppliants*, in particular, with its pollution threat resulting from the arrival in Argos of the virginal Danaids, has provoked insightful comments on the theme from an anthropological perspective;[13] so, too, has Euripides' *Hippolytus* with its purity-obsessed eponymous hero.[14] And the odd purification ritual has occasionally attracted attention. Eveline Krummen, for instance, has examined the eschatological overtones of the purification Ajax intends to undertake in Sophocles' play of the same name;[15] Walter Burkert has provided a powerful reading of the symbolic force of the purification ritual so minutely described in Sophocles' late play *Oedipus at Colonus*.[16]

But very few studies indeed have made pollution and its counterparts a central reading paradigm. Robert Parker offers the barest of sketches (aptly entitled 'Some scenes from tragedy') as an afterthought to his study of pollution and purification in ancient Greece.[17] Beyond this, Charles Segal's examination of the transformation of purity concepts in the dramatic denouement of Euripides' *Hippolytus* in an article published in 1970 ploughs a rather lonely furrow (and even that furrow is subject to bifurcation).[18] Since then, no major contribution has been made in the form of a focused study of the ritual nexus of pollution, purity and purification in tragedy, with the exception perhaps of Robin Mitchell-Boyask's Girardian reading of the latter play, which, however, very quickly moves

---

[11] Important contributions include Bernays (1880), Schadewaldt (1955), Else (1957), Golden (1962), id. (1976), id. (1992) 5–39; Belfiore (1992); for a recent summary, see LaCourse Munteanu (2012) 238–50. See also Flashar (2007). For largely non-Aristotelian views of what tragic catharsis may be, see Segal (1996); see also Dubois (2002).
[12] E.g. Lesky (1931) esp. 211, Meier (1980) 160, Pòrtulas (2006). The question of purification in *Eumenides* is examined in detail by Sidwell (1996); see also the remarks on pollution and purification in Zeitlin (1965).
[13] Zeitlin (1996d), Gödde (2000a) 238–44.
[14] Zeitlin (1996d). Evidently, the list of studies which include remarks on pollution and purification is not exhaustive; further literature will be cited *in situ* and as appropriate.
[15] Krummen (1998). [16] Burkert (1985b) 8–14.
[17] Parker (1983) 308–21. [18] Segal (1970).

from the issue of pollution to the play's presentation of violence and mimetic rivalry.[19]

The lacuna is welcome because the moment to fill it is opportune. Scholarship, not only but especially on Greek tragedy, has shown an abiding interest in the interrelation of literature and religion. This interest is by no means novel – its pedigree stretches back considerably in time to include such eminent exponents as Friedrich Nietzsche and his influential answer to the vexing question of what tragedy has to do with Dionysus in the *Birth of Tragedy*; or the Cambridge ritualists and their diagnosis, inspired by James Frazer's *Golden Bough*, of a pattern involving the death and rebirth of a year-spirit, the *eniautos daimōn*, which underlies all tragedy.[20] Although studies interested in 'tragedy and religion' were unfashionable for some time, partly due to the perceived excesses of the Cambridge ritualists, partly due to the advent in Classical Studies of New Criticism and its paradigm of text-immanent close readings, the field has been flourishing, in various guises, at least since the mid-1960s.[21] With the continued appeal of culturally contextualising approaches to classical literature and the publication, within the last decade, of two important surveys of the state of the subdiscipline's art,[22] the field is now, if anything, more vigorous and rigorous than ever.

There has also recently been renewed interest in pollution and purification and their place in ancient Greek society. For a long time, Robert

---

[19] Mitchell(-Boyask) (1991). To this, one may add Scullion (1998) on *Antigone*; this is not a comprehensive interpretation of the wider function of pollution and purification in the play, however, but a hermeneutic exercise in determining the exact meaning of the chorus' famous appeal to Dionysus, in the final stasimon of the play, to 'come with purifying foot' (*Ant.* 1144) to heal the 'violent sickness' from which Thebes suffers.

[20] See Murray (1912).

[21] The mid-1960s saw the publication of two influential studies with very different methodological affiliations: Froma Zeitlin's study of ritual imagery in the *Oresteia* (Zeitlin (1965)) and Walter Burkert's reconstruction of tragedy as developing from a performance associated with a goat-sacrifice (Burkert (1966)). Both 'schools', the one looking at the function of ritual/religious forms and language in tragedy (or comedy), the other interested in origins (and what these may tell us about fifth-century tragedy and the rituals in it), have had many followers. The former includes e.g. Else (1977), Foley (1985), Easterling (1988), Krummen (1998), Gödde (2000a), ead. (2000b), and Henrichs (2004); see e.g. Bowie (1993a) on comedy. The latter includes e.g. Guépin (1968). Origins figure large also in Sourvinou-Inwood (2003) with ead. (1994), Csapo and Miller (2007), Seaford (1994) esp. 328–67 on the supposed Dionysiac pattern underlying all tragedy and deriving from its Dionysiac origins. The literature on Dionysus and the Dionysiac in Greek drama is vast: see e.g. Bierl (1991), Des Bouvrie (1993), Schlesier (1993), (2007) and (2010); Scullion (2002) argues against the Dionysiac nature of Greek tragedy.

[22] Yatromanolakis and Roilos (2004a), Bierl et al. (2007). Both include useful introductions: Yatromanolakis and Roilos (2004b) on the concept of 'ritual poetics' (on which see also Grethlein [2007]); Bierl (2007) surveying approaches to 'literature and religion'. For comparable publications on the topic in Latin literature, see Barchiesi et al. (2004) and Augoustakis (2013). Outside of Classics, see Braungart (1996). Short surveys include Graf (2007a) and (on Sophocles) Rehm (2012).

Parker's seminal study, published in 1983, seemed to have been the last word on the topic.[23] In recent years, however, it has attracted fresh attention. On the one hand, the parameters of discussion have broadened. Ritual pollution and purification have been studied alongside, for instance, medical, philosophical or poetic concepts.[24] Outside of Classics, political uses of concepts of purity have received thorough treatment.[25] On the other hand, Parker's understanding of pollution, which owes much to structural anthropology and in particular to Mary Douglas' influential *Purity and Danger*,[26] has come under attack, along with Douglas' work and indeed much of structural anthropology. In a recent publication, Robin Osborne reviews the literature on pollution and comes to the conclusion that '[i]t is time to think more radically about dirty bodies.'[27]

This book is primarily a (literary) study of the function of the thematic nexus of pollution, purity and purification in tragic drama and not a historical account of pollution in ancient Greece. Nonetheless, by thinking about pollution and its counterparts as compositional reference points that are anchored in Greek life and by determining the nature of these compositional reference points, certain lines of inquiry and ways of looking at pollution in ancient Greek culture have crystallised which I hope will contribute to 'thinking more radically' about pollution in the context of classical Greece.

Tragedy and crisis

The principal answer this study comes up with to the central question it poses – 'what is the *function* of...?' – is that the ensemble of pollution, purity and purification (and in particular pollution) constitutes a convenient tool in the negotiation of tragic crises. This answer, to be sure, only begs further questions: *What crises? What negotiations? Why this ensemble? Why pollution... and crisis? Why convenient?* It is self-evident that this study's particular take is just that: particular. It involves a number of assumptions: about the kind of thing pollution is; about the kind of thing

---

[23] Parker (1983). Moulinier (1952) is still interesting, as comprehensive sourcebook and because of the thorough analyses of the terminology of pollution, purity and purification offered; see also Ginouvès (1962).
[24] Hoessly (2001), Seidensticker and Vöhler (2007). See Molinar and Vöhler (2009), Bradley (2012b) and Lennon (2013) for recent perspectives on pollution beyond classical Greece.
[25] Sémelin (2005).
[26] Douglas (1966). On Douglas's influence, see e.g. Fardon (1999) 80, Bradley (2012a).
[27] Osborne (2011) 163.

tragedy is; about the kind of thing a tragic crisis is. It is time for a few self-reflective confessions and explanations.

Let us tackle the last two items of the above triad first: what kind of thing is tragedy? And, what kind of thing is a tragic crisis? The answer to the last question is intrinsically bound up with the first. What one considers a tragic crisis depends to a large extent on one's assumptions about what tragedy is. In view of the centuries-long controversy over the definition of 'tragedy and the tragic',[28] a quick dispatch of the question of the nature of tragedy will seem presumptuous; the wise and circumspect will be relieved to learn, therefore, that no claim is made here to the discovery of 'essence'. The most famous as well as influential attempt to come to terms with tragedy (and indeed the 'essence' of tragedy) is that of Aristotle in the *Poetics*. At *Poetics* 1449b24–8, Aristotle famously defines tragedy as the mimesis of an action (μίμησις πράξεως) which, by inspiring pity and fear, achieves a cathartic effect. The achievement of this effect depends, for Aristotle, largely on plot (μῦθος) and character (τὰ ἤθη; 1450a37). With this, the protagonists' 'thought' becomes important (διάνοια, 1449b35–1450a9); as does plot-construction, proceeding in accordance with the tripartite structure of δέσις, which we may translate as 'knotting' ('knotting into' catastrophe or near-catastrophe), περιπέτεια, 'reversal', and λύσις, 'denouement' (or 'knotting-out-of'; 1455b24–1456a2). If we consider tragedy to be such 'in essence', the questions we will ask about it will necessarily turn on plot-construction and characterisation. And the crises we will diagnose will necessarily occur on the level of the plot and as the result of a particular character constellation and these characters' aspirations, moral choices, strengths and weaknesses. Crisis will mean the conflict of characters and the point where this conflict comes to a head.[29]

The starting point of the present study is that tragedy is not just plot and character. It shares the assumption of much of recent writing on drama that tragedy, because it was produced within a specific historical context, reflects and refracts the concerns and cultural patterns of this context.[30] As a result, it considers tragedy as a complex socio-cultural

---

[28] Silk (1996); Bohrer (2009) (foregrounding the idea of 'epiphany', see id. (1991)); Judet de la Combe (2010). For reflections on 'the tragic' in Virgil, see Hardie (1997).
[29] For a defence of Aristotelian approaches to tragedy, see Radke(-Uhlmann) (2003). In the English-speaking world, defenders of Aristotle are even rarer. An exception is, for instance, Heath (1987).
[30] One may cite Froma Zeitlin and Simon Goldhill (see bibliography), among many others. These scholars are indebted to the Parisian school of historical anthropology around Jean-Pierre Vernant, Pierre Vidal-Naquet and (earlier) Louis Gernet: see especially Vernant and Vidal-Naquet (1972) and (1986); Vidal-Naquet (1986a); Gernet (1968) and (1982). For a discussion of anthropological approaches to Greek tragedy, see Goldhill (1997) 331–6 and Sourvinou-Inwood (2005); Segal (1983).

phenomenon, negotiating complex problems which need not necessarily be invoked explicitly, nor result from specific characters' strengths and weaknesses, but may be implicit, and recognisable in particular against the backdrop of fifth-century BC Greek culture, and its concerns and patterns of thought and expression.

If we consider tragedy to be such, the range of questions we will ask about it will be much broader. We can still take the Aristotelian level of character encounters, characterisation, moral dilemmas and plot-development seriously.[31] But we can also examine underlying problems and implicit concerns. Such implicit concerns are sometimes of a more abstract and philosophical nature: *Oedipus tyrannus*, for instance, has been viewed as a comment on the question of the conditions and limits of human knowledge.[32] Very frequently, they are of a concrete, socio-cultural nature: Aeschylus' *Suppliants*, for example, has been understood to be greatly interested, beneath its surface-plot revolving around the encounter between the Argive king Pelasgus and the unwed, virginal daughters of Danaus, in the relation to society of maidens on the threshold of adulthood.[33] From this non-Aristotelian perspective, the crises likely to attract interest are therefore not only those battled out on the level of plot-development, character encounters and characterisation, but also the crises associated with these underlying concerns. A central assumption of this study is, then, that each tragedy discusses, along with surface conflicts of the type Aristotle is interested in, a number of embedded crises. The acknowledgement of the existence of such embedded crises and the belief that these deserve and need to be analysed are central to this study.

Pollution, crisis, tragedy

The principal argument of this book is that it is such embedded crises which the concept of pollution in particular – but also its counterparts, purity and (to some extent) purification – negotiate. This specification

---

See Goldhill (1990) more specifically on tragedy as historically specific 'civic discourse' with the response by Griffin (1998) on the timeless quality of tragic conflict; Goldhill responds to Griffin in Goldhill (2000). Goldhill's claim that Attic tragedy was specifically democratic has also been contested: see Rhodes (2003); Carter (2004) and now Burian (2011). For theoretical reflections on the relation of tragedy to its historical contexts, see Goff (1995b).

[31] But we should also situate characterisation and moral dilemmas in the historical context of classical Athens, as Sourvinou-Inwood has demanded: see ead. (1989), (2005). Especially in her 1989 article on *Antigone*, though, she privileges historical context to the point of insensitivity to the subversive potential of drama. A sensitive account of 'character' in tragedy and its cultural conditions is Goldhill's essay in Pelling (1990) 100–27.

[32] E.g. Goldhill (1986) 205–21.   [33] Zeitlin (1996c), Gödde (2000a).

brings us to the heart of the present study. It requires that we take a closer look at pollution and its relation to crises. The two are closely connected.

It seems that wherever there is pollution, there is some sort of crisis, in the most general sense of 'difficult situation', so that pollution can be understood as a marker of such 'crises' ('difficult situations'). The scenarios most commonly associated with pollution, and which require purification, include birth, death and murder. Theophrastus' 'Superstitious Man' (*Characters* 16) will not go anywhere near a dead body or a woman in childbed (οὔτ' ἐπὶ νεκρὸν οὔτ' ἐπὶ λεχὼ ἐλθεῖν ἐθελῆσαι, 16.9) for fear of pollution (μιαίνεσθαι, 16.9). Clearly, the man is eccentric, but a number of the so-called 'sacred laws' suggest that he is not entirely wrong-headed. The well-known 'cathartic law' from late fourth-century Cyrene includes detailed specifications on the extent of the spread of pollution in the case of birth (*SEG* IX 72 A §4);[34] and a law 'concerning the dead' (οἵδε νόμοι περὶ τῶν καταφθιμ[έ]νω[ν ...]) from late fifth-century Iulis (on Keos) gives equally detailed information on pollution and its spread in the case of death.[35] The pollution of the murderer, finally, is a frequent theme not only in tragedy, but is the earliest concrete type of pollution we encounter in the literary and historical record. The purification of Achilles from murder-pollution in Arctinus' *Aethiopis* from the seventh century BC has already been mentioned. In addition, it is likely that an early inscriptional reference to pollution, a lacunose sacred law from (early?) sixth-century Kleonai refers to murder-pollution.[36] In all these cases, pollution marks a situation fraught with tensions. A woman in childbed is in a precarious and perilous state; death disrupts everyday life, especially for those closely involved; and so does the murderer 'with blood on his hands'. The insight that pollution is regularly connected with critical states and difficult situations is basic. It justifies thinking the two together.

The 'crises' most obviously connected with pollution (birth, death, murder) do not, however, *by themselves* constitute complex problems so much as isolated 'critical' or 'difficult' events. Why this study presents, and can present, the argument sketched above, that the ritual concept of pollution and its ritual counterparts serve the function of negotiating complex 'embedded crises', instead has to do with the specific interactions in the tragedies between literary texture and the ritual nexus analysed. Partly, that is, it is a matter of the playful literary artifice that is tragedy; partly, it is

---

[34] *SEG* IX 72 = *LSS* 115 = RO 97. See RO 97 for a text with translation and commentary; see also Parker (1983) 332–51.
[35] *LSCG* 97; on birth- and death-pollution, see Parker (1983) 32–73.
[36] *LSCG* 56, with Parker (1983) 112.

a matter of the specific nature of pollution as referent with *Sitz im Leben*, which makes it a particularly apt reference point in the negotiation of complex 'embedded crises'.

I take the second point first. What is pollution's nature, then? There are two ways to proceed. One would be to inquire about the essence of pollution and therefore about the common essence also of the various difficult states pollution marks. The other would be to disregard such essentialism and to inquire instead about the qualities, functions and associations of pollution.

The first direction, the 'essentialist' approach, has frequently been taken in the past. Anthropologists have devoted considerable attention to distilling the one intrinsic 'meaning' of pollution, among them structural anthropologists in particular.[37] The influential study of Mary Douglas, *Purity and danger*, published in 1966, is a case in point.[38] Her interest lies precisely in isolating a common essence of all the different phenomena which pollution marks. For her, this essence would be, with some qualification, 'category violation', the confusion of boundaries and (the threat of) disorder. She suggests that the idea of pollution is particularly strongly present in societies in which 'lines of structure, cosmic or social, are clearly defined', claiming 'a polluting person' is one who 'has developed some wrong condition or simply crossed some line which should not have been crossed'[39] and concluding that 'our pollution behaviour is the reaction which condemns any object or idea likely to confuse or contradict cherished classifications.'[40]

Douglas' view has had a profound impact upon the modern understanding of pollution;[41] and, by extension, on a number of modern readings of pollution in Greek tragedy (such as they are). Among the latter, a good example is Thalia Papadopoulou's 2005 study of Euripides' *Heracles*. For Papadopoulou, Douglas' tenet is simply established fact. When she sets out to examine the role of pollution and purification in the play, she declares: 'Pollution is associated with the confusion of boundaries, and ritual with a process of re-establishing the collapsed boundaries.'[42] End of story.

Although it is not my aim here to provide a detailed critique of Douglas' theory, its impact and influence are such that a few words are in order

---

[37] For an introductory overview, see Fornaro (2007).
[38] On Douglas in general, see Fardon (1999), ibid. 75–101 on *Purity and danger*.
[39] Douglas (1966) 113.   [40] Ibid. 36.
[41] See Fardon (1999) 80 and Bradley (2012a and 2012b) on the book's wide influence.
[42] Papadopoulou (2005b) 23. We shall encounter another such example in chapter 2, Oudemans's and Lardinois's study of Sophocles' *Antigone*: Oudemans and Lardinois (1987).

Pollution, crisis, tragedy

to evaluate its heuristic value. For the interpreter of tragedy the idea that pollution has to do with the confusion or transgression of boundaries understandably has great appeal, in view of the many anthropologically driven studies which have suggested that the negotiation of boundaries and their transgression is one of the genre's most consistent preoccupations.[43] In fact, Greek thought in general seems fond of categorisation and binary oppositions so that the Douglasian approach would appear attractive.[44] Two objections may be raised, however.

First, Douglas' theory itself is far from unproblematic. In fact, recent scholarship on pollution has uncovered major deficiencies. Valerio Valeri's re-examination in *The forest of taboos* is a point in case.[45] Valeri here takes a fresh look in particular at Douglas' treatment of the dietary rules of the biblical 'abominations of Leviticus' (the third chapter in *Purity and danger*), in which Douglas suggests that it is because they fall between categories that certain animals are considered polluted in this text. Building on the work of Jean Soler,[46] he argues that, whilst it is true that pollution is here related to classification, classification – and breaches of an ideal classificatory order – is not itself the problem which generates pollution. In the particular case of the abominations of Leviticus, the problem which renders certain animals polluted seems to be their carnivorousness. Such carnivorousness, however, renders animals polluted, not because it is anomalous in relation to some decontextualised categorial system, but because it is problematic in relation to a *normative* classification, which has it that vegetarianism, but not carnivorousness, corresponds to God's masterplan for creation. This means that:

> Taxonomy enters into play, not as an autonomous principle, as the expression of an ideal classificatory order that is entirely responsible for generating the opposition of the pure and the impure, but first and foremost as a key, that is an aid for inferring from some easily identifiable traits whether an animal is herbivorous or not.
>
> Taxonomy presupposes, in other words, something that is nontaxonomic.[47]

Pollution, therefore, has to do with categories only because these serve as a key to identify something other that is problematic. It originates from

---

[43] Sophocles' Oedipus plays have attracted particular attention in this respect. See, for instance, Segal (1981) 207–48 on *Oedipus tyrannus*; ibid. 362–408 on *Oedipus at Colonus*; Vidal-Naquet (1986b) on *Oedipus at Colonus*.
[44] See e.g. Lloyd (1966), Goldhill (1997) 336.   [45] Valeri (2000) 70–83.   [46] Soler (1973).
[47] Valeri (2000) 78.

that 'something other' which is 'non-classificatory' and around which the system of classification has been built.

Robin Osborne has recently added to the critique of Douglas.[48] He points out in particular that Douglas' theory is hard to square with the lived reality of pollution in ancient Greece. One aspect of this (and which applies not only to ancient Greece) is the existence of purification as a means to remove pollution: for if pollution is simply category-anomaly, how could purification rectify such an anomaly? 'Would purification not somehow have to move category boundaries?' Osborne rightly asks.[49] The other aspect is that what constitutes pollution often differs from *polis* to *polis*, even though these *poleis* share the same language and with this (presumably) the same categorial divisions.[50]

Observations of this kind should make us wary of positing Douglas' tenet as a given in the interpretation of tragedy. We shall see (in the chapter on Sophocles' *Antigone*) that pollution may be linked, in a specific text, with the idea of category-confusion. That link is not essential and originary, however, but the result of one dramatic text's particular engagement with pollution. The postulation of such a Douglasian-type link between pollution and category-confusion must never be *a priori*, therefore, but at best a second or third step in the process of interpretation.

The second objection has to do with Douglas' essentialism and the impoverished interpretations of tragedy that result from it. (It applies equally to another essentialist 'theory' of pollution, René Girard's postulation, outlined in his *Violence and the sacred*, of pollution as the translation into religious terms of the threat, or actual presence, of violence.)[51] 'Essentialists' assume that pollution has but one – as it were, Platonic – meaning: the term 'pollution' is dropped and immediately all we can think of – and all we think the ancient Greeks, including the (implied) authors of the tragedies we analyse, thought of – is category-anomaly (or violence). It is not merely that this seems unlikely; worse, it has a potentially detrimental effect upon our reading of tragedy. If we approach a text with such a preconceived notion of what pollution 'really is', or 'really means', every text, however much we emphasise its potential for refraction and transformation, will end up negotiating the same set of problems and the same 'essential' crisis. The essentialist approach to pollution entails readings that

---

[48] Osborne (2011) 162–6. [49] Ibid. 164. [50] Ibid.
[51] Girard (1977) esp. 33 (the French original was published in 1972); a useful introduction to Girard's theories is Palaver (2004²). Pucci (1990) offers a pertinent critique of Girard's theories; he is (rightly) worried that 'Girard desires to read the text beyond – or even against – its textuality' (ibid. 42). See also Mitchell-Boyask (1996) on the 'uses and abuses' of Girard.

would seem to be worryingly unresponsive to the multitude of problems tragic dramas discuss.

This study embraces the notion of plurality and rests upon the assumption that tragedy as well as pollution – and indeed the interaction between the two – are more complex and multifaceted than essentialist readings would allow. In thinking about the nature of pollution, it privileges the alternative path of inquiring into the multiple (observable) properties of pollution as well as the contexts with which it is associated. In other words, this study suggests abandoning the idea of definition of essence ('*what* it is', τὸ τί ἐστιν) in favour of a focus on description, '*how* it is' (τὸ ὅπως ἐστίν).[52]

With this, the qualities, functions and associations (the plurals are important here) of pollution become central: its function as sense-making device which allows establishing narratives of cause and effect, for instance; its frustrating refusal to remain stably in place; its nature as evaluative category, potentially coextensive with other evaluative categories; or its associations, in the *lived* reality of classical Athens, with civic exclusion – and, inversely, the associations of purity with civic participation and inclusion (as when participation in the assembly can be referred to as 'being within the purification', ἐντὸς τοῦ καθάρματος).[53] These qualities, functions and associations designate, not isolated events, but complex networks of problems. These complex networks of problems are of a kind tragedy frequently deals with: they constitute potential 'embedded crises' in the sense outlined above.

This study suggests, then, that it is not only some supposed essence of pollution such as category-confusion, but also the more easily verifiable 'how' of pollution – its qualities, functions and associations – which entails that is readily drawn, within the tragic texts, into negotiations of 'embedded crises'. At the same time, in privileging the 'how' over the 'what', it restores to tragedy a greater variety since it avoids approaching the texts with rock-solid preconceptions about what it might be that pollution 'does' in the plays.

Texts and contexts

An important question surfaces at this point. It concerns the nature of the relation between text and context, tragedy and the ritual nexus in

---

[52] The terms are borrowed from the orthodox Church Fathers of the fourth century AD who emphasise this distinction in their discussion of the nature of God. See e.g. Basil of Caesarea's *Contra Eunomium* 1.15.
[53] Ar. *Ach.* 44 with Σ ad loc.

question. The preceding remarks may have suggested that pollution is treated in this study as an external referent whose qualities, functions and associations, for all their diversity, wholly determine the kind of textual negotiations pollution (and the nexus of which pollution forms part) can enter as it is integrated into tragedy. Such a view has recently been attacked by Denis Feeney, who points out that it implies a failure 'to do justice to the texts' actual capacities'[54] as medium not only of reflection, but also of transformation and play. Similarly, Gerhard Neumann has emphasised the *Differenzstruktur* of the literary text as against the 'cultural text' as the result of aesthetic refraction.[55] The present study finds itself largely in agreement with these concerns. The view adopted here is that cultural context – in this case the qualities, functions and associations of pollution in this context – is never simply reflected, but may constitute the backdrop against which tragedy's textual renegotiations emerge in a clearer light. At times, though, this backdrop may be perceived even to recede largely behind tragedy's literary play, without, of course, ever vanishing entirely out of sight.

This view of the dynamics between text and context must be considered in conjunction with the previous remarks about the concept of pollution (and its ritual counterparts) as a subtext with diverse qualities, functions and associations stemming from its *Sitz im Leben*. The result is the following model: as tragedy incorporates into its literary texture a subtext with *Sitz im Leben* and multiple socio-cultural associations of its own, all of these associations reverberate, in refracted form, through tragedy. The result of the encounter of one multifaceted text (the literary text) with another (the multifaceted subtext 'pollution') is a Protean whole 'of many turns'. These 'turns' include 'refracted reverberations' of the subtext's diverse qualities, functions and associations connected with its *Sitz im Leben*; but the encounter may produce yet other 'turns' as the literary text engages the subtext in negotiations that transcend the subtext's *Sitz im Leben*. All of these turns coexist and any one of them could be analysed.

Clearly, this Protean model is too much for any study to stomach. The raft this study clings to as it steers between the acknowledgement of this πολυτροπία and the need for a narrative consists of a hierarchisation of the potentially endless play of meaning intimated by the model outlined above. This hierarchisation, while not entirely beyond debunking (or 'deconstruction'), is not arbitrary: the tragic dramas, so the present study assumes, are crafted artifices with a specific texture which, for all its diversity and

---

[54] Feeney (2007) 175. See also id. (2004) 10–11, 19–20.   [55] Neumann (2000) 34.

openness, to some extent suggests privileging certain concerns over others.[56] This study therefore listens carefully to the plays' concerns and, translated into the terms used above, 'embedded crises'. A particular embedded crisis may gain particular urgency and in this way suggest the profit of a particular way of looking at the 'turns' pollution takes between activation of refracted reverberations of its socio-cultural associations and response to a particular tragedy's literary play.

The plot

The title of this study is '*Pollution* and crisis in Greek tragedy' and it is programmatic: it should have become obvious by now that the concept of pollution is the study's gravitational centre as the element of the ritual nexus in question which is the most prominent in tragedy and – or indeed *because* – most closely associated with the kind of crises tragedy negotiates. Accordingly, this study is organised in the main around pollution. Its qualities, functions and associations afford the thematic plotting, in four chapters. Each of these contains extended analyses of individual plays in which the prominence of a specific 'embedded crisis' suggests the utility of paying particular attention to a corresponding association of pollution.

Chapter 1 focuses on the nature of pollution as a religious interpretative model which 'affords understanding'. By and large, by this slightly oracular shorthand I refer to the idea that, because ritual pollution is readily conceived of as a potential source of disaster, the assumption of such pollution makes present misfortune comprehensible as the consequence of past transgression: it allows establishing narratives of cause and effect. Struggling for such narratives, and for understanding, in the face of disaster is a frequent preoccupation of tragic characters. The chapter focuses on two plays in which this struggle for understanding is particularly urgent and the role of pollution conspicuous: Euripides' *Hippolytus* and Sophocles' *Oedipus tyrannus*. Juxtaposing these two plays makes for an intriguing contrast: *Hippolytus* offers a whirl of competing causation models, from religious to secular and even 'scientific'; pollution, not limited in this play to the ritual, partakes of several of these causation models and is in this way (ironically?) bi- or tri- or even further-furcated; an interest in contemporary intellectual discourses is evident. *Oedipus tyrannus*, by contrast, while starting from

---

[56] This view is also adopted by Gödde (2000b) 37: 'Ein literarischer Text legt durch seine motivische, rhetorische und stilistische Verfaßtheit – ich möchte dieses Ensemble von strukturellen Momenten die 'Textur' nennen – bestimmte Fragestellungen und Diskussionen nahe.'

the above scenario, foregrounding the notion of ritual pollution as 'sense-making device', soon takes a decisive turn inwards, recasting pollution in the process. Suggested as the term by which to comprehend the protagonist Oedipus, it is eventually found lacking in this regard.

Chapter 2 is interested in the worrisome resistance to fixation that is characteristic of pollution. Fixity and stability are paramount for the civic community; disrespectful of fixed boundaries in its (contagious) spread, pollution readily sits uneasy with these civic needs – until (or unless) civic authority intervenes by defining pollution's reach. The opening section of this chapter offers a brief historical stage-setting. It focuses in particular on law as one prominent form of expression of the community's desire for stability – as its physical appearance and the ancient city's discourse about it would seem to suggest; pollution is mapped against this background as alarmingly 'transgressive'. The main body of the chapter is then devoted to *Antigone*. This play can be understood to revolve around a 'crisis of civic stability'; poised between radical transgressiveness and delimitation through civic authority (Creon, in this case), pollution in complex ways articulates this crisis and, not least, the failure of Creon's intransigent vision of a civic space defined by inflexible boundaries.

Perhaps the most basic aspect of pollution comes into focus in chapter 3: its nature as evaluative category. The designation of an act as 'polluting' rescues that act from the obscure depths of meaninglessness and draws it into the light of meaning and categorisation. Critically, such categorisation as is afforded by the concept of ritual pollution may overlap to some extent with non-ritual categorisation, and not least that provided by concepts of (legal) justice. It is before this background that we may understand pollution in Aeschylus' *Oresteia*. Owing to the particular intertwining of crises in the trilogy, the chapter is divided into three parts. The first examines the *Oresteia*'s concern with evaluation, the place of the concept of justice within it and the relation to such justice of pollution. The second part looks at the same ingredients, but from a different perspective, foregrounding the trilogy's interest in notions of stability: one may associate this interest with the uncertainties ('instabilities') which revolve around the attribution of meaning to revenge murder; pollution comes into the picture, not because of any inherent associations with instability (as in *Antigone*), but through its approximation to one particular system of evaluation (that of 'retributive justice'). An appendix briefly looks at the devaluation of purification as means of release for the matricide Orestes.

Chapter 3 is followed by an excursus. The *Oresteia* was subject to close (intertextual) engagement on the part of the later tragic poets and in particular Euripides. His Atreid plays betray a close dialogue with the Aeschylean paradigm. One aspect of this is the Euripidean reconsideration of the Aeschylean presentation of the ritual nexus of pollution and purification or of the problems negotiated through it, using the same ritual nexus for the reconsideration of these problems. This latter is the case in *Iphigenia among the Taurians*, on which the excursus largely concentrates. At the centre of the discussion of this play is not any particular quality of the concept of pollution, but the question how Euripides uses the ritual nexus of pollution and purification in the renegotiation of a problem that in the *Oresteia* was prominently associated with it: the 'release from toils' (ἀπαλλαγὴ πόνων) of the matricide Orestes.

In chapter 4 we (re)turn to socio-cultural associations of pollution and – now, too – its counterpart, purity. In particular, this final chapter is concerned with negotiations of civic identity into which the concepts of pollution and purity are sometimes drawn. As was the case in chapter 2, the discussion opens with a historical sketch. It suggests a general association of pollution with civic exclusion and of purity with civic inclusion. More specifically, it argues that in the classical city (the example is Athens) 'privileged space associated with the responsibilities of citizenship'[57] was often also associated with purity. Since civic participation was therefore frequently a matter of being inside such pure space, civic participation and indeed civic identity is readily in dialogue with the concept of purity. The second part of the historical introduction focuses on quite a different aspect: the city's discourse about ethnic purity, which crops up already in Herodotus and gains in prominence in the fourth century. This historical stage-setting provides the background for discussions of three plays which revolve around reconfigurations of civic identity in critical encounters of representatives of a civic collective with outsiders embodying in various ways foreignness and/or marginality: Aeschylus' *Suppliants*, Sophocles' *Oedipus at Colonus* and Euripides' *Ion*. In these reconfigurations (we may speak of 'crises of identity'), pollution and purity, in part in the form of pure (and impure) space, occupy a prominent role. The chapter traces how pollution and purity function as vehicles for (re-)definitions of civic identity and in the process provides a nuanced picture of similarities and differences of the three tragedians in the dramatisation of analogous tragic conflicts.

[57] Cole (2004) 47.

CHAPTER I

Pollution, interpretation and understanding

Herodotus (7.188) relates a remarkable incident which occurred during the second Persian expedition against Greece. During its advance southwards, towards Athens, Xerxes' fleet on one occasion anchored on the Magnesian coast between the city of Casthanea and Cape Sepias. It was not a good idea. The next morning a violent storm gathered, making the sea 'boil' (τῆς θαλάσσης ζεσάσης). No fewer than 400 ships were destroyed. Was this disaster mere coincidence? Not if we are to trust a certain story about the event. Herodotus notes (7.189):

> There is a story (λέγεται δὲ λόγος) that the Athenians had called upon Boreas to help them, in consequence of another oracle, by which they were advised to 'ask the assistance of their son-in-law'. Boreas, according to the Greek account, married a woman of Attica, Erechtheus' daughter Orithyia, and in consequence of this marriage the Athenians (so the tale goes) supposed Boreas to be their son-in-law; so when they observed from their station at Chalcis in Euboea that a storm was coming or possibly even sooner (ὡς ἔμαθον αὐξόμενον τὸν χειμῶνα ἢ καὶ πρὸ τούτου) they offered sacrifice to Boreas and Orithyia and begged to come to their aid... destroying the Persian fleet... The Athenians are quite positive about it:... it was Boreas who was responsible for what occurred on this occasion...[1]

This is not the only storm we encounter in the historical record of ancient Greece. The Persian invaders attract such disaster in succession.[2] But Greeks are not exempt either: sometime in the late fourth or early third century BC, the inhabitants of Dodona suffered from similarly adverse, if presumably not quite so destructive, weather conditions.

Though less positive about the origins of their affliction and unable to supply a neat and ready-made story, the Dodoneans are not clueless. Craving a concrete *logos*, presumably more so than the Athenians of Herodotus'

---

[1] Trans. Aubrey de Sélincourt, rev. John Marincola (London, 1996).
[2] See e.g. Hdt. 8.12–13 (where the storm is also attributed to divine intervention: ἐποιέετό τε πᾶν ὑπὸ τοῦ θεοῦ ὅκως ἂν ἐξισωθείη τῷ Ἑλληνικῷ τὸ Περσικὸν μηδὲ πολλῷ πλέον εἴη, 8.13).

account, they consult their story-dispensing institution around the corner, the local oracle of Zeus. Because oracles are sometimes prone to providing confused and ill-focused stories, the Dodoneans approach the oracular deity with a pointed question, proposing a possible plot-line: 'Is it because of some mortal's pollution that the god sends this storm?'

> Ἐπερωτῶντι Δωδωναῖοι τὸν
> Δία καὶ τὰν Διώναν ἦ δι' ἀνθρώ-
> που τινὸς ἀκαθαρτίαν ὁ θεὸς
> τὸν χειμῶνα παρέχει·[3]

Of chaos, disorder, incoherence, meaninglessness and inexplicable suffering the human being, including even postmodern man, can probably bear only so much. Making sense of, and ordering, experience would seem to be a paramount human activity, not for the fun of it, or the intellectual excitement, but as an elemental survival strategy. The 'Greek experience' clearly involved the confrontation with a substantial amount of potential chaos, disorder, incoherence, meaninglessness and inexplicable suffering.

In the face of this, it was arguably important, for the individual as well as for the community, to make sense of their lot by finding appropriate stories to explain it. Several answers to the challenge existed. One of them was religion. It provided an efficacious 'system of explanation'[4] by which to impose order and restore meaning. Herodotus in particular mirrors a world in which the incomprehensible – and more frequently than not the disastrous – could always be the result of divine intervention.[5] Religion in this way allowed narratives of cause and effect to be established and afforded the kind of stories which returned meaning to where there threatened to be none.

Within this 'system of explanation', the assumption of ritual pollution, and the concomitant assumption, however vague, of the potentially dangerous consequences of pollution constituted a 'sub-system of explanation'. A violent storm could be the positive result of prayer and sacrifice, as the Athenians assumed to be the case in 480 BC; but it could also be the result of pollution, as the Dodoneans suspected much later. Pollution, in fact, could be taken to underlie a wide range of disastrous and potentially inexplicable incidents. For instance, according to Antiphon the presence aboard a ship of 'a man with unclean hands or some other form of pollution' (μὴ καθαροὶ <τὰς> χεῖρας ἢ ἄλλο τι μίασμα ἔχοντες, 5.82) could

---
[3] *SEG* XIX 427.   [4] Gould (1985) 14.
[5] On religion in Herodotus, see for instance Gould (1994), Harrison (2000), Mikalson (2003).

readily cause that ship to wreck. Earthquakes, too, may result from it: the one that struck Sparta in 464 BC, at any rate, could be seen as the potential result of an *agos* the Spartans had contracted by dragging away, and putting to death, certain helots who had taken refuge at the temple of Poseidon at Taenarus (Thuc. 1.101 and 128).[6] In Euripides' *Medea*, finally, we encounter a rather wide formulation: pollution, at least of kin-murder, could result in (unspecified) 'woes', ἄχη (Eur. *Med.* 1268–70).[7] The concept of pollution in this way allowed establishing a link between the present and the past and constituted a mode of understanding and interpreting the world,[8] a tool to 'construct worlds of meaning'[9] and coherence out of incoherence, chaos and disorder.

It is apt that the present study should take its starting point here: though not necessarily its defining, 'essential', characteristic, a striking feature of Greek tragedy is, after all, that it frequently deals in a fair amount of *miseria*,[10] of 'suffering under the sun'[11] and the 'ennobling solicitations of sorrow, of mourning, of drastic loss'.[12] Therefore, as Stephen Halliwell puts it, '[c]entral to the concerns of tragic drama... is a confrontation with extremes of action and experience that stretch comprehension to its limits.'[13] Indeed, as chaos, disorder and meaninglessness loom large, we often encounter in these plays agonised human protagonists struggling for understanding.

Among all extant tragedies, two stand out in which such search for meaning is particularly urgent: Sophocles' *Oedipus tyrannus* and Euripides' *Hippolytus*. It is these two tragedies on which the present chapter focuses. Both very likely date from the first half of the 420s BC. *Hippolytus* was produced in 428 BC; and although the precise dating of Sophoclean plays is

---

[6] The term *miasma*, rather than *agos*, is used in reference to a similar sacrilege in Aeschylus' *Suppliants*: here, rejection of the Danaids, who have taken refuge at Argos's altars, threatens to 'pollute the city in its entirety', τὸ κοινὸν δ' εἰ μιαίνεται πόλις, A. *Suppl.* 366. For the differences between *miasma* and *agos*, see Parker (1983) 5–10.

[7] The text of the passage is probably corrupted. See Mastronarde (2002) ad 1268–70.

[8] This is emphasised by Bendlin (2007) 183, who (ibid.) lists a number of inscriptions from West Asia Minor, dating from the Roman period, which link disaster to pollution and in this way provide 'pollution plot-lines' (e.g. *SEG* VI 250 and 251).

[9] Burkert (1996) 128.

[10] At *Confessiones* 3.2, Augustine is concerned with the paradoxical lure of tragedy (*quid est, quod ibi homo vult dolere cum spectat luctuosa et tragica, quae tamen pati ipse nollet?*); *miseria* is one of the terms he uses to refer to the 'tragic experience'.

[11] *Ecclesiastes* 4:1. For Edith Hall such 'suffering under the sun' would after all seem to be (a defining?) characteristic of Greek tragedy; the quote serves as the subtitle of her introduction to Greek tragedy: Hall (2010).

[12] Steiner (1996) 534. Steiner here speaks of our idea of 'the tragic', however, not of Greek tragedy.

[13] Halliwell (2005) 394.

notoriously difficult, it is not unlikely that *Oedipus* dates from roughly the same time.[14] The period would seem to be fitting. In these years, Athens was repeatedly struck by a devastating plague. As Thucydides intimates, at the time 'making sense' was pressing business for the Athenians, who flocked to sacred shrines and turned to 'divination and the like' (μαντείοις καὶ τοῖς τοιούτοις ἐχρήσαντο, Thuc. 2.47). With their parallel (if differing) obsessions with interpretation in a struggle for meaning and understanding, both *Hippolytus* and *Oedipus tyrannus* would seem to reflect these concerns.

In both plays, too, pollution, as a mode of understanding and interpreting the world, plays a paramount role. This chapter is devoted to the role of pollution in these plays as a medium of negotiation of what may be labelled 'crises of comprehension'. Two very different scenarios will emerge, however. In Euripides, pollution, in its familiar ritual but also in other forms, is integrated into a wider discussion of causation and constitutes a complex voice in a chorus of competing modes of interpreting external events. What is at stake here are the limits of the ability of humans to construct of 'worlds of meaning' out of chaos and disorder. Sophocles, not surprisingly perhaps, starts with external disaster but swiftly moves inwards. As the play zooms in on the protagonist and his horrific plight, pollution is first suggested, but then found lacking, as a concept by which to make sense of the human being that is Oedipus.

Euripides' *Hippolytus*

For an appreciation of *Hippolytus*, it is indispensable to enlarge the view outlined above. Religion was one answer to the challenge posed by chaos, disorder, potential meaninglessness and inexplicable suffering. But it was not the only one. In the course of the fifth century, other, more 'scientific' systems of explanation became available, which at times set themselves in direct opposition to religious ones.[15] Hippocratic medicine constituted

---

[14] On the dating of Sophocles' plays, see Easterling (1982) 19–23. There is no external evidence for the dating of *OT*. Bernard Knox (1956) 133–47) argues for 425 BC, viewing the play's scenario as a reflection of the time when Athens was struck by the plague for the second time. If one argues for a (prompt) reflection of the plague of Athens, one needs to date the play to the first half of the 420s. Kamerbeek (1967) 29 notes that '[w]ith regard to structure a date half way between *Antigone* and *Philoctetes* seems satisfactory.' (In agreement with many other scholars, Kamerbeek considers 442 BC a likely date for the production of *Antigone*; *Philoctetes* was staged in 409 BC.)

[15] Segal (1993) 136: '[d]educing hidden causes and invisible truths that lie beneath the surface phenomena of the visible world was a major intellectual concern of the late fifth century.' See also Diller (1932). On the backdrop of the 'Athenian cultural revolution', see Osborne (2010). For the inverted commas around 'scientific', see Lloyd (1983).

one such alternative. Not least because they felt the need to carve out their territory in competition with traditional figures such as the healer-priest, whose practices combined elements of medicine, 'religion' and 'magic',[16] Hippocratic doctors (polemically) defined their art of 'secular' diagnosis in sharp opposition to religious ideas of causation.[17] The *locus classicus* is the beginning of the Hippocratic treatise *On the Sacred Disease*:

> I am about to discuss the disease called 'sacred' (ἱερῆς). It is not, in my opinion, any more divine or more sacred than other diseases, but has a natural cause (ἀλλὰ φύσιν μὲν ἔχει καὶ πρόφασιν), and its supposed divine origin (ἐνόμισαν θεῖόν τι πρῆγμα εἶναι) is due to men's inexperience, and to their wonder at its peculiar character.[18]

Instead, Hippocratic doctors located the origin of illness in what they perceived as the profane mechanisms of the human body.[19]

But the fifth century also saw the rise of historiography. This is a genre with an immense interest in patterns of cause and effect. Herodotus, we have seen, may resort to religious models of causation. Frequently, however, he offers 'secular' explanations as alternatives to religious ones and remains non-committal as to which he prefers.[20] The madness of the Spartan king Cleomenes, for instance, may be god-sent; but it may also result from heavy drinking (6.75–84).[21] Thucydides is decidedly more scientific in his approach to both underlying patterns of long-term historical processes and explanation of specific human misfortune. Divine causation only rarely has a place here. In his preface, Thucydides develops a nuanced model of historical causation at the heart of which stands the ἀνθρωπεία φύσις. To understand 'human nature' is to understand the patterns behind history.

---

[16] It is notoriously difficult to draw a line between 'religion' and 'magic' in ancient Greece. The category of 'magic' is controversial. See e.g. Graf (1997).

[17] Holmes (2010) 9 n. 28 points out that the medical writers never present the gods as causes of disease. The Hippocratic doctors' self-distancing from healer-priests may be considered 'a rhetorical stratagem in an agonistic "medical marketplace"' (ibid. 10) in view of the continuities that have been shown to exist between Greek medicine and traditional beliefs: see esp. Lloyd (1983) and Holmes (2010) 10 n. 32 for further bibliography. Still, 'a shift from personal, daemonic explanation to naturalizing explanations remains basic to our understanding of learned medicine in this period' (Holmes (2010) 38).

[18] Trans. W. H. S. Jones, Loeb Classical Library (Cambridge, MA, 1923).

[19] At the same time, Hippocratic views of the (female) body provide an example of continuities between Hippocratic medicine and traditional beliefs in that they are sometimes rationalisations of them: Lloyd (1983); Faraone (2011); and Holmes (2010) 10 n. 34 for further bibliography.

[20] This has been called the 'uncertainty principle' by Gould (1994) 94.

[21] See also Hdt. 3.33 on the madness of Cambyses as the result of religious offence against the Apis bull or 'some other reason', εἴτε δὴ διὰ τὸν Ἄπιν εἴτε καὶ ἄλλως. On such passages Harrison (2000) 115 comments: 'It is precisely . . . the potential for two contradictory but parallel forms of explanation, that allows for the belief in the possibility of divine intervention to be maintained.'

Specific human suffering, too, usually calls for 'rational' rather than divine explanations. His account of the Athenian plague is a case in point (2.47–54). The historian displays great interest in the origin of the plague. But instead of a Sophoclean scenario of ritual *miasma* as the result of human transgression, we find talk of quasi-bacterial infection and an abundance of technical Hippocratic terminology.[22]

Euripides' *Hippolytus*, produced as the playwright's second (and successful) dramatisation of the myth about Phaedra's illicit love of her stepson Hippolytus in 428 BC,[23] must be seen in this context. It reflects, and plays with, the age's intense interest in causation, poised between religion and 'science'. The play opens with the prologue-speech of vengeful Aphrodite: Hippolytus, we are told, refuses to pay her due respect 'alone among the citizens of the land of Troezen' (12). But the goddess of love will not suffer such outrageous behaviour. Sweet revenge, she informs us, will soon be hers (τιμωρήσομαι | Ἱππόλυτον ἐν τῇδ' ἡμέρᾳ, 21–2): by the goddess's cunning design, Phaedra has fallen in love with her stepson; but this love shall prove disastrous, taking down, first, innocent Phaedra; and then, through Theseus as unsuspecting intermediary, Hippolytus himself. With this beginning, the question of causation is settled, at least for the audience: all is the doing of the goddess. For the human characters in the play, however, nothing is settled. As disaster makes headway, along the predicted paths, these characters struggle hard to understand and to 'construct worlds of meaning' out of the disorder they experience. In the process, religious as well as scientific (and other) models of causation are rehearsed. The notion that all is the work of the gods is juxtaposed with 'Herodotean' uncertainty and 'Hippocratic' and 'Thucydidean' secular 'rationalism'.[24] Like other Euripidean tragedies (but more intensely), *Hippolytus* 'cultivate[s] uncertainty about divine agency, thereby opening up space to explore other possibilities'.[25]

The play's decided interest in causation is clear by the end of the parodos. We have heard Aphrodite; we have encountered Hippolytus, neatly

---

[22] On Thucydides' description of the plague, see Page (1953). On the nature of the Athenian plague and the influence of the Hippocratic outlook on Thucydides' account, see Poole and Holladay (1979). On the plague, see also Holladay (1988). On Thucydides' historiographical principles in connection with Hippocratic medicine, see Rechenauer (1991).

[23] With the second (our) *Hippolytus*, Euripides won one of the only four first places of his career. On the lost Euripidean play and Sophocles' version of the myth (the lost *Phaedra*), see Barrett (1964) 10–45.

[24] On the importance of Hippocratic subtexts in the play, see Kosak (2004) 49–65 (and *passim* on Hippocratic medicine and Euripidean tragedy in general); see also Jouanna (2012c) 61–5.

[25] Holmes (2010) 238.

displaying his scornful rejection of the goddess and expressing reservations about gods 'worshipped at night' (οὐδείς μ' ἀρέσκει νυκτὶ θαυμαστὸς θεῶν, 106). Now the chorus come on stage. The question of causation, of finding the appropriate narrative to account for the inexplicable, is immediately foregrounded. Phaedra, the chorus tell us, suffers from a 'hidden grief' (κρυπτῷ πάθει, 139), is worn out and threatens to starve herself to death (131–40). Why all this? they wonder. Has their mistress committed some fault against Dictynna (†σὺ δ'† ἀμφὶ τὰν πολύθη-|ρον Δίκτυνναν ἀμπλακίαις | ἀνίερος ἀθύτων πελανῶν τρύχῃ, 145–7)? Has Theseus betrayed her (ἢ πόσιν... ποιμαίνει τις ἐν οἴκοις | κρυπτᾷ κοίτᾳ λεχέων σῶν; 151–4)?[26] Alas, they declare in resignation, some kind of 'uneasy harmony' (δύστροπος ἁρμονία, 161–2) is characteristic of woman's nature, what with the 'unhappy helplessness of birth-pangs and their folly' (161–9).[27] We are only at the doorstep of disaster, but a comprehensive struggle for understanding is already well on its way, deploying religious models of causation (fault against Dictynna) as well as secular ones, including pointed 'scientific' explanations (female biology). With its juxtaposition of Aphrodite's explanations and the chorus' groping quest, already the opening of the play suggests reading *Hippolytus* in terms of a 'crisis of comprehension', unfolding in terms of an (inter-)play of different causation models.

An analysis of the role of pollution in the play cannot but take notice of this wider concern. There is in *Hippolytus* a strong presence of notions of pollution as well as purity.[28] It has long been recognised that in this 'Aphroditean play' these notions frequently revolve around questions of sexual purity and impurity.[29] But that is not all. These sexualised notions are integrated into a wider framework of ritual and other types of *miasma* which throws the question of causation into stark relief. The present

---

[26] The parodos' repeated references to something 'hidden' (139, 153–4) anticipate the play's interest in the search for hidden causes. It is apt that the interplay of concealment and revelation constitutes a major dynamic of the play: Goff (1990) 12–20. On signs and their (difficult) decipherment in *Hippolytus*, see Segal (1992) 425–34.
[27] Translations are taken from Kovac's Loeb (*Euripides*, vol. 2, Cambridge, MA, 1995).
[28] Segal (1970).
[29] E.g. Segal (1970), Burnett (1986), Roisman (1999) 27–45. Considerable attention has been given to the 'pure meadow' in the parodos: Bremer (1975), Cairns (1997), Goff (1990) 58–65. It recalls the flowery surroundings in which Hera seduces Zeus in Homer *Il.* 14 (esp. vv. 346–51) or the meadow where Hades abducts Persephone in the *Homeric Hymn to Demeter*. For Goff (1990) 59 the 'paradigmatic narrative set in the meadow provides a shared and available way to talking about access to sexuality.' See also Swift (2006) on this meadow and the *chloē* of the third stasimon and the language of female transition. On the theme of sexuality in the play, see e.g. Goldhill (1986) 117–37; Craik (1998) on sexual innuendo.

chapter, consequently, shall pay close attention to the context of the play's, and the age's, interest in causation.

The picture that will emerge is one of a complex play with different models of causation. *Miasma* binds these models together. Notions of inherited evil are expressed in the language of *miasma*; but ritual *miasma* has a place in this, too, as well as medical notions, according to which *miasma* is the result not of religious transgression but of physical dysfunction. Tracing the twists and turns of this complex play shall be the main business of the following discussion. But the analyses offered here also suggest reconsidering what may be called the play's 'challenge of causation'. This I shall attempt in a brief epilogue. I suggest that Euripides' play, like Herodotus, invites us to acknowledge the human inability to establish incontestable narratives of causation.

Inherited evil and pollution

As *Hippolytus* unfolds, chaos and mayhem multiply. Phaedra's condition worsens, with bouts of near-insanity (as when she 'casts out' words 'mounted on madness', μανίας ἔποχον ῥίπτουσα λόγον, 214). Fatalities follow, in the form, first, of the heroine's suicide; and of her stepson's destruction hereafter.

There is much for the characters to understand and to make sense of, but they do so differently. We have already seen that the first parodos juxtaposes the religious and the secular, including even the 'scientific', as the chorus attempt to make sense of their mistress's suffering. In the subsequent scene, too, secular and more or less scientific models of explanation are invoked as the sly nurse, apparently very familiar with the crafts her of day, cross-examines Phaedra in search of the origins of her 'hidden grief'.[30] Those more directly involved in the suffering, however, will have nothing to do with such sophistries.

Phaedra, Theseus and Hippolytus at different points in the drama's denouement all favour one specific model of causation: that provided by the idea of an inherited evil.[31] Phaedra is the first to do so, albeit in an idiosyncratic and modified form. As she is about to reveal the truth about her present distress, Phaedra, in terms too opaque for the nurse to understand, alludes to two other cases of illicit and violent sexual passion in

---

[30] On the nurse as doctor and charlatan, see Kosak (2004) 49–65 (and below in this chapter).
[31] On inherited evil, see Gagné (2013); Sewell-Rutter (2007) on tragedy. On generational schemes in Aeschylus, see Föllinger (2003). On the related issue of demons and avenging spirits (in Aeschylus), see Geisser (2002).

her family, her mother Pasiphae's encounter with the bull (ὦ τλῆμον, οἷον, μῆτερ, ἠράσθης ἔρον, 337) and her sister Ariadne's unhappy affair with Dionysus (σύ τ', ὦ τάλαιν' ὅμαιμε, Διονύσου δάμαρ, 339); 'it is thence that woe has come upon me, it's nothing new', she concludes (ἐκεῖθεν ἡμεῖς, οὐ νεωστί, δυστυχεῖς, 343). She seems to suggest in this way that her present plight is a matter of inheritance (which implies the inheritance of a certain proneness to errant erotic desire) – a type of family curse, one might say.[32] Theseus' and Hippolytus' later references to the idea of inherited evil are more straightforward. Theseus, confronted upon return to Troezen with the shocking news of Phaedra's suicide, attributes present disaster to the workings of an avenging spirit, in retribution for some ancestral crime (820, 831–3: ἀμπλακίαισι τῶν πάροιθέν τινος). Hippolytus, in the face of his own impending death, takes recourse to the same idea, surmising that 'some inherited evil of long-ago ancestors breaks its bounds and does not stay in place but has come upon me' (1379–83: παλαιῶν προγεννητόρων . . . κακόν).[33]

With this, pollution becomes central in the protagonists' attempts to make sense of their experience. Although the idea of an inherited evil is not a straightforward ritual pollution and is elsewhere often referred to in language which, although adumbrating pollution, remains decidedly vague,[34] here in *Hippolytus* the protagonists, with the exception of Theseus, draw inherited evil and the terminology of pollution closely together. Theseus' words are characterised precisely by the vague adumbration of pollution which often crops up when the idea of inherited evil is at stake. Confronted with Phaedra's death, his thoughts immediately turn to 'an unperceived stain from some avenging spirit' (κηλὶς ἄφραστος ἐξ ἀλαστόρων τινός, 820). Both Phaedra and Hippolytus, the two who suffer most, have fewer qualms about directly invoking the terminology of *miasma*.

Phaedra connects inherited evil and pollution when she refers to her passionate desire as '*miasma* of the mind' (317). Even though at first this striking formulation seems to be but the fitting reply to the nurse's probing

[32] On Phaedra's 'inherited evil' and her Cretan past, see Reckford (1974). Crete stands for sexual passion, but also for a 'pull backward into personal failure' (ibid. 318).

[33] According to Barrett (1964) ad 1378–83 Hippolytus, like Theseus, has no particular crime in mind: as he is but a distant member of the Pelopid family (through his grandmother Aithra, daughter of Pittheus, son of Pelops), it would be 'absurd to allege that he thinks of himself as a Pelopid' (and thus thinks of a specific curse/crime).

[34] The idea of inherited evil is referred to in terms of the language of *miasma* only rarely in our extant sources: among the few relevant passages, see e.g. A. *Supp.* 265 (παλαιῶν αἱμάτων μιάσμασι | χρανθεῖσ[α] . . . γαῖα); Thuc. 5.1 (κατὰ παλαιάν τινα αἰτίαν οὐ καθαρούς). On inherited guilt and pollution, see Parker (1983) 198–206.

question about whether it was perhaps some blood clinging to her hands that caused her present suffering (nurse: ἁγνὰς μέν, ὦ παῖ, χεῖρας αἵματος φορεῖς; | Phaedra: χεῖρες μὲν ἁγναί, φρὴν δ' ἔχει μίασμά τι, 316–17),[35] the play soon suggests that what Phaedra may also have in mind when she speaks of pollution is her problematic Cretan inheritance that comes into sharper focus some twenty lines later. After all, both this inheritance and the 'pollution of the mind' relate to Phaedra's passionate desire; and even though the idea of inherited evil is not frequently expressed in terms of the language of *miasma*, the link between the two is arguably close enough to allow the connection to be established even here, where inherited evil takes the form of 'inherited disposition towards errant erotic desire'. This 'family curse', Phaedra seems to imply, is her pollution.

Though unable to establish such precise connections, Hippolytus, too, couches the idea of inherited evil in the language of *miasma*. He qualifies the 'inherited evil of long-ago ancestors' to which he attributes disaster as he approaches death as one 'resulting from polluting violence'. Let us quote the passage in full now (1379–83):

> μιαιφόνον τι σύγγονον
> παλαιῶν προγεννη-
> τόρων ἐξορίζεται
> κακὸν οὐδὲ μένει,
> ἔμολέ τ' ἐπ' ἐμέ.

> Some inherited evil of long-ago ancestors breaks its bounds and does not stay in place but has come upon me.

It is with the force of careful symmetry that the idea of inherited evil, and with it one specific version of pollution, is presented as the preferred causation model in the characters' quest for sense in tragic chaos. For these references are distributed evenly, not only among the characters, but also over the play. They occur at important junctures: as the nurse's cross-examination reaches its climax in the opening parts of the play; upon

---

[35] More on this formulation below. For now, let us note that pollution as a matter of intentions rather than acts seems unusual in the fifth century context; see Barrett (1964) ad loc. A similar formulation crops up at Eur. *Or.* 1604, where Orestes accuses Menelaus of an 'unclean mind' (Menelaus: ἁγνὸς γάρ εἰμι χεῖρας· Orestes: ἀλλ' οὐ τὰς φρένας). For the development of the notion of a purity of the mind, see Chaniotis (1997) and (2012). The earliest (non-literary) evidence for the concept of a 'pure mind' comes in the form of the verse inscription above the entrance of the temple of Asclepius in Epidaurus: ἁγνὸν χρὴ νηοῖο θυώδεος ἐντὸς ἰόντα | ἔμμεναι. ἁγνείη δ' ἐστὶ φρονεῖν ὅσια, cited in Porphyry *Abst.* 2.19; the inscription probably dates from the fourth century BC: Chaniotis (1997) 152. See also Graf (2007b) 113–15 (quoting e.g. *LSCG* 139 (Lindos, second century AD), where we find the striking formulation γνώμην καθαρός).

Phaedra's suicide at midpoint; in the closing scene, when disaster has come full circle.

This preferred causation model is ironically incongruent with the play's divine frame.[36] But this is not the only irony that emerges. The play's surface engagement with pollution as inherited evil is intertwined with subtexts, some more ironic, others less, which suggest pollution, and in forms other than inherited evil, as the cause of disaster, in this way providing yet more causation models potentially in ironic tension with the play's frame of Aphroditean causation.

Ritual pollution as subtext of causation

One of these subtexts revolves around ritual pollution. This subtext is itself subject to bifurcation, however. It appears in the form of an implicit suggestion of pollution as the result of ritual transgression. But it also appears in the form of more explicit pollutions and in part in the form of an ironic play with the notion of contagious pollution. Let us begin with the concrete pollution of ritual transgression.

Phaedra's suicide during Theseus' absence as 'sacred ambassador' (θεωρός) constitutes such a ritual transgression. This embassy may be seen to evoke embassies well known in classical Athens and which mark a time of particular ritual precariousness, associated with especially strict requirements of purity. Since this 'holy time' is infringed, *Hippolytus* seems to imply, disaster proliferates. Pollution here appears, not as the ultimate source of disaster, but as the guarantor of its continuity.

Theseus' θεωρία has been associated with *miasma* in the past. Starting from W. S. Barrett's assumption that this θεωρία must have implied oracular consultation (in Barrett's view an effective way of getting Theseus out of the way, while also allowing for the dramatically effective juxtaposition of Theseus' auspicious return and the disaster which greets him),[37] Robin Mitchell-Boyask speculates that Theseus consulted the oracle about the *miasma* he had contracted as the result of his killing of the Pallantidai, which Aphrodite mentions in the prologue (34–7; see my discussion below).[38]

---

[36] See also Janka (2004) 298 on Theseus' reflections at 820 and 831–3: 'Damit stellt Theseus hypothetisch ein Aischyleisches Plot-Pattern in den Raum, das für *seine* Tragödie gerade nicht zutrifft.'
[37] Barrett (1964) 31 and ibid. ad 790. For Barrett, the idea that Theseus' embassy implied oracular consultation is simply established fact: see e.g. ibid. ad 790.
[38] Mitchell(-Boyask) (1991) 100.

Euripides' Hippolytus

Mitchell-Boyask's interpretation certainly has much to commend it. If, as is at least not entirely out of the question, *Oedipus tyrannus* was produced before the second – our – *Hippolytus*,[39] the return of a garlanded hero might have reminded the audience of Creon's 'garlanded' return from the Delphic oracle in Sophocles' play and hence of oracular consultation. That Theseus inquired about *miasma* might likewise suggest itself to the audience, despite Mitchell-Boyask's reservations about his own proposition. Theseus would have reason to do so: we see elsewhere, in historical as well as in literary sources, that exile forms part only of a more complex nexus of ritual provisions to remove *miasma*;[40] and a visit to Delphi for the purpose of purification, if not attested in historical sources, is part of the tragic imagination at least since Orestes' memorable visit to his patron god's shrine for this very purpose in Aeschylus' *Eumenides*. Also, if there is in this scene something of the *Oedipus tyrannus*, the notion of an oracular consultation in matters pertaining to *miasma* cannot be far from the audience's mind.

On this reading, the disasters in Troezen, the incurrence of new *miasma*, would coincide with the removal of Theseus' old *miasma*. 'Perhaps', Mitchell-Boyask notes, 'Theseus, because of his pollution, cannot come into contact with the oracle's divinity without something terrible happening.'[41] In this way, the play would seem to establish a close link between Theseus' *miasma*-infested past and present misfortune.[42]

This is not without significance, but there exists another association which Theseus' θεωρία might have evoked in an Athenian audience, which has a very different and arguably more intriguing connection with the theme of pollution. Renate Schlesier has pointed the way here.[43] Every year, the city sent a sacred embassy (θεωρία) to Delos. The *aition*, and

---

[39] For the dating of *OT*, see Bernard Knox, *AJPh* 77 (1956), 133–47; Kamerbeek (1967) 28–9; Easterling (1982) 19–23. *OT* may well have been produced after *Hippolytus*.
[40] See Dem. 23.72; Parker (1983) 118 (and see my discussion of the end of Sophocles' *OT* at the end of this chapter).
[41] Mitchell(-Boyask) (1991) 100.
[42] Theseus generally appears unable to escape his past. In particular, his return from the embassy is reminiscent of his earlier ill-starred return from the Minotaur. In high spirits and bearer of good news, Theseus is greeted by wailing (*Hipp.* 792–3). The return from Crete was a similarly bitter-sweet affair, as the joyful return of the hero was dimmed by the demise of father Aegeus (according to Plutarch *Thes.* 22.4, it was therefore customary to cry *Woe! Woe!* amidst libations commemorating Theseus' safe return at the Oschophoria; on allusions in *Hippolytus* to the Oschophoria and its myth, see Mitchell-Boyask (1999) 50–3). The parallel is underscored when Theseus inquires about the well-being of another father, aged Pittheus, at 794.
[43] Schlesier (2002b) 72–3.

the wider implications, are given by Phaedo in Plato's dialogue of the same name (58a–c):

> This is the ship, as the Athenians say, in which Theseus once went to Crete with the 'Fourteen' and saved them and himself. Now the Athenians made a vow to Apollo, as the story goes, that if they were saved they would send a sacred embassy every year to Delos. And from that time even to the present day they send it annually in honour of the god. Now it is their law that after the sacred embassy begins the city must be purified and no one may be publicly executed until the ship has gone to Delos and back (ἐπειδὰν οὖν ἄρξωνται τῆς θεωρίας, νόμος ἐστὶν αὐτοῖς ἐν τῷ χρόνῳ τούτῳ καθαρεύειν τὴν πόλιν καὶ δημοσίᾳ μηδένα ἀποκτεινύναι, πρὶν ἂν εἰς Δῆλόν τε ἀφίκηται τὸ πλοῖον καὶ πάλιν δεῦρο); and sometimes, when contrary winds detain it, this takes a long time. The beginning of the sacred embassy is when the priest of Apollo crowns the stern of the ship.[44]

The triad, offered by the play, of 'sacred embassy', 'Theseus' and 'return' make it difficult not to think of the Delian θεωρία commemorating the safe return home of Theseus (and the 'Fourteen') from the Cretan labyrinth and the Minotaur.

If Theseus' embassy is understood to imply the Delian scenario, Phaedra's suicide and the pollution resulting from it would appear particularly out of place and may be taken as a ritual disruption which causes further disaster. After all, as Plato's Phaedo informs us, the period of the θεωρία was perceived to be worthy of particular ritual precautions: Athens was anxious to keep herself pure, free from the stain of pollution; 'purifications of the city and no public executions' is the order of the day. Theseus' θεωρία would not simply constitute a cunning trick by the poet to remove Theseus from Troezen, then, but would mark the time wherein the disastrous dramatic knot is tied as a period of particular vulnerability, and certainly incompatible with the kind of pollution which ensues from Phaedra's suicide.[45]

We may detect pointed irony in the poet's manipulation of the need for purity associated with the Delian θεωρία. In particular, there is perhaps some significance in the language the chorus choose to describe Phaedra's suicide. In conclusion to the much-admired escape ode,[46] the Troezenian women turn their attention to present plight, their distressed mistress's brokenness (767–71):

---

[44] The translation is adapted from H. N. Fowler, *Plato in Twelve Volumes*, vol. 1, Cambridge, MA, 1966.
[45] This is also implied by Schlesier (2002b) 73.
[46] On the escape ode, see especially Padel (1974) 227–35.

χαλεπᾷ δ' ὑπέραντλος οὖσα συμφορᾷ τεράμνων
ἀπὸ νυμφιδίων κρεμαστὸν
ἅψεται ἀμφὶ βρόχον λευκᾷ καθαρμόζουσα δειρᾷ·

> And charged with an overload of hard misfortune she will fasten about her a noose hanging from the beams of her bridal chamber, fitting it to her white neck.

Consider in particular the expression λευκᾷ καθαρμόζουσα δειρᾷ. Cultural critics, indebted to the writings of Nicole Loraux and Helen King,[47] will discover in this strangulation of a white female neck a comment on one of the pressing issues of the drama: Phaedra's sexual purity. Loraux has taught us that for ancient Greeks the female δέρη (throat) was 'a strong point of feminine beauty' and also, it seems, imbued with sexual values.[48] In particular, a virginal throat severed by a knife may have evoked associations of defloration.[49] Strangulation, on the other hand, may have implied a particularly virginal death as it avoids the bloodshed of rape or defloration.[50] In King's view, Phaedra 'by choosing this death... inserts herself into an established tradition and thus strengthens her false claim that Hippolytus has raped her'.[51] A comprehensive reading of the scene in these terms is not my objective here, but it should be pointed out that such a reading would need to pay greater attention to the fact, and the irony that ensues, that Phaedra is not a virgin, but a married woman – albeit one (and here I agree with what I take to be King's meaning) who has an interest in suggesting to her husband a preoccupation with the maintenance of chastity in the face of the alleged attack on that chastity by Hippolytus.

But the expression may also be understood to imply a wordplay which in turn may be seen to draw attention to purification only to emphasise its absence, or uncanny corruption. In particular, but not only, if Phaedra's 'white neck' really evoked the (displaced and ironic) notion of virginal purity, the word used to describe the 'fitting around' the neck of the noose, καθαρμόζουσα (καθ-αρμόζω), appears striking. That Greek writers made use of wordplay no longer needs to be defended, not least thanks to 'Swell-Foot'/'Know-Foot' Oedipus whose various etymological affiliations

---

[47] King (1983), Loraux (1987).   [48] Loraux (1987) 50 (on feminine beauty); 41, 61 (on sexual values).
[49] Ibid. 40 on Eur. *Hec.* 352–3, 368, 414–16, 611–12, *Hcld.* 591–2 and *IA* 460–2 (the sacrificial deaths of Polyxena, Macaria and Iphigenia). She thinks (ibid. 41) that in Euripides 'the blood-stained death of *parthenoi* is considered as an anomalous and displaced way of transforming virginity into womanhood – as though the throat-cutting equaled a defloration.'
[50] King (1983) 119; see also (slightly differently) Loraux (1987) 15.
[51] King (1983) 119. The point is taken up by Goff (1990) 38.

we will encounter later in this chapter.[52] Here, the term expressing the horrifying act of fitting noose to neck (καθαρμόζουσα) may be seen to recall something rather less troublesome: purification (καθαρ-, καθαρμός). In a loose associative reading we might suggest that Phaedra's suicide is a purification of sorts: of her pollution of the mind in the first place, but in a sense perhaps also of her reputation; it restores her 'purity', which, as she pointed out to the nurse, was under attack by the *miasma* of sexual desire (317). But there is the corpse, there is the disaster, there is the returning hero casting down his garland in dejection: this 'purification' is no purification but results in the first concrete manifestation of *miasma* in the present of the play. In the absence of Theseus as θεωρός, this seems to be the best those left behind can offer in terms of 'purifying the city'.

The gulf between ritual norm, or ideal, and corrupted reality deepens. And it is this ritual infringement which the audience is invited to view, if not as the ultimate cause of *Hippolytus*' tragic action, then at least as a potential contributing factor.

The spread of pollution and excessive characters

The more immediate (albeit not – on the play's terms – ultimate) source of disaster is Phaedra's 'pollution of the mind' (φρὴν δ' ἔχει μίασμά τι, 317) to which we return in this and the next section. The present section will be concerned with two interrelated concerns of the play, the fatal – albeit largely apparent rather than real – spread of pollution, on the one hand; and excessive mental states, on the other. These two concerns may to some extent be considered in conjunction as feeding into another causation model complementary to, or even potentially in (ironic) tension with, the play's divine frame.

Let us first provide the frame of reference necessary for setting the following discussion within the play's wider perspective. In addition to ideas of inherited evils and implicit (polluting) ritual transgressions, more straightforward ritual purities and impurities play an important role in *Hippolytus*, albeit in different forms. Frequently expressed in the same language (and in the case of purity in particular by the adjective ἁγνός),[53] ideas of purity and pollution circle on the one hand around bloodshed (as for instance at 316, when the nurse asks Phaedra whether her hands are free

---

[52] S. *OT* may be seen to make extensive use of wordplay. See for instance the extensive list of references in the general index s.v. 'wordplay' in Ahl (1991) 297.
[53] 11, 102, 138, 316, 317, 1003, 1448 (here ἄναγνος).

from bloodshed, ἁγνάς ... χεῖρας αἵματος);[54] they circle on the other hand around one particular form of ritual purity, abstinence and in particular sexual abstinence.[55]

This latter type of purity is in fact particularly important within the dynamics of the play. Most importantly, Hippolytus' slightly esoteric adherence to permanent chastity as the expression of his devotion to virginal Artemis becomes the offence against Aphrodite by which the tragic denouement is set in motion: problematically, 'being chaste' (ἁγνὸς ὤν) he will 'greet [Aphrodite] only from afar' (102). But Phaedra, too, practices a *hagneia* that is connected with sexual abstinence, if more obliquely. As the chorus informs us, Phaedra keeps her 'body ἁγνός from the corn of Demeter' (135–8).[56] Certainly, Phaedra's *hagneia* is a ritual fast. Yet, the idea that this abstinence from food has to do with (abstinence from) sex is not far off. It is arguably fair to say that Phaedra's fast is but one form in which her struggle to repress her sexual desire for Hippolytus manifests itself. Ancient evidence sometimes suggests a correlation between inordinate eating and sexual licence.[57] Not least, Semonides, in his infamous diatribe against women, identifies a certain donkey-like woman who 'eats ... all night and all day ... and just so, when it comes to sex (ἔργον ἀφροδίσιον), welcomes any man who passes by' (Semonides 7.46–9). Conversely, a case may perhaps be made for the ritual fast on the second day of the Thesmophoria (the Nesteia) to be bound up with the participating women's chastity.[58] In the case of *Hippolytus*, eating, speech and sex are particularly closely associated, with Phaedra attempting to patrol, and indeed shut off, the

---

[54] See also 1448, where Theseus asks Hippolytus whether he will leave him with hands unclean (he considers himself polluted because he is responsible for his son's imminent death), ἢ τὴν ἐμὴν ἄναγνον ἐκλιπὼν χέρα.

[55] For a more detailed discussion of ἁγνός, see Parker (1983) 147–51. Words deriving from καθαρ-, too, may sometimes refer to sexual abstinence; see e.g. the Lucian scholion on the Thesmophoria (Σ Lucian *DMeretr.* 2.1; also quoted by Deubner (1932) 40 n. 5). On notions of chastity and purity in *Hippolytus*, see Segal (1970) and Roisman (1999) 27–45.

[56] Schlesier (2002b) 53–5 holds that Phaedra's fast alludes to Demeter's fast, described in the Homeric Hymn, resulting from her grief at the abduction of Korē (49–50). If the Demeter–Korē-story is the paradigm and Phaedra another Demeter, then Hippolytus corresponds to Korē – the significant difference being that a mother's love of her daughter is replaced by a woman's erotic desire for her stepson.

[57] Loraux (1993) 100.

[58] Incidentally, Phaedra's fast is faintly reminiscent of Thesmophoric practice. For one, Phaedra fasts, like the women on the Nesteia. In addition, Demeter, the patron-goddess of the Thesmophoria, and the suggestive number 'three' (τριτάταν ... ἀμέραν, 135–7) are invoked. The festival stretched over three days and, if we trust the scholiast on Lucian (Σ Lucian *DMeretr.* 2.1), those most involved in the rites had abstained from sexual intercourse for three days (καθαρεύσασαι) in preparation for the festival. A balanced account and interpretation of the Thesmophoria can be found in Parker (2005) 270–83; Zeitlin (1982) 138–53 also remains fundamental.

various boundaries of, and access to, her body,[59] so that it seems that Phaedra's *hagneia*, though designating a ritual fast, has something to do with (the repression of) her sexuality, too. In the refreshingly sweeping words of ethno-psychoanalyst and literary aficionado George Devereux, therefore, '[i]t cannot be said clearly enough that the *Hippolytos* is about love-and-sex.'[60]

Fittingly, at the epicentre of doom and destruction sits, next to Aphrodite, Phaedra's sexual passion, which is designated as pollution (317), and for better reasons than I have hitherto acknowledged. For one, even if the choice of terminology is not understood within the framework of inherited evil, it is in general not surprising that Phaedra's desire should be designated as pollution. Arguably, the term aptly designates something that is both worrying and frustratingly elusive. More specifically, considering Ruth Padel's (and other scholars') insights about the perturbing (and/because inscrutable) 'inside' of women in fifth-century BC (male) perception and the notion of a particular impurity attaching to, or residing within, the female body, which certain sources intimate, something ominous lodged in the female inside is quite logically referred to as pollution.[61]

But Phaedra's particular pollution is not only a disconcerting and illusory affliction of the heroine's interior, it also reaches out and 'infects'; the play retains, that is, the idea of contagion associated with ritual pollution and exploits it in ironically twisted ways. As the result of Phaedra's 'pollution of the mind' Hippolytus soon loses his particular type of purity, the *hagneia* he keeps in honour of Artemis; or rather, he loses the *appearance* of this purity. Upon hearing of his stepmother's wayward love from the nurse as intermediary, the youth feels the need for purification and considers his *hagneia* under attack, indeed claims that he appears no longer ἁγνός (to himself; 653–5):

> ἁγὼ ῥυτοῖς νασμοῖσιν ἐξομόρξομαι,
> ἐς ὦτα κλύζων. πῶς ἂν οὖν εἴην κακός,
> ὃς οὐδ' ἀκούσας τοιάδ' ἁγνεύειν δοκῶ;

> I shall pour running water into my ears to wipe away your proposals! How could I be base when I no longer seem clean (to myself) as a result of simply hearing such things?

---

[59] Rabinowitz (1993) 160.
[60] Devereux (1985) 6. See also Goldhill (1986) 117–37, Craik (1998), Roisman (1999) 27–45.
[61] Worrying female interior: Padel (1983); Hippocratic gynaecology largely confirms this picture: King (1998); Blundell (1995) 98–112 (esp. 101). Women associated with impurity: Parker (1983) 101, von Staden (1992b) esp. 13–5 (both quoting Semonides fr. 7 and Ar. *Equ.* 1284–5; von Staden also draws attention to the fact that birth is considered polluting); more widely: Carson (1999).

Word about Phaedra's 'pollution' (her illicit desire) impairs Hippolytus' *hagneia*. To see the point here and indeed realise that the notion of actual transmission of pollution is arguably toyed with here, we need to take this formulation literally. It is, very concretely, *words*, originating from Phaedra's polluted mind and transmitted by the nurse, that attack the youth's purity.

Though Hippolytus' loss of purity is apparent rather than real, the process behind this loss, real or apparent, transmission through words, is eminently fitting within the context of *Hippolytus*. For words are especially powerful in this play. It is not merely that Phaedra's tablet contains (written) words that 'scream out' and incriminate Hippolytus (more below); or that Theseus possesses curses, granted to him by Poseidon, which prove very efficient in the play's denouement.[62] Throughout, speech is a 'matter', quite literally, not to be treated lightly.[63] Hippolytus, for example, warns his servant not to pronounce the name of Aphrodite (εὐλαβοῦ δὲ μή τί σου σφαλῇ στόμα, 100). More importantly, words are constantly referred to in terms which suggest that we are dealing with quasi-material objects. For instance, delirious Phaedra 'casts out an ἔπος' (ἔρριψας ἔπος, 232);[64] a λόγος threatens to venture towards dangerous regions (ποῖ προβήσεται λόγος; 342); and Theseus' words are 'unsettled from the mind' (λόγοι... ἔξεδροι φρενῶν, 935). It is appropriate, then, that words should destroy (the appearance of) Hippolytus' purity. It is as though words, like invisible but nonetheless concrete objects, 'unsettled from Phaedra's polluted mind' and infested with that pollution, have been 'cast out' and, transmitted by the nurse as the intermediary, 'ventured towards' the chaste youth, taking away (the appearance of) his purity in the process.

Ironically, further apparent rather than real losses of purity ensue, precipitated by Phaedra's pollution; problematically, these cease to concern merely Hippolytus himself. At 655, Hippolytus 'appears no longer *hagnos*' only to himself.[65] After Phaedra's suicide, however, the rift between appearance and reality that is toyed with stops being a private concern.[66] Hippolytus

---

[62] On these curses, see Gregory (2009).
[63] It is also 'an explosive force, which, once released, cannot be restrained': Knox (1952a) 16. On speech in *Hippolytus*, see Goff (1990) 1–26, 30–9, Segal (1993) 115–17, Zeitlin (1996d) 257–61, McClure (1999) 112–57.
[64] See Goff (1990) 30–9 on speech and desire: Phaedra's delirious utterances are one instance where desire becomes as a 'generator of narrative' (ibid. 30).
[65] Both Barrett (1964) and Halleran (1995) take line 655 in this sense, supplementing ἐμοί.
[66] The idea of a rift between appearance and reality is pervasive in the play. Hippolytus' line 'my tongue has sworn, but my mind is unsworn' (612) has been notorious since antiquity. It is alluded to three times in comedy (Ar. *Th*. 275–6; *Ra*. 101–2, 1471). On this line, see in particular Avery (1968). Related dichotomies and duplicities manifest themselves in various guises. See e.g. Meltzer (1996) on truthful and counterfeit voices; also Goff (1990) esp. 12–20; Segal (1988).

no longer seems to have lost his *hagneia* only on his own view; and further inversions of appearance and reality follow. Because of the oath of silence he had sworn, Hippolytus has little to say in response to Phaedra's writing tablet which 'screams out' at Theseus (βοᾷ βοᾷ δέλτος ἄλαστα, 877) and accuses Hippolytus of rape. As a result, Hippolytus becomes 'obviously the most devious man' alive (ἐμφανῶς κάκιστος, 945) for Theseus, guilty of attempted rape and responsible for Phaedra's suicide. As a matter of this 'obviousness', the virginal youth's body to Theseus 'appears' no longer pure despite his inner 'virginal soul' (ἑνὸς δ' ἄθικτος, ᾧ με νῦν ἔχειν δοκεῖς· | λέχους γὰρ ἐς τόδ' ἡμέρας ἁγνὸν δέμας, 1002–3; παρθένον ψυχὴν ἔχων, 1006). But Hippolytus has not only lost the appearance of his *hagneia*. In his father's eyes, he has contracted worse pollution on top (ἐς μίασμ' ἐλήλυθα, 946).

From here on, irony becomes sinister. For Theseus, the loss of *hagneia* and the attraction, in the process, of worse pollution is a fact. As we shall see later in this chapter, in *Oedipus tyrannus* the invisibility of pollution prevents the characters from establishing a connection between pollution and 'culprit'; in *Hippolytus*, by contrast, it allows Theseus to establish a connection between pollution and non-culprit. In *Oedipus tyrannus* the invisibility of pollution delays disaster; in *Hippolytus* it precipitates it. The outcome is a replication, but with fatal results, of the polluted father's fate by the seemingly polluted son: like the polluted father, the son is sent into exile (ἔξερρε γαίας... φυγάς, 973).[67] Though a matter, it would seem, of appearance rather than of reality, Hippolytus' loss of purity propels him ἐκ δήμου, and towards doom. In an ironic twist of events, the pollution which has reached out from Phaedra to attack Hippolytus' *hagneia*, despite attacking, it seems, only the appearance of this *hagneia*, precipitates a fatal course of events that is predicated on the mistaken assumption that the youth has really lost his *hagneia* and incurred worse pollution in the process. A final irony is in store. This devious 'spread' of Phaedra's 'pollution of the mind' results in the first real pollution since the play's prologue: that which Theseus, at the end of the play, will be freed from and which he has contracted as the one responsible for Hippolytus' (imminent) death (ἢ τὴν ἐμὴν ἄναγνον ἐκλιπὼν χέρα; 1448).[68]

---

[67] This is also noted by Mitchell(-Boyask) (1991) 110.
[68] Attic law stipulated that the dying victim could absolve the killer from the consequences of the killing (Dem. 37.59 cited by Barrett (1964) ad 1449). A number of manuscripts print φρένα instead of χέρα. Barrett (ad 1448) dismisses this variant (because 'plain man's language is needed' and '[t]he uncleanness of the φρήν... is not plain man's language but sophistication'). I am inclined to agree with Barrett's (and Diggle's) text; but the variant would fit with, and add further irony to, the play's concern with the reality vs. appearance of pollution.

What are we to make of this? In part, it is probably fair to say, we are 'simply' dealing with Euripidean irony and a plot that is cleverly constructed around the notion of pollution and loss of purity. But is there a point to this irony? This is arguably the case, in two senses, which are to some extent connected. I would like to suggest, first, a parallel between *miasma* and desire, which *Hippolytus* plays with; and second, that *Hippolytus* toys with the notion of a shared 'excessive character', and in particular in the case of desiring heroine and obstinate youth.

As Phaedra's pollution reaches out and 'infects', it reproduces in the terms of transmissible *miasma* the mechanisms of (Phaedra's) desire. In other words, because pollution, as a result of its easy transmissibility, is associated with the refusal to stay put and fixed (I anticipate aspects of the next chapter here), it provides an apt analogy for Phaedra's desire. For, as Barbara Goff has shown, this desire reaches out from the desiring subject, escapes that subject's control, generates narrative, perpetuates itself in speech (I borrow Goff's terms) and in this way affects, and 'infects', its environment;[69] eventually it produces mayhem. In view of Goff's excellent study, there is no need for extended illustration. Suffice it to point out that, for all Phaedra's attempts to conceal and indeed confine desire (an activity at which, in Greek – male – perception, women were particularly ill-equipped to succeed, what with their physical and emotional porousness),[70] it is ultimately desire which impels Phaedra to 'cast out' delirious fantasies about exchanging *polis* and *oikos* for the wilderness;[71] this first 'casting out' leads to the revelation of Phaedra's illicit love, which in turn precipitates disaster. There is a parallel between *miasma* and desire in that both resent, and worse, defy, containment, which *Hippolytus* exploits.

The second point comes into focus as a certain quality of the desire which Phaedra harbours is not only not confined, but in fact transmitted. That quality is 'excessiveness'.

Phaedra's 'pollution of the mind' denotes such 'excessiveness'. More precisely, it denotes an excessive mental disposition incompatible with the civic community. The point emerges with some force in the prologue. Much like the pollution Theseus had contracted as the result of killing the Pallantidai (μίασμα φεύγων αἵματος Παλλαντιδῶν, 35) and which, as Aphrodite informs us in the prologue, entails a year-long exile 'outside of

---

[69] Goff (1990) 27–54.
[70] On this porousness as inherent in female physiology (the female body is wetter; the wet is seen as unbounded: Aristotle, *De gen. et corr.* 2.2.329b31–3) and stretching out to the sphere of emotions, see Carson (1999).
[71] Goff (1990) 32–3.

the community' (ἐνιαυσίαν ἔκδημον αἰνέσας φυγήν, 37),[72] what Phaedra later designates as her 'pollution' – her illicit desire – implies a state 'outside of the community' (29–32):

> καὶ πρὶν μὲν ἐλθεῖν τήνδε γῆν Τροζηνίαν,
> πέτραν παρ' αὐτὴν Παλλάδος, κατόψιον
> γῆς τῆσδε, ναὸν Κύπριδος ἐγκαθείσατο,
> ἐρῶσ' ἔρωτ' ἔκδημον...

> And before she came to this land of Troezen, she built, hard by the rock of Pallas, a temple to Kypris, looking out over this land, because she loved a love outside the *dēmos*.

What is mostly literal in the case of Theseus is metaphorical in the case of Phaedra. In the context, W. S. Barrett takes the adjective ἔκδημος to mean 'foreign' and to refer, quite simply, to the fact that the object of Phaedra's desire – Hippolytus who resides in Troezen, not in Athens – is 'not from her country'.[73] Though certainly not incorrect, this interpretation, it seems to me, misses the particular thrust that is conveyed by the adjective ἔκδημος. I suggest that we retain the strong literal sense of a movement 'across the borders of the community' (ἔκ-δημος) and take the adjective to indicate that Phaedra's love implies an excessive mental state, one which propels her, spatially, beyond the confines of her marriage-bed and, socially, beyond the limits of what is acceptable to the *dēmos*, the civic community. As the term of choice to denote this troublesome desire, Phaedra's 'pollution' implies this excessiveness.

Against this background, it is arguably apposite that Hippolytus should suffer as the result of the (literally mistaken) assumption that he has lost his *hagneia* and incurred worse pollution on top. In the play's terms, and in particular those developed in reference to Phaedra's pollution, he *is* 'polluted' – mentally. As many have commented, Hippolytus, the chaste youth who refuses to participate in the life of the civic community and chooses to roam the wilds instead, hubristically rejecting 'the works of Aphrodite' and maintaining a strict purity,[74] also betrays a beyond-the-*dēmos* disposition,[75]

---

[72] Euripides is at pains to integrate this story of violence, pollution and exile with the myth of Phaedra and Hippolytus. The episode seems to belong to Theseus' early exploits and a link to the later story of Phaedra and Hippolytus is not attested elsewhere: Barrett (1964) ad 34–7; in Plutarch and Ps.-Apollodorus the killing of the Pallantidai occurs before or shortly after Aegeus' death, i.e. many years before the action of *Hippolytus* (ibid.). The first *Hippolytus* was probably set in Athens (ibid. 11); also 'it is difficult to bring the king and queen of Athens into residence at Troezen, but easy to bring the king's son into residence at Athens' (ibid. 32).
[73] Barrett (1964) ad 29–32.
[74] Grube (1961) 179 speaks of 'a curious mixture of purity and insolence'.
[75] Goldhill (1986) 118–21, Mitchell-Boyask (1999), Burnett (1986), Zeitlin (1996d).

albeit one initially perhaps lacking the particular violence and excessiveness that characterises the kind of mental state associated with pollution in the earlier parts of the play. But such violence and excessiveness flares up as (word of) Phaedra's 'pollution', her ἔκδημος desire, reaches the youth. Then, intemperance knows no bounds: in response to the nurse's revelations Hippolytus launches into the most violent denunciation of womankind (616–50), 'full of furious anger'.[76] As his *hagneia* is under attack from Phaedra's 'pollution', his un-civic disposition is ignited and bursts out in the crassest form. In that form, it would seem to resemble to some degree the kind of un-civic mental disposition associated with pollution in Phaedra's case. In the play's terms, then, Phaedra's 'pollution' seems to 'infect' Hippolytus quite concretely after all, reproducing in the youth a kind of 'pollution', albeit one that was already encapsulated in his refusal to engage in civic life and in his endeavour to maintain instead his ἁγνεία in honour of Artemis. In a final twist of irony, the loss of purity Hippolytus laments upon his violent outburst is perhaps more real than it would appear.

Medicine and miasma

In the preceding analyses, Phaedra's *miasma* of the mind has emerged as pivotal, the point of connection between different contexts into which *miasma* is drawn in the play. It binds together the idea of inherited evil with notions of contagious *miasma*; but it is also, in different ways, associated with the idea of intemperate mental dispositions by which disaster is precipitated. These different directions in which pollution points also represent models of causation, which may be seen to stand in (a more or less) ironic tension with the play's divine framework. But we are not done yet with Phaedra's *miasma* of the mind.

To these layers of meaning, and models of causation, we must now add another: 'science', or, more precisely, medicine. Euripides has often been said to be greatly interested in medicine, from antiquity to today.[77] *Hippolytus* gives particular prominence to the topic. The chorus turn their minds 'science'-wards as early as the parodos, in the form of biological ruminations about women's 'uneasy harmony'. And (from her limited human perspective) the nurse explicitly suggests that there may be a rational, medical explanation to account for her mistress's distress and styles herself as a doctor to whom the cause of the sickness may be revealed (λέγ', ὡς ἰατροῖς

---

[76] Grube (1961) 184.   [77] Kosak (2004); Holmes (2010) 234 with references.

πρᾶγμα μηνυθῇ τόδε, 296).⁷⁸ But beyond the explicit, there is, again, the implicit. Phaedra's affliction has affinities with disease patterns we find in Hippocratic writing and the language of *miasma* is perhaps not unfitting within this medical frame of reference. Phaedra's 'pollution of the mind' may be understood against this background. As a result, the play toys with a 'scientific' pattern of explanation which (ironically) sits uneasily alongside the specific pattern of divine causation developed by Aphrodite in the prologue. Thus, to adapt Brooke Holmes's words, 'medicine... enriches [*Hippolytus*'] resources for representing the conundrum of responsibility while also complicating that conundrum.'⁷⁹

I start with an excellent observation by Froma Zeitlin in her classic 1985 study of *Hippolytus* (I quote from the extended 1996 version). Developing Bernard Frischer's conception of the play in terms of *concordia discors*,⁸⁰ she proposes that the organising principle of *Hippolytus* is to be sought in female physiology. If, as Frischer argues, *concordia discors* organises the plot, the plot is based on the principle of δύστροπος ἁρμονία which the chorus-women consider the basic female condition (161–4). Zeitlin writes:

> Woman herself can therefore be construed as a self-reflexive microcosm of the differential relations between the various characters in the play... she is in a sense the 'topocosm' of the world of the here and now upon which can be mapped life's conflicts and ambiguities.⁸¹

This has many implications for our reading of the play. Zeitlin herself develops above all the idea of the female body as frame of reference for, or 'symbolic locus' of, the play's tragic ambiguities, duplicities and conflicts.⁸² My concern may appear crude by comparison. If female physiology becomes a central organising principle of the play, this suggests that the female body may be more than a mere symbol of conflict. It may be understood, rather more literally, as the actual potential origin of conflict.

With this in mind, let us inspect Phaedra's νόσος. The symptoms include the following: Phaedra does not eat (ἄσιτος, 275); her skin has changed colour (δέμας ἀλλόχροον, 175); she is thirsty (208–9); her speech is

---

⁷⁸ See Kosak (2004) 49–65 on the nurse as a 'charlatan' familiar with the rhetoric of the medical profession. She gives 'Hippocratic advice', using Hippocratic language. But she also invokes the language of divination (at 236) and magic (509): ibid. 59–61.
⁷⁹ Holmes (2010) 230–1.
⁸⁰ Frischer (1970). He reacts against earlier views considering characterisation in *Hippolytus* to be controlled by *discordia*, opposition (ibid. 85–6). He argues instead that opposite characters share in images, words and deeds as well as values and 'laws'.
⁸¹ Zeitlin (1996d) 237.   ⁸² Zeitlin (1996d) 237.

incomprehensible; she is delirious (ἐμάνην, 241); she changes her mind by the minute (181–5); she wishes to die (κατθανεῖν ἔδοξέ μοι, 401). The play gives considerable space to these precise symptoms. Commentators have dropped the odd remark about connections to Hippocratic medicine but it has rarely been recognised that these symptoms add up to a pattern of disease associated with the most common malfunctions of the female *physis* in Hippocratic writing.[83]

These malfunctions are 'excess of blood' and the infamous 'wandering womb' as the result of sexual abstinence, which we encounter in particular in the Hippocratic treatises *On the diseases of women* (*Mul.* 1 and 2) and *On the diseases of young girls*.[84] In Hippocratic physiology, the female body is particularly 'soft' and 'spongy' and therefore draws great quantities of moisture from nutrition.[85] It needs this moisture not least to nourish a foetus, but it also requires release of excess fluids – hence menstruation.[86] If menses do not exit, blood will overflow and wreak havoc in the female body, not least because female blood is also warmer than male blood and hence brings with it the danger of excess heat.[87] As *On the diseases of young girls* specifies, such excess blood may beset the heart (καρδία) and the midriff (φρένες) from where it will return only slowly.[88] Penetration will widen and/or straighten the uterine mouth and is therefore considered a remedy and, more frequently, a prophylaxis for this type of physical malfunction.[89] The 'wandering womb' is similarly connected to fluids.[90] The womb needs moisture. If it desiccates, it becomes lighter and will go astray towards the upper parts of the body in search of the required moisture. In these cases, 'uterine suffocation' will ensue. Again, intercourse does the trick. The male sperm will irrigate the womb and, in this way, prevent it from desiccating.

---

[83] Hanson (1990) 320 points towards a Hippocratic interpretation of Phaedra's affliction; see also Lefkowitz (1981) 16–18. Jouanna (2012c) 64–5 draws attention to a case in *Epidemics* 3 where psychological distress causes symptoms similar to Phaedra's (3.142,5ff. Littré).

[84] The following summary is indebted to Hanson (1990) 314–24, ead. (1991) 81–7, Demand (1994) 55–7, Dean Jones (1996) 41–109, King (1998) 21–39 and 214–21, Faraone (2011).

[85] King (1998) 28–9; Hanson (1990) 317 with references.   [86] E.g. King (1998) 29–30 with references.

[87] On the hotness of female blood, see e.g. King (1998) 32 (in Aristotle, women are seen as 'colder'). Dean-Jones (1996) 46 warns against overemphasising the role of temperature in Hippocratic gynaecology.

[88] E.g. King (1983) 113–14.

[89] Intercourse is only one of the recommended remedies: King (1998) 220.

[90] On the wandering womb, see Hanson (1990) 317–19, Demand (1994) 55–7, King (1998) esp. 214–21, Faraone (2011) 3–9. The womb wanders also in Plato's *Timaeus* (91c), here because it is believed to be a 'creature desirous of childbearing' (ζῷον ἐπιθυμητικὸν ... τῆς παιδοποιίας), which begins to stray though the body once it has been without seed for a long time: see Hanson (1990) 319, King (1998) 222–5.

The symptoms, in both cases, are similar and closely match those of Phaedra. As the effects of wandering wombs *Mul.* 1.2 specifies suffocation (πνῖξ), an alternation of chills (φρίκη) and fever (πῦρ), lack of appetite (ἀσιτήσει), incomprehensible speech (τὴν γλῶσσαν αὐτῆς χαλινοῦται, καὶ ἀσαφῆ ταύτην ἔχει), thirst (δίψα ἰσχυρή μιν λήψεται), and derangement (ἀλύξει τε καὶ ῥίψει ἑωυτὴν ἄλλοτε καὶ ἄλλοτε, καὶ λειποθυμήσει). As the result of excess of blood, *On the diseases of young girls* specifies visions (φαντάσματα), ill-boding speech (φοβερὰ ὀνομάζει), mental derangement, and a desire for death (ἐρᾷ τοῦ θανάτου).

The play toys here with Hippocratic explanatory models. The space allowed to the presentation of Phaedra's symptoms, the conspicuousness of the parallels, the simple fact that the nurse presents herself as a doctor (296) and the circumstances of Phaedra's revelation, which are reminiscent of Hippocratic scenarios (inquisitive cross-examination of a reluctant patient),[91] render it unlikely that we are witnessing here simply the results of the cultural context Euripides shared with the Hippocratics.[92] The underlying suggestion is that Phaedra may be sick because her husband is absent. Sex would help – and it is arguably in this Hippocratic framework where intercourse becomes a remedy that the audience is invited to understand the nurse's emphatic 'It's not fine words that you need, but the man' (οὐ λόγων εὐσχημόνων | δεῖ σ' ἀλλὰ τἀνδρός, 490–1).[93]

Certainly, the play leaves room for diagnosing greater or lesser degrees of irony in this toying with Hippocratic models. A sober interpretation would favour 'great irony': for, not only does the audience know the actual reason of Phaedra's ailing, but even the symptoms which so neatly map onto Hippocratic patterns of female disease are in the course of the play revealed as partly self-induced; thus, her weak appearance results most immediately from Phaedra's abstinence from food; at 401–2 it emerges, moreover, that this abstinence is not the symptom ('lack of appetite') of some affliction (as is still considered a possibility at 274–7) but Phaedra's means of choice to end her life.[94] From this perspective, the conclusion which most readily suggests itself is that *Hippolytus* playfully gestures towards this explanatory model in its complex engagement with causation only to divest it entirely of plausibility as the play progresses (while the cultural frame of reference

---

[91] In Hippocratic writings reluctant female patients call for exact questions: see *Mul.* 1.21 (= L 8.60.15f) εἰδείη δ' ἄν τις τουτέων ἕκαστα, εἰ ἐρωτῴη ἀτρεκέως ταῦτα. For further references, see Lloyd (1983) 76 n. 68.
[92] This objection to Hippocratic interpretations of tragic symptoms is raised by Holmes (2010) 235–6.
[93] See Hanson (1990) 320 proposing that a doctor would have prescribed Phaedra intercourse as a therapy.
[94] This point is fundamental to Holmes (2010) 252–60.

is to some extent upheld, as at 490–1). A more obstinate reading would still lead to the first part of this conclusion, but not necessarily to the second: a literal-minded person determined to read Phaedra's affliction in Hippocratic terms may, after all, find in the heroine's death wish itself, not the rational resolve of a resolute mind, but a symptom of disease (ἐρᾷ τοῦ θανάτου) parallel to mental confusion.

In any case, Phaedra's *miasma* of the *phrēn* (φρὴν δ' ἔχει μίασμά τι, 317) may be understood within this medical context (which at 317 is still untarnished by the revelation of Phaedra's resolve to die). What is at stake is not necessarily, and certainly not exclusively, an abstract, moralised pollution of an equally abstract 'mind', or the 'pollution' of an inherited evil. As *On the diseases of young girls* in particular (where excess blood besets heart and *phrēnes*) illustrates, the φρήν, in the fifth century, was still conceived of as something very concrete, not so different in many respects from the Homeric 'midriff' (*phrēn*) which could be pierced by a weapon. Ruth Padel, after a thorough analysis of Greek concepts of the mind, 'suspect[s] that all fifth-century uses of these words [i.e. words referring to the 'mind'] have some somatic tinge, more or less strong in different contexts, but always available in direct relationship . . . with what Greeks believed was inside people.'[95] The notion of a *polluted phrēn* is not out of place in this context. It fits particularly well with Hippocratic ideas about female dysfunctions. Up to this point the play has made much of symptoms reminding the audience of 'wandering wombs' and 'excess of blood' as the result of sexual abstinence. The idea of a *miasma* of the *phrēn* might readily evoke notions of excess blood affecting, very physically, Phaedra's *phrēn*. The terminology of *miasma*, too, though not used in Hippocratic writing on women's diseases, is not misplaced within a medical context.[96]

---

[95] Padel (1992) 36. On φρήν and φρένες see especially ibid. 20–3. She also draws attention to Aristotle *De anima* 427a22–b7 where the author attacks the Presocratics for conceiving of 'thinking' (νοεῖν) as a somatic activity. She notes that a somatic conception of 'thinking' was probably still the norm in the fifth century. Kosak (2004) 53 n. 19 draws attention to Hipp. *On the sacred disease* 17, 'where the author attacks those who believe people think with their *phrēn*, rather than with their brain'. On this notion, see esp. *On the sacred disease* 20, 'Wherefore I assert that the brain is the interpreter of consciousness (τὸν ἐγκέφαλον εἶναι τὸν ἑρμηνεύοντα τὴν σύνεσιν) . . . I do not know what power the *phrēnes* have for thought and intelligence (οὐδὲ οἶδα ἔγωγε τίνα δύναμιν ἔχουσιν αἱ φρένες ὥστε νοεῖν τε καὶ φρονεῖν). It can only be said that, if a man be unexpectedly over-joyed or grieved, the *phrēnes* jump and cause him to start.' Trans. adapted from W. H. S. Jones, Loeb Classical Library (Cambridge, MA, 1923).

[96] The word *miasma* is used in Hippocratic writing to refer to 'pollutions' in the air which may affect the body: see Hoessly (2001) 274–8; also Hankinson (1995) esp. 45; see esp. Jouanna (2012a) 122–9 on the continuities and discontinuities between religious and Hippocratic *miasma* (and see Hankinson (1995) on pollution and infection, noting the Hippocratic doctors' silence on the infectious transmission of disease). This type of pollution is not intimated here, but the word is

The observation frequently raised by commentators in reference to Phaedra's 'polluted mind', that the formulation entails a moralised pollution of intent at odds with fifth-century notions, is not wrong, but it is one-sided, ignoring the complex web of referential frameworks into which the heroine's *miasma* is drawn. The strong medical subtext of female bodily dysfunctions also allows for a more concrete interpretation, albeit one that is medical rather than ritual. I note as an aside that this affects our understanding of the implied dichotomy: if viewed from a concrete medical perspective, the gulf which opens up is not so much one between body and mind (because the 'mind'/*phrēn* is to some extent part of the body) but between inside (reality) and outside (appearance).

The question of causation

Within the divine framework of utter predetermination, then, *Hippolytus* plays with alternative models of causation which are tied together by the language of *miasma*. The idea of inherited evil, partly in the form of inherited character, is juxtaposed with a playfully developed subtext of contagion (which may in part be taken to point in the direction of character and mental disposition) as well as medical explanations. At least in their concern with inherited evil, 'character' and (to some extent) medicine, these models are indeed alternatives to the divine frame (albeit not within the fiction of the play). This observation suggests the utility of ending the present discussion with a brief comment on the 'question of causation'.

It is an old question.[97] In particular, scholars have long been interested in the play's striking juxtaposition of complete divine predetermination and the decided 'depth and solidity in this tragedy upon the human plane'.[98] In Bernard Knox's view, for instance, the result of the play's juxtaposition of divine predetermination and nuanced human motivation is dramatic irony.[99] He works from within Euripides' fictional world, takes Aphrodite as a literal and incontestable given and consequently homes in on the sense of the human characters' tragic limitation in the face of an inscrutable

---

nonetheless appropriate in the medical context: the idea of 'purification', in the form of the word *katharsis*, is ever-present in Hippocratic writing on 'female diseases': see Föllinger (2007) and von Staden (2007).

[97] For its wider context, see Mastronarde (2010) 153–206; early: Decharme (1893/1966) 59–103, esp. 79–87. See also Verrall (1895) with Dodds (1929).
[98] Winnington-Ingram (1960) 183.
[99] Knox (1952a) 5. A similar view is adopted by Mastronarde (2010) 108–09, 177–8.

Euripides' Hippolytus

(divine) reality.[100] It is a grim vision of human nothingness, worthy in its darkness of Shakespeare's *Macbeth* (where, famously, 'Life is... a tale told by an idiot, full of sound and fury, signifying nothing'). Reginald Pepys Winnington-Ingram, in his classic 'study in causation', takes the diagnosis of dramatic irony in a different direction.[101] As is typical for his approach, evinced most famously in his study of *Bacchae*,[102] he does not feel obliged to take the poet at his word in matters divine but feels free to abstract. He emphasises that, in contrast to the complex web of factors contributing to the tragic denouement on the human plane (character but also convention and social influences), Aphrodite's and Artemis' explanations appear 'thin and oversimple'[103] and concludes that *Hippolytus*' gods are mere 'symbols', or rather 'artistically satisfying representatives of the realities which condition human life'.[104]

My own opinion is that there is perhaps more to the juxtaposition of divine frame and alternative models of causation than merely 'dramatic irony', as Knox maintains in focusing on 'character' as an alternative model. But I do not think that we need to question these Euripidean gods *as gods* and take them as mere 'representatives of the realities which condition human life', as Winnington-Ingram does.

It seems to me that we should take seriously the idea of a polyphony of different causation models; and that the play may be understood to entail a lesson about the human inability to hierarchise such polyphony and establish incontestable narratives of cause and effect. *Hippolytus*, to be sure, hierarchises this polyphony by privileging the model of divine causation, putting on stage the two goddesses to frame the action. It is an important point that in so doing *Hippolytus* invites the audience to evaluate them, as Mastronarde recently argued,[105] and also to think more widely about the divine. But this may not be the only point. It was presumably not very often that gods would appear to reveal narratives of causation outside of the theatre. *Hippolytus* could be seen to draw attention to such an idea. The play's gods are not only strikingly determinative; they are also strikingly marginal, confined to the play's frame. This may be the case in other Euripidean plays, too;[106] but no other play matches the degree to which *Hippolytus*, within this frame, is interested in ignorant humans

---

[100] See Knox (1952a) 24: 'All four characters live, and two of them die, in a world in which purpose frustrates itself, choice is meaningless, moral codes and political attitudes ineffective, and human conceptions of the nature of the gods erroneous.'
[101] Winnington-Ingram (1960).
[102] Winnington-Ingram (1948). In this study Dionysus becomes an emblem of man's hidden desires.
[103] Winnington-Ingram (1960) 188.   [104] Ibid. 190.   [105] Mastronarde (2010) 190–1.
[106] On Euripidean 'prologue gods' and 'epilogue gods', see Mastronarde (2010) 174–95.

struggling for understanding. The play arguably invites the audience to identify these characters' uncertainties as their own, reflecting their reality wherein mental derangement may be the result of divine intervention or of 'something else' (as in Hdt. 3.33); and wherein the hierarchisation of causation models cannot but be a matter of δόξα.[107]

Let me end on a contentious note. Perhaps the play can be seen to intimate more specifically that the establishment of an incontestable causation narrative is a 'fiction'. After all, it is not impossible to expose *Hippolytus'* gods as literary constructs. Bernard Knox has drawn attention to the striking parallels between Aphrodite and Artemis.[108] Integrated into the play as mirror-images in neat ring-composition, both adhering to the same moral principles (to reward the reverent and punish the wrongdoer; 5–6 ~ 1339–41), they are presented through a number of verbal repetitions: both are said to 'roam over the water' (148–50 ~ 447–8); more strikingly, Aphrodite and Artemis themselves use the same words in reference to present and future action, among them προκόπτω (προκόψασ', 23; προκόψω, 1297), δείκνυμι (δείξω, 6; ἐκδεῖξαι, 1298) and τιμωρέομαι (τιμωρήσομαι, 21 = 1422). In addition to many other things, these parallels may be taken to indicate that the two goddesses are not autonomous figures but subordinated to a crafted whole. On this reading, however, the play necessarily implies that for its specific divine model of causation to exist a creative effort is required. Were it not for the poet's intervention, *Hippolytus'* tragic denouement may just be understood to result from beyond-the-*dēmos* characters, inherited stains or physical dysfunction. Not that any of these causation models would ever be certain: to establish one over the other would once more involve the invention of a fiction, with the diagnostician as another 'Euripides'.

A journey inwards: Sophocles' *Oedipus tyrannus*

'The horror! The horror!' (Mr Kurtz in Joseph Conrad, *Heart of darkness*)

Oedipus tyrannus, dating in all likelihood from roughly the same period as *Hippolytus*,[109] shares with that play an intense interest in interpretation and

---

[107] Herodotus acknowledges this to be the case in his account of Cleomenes' madness (Hdt. 6.84).
[108] Knox (1952b) 28–9 (the following parallels are those listed by Knox). Knox (ibid. 29) concludes that the two goddesses 'are opposites, but considered as divinities directing human affairs they are exactly alike.'
[109] In the absence of external evidence any dating must eventually remain speculation. See Kamerbeek (1967) 29 (reconsidering Bernard Knox's argument for 425 BC in *AJPh* 77 (1956), 133–47). See Winnington-Ingram (1980) 341–3 and Easterling (1982) 19–23 for the dating of Sophoclean plays in general.

Sophocles' Oedipus tyrannus

'[d]educing hidden causes and invisible truths that lie beneath the surface phenomena of the visible world'.[110] And it shares with *Hippolytus* a concern with 'comprehension' in the face of human misfortune.

The play's opening tableau, the deadly plague at its centre, immediately throws the theme of detection, and comprehension, of 'invisible truths' into high relief. Oedipus enters the stage; the priest, in the company of a choice selection of Thebans, supplicates him to help, seeing that the city is no longer able to 'lift her head from beneath the angry waves of death' (23–4; Jebb's translation). Yet help requires comprehension of present misfortune. The project of seeking such comprehension, it turns out, is already well on its way: Creon has been sent to Delphi, for diagnostic purposes.

But *Oedipus* quickly takes a decisive turn, and soon enough comprehension no longer relates to external events, as in *Hippolytus*, but to (the) wretched man himself. The diagnosis of one sickness, the plague, is replaced by the diagnosis of another, Oedipus'. As mantic word reaches the city, and with it the revelation that a murderer in their midst is the cause of the plague, the play, for its characters, turns into a detective story: the culprit must be found and so Oedipus goes in search of a man;[111] the audience, with its superior knowledge, witnesses. The theme of interpretation and comprehension is now bifurcated. On the surface level, it relates 'simply' to piecing together a story, bit by bit, until truth is arrived at. On another level – the audience's level, dependent upon its superior knowledge – this piecing together, this inexorable zooming in on the man that the audience knows is Oedipus, is but a continuous gazing at the misfortune that is the very identity of one man. As the play presents that man in search of himself, the audience is invited to join in that search; as Oedipus comes to comprehend himself, the audience is challenged to reflect on its comprehension of Oedipus and his wretched plight. The challenge is there from the beginning: 'I have come myself', says a self-confident Oedipus upon his taking stance (presumably) centre stage, 'I, Oedipus by name, known to all' (αὐτὸς... ἐλήλυθα, | ὁ πᾶσι κλεινὸς Οἰδίπους καλούμενος, 7–8). For the audience the assertion implies a question: do they really know the man? Do they understand him? Sophocles' play takes the audience on a journey inwards.

---

[110] Segal (1993) 136.
[111] Lewis (1989) identifies the legal procedure of ζήτησις ('searching') as a structural basis of the play. The ζήτησις involves the appointment of ζητηταί to investigate a crime of public import committed by an unknown person and to gather evidence to identify, and then prosecute, the criminal. On the legal background of *OT*, see also Knox (1957) 84–98. Incidentally, for many the central question of the play has been whether or not Oedipus is guilty: see Manuwald (1992) (with references to earlier literature) and the study of this tradition of interpretation by Lurje (2004).

But *Oedipus* is different from *Hippolytus* in another respect. Comprehension of misfortune is here complemented by a concern with 'coping'. Just as the suffering ensuing from the plague requires not only *analysis* but also *lysis*, 'release',[112] so the discovery of Oedipus' identity requires coming to terms with such utter human misery. Diagnosis has come to an end with lines 1183–5, Oedipus' agonised cries of final self-recognition (ὢ φῶς, τελευταῖόν σε προσβλέψαιμι νῦν κτλ.). But the play does not end at this point: the following 350 lines are an indispensable part of Sophocles' treatment and interpretation of Oedipus' story. These lines present to the audience Oedipus', and the other characters', struggle to come to terms with his 'new' identity.[113] *Oedipus tyrannus* may not be the only tragedy in which processes of 'coping' constitute an important element. Sophocles' *Philoctetes* and *Oedipus at Colonus* spring to mind; *Ajax* and *Trachiniae*; and perhaps Euripides' *Heracles* and *Hippolytus*.[114] But 'coping' in *Oedipus tyrannus* stands out in that its presentation is drawn out to greater lengths than in other plays where characters are shown struggling to come to terms with acute pain following sudden comprehension and insight. More than any other tragedy, *Oedipus tyrannus* is about human efforts to 'make sense' and, in turn, about coping with what is made sense of. Despite the focus of this chapter on the former, the latter cannot be disregarded when we turn our minds to *Oedipus*.

Pollution and purification occupy a privileged place in *Oedipus* and are central to these concerns, but as object rather than as vehicle of commentary. The relation between these concerns and the ritual nexus in question, that is, is different in emphasis from the relation that emerges in Euripides' play. In *Hippolytus*, we have seen, notions of pollution are the vehicle of a discussion of causation. As such a vehicle, pollution is arguably replaceable. In *Oedipus tyrannus*, as we shall see, the concept of pollution and the ritual practice of purification are much more closely intertwined with the play's interests in interpretation, understanding and coping. Charles Segal once wrote about a line which, at least since Albert Henrichs' seminal article on choral self-reference in Greek tragedy,[115] may be counted among the most

---

[112] On the term *lysis* in Sophoclean tragedy, see Goldhill (2012) 13–25.
[113] Budelmann (2006) 49–53 argues that the play's final scenes (from anapaestic *kommos*, in which Oedipus reviews his plight, to the posture Oedipus assumes in the encounter with Creon) enact various stages in the process of 'coping with loss': from shock to awareness of loss, to withdrawal, to healing and, finally, to renewal.
[114] *Philoctetes* and *Oedipus at Colonus* are different in that these plays concentrate on the hero's long-term suffering, his endurance, rather than the acute pain caused by sudden insight into, or encounter of, 'tragic fate'.
[115] Henrichs (1994/5).

famous of the play, the chorus's urgent 'If such practices (of impiety) are held in honour, why should I dance?' (895–6); he commented: 'through the reflected rituals of the tragedy the society is able to contemplate... the mediating function of its own ritual... forms'.[116] This is true as well of pollution and purification in *Oedipus*. In a tragedy which is centrally about understanding, and coping with, human misfortune, pollution and purification are presented as ritual mechanisms whose function is precisely to allow understanding and to provide the (ritual) means for coping. Yet the dramatic denouement suggests that pollution and purification fall short of satisfactorily fulfilling these functions.

Overture and minor key: the story of the plague

Oedipus' dramatic structure requires that the play's opening, the plague narrative, be discussed first. For the themes of 'understanding' and 'coping' and the nature of the connection to these of the ritual nexus of pollution and purification are first laid out here, as an overture, before they are developed, in a different key, in the story of Oedipus' self-discovery. *Oedipus* is in this respect much like the exposition of a fugue. One voice first states the subject, in the tonic key. Then a second voice restates the subject, in a different, but usually closely related, key. Likewise, in *Oedipus* the themes in which this study is interested are first stated in one key, and then restated in another. The connection between these keys is emphasised. The play opens with the city's νόσημα (307); it then moves to Oedipus' νόσημα (1293).[117]

The play's opening first throws into high relief the themes of understanding and making sense of misfortune as well as of coping with it. The first of these themes, we shall see, is manifest at the surface of the dramatic text; the second appears largely in the form of 'finding release', which, I submit, is an activity which expresses, precisely, the need for coping with present misfortune. In a sense, seeking release is perhaps itself already a means of coping; and actually 'finding release' may be viewed as merely a particularly effective means of coping.

---

[116] Segal (1981) 235.
[117] According to Mitchell-Boyask (2008) 63 the plague does not disappear in *OT*, but 'moves into the body of Oedipus'. The city's sickness and Oedipus' converge early, for the audience, when Oedipus, in response to the priest's plea for help, says, 'I know well that you are all sick; and yet I also know that, although you are sick, there is not one among you who is as sick as I' (εὖ γὰρ οἶδ' ὅτι | νοσεῖτε πάντες, καὶ νοσοῦντες ὡς ἐγὼ | οὐκ ἔστιν ὑμῶν ὅστις ἐξ ἴσου νοσεῖ, 59–61). See Goldhill (1984a) 182 on the irony of these lines. On irony in *OT* more generally, see Kitzinger (1993).

The two themes are consecutively introduced in the play's first lines. Oedipus comes onstage to encounter a choice selection of Theban youths asking for his help to find means of release. The king's reference to 'incense offerings, paeans and cries of woe' filling Thebes (πόλις δ' ὁμοῦ μὲν θυμιαμάτων γέμει, | ὁμοῦ δὲ παιάνων τε καὶ στεναγμάτων, 4–5) immediately draws attention to the city's need to cope with present misfortune. 'Understanding' swiftly follows into the limelight as the priest, serving as the youths' spokesperson, first describes the city's plight, then formulates the city's plea. Oedipus, as solver of the Sphinx's riddle, is the sense-maker par excellence, the man most likely to 'find a defence' to 'raise the city' (31–46):[118]

> θεοῖσι μέν νυν οὐκ ἰσούμενόν σ' ἐγὼ
> οὐδ' οἵδε παῖδες ἑζόμεσθ' ἐφέστιοι,
> ἀνδρῶν δὲ πρῶτον ἔν τε συμφοραῖς βίου
> κρίνοντες ἔν τε δαιμόνων συναλλαγαῖς·
> ὅς γ' ἐξέλυσας ἄστυ Καδμεῖον μολὼν
> σκληρᾶς ἀοιδοῦ δασμὸν ὃν παρείχομεν,
> καὶ ταῦθ' ὑφ' ἡμῶν οὐδὲν ἐξειδὼς πλέον
> οὐδ' ἐκδιδαχθείς, ἀλλὰ προσθήκῃ θεοῦ
> λέγῃ νομίζῃ θ' ἡμὶν ὀρθῶσαι βίον.
> νῦν τ', ὦ κράτιστον πᾶσιν Οἰδίπου κάρα,
> ἱκετεύομέν σε πάντες οἵδε πρόστροποι
> ἀλκήν τιν' εὑρεῖν ἡμίν, εἴτε του θεῶν
> φήμην ἀκούσας εἴτ' ἀπ' ἀνδρὸς οἶσθά που·
> ὡς τοῖσιν ἐμπείροισι καὶ τὰς ξυμφορὰς
> ζώσας ὁρῶ μάλιστα τῶν βουλευμάτων.
> ἴθ', ὦ βροτῶν ἄριστ', ἀνόρθωσον πόλιν.[119]

It's not because we consider you equal to the gods that I and these children are seated at your hearth, but because we judge you to be the first among men both in the events of life and in dealing with higher powers. After all, it was you who came to the city of Cadmus and released us from the tribute that we paid to the cruel songstress. And you did this without any special knowledge or instruction from us; rather, the story is that it was with the aid of a god that you set aright our life again. So now, Oedipus, mightiest man for all of us, we implore you, all the suppliants here before you, to find some protection for us, whether it is by receiving word from one of the

---

[118] Thus Knox (1957) 117: 'Oedipus investigates, examines, questions, infers; he uses intelligence, mind, thought; he knows, finds, reveals, makes clear, demonstrates; he learns and teaches; and his relationship to his fellow men is that of liberator and savior.' On the prominence in *OT* of the vocabulary of investigating, examining, finding etc., see ibid. 116–38.

[119] Lloyd-Jones/Wilson, in their OCT, print νῦν δ' in v. 40. This is Dawe's text (Dawe [2006]) and that of most manuscripts. The sense of continuity conveyed by νῦν τ' to me seems apt.

gods or by gaining knowledge from a human. For I see that when men have experience the results of their counsels, too, have effect. Come, best of men, raise up our city again!

Processes of 'making sense' and 'understanding' are immediately central, as is the desire for release. Oedipus, the one who once came to Thebes 'knowing nothing' (οὐδὲν ἐξειδώς) nonetheless knew how to secure release (ἐξέλυσας). Now his ability to 'find' (ἀλκήν τιν' εὑρεῖν) and to 'know' (οἶσθά που) is challenged anew in the face of the plague and the concomitant need to find a cure.

The theme is taken up by Oedipus in his reply. It appears that the riddle-solver has already turned his mind to the task of making sense (66–72):

> ἀλλ' ἴστε πολλὰ μέν με δακρύσαντα δή,
> πολλὰς δ' ὁδοὺς ἐλθόντα φροντίδος πλάνοις.
> ἣν δ' εὖ σκοπῶν ηὕρισκον ἴασιν μόνην,
> ταύτην ἔπραξα· παῖδα γὰρ Μενοικέως,
> Κρέοντ', ἐμαυτοῦ γαμβρόν, ἐς τὰ Πυθικὰ
> ἔπεμψα Φοίβου δώμαθ', ὡς πύθοιθ' ὅ τι
> δρῶν ἢ τί φωνῶν τήνδ' ἐρυσαίμην πόλιν.

> You know that I have shed many a tear and travelled numerous roads in the wanderings of reflection. I considered the matter carefully; and the only cure I could find I have applied: for I sent Creon, the son of Menoeceus and my wife's brother, to the Pythian houses of Phoebus, that he may learn by what deed or word I may rescue the city.

The importance of 'understanding' is underscored at two levels. The one is the explicit level of what is said: Oedipus' intellectual abilities falter to some extent, it seems, but through many 'wanderings of the thought' and 'looking around' he 'found' at least the solution to send Creon to the Delphic oracle. The other is the implicit level of how it is said: as a result of the pun drawing together the Pythian oracle (Πυθικά) and the theme of 'acquiring knowledge' (πύθοιθ'), the oracle emphatically emerges as a place connected with the acquisition of knowledge, affording the kind of understanding the Thebans need in the face of present misfortune. Although some commentators have been hesitant to acknowledge the pun,[120] I think Jean Bollack is correct in holding that '[l]a reprise, éclairant le mot, montre

---

[120] Dawe (2006) ad 70–1; see Bollack (1990) vol. II ad 70–2 for other sceptics. Dawe is hesitant not least because of the difference in quantity between Πῡθικά and πῠθοιτο, but Bollack remarks that 'les étymologies poétiques ne se préoccupent pas de cette exactitude phonétique: il suffit qu'un mot éclaire, par le rapprochement des sons, la signification de l'autre'. Note Plut. *The E at Delphi* 385b (cited by Ahl (1991) 44), where Apollo's epithet 'Pythian' is explained as follows: 'He is *Pythios* for those who are trying to learn and ask questions (διαπυνθάνεσθαι).'

52 Pollution, interpretation and understanding

que la maison de Phoibos est désignée non sans familiarité comme un lieu (connu d'Œdipe) où l'on va pour savoir.'[121]

Pollution enters the picture as part the oracle's story of cause and effect to account for present misfortune. In a striking anticipation of the suspicions harboured by the inhabitants of Hellenistic Dodona, Creon reports that according to Apollo the cause of present disaster is a pollution 'nurtured in this land' and which needs to be 'driven out' (96–8):

> ἄνωγεν ἡμᾶς Φοῖβος ἐμφανῶς ἄναξ
> μίασμα χώρας ὡς τεθραμμένον χθονὶ
> ἐν τῇδ' ἐλαύνειν μηδ' ἀνήκεστον τρέφειν.[122]

> Lord Phoebus commands us in transparent terms that we drive out from this land a pollution which has been nurtured on this very soil and not to nourish it until it is beyond cure.

Miasma here figures as cause to present effect. It is introduced as the narrative pivot that is needed to make sense of the experience of misfortune and which allows us to impose the desired narrative logic of cause and effect. Taking the cue from Oedipus' question to Creon, 'what kind of word is it, then [which Apollo has provided]?' (ἔστιν δὲ ποῖον τοὔπος; 89), we may hold that *miasma* becomes the catchword, τοὔπος, by which to comprehend what would otherwise be incomprehensible.

The point is emphasised, ultimately, by the medical language and imagery which permeate the opening sequence. Such language and imagery crop up from early on, albeit initially divorced from *miasma*.[123] Thus, the plague-ridden city of Thebes may be seen to be cast as a patient suffering from a sickness. Too weak from physical exhaustion, she 'can no longer raise her head from the depths of the deadly tossing' (κἀνακουφίσαι κάρα | βυθῶν ἔτ' οὐχ οἵα τε φοινίου σάλου, 23–4). Though the image here suggests perhaps primarily a man drowning at sea,[124] there is a suggestion, too, as Bernard Knox points out, of a sick man no longer able to lift his head, particularly in view of the verb ἀνακουφίζω, which Euripides, for

---

[121] Bollack (1990) vol. 2 ad 70–2. See Kamerbeek (1967) ad 70, 71: '[t]he parechesis is doubtless meaningful and certainly intended to convey something of the real character of Apollo's oracle'.
[122] The syntax allows construing χώρας with *miasma* ('*miasma* of the land') or with ἐλαύνειν ('driven from the land'): see Bollack (1990) vol. II ad 96–8. For translation I privilege the second option, but suggest that both resonate in the Greek. I follow Dawe's punctuation for 96–8.
[123] On medical language and imagery in *OT*, see Knox (1957) 139–47. On wider implications of medical imagery in Greek tragedy, see Mitchell-Boyask (2008); id. (2012) on Sophocles. See also Padel (1992).
[124] Kamerbeek (1967) ad 23 notes (in reference to 22–4) that 'the image shifts from a sinking ship to a drowning man' and speaks of a 'metaphor within a metaphor'. Bollack (1990) vol. II ad 22–4 shares this view.

instance, uses in reference to Orestes lying low from disease (*Or.* 218) and which, in the form κουφίζω, 'is used almost as a technical term in medical language to describe "improvement" on the part of the patient, especially relief from fever'.[125] Consequently, Thebes needs to be 'raised' (ἀνόρθωσον πόλιν, 46), like the ailing patient from his sickbed. The symptoms are visibly perceptible (εἰσορᾷς, 22) in the form of death and barrenness. The engagement with the world of medicine becomes explicit in Oedipus' reply to the priest. Now that everyone suffers (νοσεῖτε πάντες, 60) the point has come where 'healing' (ἴασις, 68) is sorely needed. Creon's subsequent δύσφορ' ('hard to bear') at 87 and χειμάζον ('distressing') at 101 arguably feed into this, as faint echoes of the language of medical literature.[126]

But medical imagery is present also in the reported announcement of *miasma* by the Pythian god, in this way establishing a parallel between the announcement of *miasma* through Apollo and the sense-making system that is medical diagnosis. Apollo's words specify that a *miasma* 'nurtured on home soil' (τεθραμμένον χθονί, 97) be driven out lest it be nourished 'until it is beyond curing' (μηδ' ἀνήκεστον τρέφειν, 98).[127] The image of the sick patient is continued: like a sick body, Thebes has 'nurtured'[128] within its territory a *miasma* which needs 'curing'. By thus putting the announcement of *miasma* in the context of a medical diagnosis of visible symptoms of suffering, the opening of *Oedipus* highlights the fact that the notion of *miasma* is part of a pattern-creating 'diagnostic' system analogous to that of Hippocratic medicine;[129] that the assumption of ritual *miasma*, like the assumption of a certain physical malfunction in Hippocratic diagnosis, affords understanding and comprehension of the individual's (or the society's) experience of disorder by providing a cause to the visible effect.

It is important to note the great significance that is attached to pollution at this point and as the concept which allows us to rationalise the plague. 'Our' *Oedipus* is hardly imaginable without pollution. Significantly, however, the story of Oedipus as such *is* imaginable without reference to pollution.[130] Two scenarios are possible. First, there is no plague to trigger

---

[125] Knox (1957) 140–1. On κουφίζω esp. in Hippocratic writing, see ibid. 244–5 n. 102 (citing e.g. Hippocrates, *Epidemics* 1.7).
[126] Knox (1957) 141 with references.   [127] Dawe (2006) ad loc. suggests 'without curing it'.
[128] Note that τρέφω properly refers to the nurturing activity of a living organism. Sickness, too, can be nurtured. See the formulation in S. *Ph.* 795: τρέφοιτε τήνδε τὴν νόσον.
[129] On Hippocratic medicine as a diagnostic system deducing hidden causes from visible effects, see von Staden (2007).
[130] For the variants of the Oedipus-story in myth and the innovations of the tragedians, see March (1987) 121–54.

Oedipus' search for the culprit: in fact, the association of the story of Oedipus' self-discovery with the plague was probably Sophocles' innovation.[131] Oedipus might discover his true identity in some other way, for instance through the arrival of an informant like the Corinthian messenger. Oedipus' pollution might be mentioned, but not in such a prominent place. Second, there is the plague, there is Apollo's oracle-narrative pointing to the act of murder and the need to find the culprit, but *miasma* is left out of that narrative, does not become the 'catchword' and remains merely implicit and/or is relegated to less central passages. *Oedipus tyrannus*, by contrast, has both the plague and a *miasma* which is spelt out, at a crucial dramatic moment, to set off the actual Sophoclean plot. *Oedipus* does two things: it introduces the sequence '*miasma* causes plague' as the play's Ur-pattern of cause and effect. And by having *miasma* spelt out so explicitly, the play draws attention to *miasma* as a concept through which to make human misfortune comprehensible and sets it up as the exemplary concept to afford such understanding.

Purification, complementarily, is presented as the means of choice to cope with present Theban misfortune: unsurprisingly in view of the malady diagnosed, the prescribed countermeasure is a καθαρμός, at least upon the terms introduced by the protagonist who asks 'by which kind of purification' the *miasma* may be driven out (ποίῳ καθαρμῷ, 99), to which Creon specifies 'death or exile' (ἀνδρηλατοῦντας, ἢ φόνῳ φόνον πάλιν | λύοντας, 100–1) as the required purification (applying to the man, or the men, who killed Laius). It is, to be sure, a singularly effective means for the Thebans to cope with present misfortune. It allows coping with misfortune by eventually removing that misfortune and providing (or at least promising) release.[132] Much like *miasma*, purification is given great weight here. It, too, is set up as the 'arch'-measure, this time to afford a solution, the 'arch'-means to regain control over, and therefore cope with, disaster. It is intimated that with the purification executed all will be well.

It should be added here that this central, and explicit, reference to purification as means of release (and therefore of coping, too) is complemented by two rites closely related to purifications, both intended to afford relief from disaster. As we have seen, the play begins with a reference to offerings of incense and paeans which fill the city, along with cries of woe (πόλις δ' ὁμοῦ μὲν θυμιαμάτων γέμει, | ὁμοῦ δὲ παιάνων τε καὶ στεναγμάτων,

---

[131] See Ahl (1991) 35.
[132] The play mirrors this as purification and release become inextricably intertwined. At 306, for instance, the purificatory measures of 'exile or death' for Laius' murderer(s) are seen as the condition of 'release' (ἔκλυσις).

4–5).¹³³ Upon the second stasimon, as a turn for the worse seems imminent, the queen, with forebodings of ill to come, enters the stage with just such incense offerings (and wreaths: τάδ' ἐν χεροῖν | στέφη λαβούσῃ κἀπιθυμιάματα, 912–13) and proceeds to pray to Apollo to provide 'release "free from defilement" (or "pious" release?)' (ὅπως λύσιν τιν' ἡμὶν εὐαγῆ πόρῃς, 921).¹³⁴ These offerings are arguably cathartic; they, too, aim at the ultimate type of coping that is afforded by λύσις.

Jocasta's purificatory offerings drive home another point, though: the 'doing' itself, the carrying out of the rite, is a means of coping – precisely in that it allows one to 'do' something in the face of (dreaded) disaster. To use Walter Burkert's succinct formulation, 'whatever is able to be done is thereby externalised, objectified, and can be set aside at a specified time.'¹³⁵

Crescendo and major keys: the story of Oedipus

From the overture we now turn to the play's principal interest: from the sickness harboured by the city to the sickness harboured by Oedipus, the one sicker than anyone else in Thebes.¹³⁶ It is soon clear that this is another sickness that requires diagnosis, understanding as well as, eventually, coping; but pollution and purification now emerge as inadequate. Let us take this step by step. I shall first say more about the specific quest for understanding *Oedipus* takes us on: the nature of the transformation of the theme as it is transposed from minor to major key. I shall then analyse the role pollution plays in this. It is transposed, too: it reappears as a concept through which to understand; but this time, understanding is not directed at external misfortune, but the unfortunate identity of Oedipus. There, it fails. Finally, we shall turn to purification. Though suggested in the plague narrative as all-powerful cure, it can no longer provide the desired means of coping.

---

¹³³ Vernant (1988) 117 associates this scenario with a rite at the Athenian Thargelia which involved olive or laurel branches wound around with wool (the εἰρεσιώνη) being carried through the streets and deposited at Apollo's temple or hung up outside private dwellings; paeans were also sung at the Thargelia. The Thargelia was the 'purification festival' par excellence (Parker (2005) 203). It centrally revolved around the *pharmakos*-ritual (which is central to our understanding of *OT*: Vernant (1988)). Aetiology has it that the *pharmakos*-ritual was instituted to remove the pollution incurred through the killing of one Androgeos: Parker (2005) 382.

¹³⁴ The adjective εὐαγής has provoked some discussion. According to Kamerbeek (1967, ad 921) Jocasta asks for 'release which leaves us free from ἄγος (defilement)'. Some hold that Jocasta asks that Oedipus be delivered from defilement (see Bollack (1990), vol. III p. 602). I follow Bollack (1990), vol. III ad 918–21 (pp. 602–3) who holds that '[c]'est... la nature de l'intervention divine qu'ajoute l'adjectif'.

¹³⁵ Burkert (1985a) 80.

¹³⁶ See *OT* 59–61. On the language of disease in *OT*, see Mitchell-Boyask (2012) 320–3.

The corollary of the move from external to internal νόσημα is that diagnostic efforts quickly move away from that external disease and towards the internal one and its bearer. *Oedipus* could in fact be seen as a dramatisation of the Delphic 'Know thyself'.[137] This, after all, is the story of Oedipus, most exalted of all men, of his fateful *méconnaissance* and subsequent discovery – gradual, inexorable and painful – of his true identity.[138] As *Oedipus* unfolds, the diagnosis of the one sickness is replaced by the diagnosis of the other sickness, Oedipus' wretched identity as parricide and incestuous bedfellow of his mother.

At the outset of the play, we encounter an Oedipus seemingly in full control of who he is. Oedipus comes onstage and introduces himself as 'that man known to all who goes by the name of Oedipus' (αὐτὸς... ἐλήλυθα, | ὁ πᾶσι κλεινὸς Οἰδίπους καλούμενος, 7–8). The hero here resembles, not least, Odysseus among the Phaeacians.[139] In book 9 of the *Odyssey*, the Homeric hero, upon hearing Demodocus' song about the fall of Troy, finally reveals his identity to his hosts: 'I am Odysseus, son of Laertes... and my fame reaches unto heaven' (εἴμ' Ὀδυσεὺς Λαερτιάδης... καί μευ κλέος οὐρανὸν ἵκει, 9.19–20). Odysseus, at this point, has recovered a sense of who he is and now reasserts his identity. In just this way, Oedipus asserts his identity, confidently.[140] In the terms provided by the play's notorious etymological games with the name of Oedipus,[141] we may say that Oedipus trusts that he is 'Know-Foot' (Οἰδί-πους), the riddle-solver, the 'know-nothing' who knows, against all odds (ὁ μηδὲν εἰδὼς Οἰδίπους... γνώμῃ κυρήσας, 'Oedipus Know-Nothing... hitting the mark with my wit', 397–8).[142]

---

[137] The play's concern with knowledge has been discussed frequently. Among the numerous discussions, I have found the following particularly enlightening: Reinhardt (1947), Kane (1975), Kitzinger (1993), Calame (1996b) with the response by Buxton (1996). See also Lefèvre (2001) 119–47.

[138] Euben (1990) 104: 'only in this play is the finding of the self the whole action rather than a product of it.'

[139] See Segal (1981) 209 and Dawe (2006) ad 8. Oedipus also resembles some of the gods in Euripides who reveal their divinity such as Aphrodite in *Hipp*. (πολλὴ μὲν ἐν βροτοῖσι κοὐκ ἀνώνυμος | θεὰ κέκλημαι Κύπρις, 1–2) or Dionysus in *Bacchae*.

[140] Knox (1957) 21 notes that Oedipus frequently uses some form of the word 'I' or 'my' (in the first 150 lines fourteen lines end with some form of 'I' or 'my' and fifteen begin in the same way), reflecting an 'enormous self-confidence'. We may also conclude that Oedipus is 'enormously' sure of *who he is*.

[141] See Vellacott (1971) 131–4, Ahl (1991) 44 and see his index s.v. 'wordplay' ibid. 297; Griffith (1996) 70–5.

[142] As with the parechesis at 70–1, not all accept a pun with equal enthusiasm. For Calame (1996b) 22 and Vellacott (1971) the pun is undeniable. Slightly more reticent (if still inclined to accept it) are Kamerbeek (1967) ad 397 and Bollack (1990) vol. II ad 395–8 (p. 249).

But that trust is misplaced. By way of an extended diagnostic procedure, Oedipus soon discovers that his name has hidden meanings, and with the discovery of these he also discovers his own wretched identity. Oedipus is not only 'Know-Foot' but also 'Swollen-Foot' (1036), the child exposed on Mt Cithaeron, the man with a dark past.[143] To move away from etymology, in Tiresias' eerie words, Oedipus, at the outset, though 'seeing, does not see' (δεδορκὼς οὐ βλέπεις, 413) who he really is: 'the most wretched of mortals' (σοῦ γὰρ οὐκ ἔστιν βροτῶν | κάκιον, 427–8).[144] Only after a painful exercise in Delphic self-discovery does Oedipus 'see' (at which point, ironically, he blinds himself). Only after an extended piecing together of 'old' and 'new' (cf. 916: τὰ καινὰ τοῖς πάλαι τεκμαίρεται, 'judge the new in the light of the old') does he find out who he is, contrary to the wishes of Jocasta (ὦ δύσποτμ᾽, εἴθε μήποτε γνοίης ὅς εἶ, 'Ill-fated one, may you never recognise who you are', 1068).

It is important to stress, and indeed fundamental for the following analyses, that this is a diagnostic procedure in which the audience is implicated. We have already noted one aspect of this. Oedipus' words of introduction constitute a challenge directed at the audience. 'Known to all' (πᾶσι κλεινός): this is true, in a sense, since the figure of Oedipus is familiar to the audience from the mythical tradition (and to the slightly more aged amongst the audience perhaps from Aeschylus' treatment of it in his Theban trilogy some forty years earlier).[145] But the assertion also implies a question. The κλέος of κλεινός Oedipus may have reached the audience, they may have 'heard' (κλύω) of him, they may know more of Oedipus' true identity than the characters in the play. But do they *know* and *understand* him?[146] Is the audience in the theatre of Dionysus not in the same position as the Phaeacians on Scheria, whom Odysseus' κλέος may have reached, but who are mistaken if they assume that they really know the man (and who in fact are in need of Odysseus' story to get a sense of who the man before them, the ἀνὴρ πολύτροπος, 'man of many turns', is)? There is an irony in this opening and it highlights the fact that knowledge and understanding of the famous figure onstage are perhaps more limited

---

[143] On the 'Swollen-Foot' etymology, see Vellacott (1971) 131–3.
[144] On blindness and insight in this scene, see Lefèvre (2001) 123–30, Jouanna (2007) 487–8 ('voir' vs. 'savoir').
[145] On Aeschylus' treatment of the Oedipus myth, see March (1987) 139–48.
[146] They may indeed 'misunderstand Oedipus Rex', to invoke Dodds's influential *OT* article: Dodds (1966). True, the invocation is slightly misleading as I refer rather to 'not fully understanding'. Still, it has a point: it is ironic that Dodds should be so convinced that one may 'misunderstand', and inversely 'correctly understand', a play which is so concerned with interpretation and understanding and their pitfalls.

than would appear, that it is at best the end point, not the starting point, of the dramatic events presently about to unfold, for the audience as much as for Oedipus.

But *Oedipus* continues to revel in ironies which implicate the audience in the seach for Oedipus' identity.[147] Throughout, the drama plays on the tension between the audience's superior knowledge and its eventual lack of complete knowledge. The audience knows that Oedipus is the murderer; Oedipus does not. The audience knows that Oedipus is the bedfellow of his mother;[148] Oedipus does not. But then again, for us, so familiar with a masterpiece which, according to the ancient literary critic Longinus, 'no one in his right mind (οὐδεὶς ἂν εὖ φρονῶν) would give in exchange for the entire work of Ion of Chios' (*On the Sublime* 33.5), it is easy to forget that a fifth-century audience never quite knew just what to expect of their tragedians.[149] In the eerie scene between Oedipus and Tiresias, therefore, which insistently hammers home the point that Oedipus does not *know* 'where he is in evil' (367, 413) or 'from whom he is [descended]' (οἶσθ' ἀφ' ὧν εἶ; 415), despite Oedipus' claims to superior knowledge (ὁ μηδὲν εἰδὼς Οἰδίπους... γνώμῃ κυρήσας οὐδ' ἀπ' οἰωνῶν μαθών, 'Oedipus Know-Nothing... hitting the mark with my wit, not instructed by birds', 397–8), there is arguably a tension, for the audience, between a feeling of secure knowledge in matters of Oedipus' identity and the feeling that their knowledge of Oedipus goes only so far – that the particulars of the 'narrative' that makes up this Oedipus elude them.[150] Perhaps we can adopt the following model to describe the ensuing dynamics: the audience's feeling of superiority of knowledge may be seen to dominate; at the same time, the residue of insecurity arguably piques their curiosity to find out just who precisely this Oedipus is.[151]

We need to bear these dynamics in mind when approaching, always with a focus on the audience's perspective, the concept of pollution and its relation to the theme of 'understanding' as developed in the major key of the story of Oedipus' self-discovery. Let us concentrate in particular on the

---

[147] On irony and audience-implication in *OT*, see Kitzinger (1993). She does not acknowledge, though, that these ironies also test the audience's knowledge of Oedipus. See Goldhill (2012) 25–9 on the destabilising effect of irony in *OT* (prodding the audience to ask, 'to what extent should irony be seen here?': ibid. 26).

[148] But see Sommerstein (2010b) 215–19 (arguing that the identity of Oedipus' wife is not fully clear until 631–3).

[149] Sommerstein (2010b).   [150] Sommerstein (2010b) 213–23.

[151] Jouanna (2007) 471 makes a similar point: 'De fait, Sophocle ne révèle pas au début de la tragédie la véritable identité d'Œdipe... Certes, on doit tenir compte du fait que le mythe d'Œdipe est bien connu des spectateurs... Toutefois, l'absence d'une certitude totale chez les spectateurs les maintient dans un suspense.'

word *miasma*, the one which is used by Creon as he reports the Delphic oracle's announcement and which, as we have seen above, is in this way thrown into stark relief.

The word occurs five times in *Oedipus tyrannus* (97, 241, 313, 353, 1012). Four of these occurrences fall into the first quarter of the play. The first, quoted above, forms part of Apollo's oracle as reported by Creon. The god has diagnosed a μίασμα... ὡς τεθραμμένον χθονί | ἐν τῇδ᾽ ('a pollution... nurtured in this land', 97–8) and bids the Thebans expel it. The second is a quotation of this oracle; it forms part of Oedipus' much-discussed 'edict of excommunication'.[152] He instructs the Thebans as follows (241–3):

> ὠθεῖν δ᾽ ἀπ᾽ οἴκων πάντας, ὡς μιάσματος
> τοῦδ᾽ ἡμῖν ὄντος, ὡς τὸ Πυθικὸν θεοῦ
> μαντεῖον ἐξέφηνεν ἀρτίως ἐμοί.

All must drive him from their homes since this pollution is upon us, as the god's Pythian oracle has just revealed to me.[153]

The third occurrence of *miasma* is at the beginning of the Tiresias-scene. Tiresias comes on stage. Oedipus asks the seer to help in the identification of the murderer, and in this way to 'save himself, the city and [Oedipus]'. The exact words are (312–13):

> ῥῦσαι σεαυτὸν καὶ πόλιν, ῥῦσαι δ᾽ ἐμέ,
> ῥῦσαι δὲ πᾶν μίασμα τοῦ τεθνηκότος·

Save yourself and the city, save me! Keep away all the pollution from the dead man!

The fourth instance follows only a few lines later. Tiresias, accused by an upset Oedipus of conspiracy in the murder of Laius, reveals, very openly now, that Oedipus is the 'polluter' (350–3):

> ἄληθες; ἐννέπω σὲ τῷ κηρύγματι
> ᾧπερ προεῖπας ἐμμένειν, κἀφ᾽ ἡμέρας
> τῆς νῦν προσαυδᾶν μήτε τούσδε μήτ᾽ ἐμέ,
> ὡς ὄντι γῆς τῆσδ᾽ ἀνοσίῳ μιάστορι.

Really? I bid you abide by the very proclamation you made and from this day on address neither these men nor me: for you are the unholy polluter of this land.

---

[152] On the edict, see Carawan (1999).
[153] I follow the reading of Jebb in taking τοῦδ᾽ as neuter referring to the pollution ('with this pollution being in existence for us'). Kamerbeek takes it as masculine, pointing to the murderer (with μιάσματος as predicate). My remarks below apply on either reading.

The fifth and final use of the word occurs as the noose begins to tighten. The Corinthian messenger has brought the news of Polybus' death. He is astounded to learn that Oedipus is quite unaware that Polybus and Merope are not his parents and that Oedipus does not want to return 'home' to Corinth because of Apollo's oracle. Just before he reveals that Oedipus is in truth a foundling from Mt Cithaeron, he asks (1012):

> [So you don't come home . . .]
> ἢ μὴ μίασμα τῶν φυτευσάντων λάβῃς;
>
> Is it in order that you avoid incurring pollution through your parents?

I should like to make three basic observations about these passages. First, all of these occurrences of *miasma* (μιάστωρ, in one case) are heavily ironic. For the audience with its superior knowledge, it is clear that Oedipus is himself (the source of) the *miasma* each time in question. The characters in the play, by contrast, are in the dark, with the exception of Tiresias at 353. At 1012, the audience knows that Oedipus has already acquired the pollution he has set out to avoid. Such is the first level of irony.

In the first three passages, additional ironies further emphasise the audience's position of superior knowledge. In line 97, such additional irony revolves around the formulation τεθραμμένον χθονί, 'nurtured in this land'. The formulation immediately points to Oedipus,[154] but in intricate ways which provide a comment on the king's complex relation to Thebes. The verb τρέφω may simply mean, in its weak sense, 'to have within oneself';[155] or else, 'to maintain, support'.[156] This points to Oedipus the King who has been in Thebes, and been maintained on Theban soil, for a considerable time now. But the more marked sense of τρέφω is to 'bring up, rear'.[157] This suggests Oedipus' complex past: he may have received a rudimentary τροφή here, as an infant, before exposure (according to 717–18, Oedipus was exposed not even three days after birth). But really he was reared in Corinth. 'Ironically,' Segal remarks, 'the city nurtures as a pollution the one citizen who has not received its nurture.'[158]

At 241–3, where Oedipus speaks of *miasma* to refer to some general condition of pollution when in truth the (reason for) *miasma* is precisely himself, the additional irony is that his very wording points to himself

---

[154] It does so (designating the polluted person) whilst also denoting the pollution incurred: Kamerbeek (1967) ad 97, 98; see (contra) Bollack (1990) vol. 2 ad 96–8, p. 56; see also my discussion below.
[155] LSJ II.6 (with references to S. *OC* 186, *Tr.* 86, *Ant.* 1089).
[156] LSJ III (with references e.g. to A. *Choe.* 921, Pindar *O.* 9.106, Aeschines 1.13).
[157] LSJ II (with references e.g. to Hom. *Il.* 8.283, *Od.* 2.131, A. *Choe.* 908, Pl. *Republic* 565c).
[158] Segal (1981) 209 (glossing over the duplicity pointed out here).

as the *miasma, malgré lui*. Lines 241–3 are grammatically dependent on line 236, which gives us the object of Oedipus' edict of communication: τὸν ἄνδρ' ἀπαυδῶ τοῦτον. The interpretation of the line, and the entire passage, has resulted in fervent debate. Is 'this man' the informant who does not come forth? Or the murderer? Is the ambiguity perhaps intentional?[159] For the present purposes it is more important to note the irony implicit in the passage. The person indicated by the deictic pronoun οὗτος is, in reality, Oedipus himself (who is both the polluted/polluting murderer and the informant who does not (yet) give testimony).[160] The deictic pronoun οὗτος in reality points out the person presently speaking, the one closest at hand. This irony is taken up and exacerbated in 241–2, in μιάσματος τοῦδ' ἡμῖν ὄντος. The exacerbation has to do with the change from the deictic pronoun οὗτος to the deictic pronoun ὅδε. There is an important distinction between the two. Herbert Smyth notes:

> ὅδε *hic* points with emphasis to an object in the immediate (actual or mental) vicinity of the speaker, or to something just noticed. In the drama it announces the approach of a new actor. ὅδε is even used of the speaker himself as the demonstrative of the first person... οὗτος *iste* may refer to a person close at hand, but less vividly, as in statements in regard to a person concerning whom a question has been asked.[161]

From Oedipus' point of view, the use of ὅδε is arguably a matter of 'immediate mental vicinity': what Oedipus has in mind is 'this pollution' that has 'just recently' (ἀρτίως, 243) been diagnosed as the problem. From the audience's point of view, however, this ὅδε emphatically points to 'immediate actual (physical) vicinity': it points to Oedipus, and more urgently than the οὗτος before.

At 312–13, finally, additional irony emerges from Oedipus' triple use of ῥῦσαι culminating in the formulation ῥῦσαι μίασμα. Now, ῥύομαι can mean 'to save, deliver'; this is the sense required in 312: 'save yourself and the city, save me!'. It can also mean 'redeem, compensate for';[162] or denote a movement of 'dragging away'.[163] From Oedipus' perspective, it is such a sense that is implied in 313, ῥῦσαι μίασμα. Roger Dawe notes: 'obviously not "save the pestilence", parallel to "save yourself" in the line before, but

---

[159] See the account of Carawan (1999). That the ambiguity is intended, that the blurring of the identities of culprit and informant is significant, is the position advocated by Dyson (1973).
[160] Kitzinger (1993) 541 detects a similar ironic use of the deictic pronoun at 108.
[161] Smyth, § 1241.
[162] LSJ s.v. ἐρύω C 6.b (with reference e.g. to Eur. *IA* 1383 and the Sophoclean line in question).
[163] LSJ s.v. ἐρύω A (with references e.g. to Hom. *Od.* 9.99).

"keep it away"'.[164] But this is 'obvious' only from Oedipus' perspective. For the audience, the repeated and ambiguous use of ῥῦσαι is suggestive. In particular, the paralleling of Oedipus' ῥῦσαι δὲ πᾶν μίασμα with ῥῦσαι δ' ἐμέ, save *me*, in the preceding line cannot but hammer home the point that the *miasma* needs saving just like 'me' because 'me' and '*miasma*' refer to one and the same person.

The second observation I should like to make is that in the first four of these passages *miasma* relates to the very person of Oedipus. *Miasma* is basically something one 'acquires' and is in this sense not one with the person; one 'has' (contracted) *miasma*, like the matricide Orestes at the end of Aeschylus' *Choephori* (ἄζηλα νίκης τῆσδ' ἔχων μιάσματα, 'having [contracted] the unenviable pollution of this victory', *Choe*. 1017). However, the person that has acquired such *miasma* is then usually seen to become him- or herself a source of pollution. The formulation 'source of pollution' still indicates a distinction between the person that is the source of pollution and the *concept* pollution. But Greek writers often elide the distinction by calling the polluted (and polluting) person a *miasma*.[165] For instance, the chorus at the end of *Agamemnon* berate Clytemnestra as χώρας μίασμα ('pollution of the land', *Ag*. 1645). *Miasma* and person, in these cases, become one: the pollution is the person; and the person is the pollution. In *Oedipus*, the first three references all function in this way. This is not a matter of direct predication as in *Agamemnon*, however. Rather, it is a matter of the ironies noted above, which continually point to Oedipus, the 'pollution [in complex ways] nurtured in this land' (97), '*this* [physically present] *miasma*' (241–2), the *miasma* that needs to be 'saved' (312–13). Pollution, these passages suggest in their complex dynamics, is not merely something that attaches to the protagonist, or emanates from him, but is one with the person, is the essence of the person, *is* the person. Much the same is indicated in a different way in the fourth passage, in which Tiresias calls Oedipus μιάστωρ. It is only the fifth reference which makes a distinction between the person and the concept *miasma*: here it is something which one 'takes' (λάβης, 1012).

Third, *miasma* is a term which is associated, in all but one instance, with prophetic voices: it is an oracular word. It first crops up in a passage which appears to quote Apollo's oracle at 97 (ἄνωγεν . . . Φοῖβος . . . μίασμα χώρας . . . ἐλαύνειν, 96–8) and is in this way introduced as part of a

---

[164] Dawe (2006) ad 313. Some have tried to take *miasma* in 313 in the sense 'everything that is affected by the pollution'; see Kamerbeek (1967) ad 312–13.
[165] See Kamerbeek (1967) ad 97, 98; Bollack (1990) vol. II ad 96–8.

prophetic utterance. The next two occurrences strongly suggest dependence on Apollo's oracle. This is obvious at 241–3 where the use of the term *miasma* is expressly justified, by the protagonist, in reference to the oracle (τὸ Πυθικὸν θεοῦ | μαντεῖον ἐξέφηνεν ἀρτίως ἐμοί, 242–3). But at 313 *miasma* stands in a similarly close connection to the terms of the oracle; just a few lines before Oedipus referred, once more, to Apollo's injunctions (Φοῖβος ... ἀντέπεμψεν, 'Phoebus ... sent back [the message]', 305–6). Oedipus, it seems, does not choose the word himself: instead he quotes an oracular word. In the fourth passage Tiresias is the speaker, declaring the king the source of Thebes' *miasma* (γῆς τῆσδ' ἀνοσίῳ μιάστορι, 353). In contrast to Oedipus, the seer carefully chooses his words. But not only may this use of *miasma*-terminology be seen to hark back, again, to Apollo's revelation and to pay tribute to the fact that *miasma* has become the catchword for the king to sum up the *fons et origo* of present misery; significantly, it is again an oracular voice that speaks:[166] Tiresias is after all the city's seer, blind but 'divinely' clairvoyant.[167] Only at 1012, the Corinthian messenger's reference to parricide and incest as *miasma*, does the use of *miasma*-language not seem motivated by oracular authority (even though here, too, it is again closely associated with the Delphic oracle as the whole passage refers to the oracle Oedipus had received in the past).

The picture that emerges from these observations has a focal point: the suggestion – for the audience, with its superior knowledge – that *miasma* affords comprehension of the man Oedipus. For the characters the word *miasma* is certainly one of great authority, prophetically uttered, and summing up, in one oracular word, present misfortune. Such seems to be the case in particular in the first three instances: for Creon and Oedipus, *miasma* is the one (oracular) word which accounts for disaster and affords comprehension thereof. But importantly, something similar emerges, again in particular in the case of the first three passages, if we look at the dynamics of the audience's reception, but with an important difference: the term *miasma* is suggested, to the audience, as the catchword and key concept to afford comprehension, not of external disaster (the plague), but of the man Oedipus. The above-noted ironies are central in this. As these dynamics revolve around the man who does not know himself and make the audience acutely aware of its superior knowledge of that man,

---

[166] On oracular voices in *OT* and Oedipus' attempt to compete with these voices, see Bushnell (1988) 67–85.

[167] Bushnell (1988) 75 suggests that 'Oedipus and Tiresias are ... opposites, the mortal facing the riddling god ... On stage, Tiresias *is* the Oracle, the divine mind in human flesh, a figure of divinity expressed in human speech.'

they engage the audience in a process in which what is at stake is precisely their understanding of the man presently before them onstage. In that process, they are 'fed' the oracular word *miasma*, which, as the result of the play's insistent irony, is inextricably bound up with Oedipus. Finally, as part of the same process, Oedipus and *miasma* appear as 'inextricably bound up' in a particular way: they collapse into one, so that Oedipus appears not only as afflicted by *miasma*, or the source of *miasma*, but in his essence and very being as *miasma*. *Miasma* is in this way suggested, to the audience, as the oracular catchword and concept through which to make sense of Oedipus.

The first passage, Creon's report of Apollo's oracular words, may serve as illustration. *Miasma* is set up as a concept capable of elucidating present misfortune, the plague. But for the audience, in particular, the heavy irony encapsulated in the qualification 'nurtured in this land' (τεθραμμένον χθονί | ἐν τῇδ᾽, 97–8) makes clear that Oedipus is that *miasma*. For the audience, therefore, the significance at this moment of the oracle's announcement of *miasma* is less that it explains past misfortune than that it appears to sum up, in one oracular word, what Oedipus *is*. To the characters in the play, *miasma* suggests itself as the catchword and key concept which explains the plague; to the audience *miasma* is suggested rather as the catchword and key concept which expresses Oedipus' intrinsic nature.

Let us linger here for a moment. For, the point (that *miasma* expresses, or is one with, Oedipus' intrinsic nature) depends not only on what is said, and how, but also on what is seen, or not; it also depends on the striking invisibility of *miasma* in this play. Of course, the above-described ironies work only because *miasma* is not visible in this play. They both depend on and emphasise this invisibility.[168] This emerges with particular force in the first passage, where Creon reports Delphic wisdom. The characters' inability to recognise Oedipus as the *miasma* 'nurtured in this land' emphasises that *miasma* is something less than 'obvious'. The point is highlighted by Creon's reference to Apollo's oracular words as having been announced 'in transparent/obvious terms' (ἄνωγεν ἡμᾶς Φοῖβος ἐμφανῶς ἄναξ | μίασμα... ἐλαύνειν, 96–8). The adverb ἐμφανῶς refers to the particular nature of Apollo's injunction. In the light of the play's interest in ruptures in communication and in particular the gulf between the divine and the human, it is most obviously (irony intended) taken

---

[168] This invisibility is also important in that it forms part of the play's dynamic of 'revealing the potential horror beneath the surface beauty of life' (Segal (1995) 143). Oedipus later speaks of himself as 'the beautiful thing that underneath is festering', κάλλος κακῶν ὕπουλον (1396, Dawe's translation).

to throw a problematic light on the 'clarity' of Apollo's oracles and the gulf which opens up between the god's meaning, the oracular word and human interpretation.[169] But at the same time, the confident assertion of 'clarity' and 'conspicuity' draws attention to the fact that *miasma* itself is anything but conspicuous. The conspicuity of this invisibility has a point and this point is the second pillar upon which rests the emergence of the notion that *miasma* expresses the protagonist's intrinsic nature: it intimates that *miasma* is not extrinsic but intrinsic, not external and detachable, but essential and defining.

In the *Oresteia*, much the inverse is true, and it will be useful at this point to anticipate, for comparative purposes, an important point of the later chapter on that trilogy. In Aeschylus' trilogy pollution is frequently highly visible, in the form of blood. Now, if blood indicates pollution, and in particular the blood that attaches to the murderer's hands, then such pollution appears, like the blood on the murderer's hands, as external, something that (automatically) attaches to the person but is not an intrinsic part of that person, much less *is* that person. The point is borne out by the trilogy. The ritual notions of pollution and purity turn out to be inadequate when it comes to judging Orestes' matricide. The trilogy leaves little doubt that this is so because they are categories which allow no grasp of motivation or moral guilt. In the *Oresteia*, that is, the point is that pollution has nothing to do with a person's 'essence' or 'intrinsic nature', but has to do with appearance rather than being, and the point is made in part through pollution's high visibility, which is the (visual) expression of its exteriority. In *Oedipus*, by contrast, invisibility suggests being rather than appearance: essence. *Oedipus* positions *miasma* as the one concept through which one can essentially understand, and comprehensively make sense of, its tragic hero.[170]

The limits of ritual: miasma

This suggestion, however, comes with a question mark. It is a question mark which is there from the beginning, but one which deploys its real

---

[169] The passage is cited as one of the many in the play concerned with 'clarity' by Buxton (1996) 40. See Buxton (1980) on human blindness in the face of inscrutable gods in Sophocles. On ruptures of communication and the ambiguity of divine voices in *OT* (and the play's interest in language and cognition), see Segal (1981) 236–48; see Bushnell (1988) 67–85 on the gulf between divine and human voices in *OT*.

[170] Incidentally, it has been understood in this way by modern interpreters. In reference to 97, Vernant (1988) 118 remarks that the misfortune that is Oedipus is immediately referred to by its 'right name'.

significance only upon the play's climax, Oedipus' discovery of his true identity.

The presence of this question mark at the beginning is mostly a matter of the dynamics of irony outlined above and emerges in the interaction of play and audience. This irony, we have noted, is not static. There is a pull in one direction: the invitation to the audience to feel secure in their superior knowledge of the protagonist, the luring of the audience into a position where they assume they know, and know fully, the protagonist who does not know himself. This direction urges the audience to 'give in' to the play's suggestion that *miasma* is the catchword through which comprehensively to understand the tragic hero. But there is a pull in the opposite direction, too. After all, to an audience which has gathered in the theatre of Dionysus in order precisely to find out more about this (Sophoclean) Oedipus, ironies revolving around the protagonist are also a provocation to acknowledge a certain imperfection in their knowledge of the man before them on stage. From this perspective, because the *miasma* occurrences are heavily ironic and therefore provocative in the sense described above, the play invites a certain degree of resistance to the suggestion that *miasma* exhausts the man Oedipus. It does this even while putting forward such a suggestion. Confronted with the play's suggestion that *miasma* is the catchword which defines Oedipus, the more reflective types in the audience may aptly ask, 'How could *miasma* exhaust the man if I do not yet fully know him?'

The validity of this initial question mark is eventually confirmed, but on very different terms having to do with the particular integration of the *miasma* occurrences within the play's dramatic structure. Two points stand out. First, no ordinary human character in the play ever consciously uses the word *miasma* to refer to Oedipus and his plight; closely related is the fact that it is never used by ordinary human characters to designate quite the *type* of fate that turns out to be Oedipus'. For Creon and Oedipus, it is only murder that is in question; parricide and incestuous intercourse are not in question; and in the case of the Corinthian messenger, who uses the term in reference to parricide and incestuous intercourse, what is lacking is the important element of committing these deeds unawares, which is the particularly devious twist of 'Know-Foot' Oedipus' plight. In fact, the term *miasma*, when referring to Oedipus and his particular fate, is used only by the oracular deity, Apollo, as well as the city's somehow more-than-human seer Tiresias.

Second, once the characters are conscious of Oedipus' true identity, *miasma*-terminology is conspicuously absent from the play. This is striking.

Sophocles' Oedipus tyrannus

The centrality of *miasma*-terminology in the earlier parts of the play as well as the Corinthian messenger's reference to *miasma* shortly before Oedipus discovers the truth arguably raise expectations that upon discovery the terminology of *miasma* will remain central and that Oedipus will be identified, or identify himself, as *miasma*. But expectations are frustrated. After Oedipus' agonised self-recognition at 1183–5, *miasma* is not used by any speaker.[171] Creon, perhaps the least emotionally involved and the most candid, comes closest: he once uses the wider term *agos* to describe Oedipus' condition (αἰδεῖσθ'... τοιόνδε ἄγος | ἀκάλυπτον οὕτω δεικνύναι, 'Show reverence... and do not expose openly such an *agos*', 1426–7). Otherwise, we encounter only terminological vagueness, and in particular in the case of wretched Oedipus himself. Lines 1360–84 are especially striking. The audience here witnesses a character trying to grasp his 'new' identity and find the proper word by which to define, and make sense of, what he has turned out to be. But *miasma* is not one of them. Instead, Oedipus uses a plethora of imprecise terms. He calls himself 'ungodly' (ἄθεος, 1360),[172] 'child of unholy deeds/parents' (ἀνοσίων... παῖς, 1360), 'unholy' (ἀσεβής, 1382) and 'unclean' (ἄναγνος, 1383). The result of his deeds he considers a 'stain' (κηλίς, 1384), which he has brought to light through his investigation.

The general point to be gained from these two observations is that, while *miasma* may very accurately describe some of the (external) ritual qualities Oedipus has acquired as the result of his acts (in the sense of λαβεῖν μίασμα as at 1012),[173] it is problematic as a concept by which comprehensively to grasp the suffering man on stage as well as the complex misfortune that lies behind this suffering. The impression is that for the characters it remains but a distant oracular word, which cannot exhaust reality – the complex reality of the suffering hero – once it has been fully divulged; in particular Oedipus' references to himself by a variety of vague

---

[171] This absence of the terminology of *miasma* has a significant parallel in the absence of the name of Apollo from the end of the play, noted by Budelmann (2000) 174–5. The dynamic is comparable (ibid. 174): 'Critics and spectators are first emphatically directed towards Apollo as a driving force of the play, but then do not get the confirmation they may desire.' Budelmann (ibid. 175) finds that spectators and critics, like Oedipus, despair 'at being "abandoned by the gods"'.

[172] The manuscripts give ἄθλιος, but this is unmetrical. ἄθεος is the widely adopted emendation suggested by Erfurdt and Elmsley (adopted e.g. by Dawe (2006), Lloyd-Jones/Wilson (*OCT*) and Bollack (1990), vol. 1).

[173] Harris (2010b) 134–7 argues that Oedipus' parricide as described in *OT* would not fall into any category of just, and hence non-polluting, homicide. The situation is different in *OC* because in that play it is specified that in killing Laius Oedipus acted in self-defence (see my discussion of that play).

terms at 1360–84 intimate that for the agonised individual his own intrinsic self now generally exceeds conceptual definition; that impression will make the audience wonder, too, whether conceiving of Oedipus as *miasma* fully exhausts, and does justice to, the suffering man and his complex fate.

The impression is, too, that 'Sophocles' wants to convey much the same point by withholding the terminology of *miasma* when earlier he raised expectations that it would be central upon Oedipus' discovery of his true identity. We are invited to ascribe to the conspicuous blank space an interpellative function by which we are encouraged to question precisely any assumptions about *miasma* as the definitive catchword by which comprehensively to make sense of Oedipus. We are also encouraged to take cognizance of the idea that Oedipus' identity implies a misfortune that, from the human perspective at least, exceeds definition *tout court*. It is not that *miasma* is the *wrong* term; as far as terms go, it may be quite accurate, just as oracular words in *Oedipus* always turn out to be accurate.[174] But it seems to capture but a fraction of the complex story that lies behind Oedipus and appears too abstract and removed from the reality of acute human misery.

The play, at this point, suggests an important specification. On its terms we should speak of 'acute human misery' that stands *revealed* before the audience, and this includes visual as well as verbal revelation: 'Having *revealed* this stain of mine', says a self-blinded Oedipus, 'was I to look upon these with steady [lit. 'straight'] eyes?' (τοιάνδ' ἐγὼ κηλῖδα μηνύσας ἐμὴν | ὀρθοῖς ἔμελλον ὄμμασιν τούτους ὁρᾶν; 1384–5). The Greek verb used here is suggestive: μηνύω may refer to visual revelation, and this is certainly its primary meaning here, in view of Oedipus' insistence on eyesight and lack thereof. But μηνύω is associated also, indeed usually, with verbal revelation, the betraying of a (secret) story or, particularly in Athens, the laying of information before a law court.[175] *Oedipus*, that is, draws attention to the fact that the process that the characters, and the audience with them, have gone through is one of visual and verbal revelation, the revelation of his misery as spectacle as well as story. On these terms, the above observation can be reformulated: Oedipus' identity has been translated into vision and narrative; these transcend the notion of *miasma* in the moment they are 'revealed'.

---

[174] According to Knox (1957) 43, '[t]he play is a terrifying affirmation of the truth of prophecy.'
[175] For this specific legal sense, see LSJ s.v. μηνύω II.

The limits of ritual: purification

So far, we have concentrated on one side of the coin, 'understanding' and *miasma*. Let us return to the coin's other side: in the play's overture, the protagonist himself suggested purification as the corresponding means of coping adequately with present misfortune. But purification turns out to be problematic, too. The second messenger's proclamation that 'neither Istros nor Phasis could cleanse this roof by purification' seems programmatic (οἶμαι γὰρ οὔτ' ἂν Ἴστρον οὔτε Φᾶσιν ἂν | νίψαι καθαρμῷ τήνδε τὴν στέγην, 1227–8). One aspect of this is notorious. Upon the protagonist's enquiry 'by which purification' the 'pollution of the land' could be driven out, Creon suggests 'exile or death'. This is a purification, not of the protagonist, but of the city. It is never enacted. The other aspect is that the hero's early insistence on purification as appropriate means of release for the city suffering from pollution has raised expectations that it will be perceived, especially by that hero, as the appropriate means of release, and of coping, for the hero suffering from pollution, too (even though this scenario is never envisaged). But such a purification is not carried out either. Mechanistic purification seems somehow insufficient.

Let us begin with the purification of the hero. Such purification is obliquely hinted at in two different forms. One is Oedipus' desire for exile on Mt Cithaeron. This desire, expressed in the concluding encounter with Creon (ἔα με ναίειν ὄρεσιν, 1451; see 1381–3), harks back to the oracle's injunction to exile the murderer. But it brings to mind not only purification of the city: in classical Athens, exile was not only a means to 'cleanse the city'; it also formed part of purificatory processes aimed at the polluted individual. The Aeschylean Orestes, for instance, goes into exile there to receive purification (*Eum.* 448–52); a passage in Demosthenes indicates that in the case of involuntary homicide exile preceded purification upon return;[176] and the final column of the Cyrene cathartic law seems to describe the purification of the polluted murderer, 'probably a refugee from abroad' (and therefore an exile),[177] 'received' by a sponsor (ὑποδεκομένος).[178] Therefore, when Oedipus longs for exile, the idea of

---

[176] Dem. 23.72: τὸν ἁλόντ' ἐπ' ἀκουσίῳ φόνῳ ἔν τισιν εἰρημένοις χρόνοις ἀπελθεῖν τακτὴν ὁδόν, καὶ φεύγειν ἕως ἂν †αἰδέσηταί τινα† τῶν ἐν γένει τοῦ πεπονθότος. τηνικαῦτα δ' ἥκειν δέδωκεν ἔστιν ὃν τρόπον, οὐχ ὃν ἂν τύχῃ, ἀλλὰ καὶ θῦσαι καὶ καθαρθῆναι καὶ ἄλλ' ἄττα διείρηκεν ἃ χρὴ ποιῆσαι, ὀρθῶς, ὦ ἄνδρες Ἀθηναῖοι, πάντα ταῦτα λέγων ὁ νόμος.

[177] Parker (1983) 350.

[178] *SEG* IX 72 B §20.137 (= RO 97 B §20.137). For a discussion of this column, see ibid. 350–1; on the similar concerns of side B of the *lex sacra* from fifth-century Selinous, see Burkert (2000).

purification of the polluted hero is arguably afloat along with the idea of the purification of the city.

The other is, perversely (more on this below), Oedipus' self-blinding. This self-blinding is not an innovation of Sophocles. Though it may have been absent from the mythical tradition of Oedipus before the fifth century BC, it was certainly there in Aeschylus' lost Oedipus play.[179] What seems innovative, however, is Sophocles' strategy to present this blinding as the replacement of purification rites. Scholars have pointed out that this blinding is referred to in terms which recall the oracle's injunction to drive out the *miasma* through 'bloodshed' (φόνος), which on the terms introduced by Oedipus is to be understood as purification (oracle's injunction: φόνον φόνῳ, 100; self-blinding: οὐδ' ἀνίεσαν | φόνου μυδώσας σταγόνας, his eye-sockets 'did not cease to send forth sluggish drops of gore', 1277–8).[180] Charles Segal, moreover, has suggested an allusion to a choral passage in Aeschylus' *Seven against Thebes*, which, if this interpretation is accepted, gives further weight to the notion of the self-blinding as replacement of purification rites.[181] Just before the (Aeschylean) passage in question, Eteocles has left Thebes to meet his brother in combat. The chorus now express their fear that no purification will ever suffice to remove the pollution resulting from the dreaded fratricidal killing (*Sept.* 734–41):

> ἐπεὶ δ' ἂν αὐτοκτόνως
> αὐτοδάικτοι θάνωσι καὶ γαῖα κόνις
> πίῃ μελαμπαγὲς αἷμα φοίνιον,
> τίς ἂν καθαρμοὺς πόροι;
> τίς ἂν σφε λούσειεν; ὤ
> πόνοι δόμων νέοι παλαι-
> οῖσι συμμιγεῖς κακοῖς.

> But once they have died, killing each other in mutual slaughter, and the dust of the earth has drunk the black and clotted blood of murder, who can provide purification? Who can cleanse them? Ah, these fresh troubles of the house mixed with the evils of before!

There are certainly interesting parallels between this passage and *Oedipus tyrannus* 1276–81. In particular, the Sophoclean passage echoes the Aeschylean passage's concern with 'black blood' and 'mingled woes': the first we encounter in the form of a reference to the 'black shower of blood' streaming from Oedipus' eyes (μέλας | ὄμβρος... αἵματος, 1278–9); the second in the form of a reference to the 'mingled woes' that have befallen

---

[179] See March (1987) 138 with n. 101, 140; also Edmunds (1981) 232 n. 43.
[180] Howe (1962) 137; Segal (2001²) 76.   [181] Segal (2001²) 120 n. 3.

both 'man and woman', Oedipus and Jocasta (ἀνδρὶ καὶ γυναικὶ συμμιγῆ κακά, 1281).

Almost needless to say, neither exile nor self-blinding constitute actual purification, but (if anything) only corrupt versions of it. In the case of the desired exile it is important to note, not only that exile is not put into practice, but that, more importantly, if put into practice, it would at best be a truncated purification. As the Demosthenes passage in particular indicates, purificatory exile is usually but one part of wider purification processes and is followed by purification rites of the customary type, which mark the re-entry of the individual into the community.[182] But Oedipus desires permanent exile, which would isolate him forever from the community. What Oedipus desires, therefore, is a 'purification cut short', or rather, a course of action that hints at purification but in truth is not purification.

Just so with the self-blinding. If it is understood to hark back to Aeschylus' *Seven*, *Oedipus* could be seen to provide a bleak answer indeed to the chorus' agonised τίς ἂν καθαρμοὺς πόροι;[183] For Oedipus self-mutilation is not, I think, a particularly *fitting* type of purification,[184] re-enacting in a sense sexual penetration or symbolising castration, but no purification at all. While purification would 'remove' the stain of pollution, the self-blinding makes it forever visible. Purification would reintegrate the individual into the wider community; just as the intended perpetual exile would, if carried out, forever isolate the hero, the self-blinding, as realisation of the hero's wish to 'seal off [his] wretched body' (ἀποκλῆσαι τοὐμὸν ἄθλιον δέμας, 1388),[185] cuts the hero forever off from the community.

What is intimated by way of these corrupt purifications which do not constitute actual purification is not so much that Oedipus is ritually beyond purification, but that such purification is futile as a means for Oedipus to cope; that something other than the traditional rites are required for this hero to come to terms with his misfortune. The point emerges with particular force in the case of the self-blinding. By first drawing attention to Oedipus' self-blinding as taking the place of customary rites of purification and by then displaying the agonised and mutilated protagonist onstage, the play raises the fundamental question of what solution customary ritual

---

[182] See Parker (1983) 118.
[183] *OT* could be seen to invoke the Aeschylean notion that purification will be difficult (τίς ἂν κτλ.) at the climactic moment of Oedipus' self-mutilation. Attention would be drawn to the difficulties surrounding purification: that the blinding replaces such purification; that it is something other than purification.
[184] This has been suggested by Howe (1962) 137.
[185] Taken by Kamerbeek (1967) ad loc. as 'suggestive of self-willed isolation'.

purification would offer Oedipus; what 'release' (λύσις) it would bring; how effective, finally, it would be as a means of coming to terms with the experience of such misfortune.

Something parallel may eventually be seen to be suggested by the non-enactment of the purification of the city through removal of the culprit by 'exile or death', to which I turn in conclusion to this discussion. This non-enactment, which is a matter of Oedipus' being kept alive and in Thebes, has acquired major notoriety: after all, in view of the earlier insistence on 'exile or death', it constitutes a major inconsistency. Many have suspected the ending to be spurious, among them the most recent editor of the play, Roger Dawe, who in the second edition of his commentary rejects most of the transmitted text from line 1424 onwards.[186] Those who are in agreement with him tend to adopt a theory first propounded by Graffunder in 1885, who proposed that the original *Oedipus tyrannus* ended with exile, but that the ending was later altered so as to make it possible to stage the play together with *Oedipus at Colonus*, in which we encounter, not voluntary exile, as the plot of *Oedipus tyrannus* before 1424 would seem to demand, but involuntary exile – such as is made possible by the ending of *Oedipus tyrannus* as we have it.[187] Certain philological oddities that mark the end have been invoked to bolster the case against the transmitted ending.[188] Scholars who argue for the ending's authenticity do so mostly on literary grounds,[189] although recently philological reasons for keeping the end have been expounded by Patrick Finglass.[190] I take the side of those defending authenticity on literary grounds.

Importantly, the drama's development is such that by its end the focus has shifted entirely from the one νόσημα (the city's) to the other (Oedipus'). By the end of the play, the sickness that matters, not only for Oedipus but for the wider Theban community, is not so much the one from which the city suffers, but the one from which Oedipus suffers. The clearest external marker of this shift is that in the parodos the chorus of Theban elders are solely concerned with the plague and the 'woes beyond reckoning' (ἀνάριθμα... πήματα, 168–9) ensuing from it. However, (at least) from the

---

[186] Dawe (2006). For his reasons for rejecting the end, see id. (2001) and the brief summary in id. (2006) 193. See also (slightly differently) Kovacs (2009).
[187] See Graffunder (1885); see Hester (1984), Dawe (2001) esp. 14–15.
[188] See esp. Dawe (2001) 6–11.
[189] See e.g. Foley (1993) on the centrality of the question of leadership in *OT* and the renewed negotiation of that question at the end; Segal (2001) esp. 108–22 on tragic endurance; Budelmann (2006) on a mediation 'between the relentless movement leading up to the all too foreseeable catastrophe, and the less predictable ordinary world outside the theatre' (ibid. 49).
[190] Finglass (2009). See also Sommerstein (2011) in response to Kovacs (2009).

revelation of Oedipus' true identity at 1182–5 onwards they are concerned solely with their leader's plight. The plague, at this point, has long faded out of sight (the last we hear of it is at 635–6). It is in line with this that Oedipus refers to the *polis* of Thebes eleven times in the first half of the play, but not once in the second half.[191]

This shift, however, implies a change of the primary object of coping, too: Oedipus, the play intimates, has superseded the plague as the misfortune that requires coping, and not only on the part of the hero, but on the part of the city, too. The Thebans, too, need to come to terms with the fate of Oedipus, this twisted story, and the lesson this story teaches them about the frailty of the human condition more generally. (The lesson is bleak, of course, and so is the chorus' conclusion that one should 'call nothing in the life of mortals blessed', τὸν σὸν τοι παράδειγμ' ἔχων . . . ὦ τλᾶμον Οἰδιπόδα, βροτῶν οὐδὲν μακαρίζω, 1193–5).

But from this perspective, the inconsistency of the ending's non-compliance with the strict ritual logic set out earlier in the play makes sense. It is consistent with the implications of the perverted purification that is the self-blinding. Customary, mechanistic purification seemed insufficient for Oedipus to cope with his misfortune; so, too, the purification that is ritual expulsion seems insufficient for the Theban community to come to terms with Oedipus. And so Oedipus remains in Thebes. Instead of expulsion, the oracle is consulted once more to 'acquire comprehensive knowledge of what needs to be done' (ἐκμαθεῖν τί πρακτέον, 1439). Instead of sending away the problem that is Oedipus, the Thebans scrutinise it. Complex processes of interpretation and comprehending begin afresh. This seems fitting. It corresponds to the complex nature of wretched Oedipus and his plight.

[191] Ahrensdorf (2009) 27–8.

CHAPTER 2

Pollution and the stability of civic space

Troy was famous for its walls. In the *Iliad* they occupy a conspicuous place. Poseidon and Apollo built them, serving Trojan Laomedon for a year, 'wide, and very splendid, that none could break into their city' (εὐρύ τε καὶ μάλα καλόν, ἵν' ἄρρηκτος πόλις εἴη, 21.447; Lattimore's translation). In the *Iliad*, these walls remain erect. But they are eventually razed to the ground, through the cunning of Odysseus. Tragedy frequently focuses on the aftermath of this event, on their smoke-filled and shattered remnants. Poseidon, in *Trojan Women*, can only bid them farewell: ὢ ποτ' εὐτυχοῦσα, χαῖρέ μοι, πόλις | ξεστόν τε πύργωμ' (45–6). With the wall gone, the city is no more; its people are set adrift. *Hecuba* offers a particularly striking scenario. Before Troy was taken, Priam had sent his son Polydorus to Thracian Polymestor, with gold. As long as the walls stood erect, we are told in the prologue, ἕως μὲν οὖν γῆς ὄρθ' ἔκειθ' ὁρίσματα | πύργοι τ' ἄθραυστοι Τρωϊκῆς ἦσαν χθονός (*Hec.* 16–17), all was well. But when Troy fell, the desire for riches became too strong for Polymestor to resist: he killed Polydorus, kept the gold and threw the corpse into the sea. Anchorless, the corpse is borne hither and thither, at one time lying on the beach, 'at another afloat in the sea's surge, carried up and down the waves' (ἄλλοτ' ἐν πόντου σάλῳ, | πολλοῖς διαύλοις κυμάτων φορούμενος, *Hec.* 28–9). The body adrift may be understood symbolically to stand for the loss of fixity and stability afforded by the city's walls. With the anchorage of the city gone, we may say, dispersal, drifting and floating ensue.

The present chapter focuses on the central point of the story: that secure anchorage – stability and fixity – is paramount for the civic community. Walls are one aspect of this. But within such walls, other elements of civic life are fixed, too. To remain with the Homeric city for a moment, it is noteworthy that the institutions of the civic community – in particular assembly places where civic business of various sorts is conducted – are repeatedly described in terms which place emphasis on their stable fixation

Pollution and the stability of civic space

in space.[1] The Phaeacians' *agora*, for instance, is 'fitted with huge stones set deep in the earth' (ῥυτοῖσιν λάεσσι κατωρυχέεσσ' ἀραρυῖα, *Od.* 6.267).[2] Similarly, in one of the cities depicted on Achilles' shield in *Iliad* 18, the assembly place of the council of the city's elders consists of 'polished stones in a sacred circle' (ἐπὶ ξεστοῖσι λίθοις ἱερῷ ἐνὶ κύκλῳ, *Il.* 18.504).

But as we shall see in greater detail below, the desire and need for stability extends yet much further, comprising immaterial notions of stability, too. Law springs to mind, often referred to today as the community's '*pillar* of order', and which itself needs to be fixed – like a pillar – but in turn may also provide the community with fixed boundaries and points of orientation. From law, in turn, it is but a small step to the (fixed) organisation of the community's larger 'conceptual space', moral attitudes and other categorisations.[3] We may refer to this ensemble, of which walls and laws form a prominent part and which includes the community's actual and conceptual space, as 'civic space'. Its stability appears to be paramount.

Pollution comes into the picture by way of its awkward relation to such stability. It is often resistant to spatial fixation and readily cuts across boundaries: it is 'transgressive'. In anthropological writing, and most famously in Mary Douglas' structuralist study *Purity and danger*,[4] pollution is frequently associated with 'transgression' of the cognitive structures of a given society, the confusion of categorial boundaries. Pollution, in this model, emanates from everything that violates systems of classification.[5] As we have seen in the introduction, such a taxonomical, cognitive approach cannot do full justice to, and perhaps even misses the point of, pollution (if there is *one*).[6] When it comes to tragedy such taxonomical concerns may still enter the picture (albeit not by way of the *a priori* and essentialist assumption that pollution necessarily means category-confusion). But the term 'transgressive' may also be used to denote something less abstract, designating, instead of a perceived Douglasian connection between pollution and the confusion of cognitive structures, the behaviour of pollution in actual space: the fact that pollution implies movement across and beyond the tangible, and ideally stable, boundaries which constitute civic space.

[1] See Hölkeskamp (2002) esp. 318–27.
[2] Their walls are awe-inspiring, too: see *Od.* 7.43–5, where Odysseus marvels at the Phaeacians' market places and walls, 'high and steep, fitted with palisades, a marvel to look at' (θαύμαζεν δ' Ὀδυσεὺς... αὐτῶν θ' ἡρώων ἀγοράς καὶ τείχεα μακρά, ὑψηλά, σκολόπεσσιν ἀρηρότα, θαῦμα ἰδέσθαι).
[3] On law and morality in classical Athens, see Cohen (1991). [4] Douglas (1966).
[5] See e.g. Douglas (1966) 36: 'In short, our pollution behaviour is the reaction which condemns any object or idea likely to confuse or contradict cherished classifications.'
[6] See Valeri (2000) 70–82, Osborne (2011) 158–84 and my own earlier complementary remarks in the introduction.

This chapter is ultimately about Sophocles' *Antigone*. In this play pollution occupies a conspicuous place; at the same time the play is obsessed with fixity, not least in the form of (fixed) categories, antitheses and taxonomies.[7] In order better to grasp the specific scenario underlying *Antigone*, however, we must first expand on the points raised above. It is no coincidence that law was referred to in a prominent position above: it may be understood as the epitome and concrete manifestation of the city's desire for the stability of civic space and is central as such in Sophocles' play. Therefore, instead of layering up examples of Trojan walls and assembly places 'fitted with huge stones set deep in the earth' I shall concentrate on certain aspects of law in ancient Greece which reflect a concern with stability and suggest that law should be conceived as one (prominent) point of crystallisation of the community's hopes for stability. I shall return to pollution only after these remarks: the worrying dimension of pollution as 'transgressive' and the significance of the city-states' restrictive definitions of pollution will emerge the clearer against this background.

Law and stability in ancient Greece

The shift from thinking about the walls of Troy, within which we encounter fixed market places and 'sacred circles', to the abstract notion of law is by no means arbitrary. If, as Homer and tragedy suggest, walls may be seen as central for the existence of the civic community, the same is often true of law. According to the speaker in Demosthenes 25 (*Against Aristogeiton*), 'it is agreed that, next after the gods, the laws save the city' (οἱ νόμοι μετὰ τοὺς θεοὺς ὁμολογοῦνται σῴζειν τὴν πόλιν, 25.21). Inversely, an attack on the city's laws may be taken to be tantamount to an attack upon the prosperity of the city itself.[8]

The fact is, law and walls have much in common. Both have a lot to do with a community's desire for stability, and in analogous ways. Walls are intended to afford stability in actual space, as protection, for instance, against dispersal and anchorless drifting; laws are intended to afford stability in conceptual space and over time, providing the citizens with a stable point of reference according to which to orient their conduct and distinguish between 'right' and 'wrong'. Like walls, laws (ideally)

---

[7] The most comprehensive analysis of the play in such structural terms is Oudemans and Lardinois (1987).
[8] See for instance Dem. 24.155: ὅτι τοίνυν καὶ τέχνῃ κακῶς ἐνεχείρησε ποιεῖν ὑμᾶς, ἄξιόν ἐστιν ἀκοῦσαι. ὁρῶν γὰρ ἑκάστοτε πάντας, καὶ τοὺς πολιτευομένους καὶ τοὺς ἰδιώτας, τοὺς νόμους τῶν τῆς πόλεως ἀγαθῶν αἰτίους ὑπολαμβάνοντας, ἐσκόπει πῶς λήσει τούτους καταλύσας.

provide a sense of continuity (i.e. stability over time) and, more importantly for the subsequent discussion, a fixed line of demarcation indicating what is 'within' and what is 'not within' the civic community.

The ancient Greeks were aware of the parallel. In the writings of the Athenian lawgiver Solon, it is approximated by insistent spatial metaphors: for instance, Solon thinks of himself as a boundary stone securely fixed midway between the opposing Athenian factions and their conflicting demands (ἐγὼ δὲ τούτων ὥσπερ ἐν μεταιχμίῳ | ὅρος κατέστην, fr. 37 West 9–10);[9] from this position, he writes laws which provide both parties with 'straight justice' (θεσμοὺς δ' ὁμοίως τῷ κακῷ τε κἀγαθῷ | εὐθεῖαν εἰς ἕκαστον ἁρμόσας δίκην | ἔγραψα, fr. 36 West 18–20).[10] It is explicitly addressed by Heraclitus in the sixth century: according to him, 'it is necessary that the people fight for their law as for [their city-] wall' (μάχεσθαι χρὴ τὸν δῆμον ὑπὲρ τοῦ νόμου ὅκως ὑπὲρ τείχεος, fr. 65 Kahn).[11]

But if it follows that the existence of law, like the existence of walls, may be seen as a good indicator of the importance of notions of permanence, fixity and stability within a given community, it needs to be pointed out that to do so law need not necessarily imply a coherent, systematic and comprehensive (written) codification of rules and regulations such as we find in Roman (and contemporary) law. In fact, in archaic and even in classical Greece 'law' was not entirely coherent and systematic (although recently scholars have argued that 'some degree of large-scale legislation' existed from early on);[12] nor was it necessarily written. It is this second aspect that is of concern here: in addition to such written law(s) as existed in ancient Greece, 'unwritten law', or 'nomological knowledge' as Karl-Joachim Hölkeskamp calls it (following Christian Meier),[13] always existed, though such 'unwritten law' seems to have decreased in importance vis-à-vis written law(s) in the later fifth and certainly the fourth century BC. The existence of *both*, written and unwritten law, may be seen as an expression

---

[9] On the politics of Solon's poetry, see Irwin (2005).
[10] See Hölkeskamp (2000) 83 on the emphasis Solon puts on the fact that these laws are written (ἔγραψα): 'It becomes apparent that Solon wanted the writing of the *thesmoi*... to be seen as an act of innovation and that this aspect of his activities was actually supposed to send a message of its own and even have a certain effect on people' (my translation).
[11] Kahn (1979) 180 notes that Heraclitus was perhaps influenced by Solon. He draws attention to the parallel between Heraclitus' wall and Solon fr. 4 West 26–9, where evil is said to leap over walls to pursue people even to their bedchambers.
[12] The quote is from Gagarin (2008) 45. Hölkeskamp (1992) 89–94 makes the case for early Greek law as individual and independent enactments and specific regulations (and notes that even in classical Greece a complete codification of law never existed); Osborne (1997a) presents the counterargument, that early law involved legislation on a larger scale; see also Gagarin (2008) esp. 45.
[13] E.g. Hölkeskamp (2000) 85.

of the community's need of stability over time and stability in the form of a clearly organised civic space.[14] (In an anticipatory aside, one may note that usually these two types of law were not (perceived to be) in conflict, but that *Antigone* turns the coexistence of these two types of 'law' into a problem – albeit not so much in the form of 'written' vs. 'unwritten' law, but in the form of 'laws issued by the city's authority' vs. '(unwritten) divine law').[15]

With these remarks in mind, let us in this introductory section nonetheless concentrate on (written) law issued in a legislative process by the civic community, as it is here that one can most clearly grasp the significance of law as a manifestation and crystallisation of the community's desire for stability. Two aspects are especially interesting: the concrete physical appearance of law in ancient Greece; and, even more importantly for the present argument, classical Athens' discourse about law. Both would seem to reflect a concern with stability.

Let us take a look at physical appearance first. Written laws begin to appear in the archaeological record from the mid-seventh century onwards,[16] not long after the reintroduction of writing in ancient Greece, and within a few decades of Homer and Hesiod (whose poems, it has been argued, show no awareness of written law: disputes are settled ad hoc and orally and adjudication appears to be primarily a matter of verbal negotiation).[17] Early laws were often recorded on bronze plaques or even wooden *axones* and deposited in sanctuaries (where they were probably accessible to the public);[18] or they were inscribed on the (outside of the) walls of a given community's major temple, where they were easily accessible to the public, as was the case in Gortyn, for instance, where early laws

---

[14] However, written laws probably came to be seen as more important, and as the source of greater stability, at least in Athens. Theseus in Euripides' *Suppliants*, for instance, perhaps reflects slogans of democratic Athens in praising *written* laws, which guarantee that the weak and the strong have equal justice (*Suppl.* 429–37).

[15] For an instance where written and unwritten law are after all in conflict, see Andocides 1.115–16 (cited by Gagarin (2008) 179): here the *patrios nomos* (interpreted to prescribe death if someone placed a suppliant branch in the Eleusinium) is in tension with the written laws (which prescribes in this case a fine of 1,000 drachmas). For the usual peaceful coexistence of both types of law (at least in the law courts), see Gagarin (2008) 204: '[n]o litigant ever suggests that written laws are opposed to what is reasonable or to the general law . . . On the contrary, when general or unwritten laws are mentioned, they either reinforce written rules (Dem. 18.275), or have authority (in matters of piety) only in the absence of written laws (Lys. 6.10), or they work together with written laws'. See also Harris (2010a) 12–13; id. (2010b) 124–6.

[16] Gagarin (2008) 39; Osborne (2011) 170. [17] Gagarin (1992).

[18] See Hölkeskamp (1992) 100 on the practice of depositing laws inscribed on plaques in sanctuaries; public accessibility is assumed e.g. by Sickinger (1999) 30; Robin Osborne also advocates public accessibility as the norm (private correspondence).

were inscribed on the walls of the temple of Apollo Pythios;[19] in Dreros, too, a group of early laws was inscribed on the walls of the temple of Apollo Delphinios, at the edge of the local *agora* (or some other type of public assembly place).[20] Stelae, too, were sometimes used for early laws,[21] but it seems that this very conspicuous type of fixation of law became more common, at least in Athens, only in the later fifth and the fourth centuries.[22]

A quick word on written laws in Athens, then.[23] It is true that drawing conclusions about Athens is always difficult because little evidence survives (and even in classical times and especially the 'age of litigation', the fourth century, evidence comes mostly in the form of forensic speeches rather than material records),[24] but one may tentatively outline as follows: it would seem that Solon's and Draco's laws were kept in various places; and Solon's, at least, were inscribed on the famous (wooden) *kyrbeis* and *axones* (as perhaps were Draco's)[25] and apparently kept on the Acropolis (but were brought, perhaps by the democratic reformer Ephialtes and around 460 BC, to civic spaces such as the *agora*, the prytaneion, the bouleuterion and the stoa where they were more readily accessible to the public).[26] Quite certainly, in the last decade of the fifth century BC efforts were made partially to regroup Athens' scattered laws: Andocides 1.83–4 suggests that at least newly passed laws were inscribed on a wall on the Stoa Basileos;[27] and perhaps the city's laws were at this time more generally collected and inscribed on stelae in the stoa.[28]

Two points can be made about these written laws. First, whether these laws were deposited in temples in the form of inscribed wooden *kyrbeis* or displayed in more easily accessible public spaces, the fact that they were

---

[19] Hölkeskamp (1992) 100; the markedly public display of the Gortynian laws is stressed by Gagarin (2008) 80.
[20] Gagarin (2008) 45–6. The area (within it the temple) was probably laid out and constructed when Dreros expanded control over the surrounding territory: ibid. 76.
[21] For instance on Chios, where a free-standing stele, inscribed on all four sides, was set up in the centre of the *polis*: see Hölkeskamp (1992) 100.
[22] See Hölkeskamp (1992) 100; see id. (2000) 88–91.   [23] More in Gagarin (2008) 176–205.
[24] Gagarin (2008) 176.   [25] Gagarin (2008) 99.
[26] On the *axones*, see Owens (2010) 140–1; on the relocation of the *axones* and *kyrbeis*, see Hölkeskamp (2000) 94; also Sickinger (1999) 29–31; the source for this relocation is Anaximenes of Lampsacus (*FGrHist* 72 fr. 13; see also Pollux 8.128 with Ps.-Aristotle, *Ath. Pol.* 7.1). This relocation perhaps had to do with making these laws more easily accessible: see Pollux 8.128 with Sickinger (1999) 30. The public visibility of Solon's *axones* and *kyrbeis* is noted also by Thomas (2005) 47, Gagarin (2008) 181–2.
[27] See the comments of Gagarin (2008) 182–4.
[28] Shear (2007) 102–03; see Dem. 20.94, 24.25 on the display of laws in fourth-century Athens (in Harris (2010a) 2).

written down may be seen as the concrete expression of the desire for stability and permanence (Hölkeskamp points out that these laws often refer to the fact that they are written; sometimes, they even refer to the material on which they are written).[29] If we return at this point to 'unwritten law', one may provisionally say, perhaps, that while 'unwritten law' was perceived to be by its very nature timeless and therefore secure and a source of stability,[30] these issued (written) laws, regulating specific matters and concerning problems whose solution was not self-evident in terms of wider 'custom'/'unwritten law', needed fixation to achieve – and, by the same token, provide – such stability. *Mutatis mutandis*, the written, fixed nature of these laws may be taken also to express the community's desire for stability (again, temporal and conceptual).

The second point is more specific and relates to the practice of inscribing laws on marble stelae or walls: we may arguably speak here of a monumentalisation of law which translates the abstract idea of 'the law' into an imposing presence that is firmly anchored in space in concrete visual terms.[31] Inscribed on marble stelae or walls 'set deep in the earth', these laws become a symbol for the permanence and stability of the rule of law as upholder of the civic community;[32] and, by extension, for the desired stability of the civic community itself. One is presumably not too far off the track if one understands this practice of inscribing law on walls and marble stelae as the translation into practice of the (modern) saying that 'law is the central pillar of order'.

This implicit association of law with notions of fixity and stability is made explicit in the terms in which law, in ancient Greece and especially in classical Athens, was talked about. The development of Greek legal terminology, and in particular of the various terms for 'law', has received considerable scholarly attention.[33] Although arguments are complex, it can be asserted without undue oversimplification that one of the traditional, and early, terms for 'law' was θεσμός, used in particular (but not exclusively)

---

[29] Hölkeskamp (2000) 88 with n. 94.
[30] Such may be Aristotle's view at *Politics* 1287b (it certainly is Antigone's view in Sophocles' play).
[31] See Hölkeskamp (2000). Such imposing stelae are important on Plato's Atlantis (Pl. *Critias* 119c–d): the law by which its ten kings abide is written down on an orichalcum stele and kept 'in the middle of the island in the temple of Poseidon' (ἐν στήλῃ γεγραμμένα ὀρειχαλκίνῃ, ἣ κατὰ μέσην τὴν νῆσον ἔκειτ' ἐν ἱερῷ Ποσειδῶνος).
[32] Hölkeskamp (2000) 88–91. He notes (ibid. 88): 'More important than the readability of a statute was evidently its visibility in the concrete sense, as a symbol and guarantee of its unchanging and lasting validity' (translation by Gagarin (2008) 68).
[33] See e.g. Gehrke (1995) and Hölkeskamp (2000) with further references.

in reference to written statutes.³⁴ This means that from early on, laws were referred to in terms which draw attention to the idea of stability. Θεσμός, after all, is literally 'that which is laid down', deriving from τίθημι,³⁵ and therefore reflects secure, permanent placement, arguably designating something that is set up not to be (re-)moved.³⁶ We need not necessarily understand this to denote a concrete physical reality. In any case, what is emphasised is the idea of law as something that occupies a permanent position, above and beyond dislocation and change, a stable point of reference. (That the term may refer to wider 'custom', too, and not only to written law, underscores the wider point of this discussion, that stability is paramount for the civic community; for if θεσμός, and in particular θέσμια, may stand, not only for issued, written law, but also for wider unwritten 'custom',³⁷ such custom, too, is referred to in a language that suggests permanence, reflecting the idea, or giving expression to the ideal, that this custom is a source of stability for the civic community.)

While especially in the archaic period many other terms were used to refer to laws which do not betray a similar concern with set-in-placeness and stability (such as ῥῆτρα or ψῆφος),³⁸ in classical times it is precisely this language of 'placed-ness' which becomes part of the official Athenian terminology. Thus, to speak of '*established* laws', οἱ προκείμενοι νόμοι, is the standard way of referring to the legal statutes of the classical Athenian *polis*: the expression is ubiquitous in Attic oratory;³⁹ and according to Andocides, it formed part of the oath formula by which jurors swore allegiance to Athenian law.⁴⁰ With this expression, the associations with stability and fixity of the verb τίθημι, of which κεῖμαι serves as the perfect passive form, become standard in the classical Athenian rhetoric about law. As in the case of θεσμός, we need not assume the specification προκείμενοι to denote an actual physical reality: spatial stability, a sense of something 'set down' that is beyond dislocation, is underscored in any case.

---

³⁴ Hölkeskamp (2000) 78–81. The word appears for instance on the 409/08 BC redraft of Solon's law in the form of a self-reference to 'this law' (ὅδε θεσμός), which very likely reproduces the language of the original law dating from *c.* 620 BC (*IG* I³ 104); see also ML 13 (Naupactus, *c.* 500 BC).
³⁵ See LSJ s.v. θεσμός ('that which is laid down, law, ordinance').
³⁶ See Thomas (2005) 51 on θεσμός as something laid down for the future and set aside from customary rules.
³⁷ See e.g. Pindar *P.* 1.62ff. See also Hdt. 1.59.6, where it is stated that Peisistratus did not change Athens' θέσμια, but abided by the 'established' (κατεστεῶσι) ones; it is unlikely that θέσμια is used in the narrow sense of 'written laws' here.
³⁸ Hölkeskamp (2000) 81–3.
³⁹ Among the countless examples, see e.g. Antiphon 5.96, Aeschines 1.4.
⁴⁰ Andocides 1.91: καὶ οὐ μνησικακήσω, οὐδὲ ἄλλῳ πείσομαι, ψηφιοῦμαι δὲ κατὰ τοὺς κειμένους νόμους.

Other, rarer turns of phrase point in the same direction. The particular phrasing of the Athenian ephebes' oath of allegiance to the city's laws is a point in case. The ephebes swear to 'obey the established laws and all those which may be established in the future' (εὐηκοήσω... τῶν θεσμῶν τῶν ἱδρυμένων καὶ οὓς ἂν τὸ λοίπον ἱδρύσωνται ἐμφρόνως).[41] Here, a concrete spatial connotation may more clearly be felt. Of particular importance is the qualification of the city's θεσμοί as ἱδρύμενοι. The verb ἱδρύω denotes acts of 'setting down' – in Homer often, quite literally, of 'making to sit down';[42] it is then used to express the idea of 'establishing', in the fifth century in particular in reference to the 'establishment', 'institution' or 'foundation' of temples and/or cult.[43] The idea of stability in space is strongly present, therefore. The ephebes swear the oath as they enter upon their training, the endpoint of which will be full civic participation; law here arguably appears as the epitome of civic stability, the fixed centre towards which civic life is oriented.

It seems advisable, in view of these observations, not to dismiss the spatial dimension of the conventional phrase, οἱ προκείμενοι νόμοι, as a mere *façon de parler*, but as indicator of the importance which the civic community attributed to the idea that these laws be fixed, like walls, providing secure points of reference and fixed coordinates along which to stake out a clearly, and stably, defined civic space.

Pollution and civic stability

Pollution relates awkwardly to such stability of the city's civic space, both actual and conceptual. One aspect of this is that pollution may potentially be associated with confusion of categories and therefore designate infringements of boundaries. In the introduction, I drew attention to the difficulties that arise if such an assocation is postulated *a priori* and as the essential characteristic of pollution. I noted that such an association may nonetheless exist in tragedy, but as the result of a tragedy's particular engagement with pollution and not because of any essential link between pollution and category-confusion. I abide by this and shall leave all further remarks on the matter to the discussion of concrete instances in *Antigone*.

The other aspect is less theoretical, concerning a concrete and decidedly 'physical' property of pollution: by inclination it is rather less fixed than the city's inscribed stelae. There is no need to elaborate the point at great

---

[41] Lycurgus 1.77. For the ephebic oath (with text, translation and commentary), see also RO 88.
[42] See e.g. Homer *Il.* 2.191, 15.142.   [43] See e.g. Herodotus 6.105; Eur. *IT* 1453.

length: pollution is potentially contagious and as such apt to travel across distances. We may recall Theophrastus' superstitious man, somewhat of a boundary-obsessed neurotic *avant la lettre*, who will not go anywhere near a corpse or a woman in childbed for fear of pollution (*Characters* 16.9); but we may also think of the many references in tragedy to the ready transmissibility of pollution. Touch may transmit pollution, but even sight or speech is potentially worrisome.[44] Pollution, it is true, is perhaps not usually as aggressively transgressive as the pollution we shall encounter in Sophocles' *Antigone*; but a certain resistance to fixation is nonetheless central to its character as 'contagious religious danger'.[45] There is always the threat for it not to remain an isolated, circumscribable event, but to spread. Consequently, it is readily at odds with the civic community's desire for fixity.

In view of both the preceding and the subsequent comments, it is important to point out that pollution, as we encounter it in historical reality, is rarely endlessly contagious, however. It is, quite literally, defined and circumscribed. In terms of the above remarks, we may say that it is aligned with, and integrated within, civic space and its need of fixity and stability. Incidentally, other than from tragedy our knowledge about pollution derives largely from 'sacred laws' frequently issued by some civic authority: it therefore derives from decrees issued by representatives of the civic community for which fixity is paramount. Pollution does not remain unaffected by this encounter with regulatory powers. In Iulis on Keos, for instance, 'these laws about the dead' (οἵδε νόμοι περὶ τῶν καταφθιμ[έ]νω[ν . . .]) specify that in the event of death 'the mother, the wife, the sisters and the daughters are polluted, but in addition to these not more than five women, the children of daughters and cousins, but no one else';[46] and according to the Cyrene cathartic law,

> the woman who gives birth pollutes the house. She pollutes anyone within the house, but she does not pollute anyone outside the house, unless he comes inside. Anyone who is inside will be defiled for three days, but he will not pass on the pollution to another, no matter where this person goes.[47]

An extreme, if perhaps not quite verifiable example, finally, is Plutarch's Lycurgus. According to his biographer, the Spartan lawgiver confined pollution, at least in the case of death, to the realm of the 'as though' (ὡς) and

---

[44] Touch: e.g. Eur. *Or.* 46–8; hearing: e.g. A. *Eum.* 448–52, Eur. *HF* 1218–20, *Or.* 75–6; sight: e.g. Eur. *HF* 1155–6, *Hipp.* 945–6, *Or.* 512–5.
[45] Parker (1983) 6.   [46] *LSCG* 97 A 25–9, trans. in Arnaoutoglou (1998) no. 109.
[47] *SEG* ix 72 A §4 (= RO 97 A §4). The translation is that provided in RO.

superstition. In the process, its transgressiveness is essentially denied (Plut. *Lycurgus* 27.1):

> Lycurgus also made most excellent regulations in the matter of their [the Spartans'] burials. To begin with, he did away with all superstitious terror by allowing them to bury their dead within the city, and to have memorials of them near the sacred places, thus making the youth familiar with such sights and accustomed to them, so that they were not confounded by them and had no horror of death believing it to pollute those who touched a corpse or walked through a graveyard (ὥστε μὴ ταράττεσθαι μηδ' ὀρρωδεῖν τὸν θάνατον ὡς μιαίνοντα τοὺς ἁψαμένους νεκροῦ σώματος ἢ διὰ τάφων διελθόντας).[48]

Sophocles' *Antigone*

> iusque datum sceleri canimus, populumque potentem in
> sua vitrici conversum viscera dextra. (Lucan, *De bello civili* 1.2–3)

In the preceding sections, we have established spatial notions of stability and instability as inherently 'political', central to how the *polis* was thought of and talked about; we have noted that these spatial notions, and in particular the desire for stability, crystallise in conceptualisations of law as a permanent and fixed point of reference; and we have observed that the space which pollution occupies in relation to this civic need for stability is ambiguous, because it is by nature prone to instability.

Sophocles' *Antigone* is a singularly apt play to analyse within the framework of such concerns. *Antigone* is in an important sense one of the more obviously 'political' (in the sense of '*polis*-centred') of the extant tragedies and has often been understood as something of a philosophical treatise-turned-theatre-play on the concept of the *polis*. The story is well known: in the aftermath of Polyneices' attack on Thebes and his death in unison with city-defending Eteocles, Creon, the new ruler of Thebes, issues the order that Polyneices, as enemy of the city, be left unburied. Antigone, undaunted (stubborn, according to some),[49] defies the order. The antagonists Creon and Antigone meet. Disaster ensues. The encounter between the two (as well as the later encounter between Creon and his son Haemon) is presented in terms of a negotiation of the relationship between the state (the *polis*) and its constituent elements: the *oikos*, the family; the individual. Creon claims the role of representative of the *polis*, upholder of civic

---

[48] Trans. adapted from B. Perrin, Loeb Classical Library (Cambridge, MA, 1914).
[49] See Knox (1964) 67. More positively: Ahrensdorf (2009) 90–105.

order; Antigone foregrounds the importance of the family – by no means an 'apolitical' stance[50] – and appears as the upholder of another (opposed? complementary?) order, one sanctioned by the gods. In all this, the questions of what the *polis* is and how it is to be ordered and/or ruled as well as what it means to be a member of that *polis*, a citizen, take centre stage, more explicitly and more directly than in any other tragedy.[51]

This debate about the state and the nature of civic order and citizenship unfolds, most memorably, along the central theme of the role of law in the maintenance of order, the rule of law as guarantor of the *polis*' continued stability, the *sine qua non* of the community of ζῷα πολιτικά: 'Out of all the extant Attic tragedies, there is none that is more concerned with the role of law ... than Sophocles' *Antigone*.'[52] The specific scenario is famous and well-beloved:[53] Creon, self-proclaimed champion of the city's νόμοι, vs. Antigone, dedicated defender of the eternal, unwritten laws of the gods.[54] It is not least in relation to these two positions that the nature of citizenship, rule and the life in (and of) the *polis* is negotiated. Law appears as central ingredient in the *polis*' make-up and serves as vehicle for a dramatic discussion of civic order.

Significantly, this concern is deployed against a wider background, one that is divided up by crossings and boundaries. The stability afforded by law appears to be precarious. There is, for one, the narrative that lurks in the background about the family of Oedipus, with its history of dangerous crossings of boundaries, bodily as well as territorial; most recently Polyneices' inimical crossing of the borders of Thebes and the

---

[50] See Knox (1964) 75–7: adherence to the *genos* is just as political as adherence to the *polis*. He also notes that Antigone often uses political language (as at 46, when she refuses to become a 'traitor' of her brother).

[51] On the *polis* in Sophocles, see Knox (1983); on *Antigone* ibid. 13–16. The *polis*, he notes, is central right from the start: in the opening scene, Ismene and Antigone severally refer to the *polis*; the parodos evokes Polyneices' attack on his native *polis*; Creon enters and immediately refers to the well-being of the *polis* (vv. 162–3).

[52] Harris (2006) 42. See Harris (2010a) 18 for a list of words for law and justice in Sophocles. In *Antigone* there are eight occurrences of *dikē* and eleven of *nomos* (= highest frequency of *nomos*-terminology in Sophocles), whereas in S.'s *Electra* there are only four occurrences of *nomos*, but fifteen of *dikē*.

[53] For the *Nachleben* of *Antigone*, see Steiner (1984).

[54] Famously, Hegel saw in this encounter the collision of two principles of equal authority. Not least in the wake of the Second World War, scholars have tended to sympathise with Antigone rather than Creon; see Knox (1964) who applauds Antigone's heroism as opposed to Creon's unheroic surrender at the end (ibid. 62) and holds that Creon's motive is hatred while 'Antigone's was love' (ibid. 116). In reaction to such views, some have assigned the bad part to Antigone: see Calder III (1968); Sourvinou-Inwood (1989),140, arguing that for fifth-century Athenians Antigone must appear subversive, embodying the negative idea of the 'woman in charge'; see also Hame (2008). But such readings often miss out on important nuances of the play: see Foley (1995) esp. 143; see ead. (1996).

mutual slaughter of the enemy brothers. And there is another narrative that unfolds in the play's choral odes which maps out the space inhabited by man and ruled by law as a space that is both the product of crossings – seafaring, hunting, domestication (the latter two in particular involving crossings into and (back) from the wilderness)[55] – as well as permanently threatened by crossings, not least the dangerous crossings and *ek-staseis* perpetrated and provoked by Eros (the 'transgressor' and 'confounder' invoked in the third stasimon).[56] As the corollary to this we find (and shall see in more detail below) that Creon is obsessed with stable spatial definitions. All of which is to say that *Antigone* has it all: the political – the *polis*, the law; the spatial – the boundaries, the (fear of) transgression.

It also has pollution. Comparable in this respect to Sophocles' other Theban plays, and in particular *Oedipus tyrannus*, pollution constitutes the backdrop of *Antigone*'s action, determines the 'atmosphere' of the play and provides structure. The 'original' pollution within the play is the result of the mutual fratricide (v. 172). But pollution is not confined to that (recent) past. Rather, the play seems to confirm the fears of the chorus of Aeschylus' *Seven against Thebes* that the pollution which ensues when men of the same blood kill each other never grows old (ἀνδροῖν δ' ὁμαίμοιν θάνατος ὧδ' αὐτοκτόνος, | οὐκ ἔστι γῆρας τοῦδε τοῦ μιάσματος, *Sept.* 681–2): pollution has encroached upon *Antigone*'s dramatic present; it is exuded by Polyneices' unburied corpse, a monument, it would seem, both to the city's inglorious past as well as to its worrisome present; it confounds, in passing, Haemon's character (a 'polluted ἦθος', in the eyes of his father, 746); it preoccupies Creon's thoughts as he proceeds to devise plans for putting Antigone to death without polluting the city (775–6); and it would seem to be connected, if by no means straightforwardly, with the tragic catastrophe – just before the arrival of the messenger the chorus pray that Dionysus come with 'purifying foot' (καθαρσίῳ ποδί, 1142);[57] and upon the news of Eurydice's death a shattered, exasperated Creon realises that 'Hades' harbour is hard to purify' (ἰὼ δυσκάθαρτος Ἅιδου λιμήν, 1284).

---

[55] Crossing the sea: τοῦτο καὶ πολιοῦ πέραν | πόντου χειμερίῳ νότῳ | χωρεῖ, περιβρυχίοισιν | περῶν ὑπ' οἴδμασιν (334–7); hunting and domestication of wild animals: 342–52 (e.g. κρατεῖ | δὲ μηχαναῖς ἀγραύλου | θηρὸς ὀρεσσιβάτα, 347–9). See Oudemans and Lardinois (1987) 120–31.

[56] See Oudemans and Lardinois (1987) 120–59 on transgressions in the play's odes; ibid. 140–4 on Eros. Eros crossing boundaries: φοιτᾷς δ' ὑπερπόντιος ἔν τ' | ἀγρονόμοις αὐλαῖς (785–6). Eros encouraging transgression: φρένας παρασπᾷς ἐπὶ λώβᾳ (792); νεῖκος... ταράξας (793–4). See Oudemans and Lardinois (1987) 120–59 on the play's odes.

[57] On this passage, see Scullion (1998); on the foot of Dionysus more broadly: Schlesier (2002a).

Anthropologically inclined scholars have readily picked up on this prominence of pollution in *Antigone*. For Wouter Oudemans and André Lardinois, in particular, pollution is of paramount importance, the ritual corollary of what they identify as the play's central insight and concern: that reality is not clear and distinct but ambiguous, blurred and paradoxical; and that Man, as Antigone and Creon with their 'reckless acts, their ambiguous fates, their holy pollutions'[58] illustrate, is likewise ambiguous and paradoxical, confounding boundaries of clear-cut categorisations – Man is δεινός, 'awesome', 'terrible', 'wondrous', as the first stasimon famously has it.[59] Theirs, that is, is a classic anthropological view, owing much to the work of Mary Douglas: pollution gives expression to the confusion of cherished categorial boundaries.

Oudemans and Lardinois' insights are useful,[60] but their treatment of pollution in the play, though on the whole illuminating, is imprecise and does not go beyond generalising anthropological statements, reducing the play in this respect to little more than an anthropologist's field report. Pollution may indeed be seen to have something to do with boundaries and their transgression in Sophocles' play. But we need to pay more careful attention to the *dramatic* dynamics among the ritual idea of pollution, such spatial notions and the specific issues the play raises.

These dynamics, I contend, may be understood better if we consider *Antigone*'s pollution in close relation with the play's (and especially Creon's) concern with the *polis* as stable entity, crystallising not least in the concern with law, and the spatial mapping of these concerns. This is what the present discussion sets out to do. I shall first (re-)turn to *Antigone*'s interest in notions of civic stability and instability, focusing in particular on Creon's conception of a civic space hedged in by clearly defined and securely fixed boundaries. This will provide the necessary background for the subsequent discussion of pollution in the play. I shall argue that *Antigone*'s presentation of pollution comes to articulate the failure in particular of Creon's strict vision of a civic space defined by inflexible boundaries.

---

[58] Oudemans and Lardinois (1987) 117.

[59] In the view of Oudemans and Lardinois (1987) 78, *Antigone*'s world is determined by what they call an 'interconnected cosmology' wherein reality is indiscriminate power, which (from the human point of view) is dangerous and ambiguous; pollution gives expression to this ambiguity. Inversely, 'a degree of purity is attained by man's ordering of the cosmos, but it is realized that to a certain extent this human order violates "true" reality' (ibid. 78). For them, δεινός is 'the key word of the tragedy' (ibid. 129).

[60] Especially in that they encourage us to abandon simplistic readings of the type 'Antigone is just, Creon a tyrant', urging us instead to consider both as δεινός in the full (ambiguous) sense of the word. For reviews of the book, see R. Buxton, *JHS* 109 (1989), 216–17; S. Goldhill, *CR* 38 (1988), 396–7.

The crisis of civic space

Set against the background of the confusion of vital distinctions that is implied in Oedipus' killing of his father and sexual relationship with his mother, as well as the recent experience of the dissolution of internal boundaries as the result of civil war and culminating in the mutual fratricide of Eteocles and Polyneices, *Antigone* dramatises the failure of Creon's attempt, as man of the city, to re-establish clear-cut boundaries and in this way 'straighten the city'. The failure of this attempt is articulated in part as the failure of Creon's conception of civic space in the face of grave challenges which it is unable adequately to accommodate and respond to.

The dissolution of physical and conceptual boundaries from which Thebes suffered prior to the play's beginning was complete.[61] Oedipus' parricide and the ensuing merging of mother and wife is ancient history as the play commences; but in particular the latter is still very much on people's, and not least the immediate family's, mind (for instance, on Ismene's, at 53: μήτηρ καὶ γυνή, διπλοῦν ἔπος). More recent, and anxiously recalled by a distressed chorus of Theban elders in the parodos, is the inimical incursion into Theban territory and across its boundaries by one of her own citizens (110–16), leading to a war of 'like against like' (ταχθέντες ἴσοι πρὸς ἴσους, 142) of those born 'from one father and one mother' (πατρὸς ἑνὸς | μητρός τε μιᾶς φύντε, 144–5).[62]

Against this, Creon most prominently sets his insistence on the letter of the law as the *polis*' stable point of reference and source of fixed boundaries. Creon picks up on contemporary Athenian parlance with its spatial connotations when he designates the city's laws as 'laid down' (νόμους... τοὺς προκειμένους, 481). Thus laid down, they provide boundary lines which must not be, but presently are, transgressed: 'stepping across the [boundary line provided by] law' is Antigone's particular 'act of daring' (καὶ δῆτ' ἐτόλμας τούσδ' ὑπερβαίνειν νόμους; 449; see 481), which she commits by burying Polyneices, against the decree which Creon (if only in the form of a verbal edict) has 'laid down for the entire *polis*' (πανδήμῳ πόλει | κήρυγμα θεῖναι, 7–8).[63] Such 'stepping across the law' is the specific

---

[61] The complete dissolution of boundaries in Thebes is stressed by Böhme (2002) 115.
[62] On civil war and civic stability, see Cohen (1995) 25–33. On the monstrosity of civil war, see Thucydides' description of the Corcyraean stasis of 427 BC (Thuc. 3.81–2). On *staseis* in classical Greece, see Gehrke (1985); also Loraux (1995).
[63] That Creon's decree is not written is emphasised by Knox (1964) 95. Dalfen (1977) 10 notes that Antigone distinguishes between κήρυγμα and νόμος and never calls the edict a νόμος. For her, it seems, the edict is not even proper law. (She still invokes the language of τίθημι with its associations of stability and fixity, which may be seen to sit uneasy with the idea of one man's verbally pronounced

spectre that haunts Creon as the man of the city not only in this case, but in general: it is in fact an act of violence (ὅστις δ' ὑπερβὰς ἢ νόμους βιάζεται, 663). Law appears as coextensive with the city and its well-being when Creon asserts that 'with laws like these [underscoring the difference between friends and enemies] I will make the city grow' (τοιοῖσδ' ἐγὼ νόμοισι τήνδ' αὔξω πόλιν, 191). The city's laws have themselves clear boundaries as they are subject to the *polis* authorities' (precise) 'definition' (ὥρισεν νόμους, 452). And they afford stability in that they are somehow like a temple's columns, straight, upright, keeping apart what should be kept apart – or so Creon's close association of the burning down of 'temples with columns all round' and the scattering of laws would seem to suggest (ἀμφικίονας | ναοὺς πυρώσων... καὶ νόμους διασκεδῶν, 285–7).

This preoccupation with law is, however, but the most prominent aspect of Creon's larger concern with stability and the fixity of civic space.[64] As the crystallisation of the hoped-for stability of the city and the body politic, it does not enter the picture by itself. In its wake come a number of concerns which betray a related interest in stable boundaries which organise, in a clear and reliable fashion, the city's actual and/or conceptual space. Creon's speech about civic stability and the necessity of obedience, delivered in his encounter with Haemon (and the first line of which we have already encountered), is a neat exposition of these concerns (661–680):

> ἐν τοῖς γὰρ οἰκείοισιν ὅστις ἔστ' ἀνὴρ
> χρηστός, φανεῖται κἀν πόλει δίκαιος ὤν.
> ὅστις δ' ὑπερβὰς ἢ νόμους βιάζεται
> ἢ τοὐπιτάσσειν τοῖς κρατύνουσιν νοεῖ,
> οὐκ ἔστ' ἐπαίνου τοῦτον ἐξ ἐμοῦ τυχεῖν.
> ἀλλ' ὃν πόλις στήσειε, τοῦδε χρὴ κλύειν
> καὶ σμικρὰ καὶ δίκαια καὶ τἀναντία.
> καὶ τοῦτον ἂν τὸν ἄνδρα θαρσοίην ἐγὼ
> καλῶς μὲν ἄρχειν, εὖ δ' ἂν ἄρχεσθαι θέλειν,
> δορός τ' ἂν ἐν χειμῶνι προστεταγμένον
> μένειν δίκαιον κἀγαθὸν παραστάτην.
> ἀναρχίας δὲ μεῖζον οὐκ ἔστιν κακόν.
> αὕτη πόλεις ὄλλυσιν, ἥδ' ἀναστάτους
> οἴκους τίθησιν, ἥδε συμμάχου δορὸς

---

edict. Segal (1981) 162 notes, however, that κήρυγμα implies public and political speech). This tension does not affect my argument, however. My perspective here is Creon's, who elides the difference between his verbal edict and the city's proper νόμοι προκείμενοι (see e.g. 481): in his thought-world the edict equates to proper law – and what such law stands for.

[64] See Goldhill (1986) 96: 'it is not just the law that is at stake, but what the laws imply in and for the city.'

> τροπὰς καταρρήγνυσι· τῶν δ' ὀρθουμένων
> σῴζει τὰ πολλὰ σώμαθ' ἡ πειθαρχία.
> οὕτως ἀμυντέ' ἐστὶ τοῖς κοσμουμένοις,
> κοὔτοι γυναικὸς οὐδαμῶς ἡσσητέα.
> κρεῖσσον γάρ, εἴπερ δεῖ, πρὸς ἀνδρὸς ἐκπεσεῖν,
> κοὐκ ἂν γυναικῶν ἥσσονες καλοίμεθ' ἄν.

> For the man who manages family matters rightly will be seen to be righteous in the city also. But whoever steps across or does violence to the laws or is of a mind to give orders to those in power, that man shall clearly not win praise from me. But it is imperative that one obey the man whom the city sets up in power, in small things and just things and their opposite. And this is the man that I am confident will rule well and wish to be ruled well and when assigned his post in the storm of battle to remain steadfast, a just and noble comrade. But there is no greater evil than the absence of order and obedience. This is what destroys cities; this is what ruins houses; this is what breaks up and routs ranks of allied spearsmen. But when men remain put and straight, it is order and obedience which saves the lives of most. Thus, we must defend those who obey and in no way submit to a woman. For if die we must, it is better to do so by the hand of a man: then surely we will not be called inferior to women.

Creon effortlessly moves from the fixed boundary lines provided by law to wider issues of stability. Two aspects in particular stand out. There is, on the one hand, Creon's persistent worry about the stability of categories. In this passage, the distinction in question is that between male and female, harking back to Creon's earlier assertion vis-à-vis Antigone that he will not submit to her because this would mean 'becoming a woman' (ἦ νῦν ἐγὼ μὲν οὐκ ἀνήρ, αὕτη δ' ἀνήρ, | εἰ ταῦτ' ἀνατεῖ τῇδε κείσεται κράτη, 484–5), thus turning into the conceptual monstrosity (from his perspective) of a 'man-woman';[65] in other passages, and most prominently at 184–91 where Creon comments on the outrage of Polyneices' attack on Thebes, it is also the distinction between friend and foe that is a matter of concern for him.

There is, on the other hand, Creon's obsession with the vocabulary of ὀρθός and ὀρθόω which gives expression to Creon's desire for stable straightness as antidote to deviance and warping and which appears here in the form of the hoplites' upright bodies (τῶν δ' ὀρθουμένων | σῴζει τὰ πολλὰ σώμαθ' ἡ πειθαρχία, 675–6).[66] Such straightness is essential to

---

[65] On gender dichotomies and their transgression in *Antigone*, see Griffith (1999) 51–4; id. (2001) 126–36.
[66] This obsession is noted by Segal (1981) 179 and Goldhill (1986) 94, 101; see also Griffith (1999) ad 162–3.

Sophocles' Antigone

Creon's conception of civic space and appropriately, therefore, ὀρθόω is the first predicate verb he uses in the play. Entering upon the chorus' remarks on the perversion of civil war in the parodos, he observes that the gods 'securely straightened the city again' after a period of unsettling and destabilising 'tossing' (ἄνδρες, τὰ μὲν δὴ πόλεος ἀσφαλῶς θεοὶ | πολλῷ σάλῳ σείσαντες ὤρθωσαν πάλιν, 162–3). Ruling the city is correspondingly a matter of 'keeping it straight': Oedipus (ironically) did so in the past (ὤρθου πόλιν, 167). Creon now aims to emulate Oedipus' straightness at least as ruler and aims to 'sail on a straight ship of state' in this way to benefit the *polis* (ταύτης [= τῆς πόλεως] ἔπι | πλέοντες ὀρθῆς, 189–90). But for that ship of state to remain 'straight', straightness is required, too, of the citizens' body and their speech: the former is reflected in Creon's view, put forward at 675–6, that the hoplites' 'straight' bodies, obedient to the city's laws, are city-saving; the latter in his inquiry vis-à-vis the guard reporting Antigone as the culprit who buried Polyneices, as to whether his words are 'straight' (λέγεις ὀρθῶς ἃ φής, 403; such 'straightness is a concern of his son, too: see 685–6, 706).[67]

Creon here emerges as the champion of a type of civic space that is hedged in by clear and securely fixed boundaries. His views, in general, are by no means ill-fitted with 'the Greek map of civic space' set out in the introductory section of this chapter. His concerns reflect those of that archetypal man of the city, Solon, with 'straight justice' (εὐθεῖαν ... δίκην, Solon fr. 36 West 19), and his efforts seem to respond to Heraclitus' exhortation to 'fight for the law as for a city wall' (μάχεσθαι χρὴ τὸν δῆμον ὑπὲρ τοῦ νόμου ὅκως ὑπὲρ τείχεος, fr. 65 Kahn).

Crisis and catastrophe ensue because the particular law Creon has laid down readily invites objection, and not only by some anarchist or merely within the play. For *Antigone* turns into tragedy a tension that existed, to some extent at least, in Athenian attitudes to burial.[68] Antigone claims that it is her duty to bury kin. From an Athenian perspective, she is quite right, as Edward Harris has shown.[69] For one, the Athenians may well have taken Antigone's specific stance, considering the burial of kin to be divine law: after all, the Olympians in *Iliad* 24 (esp. 35–45) care greatly

---

[67] See Goldhill (1986) 101 on 'straightness' as 'correctness': the correct attitude of the (straight-talking) citizen.
[68] See Osborne (2008) 55: 'The clash in *Antigone* is neither about what constitutes law, nor between laws of different jurisdictional type (unwritten versus written; arbitrary decree versus popularly supported law), it is a clash which existed in classical Athens within a single lawcode... the crisis [this and other Greek] tragedy worries about is not a crisis that Athenian law solves.'
[69] Harris (2006) esp. 65–7.

for Hector's body.⁷⁰ More importantly, such divine law existed in profane form: Demosthenes 43.57 reports a law that requires that the demarch take care that relatives bury their deceased kin (and purify the deme, ἐπαγγελλέτω ὁ δήμαρχος τοῖς προσήκουσιν ἀναιρεῖν καὶ θάπτειν καὶ καθαίρειν τὸν δῆμον). But from such an Athenian perspective, Creon is not necessarily wrong either in denying burial to the traitor.⁷¹ Xenophon (*Hellenica* 1.7.22), for instance, refers to a law according to which 'if anyone shall be a traitor to the state or shall steal sacred property, he shall be tried before a court, and if he be convicted, he shall not be buried in Attica'.⁷² (Some think that Creon would have been perceived to be going a significant step further, towards outright hubristic aberration, by denying, not only burial in Attica, but burial *tout court*.⁷³ For, Creon's decree would seem to stipulate that the corpse be left as (and where) it is (ἐᾶν δ'... ἄταφον, 29; ἐᾶν δ' ἄθαπτον, 205). But to resolve the complexity of the situation in this way seems problematic.⁷⁴)

The particular crisis which unfolds around the burial of Polyneices puts at stake the 'Creonian' conception of civic space. Creon opts for taking a firm stance as champion of the side of the argument (turning it into a decree) which bolsters in particular his desire for clear-cut distinctions between friend and foe, conceived in the 'political' terms of a person's 'friendly' or 'hostile' (δυσμενῆ, 187) disposition towards the city (and not in the 'genealogical' terms of blood relation, which for Antigone defines

---

[70] This invalidates the claim of Sourvinou-Inwood (1989) 143 that there is no evidence predating *Antigone* suggesting that non-burial offends the gods.
[71] Rosivach (1983) 193–4, Harris (2006) 67.
[72] See also Lyc. *Ag. Leocr.* 113–15; Thuc. 1.138.6, cited by Lefèvre (2001) 83.
[73] Harris (2006) 67; Patterson (2006b) 34–5; see Griffith (1999) 31.
[74] There are both factual and dramatic reasons why Creon would more likely *not* have been perceived as clearly in the wrong. On the factual side, it is not entirely self-evident that even denial of burial *tout court* would be seen as clear hubristic misconduct. The standard term to refer to criminals of the type who were denied burial in Attica, ἄταφος, may be taken to express that burial outside Attica, though perhaps possible, was not normally expected to follow (see Griffith (1999) 30 n. 91, with references to Pl. *Laws* 873c1, 960b2). Also, there existed in Athens a type of execution which consisted of criminals being thrown down a cliff into 'the pit': according to Parker (1983) 47, this was 'probably intended to exclude all possibility of burial'; see Griffith (1999) 30. More important is the dramatic side: Griffith (1999) 31–2 remarks that 'this fine distinction [between burial inside and outside Attic territory] is never in fact made in the play... it does not seem to have been S.'s purpose to provide a systematic analysis of, *and solution to*, these issues: instead, he composed a tragedy' (emphasis mine). Importantly, *because* the distinction is never made, 'it would be hard for an audience to be sure of the legitimacy or illegitimacy of this [Creon's] policy' (Griffith (1999) ad 26–36). See Parker (1983) 47: 'it is the justice of giving Polyneices anything other than a proper burial that is at dispute' (similar: Hester (1971) 19–21). See also Osborne (2008) 55 n. 21: 'one has only to imagine the effect on the *Antigone* as a play of having a character come and say to Antigone, "Never mind, you can just take him to the border and bury him on the other side" to see why this issue [the possibility of burial outside Attica] is not raised.'

the φίλος).[75] In the encounter with Antigone it turns out, however, that Creon, as the advocate of non-burial, would seem to transgress divine law (θεῶν | νόμιμα... ὑπερδραμεῖν, 454–5). Avoiding such transgression would require Creon to allow his conception of civic space a degree of flexibility, as Haemon in fact demands in his lengthy rejoinder to Creon's exposition of his vision of a fixed and inflexible civic space quoted above, a 'yielding' comparable to the 'life-saving' yielding of branches exposed to torrents swollen by winter rain (ὁρᾷς παρὰ ῥείθροισι χειμάρροις ὅσα | δένδρων ὑπείκει, κλῶνας ὡς ἐκσῴζεται, 712–3). But this he will not do. The enemy (of the city) – and not least this enemy who is born and bred Theban – must in no way receive the same treatment as the friend (of the city). Civic space must remain 'straight', like the hoplites defending the city and the walls encircling it. Tragedy ensues.[76]

For completeness' sake, it should be mentioned here that this tragic crisis, in which 'the Greek map of civic space' is put at stake, is framed by the mapping out of other, less fixed and less clearly defined spaces, which are related to, or immediately part of, civic space.

On the one hand, there is the divine sphere which needs to be accommodated by the *polis*. The gods themselves appear to be beyond the human need for definition. In the second stasimon, for instance, Zeus is seen as ageless (ἀγήρως δὲ χρόνῳ, 608), therefore also in a sense boundless, removed from categorisation and boundary-drawing. With this 'boundlessness' comes, according to the chorus, a certain indifference to human transgression: 'what transgression of men', they wonder, 'could (ever) inhibit your power, Zeus?' (τεάν, Ζεῦ, δύνασιν τίς ἀν- | δρῶν ὑπερβασία κατάσχοι; 604–5). Their point seems to be, not that transgression is not possible or that it is of no concern for Zeus, but that his (and the other gods'?) 'eternal omnipotence'[77] is not ultimately impaired by it.[78] This is perhaps not problematic. But other aspects are, and not least the gods' unknowability. The divine sphere is not defined and distinct and therefore no adequate object of human recognition. Divine laws, for instance,

---

[75] On these two different definitions of φίλος in *Antigone*, see Knox (1964) 80–97. See also Blundell (1989) 106–48 (= chapter 4); Ibid. 118: 'for him [Creon] *philoi* are made, not born'; see Nussbaum (2001) 63.
[76] Carter (2007) 113 rightly remarks (though on Creon's maxim 'city first'): '[t]he problem is not so much in the principle itself as in Creon's misguided interpretation of it and his intransigent pursuit of this interpretation.'
[77] Kamerbeek (1978) ad 604–5.
[78] See Kitzinger (2008) 39 on the contrast between Zeus' timelessness and human movement (ὑπερβασία, 605; ἕρπει, 613; πολύπλαγκτος ἐλπίς, 615; πρὶν πυρὶ θερμῷ πόδα τις προσαύσῃ, 619).

though *perhaps somewhere* and *somehow* determined,[79] are not defined by the city's authorities. As such they are not *straight*-forwardly discernible for humans. The tragic denouement of *Antigone* would perhaps seem to validate the notion that at least certain divine requirements (such as the requirement that dead relatives be buried) are fixed and as such adequate objects of human recognition. Nonetheless, on the whole the feeling of uncertainty in the face of the divine persists. We never encounter these gods. And their ways are mysterious, too: why, for instance, if Creon is understood to be clearly at fault, do Antigone and Haemon have to die? As in other plays, we see these (Sophoclean) gods only 'through a glass darkly': to adapt Robert Parker, 'saturated with the divine though the [play is], the . . . gods remain distant and elusive.'[80]

The other spaces that are mapped out and at odds with Creon's vision of carefully delineated and fixed civic space are those staked out by human emotion and, eventually, by human civilisatory acts. As for human emotion, love may imply trespassing, in the form of mental confusion, as the chorus' famous ode on Eros (781–800) intimates.[81] In the chorus' eyes, Haemon's mind is 'brought into excited motion' as the result of his love for Antigone (ταράξας, 794); but sympathy, in the most literal sense of the word, 'commiseration', seems to sit uneasy with Creon's boundary-obsession, too. The chorus at any rate is 'carried across the boundaries' as they watch Antigone advance towards death (θεσμῶν | ἔξω φέρομαι τάδ' ὁρῶν, 800–1). Human civilisation, finally, implies crossings, too – as the famous first stasimon, with its appraisal of 'awesome Man' intimates – into the wilds of land and sea, for instance, in the form of hunting and seafaring.[82]

These remarks on other, less clearly defined spaces and in particular the final remarks on certain necessary and unavoidable crossings underline the precariousness – and perhaps the superficial nature – of the stability of civic space as propounded by Creon. More importantly for the present purposes, however, the very fact that the play lays out in some detail spaces other than Creon's fixed, bounded and unyielding civic space gives further weight

---

[79] At 451–2 (οὐδ' ἡ . . . Δίκη . . . τοιούσδ' ἐν ἀνθρώποισιν ὥρισεν νόμους) for instance, Antigone implies that *Dikē does* determine laws for humans, only not the one Creon presently propagates in the form of his edict.
[80] Parker (1999) 11.
[81] On this ode, see Kitzinger (2008) 44–8, Winnington-Ingram (1980) 92–8; see Blundell (1989) 130–48 on reason and passion in the play.
[82] See Oudemans and Lardinois (1987) 126 on περάω at 337 (περιβρυχίοισιν | περῶν ὑπ' οἴδμασιν, 336–7). For extended comment on the first stasimon, see Rohdich (1980) 63–78; on its wider background (ancient theories about the genesis of human civilization), see Utzinger (2003).

to the idea that Creon's tragedy, and the play's crisis, is centrally about a specific spatial conception of the civic. This specific spatial conception is Creon's tragedy. It may be, in some form or other, the tragedy of all the Creons in the audience.

Pollution and civic space

Pollution, as it appears in *Antigone*, articulates this tragedy of Creon. It is not so much, and rather vaguely, a matter of the protagonists' 'holy pollutions'.[83] Rather, it is in striking ways set in relation with Creon's conception of a fixed and stably defined civic space. In the following discussion, we must distinguish between the two forms in which we encounter pollution in the play. There is, on the one hand, a pile of bodies and most prominently Polyneices' corpse as the concrete source of (what at least Creon designates as) pollution; there is, on the other hand, explicit talk of pollution. The latter is almost the exclusive preserve of Creon; in the form of the terminology of *miasma* it *is* his exclusive preserve.[84] Both these manifestations of pollution in the play are set in relation to civic space, but in ironically divergent ways.

In order to understand better the first form of pollution, let us first inspect its source, Polyneices' body. It is positioned far away from the city, at least if we take the messenger's πεδίον ἐπ' ἄκρον (1197) to mean 'at the outermost edge of the plain', as it has traditionally been understood (and not 'at the highest part of the plain' as Mark Griffith understands it).[85] Its position, therefore, is emphatically 'outside', not within, but far beyond the city proper, which is neatly defined and hedged in by the city-walls. It refuses, however, to remain in this outside position. As Tiresias informs Creon (1016–22, 1081–3), the corpse's scraps are carried into the city and upon the city's altars (1016–8; see also ἑστιοῦχον ἐς πόλιν, 1083). Therefore, the body may be something 'laid down' (κτίσον δὲ τῷ προκειμένῳ τάφον,

---

[83] Oudemans and Lardinois (1987) 117.
[84] Only in one instance does a character other than Creon refer to pollution, but using the term *agos*, not *miasma*: at 256, the guard who reports the 'burial' of Polyneices' corpse speaks of the *agos* resulting from the/an unburied corpse (λεπτὴ δ' ἄγος φεύγοντος ὡς ἐπῆν κόνις).
[85] Griffith (1999) ad 1196–8 (explicating ποδαγὸς ἑσπόμην); 'traditional': see e.g. LSJ s.v. ἄκρος 2 ('to the farthest edge of the plain'), Patterson (2006b) 34. Griffith argues that Polyneices traditionally fell before the seventh gate and that there is no indication in the text that the corpse has been moved (but concedes that Sophocles may be inconsistent). But if the corpse is still in proximity to the gate, Creon would not need a guide, the ποδαγός that appears as messenger (unless we take ποδαγός in the less specific sense of 'attendant', which is unattractive, not least in view of the specification that Creon 'follows' this ποδαγός). The point, which Kamerbeek (1978) ad 1110 and ad 1197 seems to make, that the 'well-visible place' of 1110 points to height, is not evident.

1101), like law (νόμους... τοὺς προκειμένους, 481); like law, too, it may exert pressure upon the city and require that a certain course of action be taken (in this case burial); but quite unlike law (in its monumentalised, inscribed form; and in the form of the image of law as 'laid down'), it refuses to remain stably in place.[86] It transgresses upon the city instead, unheedful of fixity, walls and boundaries.

Two points stand out about the pollution which emanates from, and with, it. The first recaps the basics: it is a concrete pollution; first and foremost, it simply *is*, ἔστιν; it *exists*, in time and space. For it to exist, it does not need words. Tiresias in fact merely evokes the image of the corpse in disintegration: the reference in the present analysis to it as 'pollution' is in a sense but a makeshift solution necessitated by the task of verbal description. Were it not for Creon and his defiant response to the seer's account, that pollution is not to be feared from the decomposing corpse since 'no man can pollute the gods' (1043-4), then 'pollution' would waft about unnamed. The second point picks up on the particular ways of the corpse's behaviour in space. If the spread of the corpse described by the seer is understood to express the spread of pollution, as it usually is (not least because Creon understands it thus),[87] pollution appears at this point eminently unstable and transgressive of the walls and boundaries so dear to Creon's heart.

In implicit contrast to this scenario of boundary-transgressing, nameless pollution stands Creon's named *miasma*. It is significant that Creon, though apparently insouciant about the pollution spreading from Polyneices' corpse, is at the same time the character most obsessed with the concept of pollution as he repeatedly draws explicit attention to it. It is significant, too, that he is the (only) one who calls pollution by its rightful name, *miasma*.

Even before turning to an analysis of the passages in question, these observations would by themselves suggest making two related inferences about the significance and place of pollution in Creon's world. First, it is *a priori* likely (or at least not unlikely) that Creon is obsessed with the concept of pollution because of its unstable, transgressive quality (in the concrete spatial sense), which sits uneasy with his concern for the integrity of boundaries and turns pollution into something of an epitome of that

---

[86] The corpse's 'expansiveness' is stressed by Rehm (2006) 191–2.
[87] Spread of corpse understood as spread of pollution: e.g. Parker (1983) 44; Patterson (2006b) 35. Creon at 1039-44 picks up on Tiresias' evocation of the spread of the corpse and connects it to the question of the reach of pollution.

which must seem worrying to the boundary-obsessed types such as Creon. We shall in fact see in the following that, for Creon, it is consistently the relation of pollution to boundaries and their potential transgression or confusion which is paramount.[88] For once, we shall see, categorial boundaries are at stake, too.

Second, and more importantly, the fact that Creon names pollution, in marked contrast to Tiresias for instance, would seem to give an indication of the particular location of pollution on Creon's map of civic space. When Oudemans and Lardinois speak of the larger-than-life protagonist's 'holy pollutions', their underlying assumption is that in *Antigone*, as well as outside of the play, 'pollution is whatever transcends the system, whether by shortage or excess.'[89] Whatever we make of this view of pollution, it only tells half the story even if accepted. For, if pollution designates something which somehow 'transcends the system', the designation itself of something as pollution, the act of naming pollution, implies nonetheless that this pollution is drawn back into the sphere of the nameable and therefore categorisable.[90] As Shadi Bartsch, in her study of Lucan's *Civil War*, writes, in reference to the 'abject' (a concept closely akin to pollution as Douglas understands it, but without the ritual overtones),[91] '[m]erely to *describe* abjection is to resist it, to trust in the orderly capacity of language to express the dissolution of conventional categories'.[92] Returning to *Antigone*, we should therefore be wary of locating pollution simply at a point beyond Creon's map of civic space as something which 'transcends the system' (i.e. the conceptual space staked out on that map). The observation that Creon speaks regularly of pollution and in the precise terms provided by the vocabulary of *miasma* should alert us, rather, to the possibility that Creon, while fearing the potentially 'transgressive' (and perhaps 'system-transcending') quality of what he designates as pollution, at the same time attempts to integrate these ambiguous margins into his concept of civic space, with its clear-cut categories and fixed boundaries.

---

[88] Followers of Douglas may be tempted to make the same point slightly differently. Consider this quotation from *Purity and Danger*: 'pollution is a type of danger which is not likely to occur except where lines of structure, cosmic or social, are clearly defined' (Douglas (1966) 113). The inference would be that Creon is the one obsessed with pollution because he is also the champion of a conception of civic space in which lines of structure are clearly defined.
[89] Oudemans and Lardinois (1987) 53.
[90] Osborne (2011) 9 comments: 'It is the beauty, but also the limitation, of language that it provides... structure.'
[91] The concept of the abject was developed by Julia Kristeva in her *Powers of horror*: Kristeva (1982).
[92] Bartsch (1997) 25 (italics hers).

An analysis of the occurrences of *miasma*-terminology supports this claim: in contrast to the nameless, transgressive pollution of Polyneices' body, Creon's *miasma*, we shall see, designates worrisome confusions but is nonetheless not only nameable but controllable in other ways, too. In this way, it comes to express a conception of civic space in which even ambiguous margins are containable.

Creon uses the terminology of *miasma* four times. In the first two cases, it is category-confusion that *miasma* is associated with. The first occurrence forms part of Creon's opening speech to the chorus of Theban elders. Entering upon the chorus' account, in the parodos, of Polyneices' recent attack upon Thebes, Creon applauds the present 'straightness' of the city, recovered after the climax of the war of brother against brother, the mutual fratricide and its aftermath, the brothers' lying in unison before the city's (seventh) gate 'with *miasma* resulting from the shedding of kindred blood' (162–73):

> ἄνδρες, τὰ μὲν δὴ πόλεος ἀσφαλῶς θεοὶ
> πολλῷ σάλῳ σείσαντες ὤρθωσαν πάλιν·
> ...
> κἀπεὶ διώλετ', ἀμφὶ τοὺς κείνων ἔτι
> παῖδας μένοντας ἐμπέδοις φρονήμασιν.
> ὅτ' οὖν ἐκεῖνοι πρὸς διπλῆς μοίρας μίαν
> καθ' ἡμέραν ὤλοντο παίσαντές τε καὶ
> πληγέντες αὐτόχειρι σὺν μιάσματι,
> ἐγὼ κράτη δὴ πάντα καὶ θρόνους ἔχω...

Men, the gods have shaken the city's fortunes with a heavy shaking; but now they have set them straight again.... When he [Oedipus] perished, you remained loyal to their children [Oedipus' and Jocasta's] with steadfast minds. So now that they [Eteocles and Polyneices] have died by a twofold fate on a single day, striking and stricken and afflicted with the pollution of kindred murder, I hold all power and the throne...

Miasma here designates an act which challenges the stability of those categories so dear to Creon's civic-minded thought, confounding in particular the vital distinctions between friend and enemy. The language of 'straightness', ὀρθότης, gains corresponding prominence, expressing the need for stability in view of the severe challenge of the brothers' mutual slaughter.

The connection between *miasma* and the idea of confusion of categories is underscored through the preceding reference to the 'twofold doom in one day' (170–1). The play delights in such juxtaposition of oneness and

Sophocles' Antigone

twoness. Before 170–1, Ismene has already repeatedly indulged in the device, occasionally adorning it with additional duals the better to carve out the contrast.[93] The chorus, too, has offered a version of it,[94] before Creon enters, agitated by the 'twofold doom in one day' (170–1). In the wider context of *Antigone*, but also the immediate context here with its insistence on the recovery of straightness and stability, we are invited to understand the formulation as an expression of the feared confusion of categories and dissolution of distinctions which haunt this Theban world. Specifically, it calls attention to the conceptual problems of oneness and twoness which underlie the mutual fratricide: two brothers of one father and one mother (who, incidentally, are also the brothers of their father) in two opposed quarters, when they should act in unison, be of one mind; but also, and equally worryingly, two brothers (who, though ideally of one mind, should still remain separate entities) forming in their twofold death a distressing oneness which stands in ironic contrast to their two opposed mindsets.[95] *Miasma* comes to be associated closely with these undertones. Placed at the end of the subordinate clause in which the 'two/one' difficulties form the central thought, *miasma* constitutes the climax of the sentence, the term, and concept, in which, so the syntax implies, the problems involved in the brothers' mutual fratricide find their definitive and final expression.[96]

This reading of 170–2, and the suggestion that *miasma* is associated here with conceptual confusion, is supported by the implications of Creon's reference to 'steadfast minds' at 169, which shifts attention in the direction of precisely such conceptual confusion, and just before 170–2. These 'steadfast minds' are attributed to the Theban elders, who displayed these minds when they 'remained around' Oedipus' children after his death (μένοντας ἐμπέδοις φρονήμασιν, 169). The formulation must be seen as part of Creon's rhetoric of stability. In his view, the chorus has safeguarded the

---

[93] See esp. vv. 13–14, δυοῖν ἀδελφοῖν ἐστερήθημεν δύο, | μιᾷ θανόντοιν ἡμέρᾳ διπλῇ χερί, with Griffith (1999) ad loc.; 55–7: ἀδελφὼ δύο μίαν καθ' ἡμέραν | αὐτοκτονοῦντε τὼ ταλαιπώρω μόρον | κοινὸν κατειργάσαντ' ἐπαλλήλοιν χεροῖν.

[94] 144–7: πατρὸς ἑνὸς | μητρός τε μιᾶς φύντε καθ' αὑτοῖν | δικρατεῖς λόγχας στήσαντ' ἔχετον | κοινοῦ θανάτου μέρος ἄμφω.

[95] Griffith (1999) ad 170–2 underlines the fact that Creon does *not* use the dual. He argues that this indicates that for Creon the two brothers are separate entities.

[96] One may go even further. Perhaps there is wordplay at work. The word μίασμα, after all, contains the female form of εἷς ('one'), μία, which time and again, and so in this passage, too, forms part of the 'two/one'-motif's rhetoric. The two words are indeed set in parallel positions here, both occurring as conclusion to their respective verses (μοίρας μίαν, 170; σὺν μιάσματι, 172), foregrounding in this way the resonance of the first word in the second. If we take this observation seriously, we may say that Creon's locution encourages us to think of *miasma* as containing not only the word μία but also the complex problems this word comes to designate in this passage in combination with the 'twofold doom'.

polis' stability through their unswerving, fixed and stable minds, that fixity and stability finding expression in the participle μένοντας and the adjective ἐμπέδοις with their respective implications of continuity over time and fixation in place. What Creon arguably means is that Thebes' elders did not succumb to anything as deviant (to be understood quite literally as *de-via*-nt, 'off the [straight] track') as 'crooked' loyalty, turning away from the Labdacid House as it is struck by disaster, but that they remained 'friends of the city' and its ruling family, as reliable advisers presumably, unswerving in their loyalty even in the face of adversity. We may render Creon's meaning by taking recourse to the idea of conceptual space: the Theban elders maintained a straight and stable definition of the category 'friend', staying clear of such conceptual confusion as would be implied in the act of revoking their 'friendship' with the city's ruling family (whose members, as long as they do not turn against the city, are necessarily its φίλοι; or else, as representatives of the city, even the yardstick by which everyone else's 'friendship to the city' is measured). The Theban elders kept their conceptual space 'straight' and 'fixed'.

In the second passage, the connection between the two, *miasma* and confusion of categories, is arguably more explicit. It occurs in the course of Creon's and Haemon's increasingly heated exchange about different styles of governance. Creon, as we have seen, endorses uprightness, steadfastness and obedience (661–80); Haemon, in response, makes a case for 'yielding' and flexibility, the abandonment of all-too-fixed positions and 'deviation' as a strategy for survival (and therefore eventually for the maintenance of civic stability, too; see 712–13: ὁρᾷς παρὰ ῥείθροισι χειμάρροις ὅσα | δένδρων ὑπείκει, κλῶνας ὡς ἐκσῴζεται, 'You see how the trees that stand beside the torrential streams created by a winter storm yield to it and save their branches', trans. Jebb). Creon is shocked at his son's views and, unyielding in his stance, levels the charge of deviance against him. He suspects that Haemon shares Antigone's illness, the confusion of good and bad, friend and foe, commending Antigone's concern for the city's fallen enemy Polyneices (730–2, 740); and, worse even, that he submits to a woman, Antigone, thereby threatening to confound his own cherished gender differentiations which require that a man must never submit to a woman since such submission amounts to being a woman, a horror and the apogee of confusion.[97] 'O you polluted character', he finally exclaims, 'taking second place to a woman!' (746):

---

[97] See *Ant.* 484–5 (ἣ νῦν ἐγὼ μὲν οὐκ ἀνήρ, αὕτη δ' ἀνήρ, | εἰ ταῦτ' ἀνατεῖ τῇδε κείσεται κράτη); 678–80 (κοὔτοι γυναικὸς οὐδαμῶς ἡσσητέα. | κρεῖσσον γάρ, εἴπερ δεῖ, πρὸς ἀνδρὸς ἐκπέσειν, | κοὐκ ἂν γυναικῶν ἥσσονες καλοίμεθ' ἄν). On gender issues in *Antigone*, see Griffith (1999) 51–4; see also id. (2001) 126–36.

ὦ μιαρὸν ἦθος καὶ γυναικὸς ὕστερον.

The adjective μιαρός is used here, not to designate ritual pollution, but as a term of abuse.[98] This non-ritual use of μιαρός is not uncommon in the classical period.[99] It is a particularly strong term of abuse and especially at home in comedy.[100] The term can denote any outrageous behaviour.[101] But here, at (and as) the climax of the preceding discussion, it is associated closely with Creon's charge of confusion of categories. In view of the second part of the line, it is associated in particular with the confusion of male–female distinctions, since 'taking second place to a woman' according to Creon's logic means that Haemon has become a woman (see 484–5). From Creon's point of view, then, the 'pollution' of Haemon's character would seem to be a matter of its yielding and unstable nature, its proneness to categorial confusions both in outlook (friend/foe) and in action (submission to Antigone).[102] It is a matter precisely of not maintaining a 'steadfast mind', a φρόνημα ἔμπεδον, such as the Theban elders maintained.[103] It should be noted here in addition that what Creon considers a loss of a steadfast mind would seem to be the result of Eros' confusion-inducing capacities, to which the chorus draw attention in the stasimon following this encounter (φρένας παρασπᾷς, 792; ταράξας, 794).[104] (And it should also be pointed out, in an aside concerning the wider picture of civic space, that the other type of 'confusion' Eros lords over, sexual intercourse, which is implicative of trespassing of bodily boundaries, is a necessary boundary-confusion and constitutive of civilisation).

In the light of these reflections, the two other passages in which Creon refers to *miasma* appear pointed: we witness in these the translation into action of what is already implied in the act of applying a name to the

---

[98] Kamerbeek (1978) ad loc. consequently translates μιαρός as 'abominable'.
[99] See Parker (1983) 4–5 with references.
[100] Occurrences in comedy include Ar. *Ach.* 182, 282, 285, *Eq.* 304, *Pax* 182–7 (culminating at 184 in μιαρῶν μιαρώτατε), *Ra.* 466 (καὶ μιαρὲ καὶ παμμίαρε καὶ μιαρώτατε).
[101] Parker (1983) 5.
[102] Oudemans and Lardinois (1987) 184 think that the use of the vocabulary of pollution here suggests that Haemon's mind has been infected by Antigone's as the result of too close contact.
[103] My interpretations of 170–2 and 746 (because they argue for an association of pollution with a certain mental disposition) in part reinforce Scullion (1998) on *Ant.* 1144, where the chorus implores Dionysus to 'come with purifying foot' and deliver the city from its *nosos*. He argues that we are to think of this *nosos*, not in terms of a plague or pollution afflicting the city (as is the case in *OT*), but as a mental sickness. I tend to agree with this reading, but think that pollution plays a greater role at the end of the play than Scullion, with his focus on mental states as the 'real problem', suggests: see the section 'Trangressing corpses' below. On disease imagery in *Antigone*, see also Goheen (1951) 43.
[104] On the transgressive power of Eros, see Zeitlin (1996a) 223 (commenting on *Hippolytus*).

marginal: control through definition.[105] What is at stake in the remaining two passages is Creon's attempt to define what does and what does not constitute pollution as well as to determine the limits of pollution's worrying (spatial) transgressiveness.

This concern with control through definition is readily identified in the third passage in which *miasma* occurs. It follows shortly after berated Haemon's departure from the scene. The chorus ask Creon how he intends to put Antigone to death. Creon replies that he 'will bring her to where the path is deserted by men and bury her alive in a rocky cavern, providing only so much food as to be expiation [Griffith's translation],'[106] so that the city in its entirety may escape *miasma*' (773–6):

> ἄγων ἐρῆμος ἔνθ' ἂν ᾖ βροτῶν στίβος
> κρύψω πετρώδει ζῶσαν ἐν κατώρυχι,
> φορβῆς τοσοῦτον ὡς ἄγος μόνον προθείς,
> ὅπως μίασμα πᾶσ' ὑπεκφύγῃ πόλις.

The assertion that through the provision of a modicum of food the *polis* will escape *miasma* constitutes an attempt at defining what constitutes pollution for the *polis*. Creon defines what does and what does not result in pollution afflicting, or even (to stay within the spatial parlance of the present discussion) 'transgressing upon', the city. Something potentially as troublesome as pollution is in this way made palpable and manageable for the city by the city's authority. It is aligned with civic space, much like the death-pollution on fifth-century Keos, which we encountered in the introductory section.

In a slight detour, it is worth pointing out here that Creon's wording is provocative. Commentators have drawn attention to the difficult line 775, which has caused trouble (and provoked emendation): for the transmitted text (which is the text given above and printed for example by Griffith) to make sense, it is necessary to take ἄγος not in its usual sense, 'pollution',[107] but in its far less usual sense 'expiation', or better, 'protection from pollution'.[108] It is arguably not too far-fetched to diagnose a deliberate ambiguity: Creon may attempt to define what is and what is not

---

[105] On Creon's desire for control, see also Rehm (2006) esp. 191–2, 197. On Creon's efforts to control (through) speech, see Bushnell (1988) 50–1 and generally 50–66.
[106] Griffith (1999) ad 775.
[107] It should be noted that this translation is somewhat cavalier. It wrongly suggests that there is no difference between *miasma* and *agos*. See Parker (1983) 5–10 on *agos*; and ibid. 8 on the difference between *agos* and *miasma*. *Miasmata* include unavoidable physical conditions; an *agos*, by contrast, is an 'offence [which] must probably be directed against the gods or their rules' (ibid. 8).
[108] For this second sense, see LSJ s.v. ἄγος 2 (with references to this passage in *Antigone*, Soph. fr. 689 Radt and A. *Choe.* 155). On this line, see in particular Griffith (1999) ad loc.; Kamerbeek (1978) also

pollution, but the very terms he uses to do so call attention to the idea that definition may not be so easy. One aspect of this is that, ironically, control over language, and clear-cut definition through language, fails him just as control and definition is at stake; another, *à la limite*, that there is perhaps an underlying suggestion that it is not at all clear that what Creon wants to posit as 'protection from pollution' is really that – and not quite the contrary, an act which results in further pollution.[109]

Similar in its concern with definition but even more radical is Creon's final reference to *miasma*. In the encounter with the city's seer and in response to his evocation of the scenario of the expanding corpse, Creon asserts that he does not fear pollution. It does not, in his view, affect the gods. Not even if Zeus' eagles carried the scraps of Polyneices' corpse to the thrones of Zeus would he be afraid, he maintains. For, so he claims, 'no human has the power to pollute the gods' (1039–4):[110]

> τάφῳ δ' ἐκεῖνον οὐχὶ κρύψετε,
> οὐδ' εἰ θέλουσ' οἱ Ζηνὸς αἰετοὶ βορὰν
> φέρειν νιν ἁρπάζοντες ἐς Διὸς θρόνους·
> οὐδ' ὣς μίασμα τοῦτο μὴ τρέσας ἐγὼ
> θάπτειν παρήσω κεῖνον· εὖ γὰρ οἶδ' ὅτι
> θεοὺς μιαίνειν οὔτις ἀνθρώπων σθένει.

> But you shall not hide him in a grave, even if the eagles of Zeus were to snatch him and carry the carrion to Zeus' thrones. Not even then shall I fear this pollution and permit that he be buried. For I know full well that no mortal has the power to pollute the gods.

Creon here effectively blunts pollution. Although he does not seem to be saying that pollution does not exist or that the worrisome expansion of Polyneices' body does not constitute pollution (which, so his words

---

accepts the transmitted text. In their OCT, Lloyd-Jones/Wilson print φορβῆς τοσοῦτον ὅσον ἄγος φεύγειν προθείς (following Blaydes/Hartung), 'providing just enough food to escape pollution', taking ἄγος to mean 'pollution'.

[109] This is the conclusion of Müller (1967) 162–3. He argues that the poet exploits the ambiguity of *agos* as 'expiation' and 'pollution' to draw attention to Creon's mad perception ('paradox unnatürlichen Wahn') that his course of action will mean escape from pollution for the city. Kamerbeek (1978) ad loc. is suspicious of Müller's reading, but accepts at least 'a strong sense of irony in 776 when one considers the consequences for the πόλις of the non-burial of Polynices'.

[110] Griffith (1999) ad 1043–4 notes: 'Here, immediately after Tiresias' [to us, utterly convincing] narrative, the claim is hollow and unpersuasive.' Kamerbeek (1978) ad 1043–44 speaks of 'a sophism of the worst sort'. The idea appears again in Euripides, in a context where it appears more convincing: see Eur. *Heracles* 1232 (οὐ μιαίνεις θνητὸς ὢν τὰ τῶν θεῶν) with Bond (1981) ad loc. on the relation to contemporary intellectual currents; see also Rohdich (1980) 204; Jouanna (2007) 455: 'Alors qu'Euripide l'attribue [sc. this theory] à un roi idéalisé, Sophocle la [sc. la théorie] met dans la bouche d'un roi, au moment où il délire.'

would strikingly seem to imply, may reach *humans*), he defines pollution in such a way that it loses its sting in the present circumstances. Essentially, he picks up on the chorus' assertion about the immense power of Zeus, which is not inhibited by human transgression (604–5), and turns it to his advantage. Whatever we make of the chorus' ultimate meaning, for Creon the gods' immense power means that they are in effect beyond human transgression, at least as far as pollution is concerned. For all its proneness to spread, pollution can never quite reach the gods themselves, but only their paraphernalia at best.

What happens here (as in the preceding passage) is twofold definition. In response to Tiresias' evocation of a nameless, transgressive ritual danger, Creon exerts control not only by applying names (*miasma*) to the nameless and in this way drawing it into the sphere of the distinct and recognisable (and categorisable), but also by setting limits to what is thus recognised. As Tiresias' nameless ritual danger turns into Creon's *miasma*, it is thus doubly 'defined': in language, first, as the nameable, classifiable concept *miasma*, worrisome perhaps but not exceeding linguistic differentiation; and second in its actual properties, no longer endlessly outward-reaching but circumscribed and therefore respectful at least of certain boundaries. Again, pollution is made palpable and manageable and is in this way integrated into Creon's vision of civic space with its need of fixed and clear-cut boundaries.

In conclusion to this section it should be pointed out that this location of pollution on Creon's map of the civic – not nameless, but definable; marginal, but still controllable – as well as the progression towards that location finds its counterpart in the position of Polyneices' disfigured corpse within Theban territory as well as, more importantly, in Creon's particular exertion of control over it. Arguably, this is so not only because the body is connected to pollution (in that it constitutes its source), but also, and at a more basic level, because it is similarly problematic and 'un-civic', provoking similar reactions on Creon's part. After all, what we are dealing with here is the corpse of the friend turned enemy; and it is decomposing matter, torn and lacerated, 'abject' as Julia Kristeva would have it.[111]

The corpse is assigned by Creon a position within actual Theban territory which corresponds to the position of *miasma* in Creon's conceptual world.[112] We have seen in the above that Creon advances towards

---

[111] On abjects and abjection and language as tool for differentiation vs. de-differentiations brought about by abject matter, see Berressen (2007).

[112] I emphasise that I speak of *correspondence* here; I do not wish to go as far as to suggest that the position of Creon's corpse *expresses* the position of pollution on Creon's mental map.

integration of pollution within (his particular version of) civic space by first drawing it out of the dark abyss of namelessness and into the light of differentiation and language and then imposing a particular definition – *his* definition – on it, which cuts its worst associations with unbounded transgressiveness. Thus, though marginal, it remains under the control of civic authority and as such within the confines of civic space. Much the same is true for the corpse and its position, as endorsed by Creon: outside the city proper, in the wilderness of the *Umland*, it is still within the borders of Theban territory and therefore within the reach of Creon's control.

More intriguing is the second point: thus positioned, Creon imposes his particular definition of the extent of its meaning upon it in an attempt to cut its worst (potential) associations with transgression. We encounter the body disfigured, marked presumably by blows received from the brotherly blade and lacerated by scavenging birds and dogs. This disfigurement may be indicative of boundary-confusion and transgression, a visual reminder of the fratricide as well as, potentially, of Creon's present turning against a family member – not unlike Polyneices' in the past. But Creon will not let such an interpretation stand. Rather, he attempts to impose a meaning onto this disfigurement that is constitutive, rather than disruptive, of civic space. Remarkably, Creon wants the body to be *seen* in its disfigurement (αἰκισθέν τ' ἰδεῖν, 206). The context, with its insistence on the distinctions between friend and foe, suggests that this display is meant as visual deterrent and is intended, more precisely, to provide an image of 'the foe' and the kind of fate that awaits him.[113] Creon, that is, defines the wounds and laceration as the visual expression of the *differentiation* between friend and foe, in a way that underpins, rather than undercuts, boundaries and categorisations.

Transgressing corpses: nameless pollution and Creon's failure

In the light of these observations on naming and namelessness, transgression and containment, as well as the underlying juxtaposition of the (namelessly) spreading corpse and Creon's *miasma*, the denouement of *Antigone* appears pointed. Corpses multiply and spread from margins to centre, replicating in this way the movement of Polyneices' expanding corpse. That we are dealing here with a spread from margins to centre of pollution is not verbalised, but some such thing is obliquely hinted at. Ironically, therefore, but appropriately and in pointed contrast to Creon's

---

[113] Rehm (2006) 191 suggests that Creon means to display the punishment that awaits the traitor after death; see also Roselli (2006) 144 (who places greater emphasis on the aspect of public humiliation of the enemy).

(conception of) *miasma*, a 'pollution' that is neither controlled now through language nor inhibited in its transgressive expansion towards the centre of civic space articulates Creon's downfall and in particular the failure of his overly rigid patrolling of boundaries.[114]

Bodies pile up, first, at the margins, in Antigone's rocky cavern 'where the path is deserted by man'. Antigone hangs herself; Haemon, after a failed attack on Creon, commits suicide, wrapping himself around his beloved's corpse as he breathes his last, spurting streams of blood on the dead maiden's pale cheek. As the image of two enwrapped bodies is conjured up (κεῖται δὲ νεκρὸς περὶ νεκρῷ, 1240), the twofold doom of the fratricides, corpse hard by corpse, looms large, and with it the idea of pollution, αὐτόχειρ as well, albeit now resulting from self-inflicted, rather than kin-inflicted murder (see 172, αὐτόχειρι σὺν μιάσματι).

The scene gestures towards pollution in a further way. It evokes not only the scenario of the fratricide: as has often been noted, the particular wording of the passage implies an allusion to the memorable scene in Aeschylus' *Agamemnon* in which the queen, blood-splattered upon the murder of her husband, returns onstage, exulting in her deed. Triumphantly she informs us that 'lying there, he [Agamemnon] gasped away his life, and as he breathed forth quick spurts of blood, he struck me with a black drizzle of bloody dew' (κἀκφυσιῶν ὀξεῖαν αἵματος σφαγὴν | βάλλει μ' ἐρεμνῇ ψακάδι φοινίας δρόσου, 1389–90; trans. adapted from H. W. Smyth). The words of *Antigone*'s messenger are strikingly reminiscent of Clytemnestra's. As Haemon collapses on Antigone, the messenger tells us, 'panting, he spurted a quick stream of bloody drops onto her white cheek' (καὶ φυσιῶν ὀξεῖαν ἐκβάλλει ῥοὴν | λευκῇ παρειᾷ φοινίου σταλάγματος, 1238–9; trans. Griffith).[115] Arguably, in Aeschylus' scene the idea of pollution, albeit not spelt out until later in the play, is strongly present. Its evocation at this point in *Antigone* underpins the effect of the back reference to the fratricide: pollution, though not verbalised, is obliquely hinted at.

---

[114] Goldhill (1986) 104, aptly: Creon's 'desire for the accurate and upright has led to the warping of tragedy'.

[115] As Griffith (1999) ad 1238 notes, some editors have emended the text in order to make the correspondence even closer (κἀκφυσιῶν instead of καὶ φυσιῶν). For Kamerbeek (1978) ad 1238–9 Aeschylean inspiration is certain. Difference rather than similarity is at stake: in Aeschylus, the act from which results Clytemnestra's being struck by blood signifies hate and disjunction of husband and wife; here, love and 'con-junction' are implied, the lovers' union in death. Latinists will be reminded of the scene in *Aeneid* 9 where the two Trojan youths Nisus and Euryalus are united in death as their nocturnal raid through Turnus' camp comes to a disastrous end: *tum super exanimum sese proiecit amicum | confossus, placidaque ibi demum morte quievit* (*Aen.* 9.444–5). On the marital and sexual overtones of the Sophoclean passage, see Seaford (1987) 107–8 and 120–1.

Bodies then advance upon the city and the very hearth of the royal house. The movement by which margins and centre are connected is the carrying into the city of Haemon's corpse in the arms of his father (διὰ χειρὸς ἔχων, 1258). The completion of the movement, as replication of the movement of the scraps of Polyneices' corpse, is achieved with Eurydice's suicide. Eurydice falls 'around', or on, the altar, as the second messenger informs us (βωμία πέριξ, 1301).[116] Whether or not she was rolled out on the altar serving as *ekkyklēma*, too,[117] the evocation in language of this scenario suffices to establish the connection with the earlier scraps of Polyneices' corpse on the city's altars (1016–18: βωμοὶ γὰρ ἡμῖν ἐσχάραι τε παντελεῖς | πλήρεις ὑπ' οἰωνῶν τε καὶ κυνῶν βορᾶς | τοῦ δυσμόρου πεπτῶτος Οἰδίπου γόνου, 'for our altars, high and low, are all full of carrion, brought by birds and dogs, of Oedipus' ill-fated son who fell').

Pollution, though not spelt out, is again hinted at. For one, the idea itself of the body on the altar cannot fail to evoke the idea of pollution, especially before the background of Tiresias' earlier graphic account of the fate of Polyneices' corpse and Creon's translation of it into the concept of *miasma*.[118] In addition, the second messenger's choice of words once more directs our attention to the brother's 'pollution resulting from kin- (or brother-) inflicted shedding of blood' (αὐτόχειρι σὺν μιάσματι, 172): Eurydice, too, arranges her death αὐτόχειρ (παίσας ὑφ' ἧπαρ αὐτόχειρ αὐτήν, 1315).[119] Finally, Creon's own words point in the direction of pollution, albeit ambiguously. In reaction to the second messenger's news he observes that 'the harbour of Hades is hard to purify' (ἰὼ δυσκάθαρτος Ἅιδου λιμήν, 1284). It is not entirely clear what Creon means. A few lines later, he speaks of his wife's death as σφάγιον (σφάγιον ἐπ' ὀλέθρῳ ... μόρον, 1291–2). Such σφάγια (which, like Eurydice's death, always involved blood-flow) were sometimes purificatory.[120] In view of the preceding reference to

---

[116] On the difficulty of the MS reading of 1301, see Griffith (1999) ad loc. (a plausible emendation would be Arndt's ἡ δ' ὀξυθήκτῳ βωμία περὶ ξίφει; see Kamerbeek (1978) ad 1301 for other emendations).

[117] For the question whether Eurydice's body was rolled on the *ekkyklēma*, draped on the altar or whether she was carried out of the palace, without *ekkyklēma* and altar, see Griffith (1999) ad 1293.

[118] Rehm (2006) 195 speaks of the 'corpse-polluted altar' (and draws attention to the contrast between containment and spread which emerges, noting that Creon's 'effort to seal off Polyneices' corpse from the earth and the living Antigone from the sun has spread to his own home').

[119] On Loraux' terms, this suicide, since it is carried out with a sword, is 'manly'; in addition, the flow of blood involved (still on Loraux's terms) points in the direction of maternity (invoking the pains of childbirth). Appropriately, Eurydice dies *for* her son. See Loraux (1987) 7–30 (14 on manly deaths; 15 on bloody suicides; 23 on Eurydice dying for her son).

[120] The Orestes of *Eumenides* speaks of such purificatory σφαγαί, for instance, at A. *Eum.* 449–50. If Froma Zeitlin is right in her interpretation of *Ag.* 1431–3, Clytemnestra's reference to her murder as σφάγιον implies a purificatory σφάγιον, too. See Zeitlin (1965) 475–80, esp. 479.

'difficult purification' (δυσκάθαρτος) and the general notion that Thebes (and its ruler) are in dire need of purification, one may just understand σφάγιον in this sense here, too: we may take Creon to conceive of Eurydice's' death as a (suitably perverted and painful) form of expiation, this painfulness being the reason for purification being δυσ-, 'difficult', 'hard'. But if such is Creon's meaning we need not agree. Eurydice's σφάγιον ἐπ' ὀλέθρῳ... μόρον is readily understood as 'new bloody death in addition to the ruin',[121] without the purificatory overtones; Hades' harbour may be hard to purify in particular for Creon, now and in the future, in view of the many deaths he has caused, resulting in a *miasma* that 'cannot be overtopped' (to borrow from Aeschylus *Suppl.* 473).[122] On either reading,[123] the notion of pollution moves provocatively into the foreground.

If Polyneices' expanding corpse is in part the tangible expression of the transgressive nature of pollution, unheedful of Creon's demands of fixity and stability, doubly worrisome in fact because unnamed and undefined, the piling up of bodies from margins to centre translates this transgressiveness into even more concrete images. Creon's final words are apt. For all his desire that the *polis* and its conceptual space be stable and clearly defined, in the end he can only observe that 'everything in my hands has become cross' (or 'slanting', 'crooked'; πάντα γὰρ | λέχρια τἀν χεροῖν, 1344–5). The presentation of pollution in the play articulates both Creon's desire for stability and definition and its failure. His obsession with boundaries, expressed in part by his desire to define and delimit even pollution, has led to their transgression, by an undefined and perhaps indefinable pollution.

Transgressive corpses: Polyneices' dissolving body and civil war

Corpses have been much on our minds in the course of this discussion, in particular Polyneices'. This body is central to the play.[124] It is not only the

---

[121] The translation given by Kamerbeek (1978) ad loc. Griffith (1999) ad loc. translates 'new bloody death piled on top of death'.

[122] Such seems to be the interpretation of Griffith (1999) ad 1284–5 ('"hard to cleanse" for Kreon because he has caused the bloody deaths of his own φίλοι'). See also Kamerbeek (1978) ad 1284: Hades is hard to cleanse because it is 'choked with the dead'.

[123] In its ambiguity, the passage may be taken to evoke the Aeschylean scenario wherein retributive murder is seen as both polluting and as purifying. See chapter 3.

[124] Bodies play an important role in Sophocles in general. One need only think of Oedipus' γεραὸν σῶμα, his aged and frail body in *Oedipus at Colonus*, subject to elaborate negotiations concerning its placement vis-à-vis the Colonean shrine of the Eumenides and in the course of the play increasingly a source of numinous power; or of disease-ridden Philoctetes' festering body in Sophocles' play of the same name. On the role of Philoctetes' diseased ('abject') body as the point of reference of a 'discourse of disease', see Worman (2000); on 'recalcitrant bodies' in Sophocles, see ead. (2012).

bone of contention in the tragic encounter between Creon and Antigone and therefore the central element in the play's progression towards disaster; evoked early in the play as a 'sweet treasure for birds that spot it' (οἰωνοῖς γλυκὺν | θησαυρὸν εἰσορῶσι, 29–30) and rotting away as the play unfolds, it also constitutes the play's most present absence, imposing itself as a vivid image upon the audience's mind. Earlier in the discussion, attention was drawn to the interpretation of the meaning of its disfigurement and the possibility that it might be read otherwise than Creon would have it. Now in conclusion and as an addendum, let us take up Creon's invitation to 'behold the mangled corpse' (αἰκισθέν τ' ἰδεῖν, 206) and take a final look at Polyneices' body and its fate of decomposition. I suggest that this look turns out to be subversive of Creon's reading. It seems to me that Polyneices' corpse and its fate of laceration may be taken to reflect the continuity of boundary-transgressing internal strife which presses hard upon the integrity of Thebes' civic space as the result of Creon's denial of burial.

As a first step, I propose that we are encouraged to understand the unburied corpse of Polyneices not only as the necessary product of Creon's edict, a sign of this ruler's particular aversion to former friends that have turned into enemies, but also as something of a visual metaphor, suggesting that the specific conflict of the past – the internal strife that, along with the brothers' bodies, has ripped apart the city's most precious boundaries – *has not yet been buried*. We have seen that internal strife, the war of brother against brother, is at the root of the pressures which endanger the stability of the city's space, tangible as well as conceptual. Through its association with the brothers' mutual fratricide (αὐτόχειρι σὺν μιάσματι, 172), pollution is closely bound up with this unsettling and destabilising internal strife. In the present of the play we find that one of the two brotherly corpses earlier lying in troubling unison hard by one of the city's seven gates (the seventh, traditionally) is still there, if now (presumably) displaced to the far reaches of Thebes' territory, exuding what we may designate as pollution. This continuity between past and present seems important. It suggests conceiving of the present conflict as a continuation of the past conflict.

Important studies of the symbolic significance of the body suggest going further, however, towards an understanding of Polyneices' lacerated body as a kind of map of the present strife as another boundary-dissolving internal strife, another 'civil war', provoked, paradoxically, by Creon's attempt to re-establish, and patrol closely, the boundaries which civil war had

On the theme of disease as dramatic device in Sophocles, see Biggs (1966). On bodies in Greek tragedy in general, see Cawthorn (2008), Fartzoff (2010).

dissolved. Such studies have drawn abundant attention to the symbolic relationship often established between the individual's body and society, the 'body politic'.[125] We have become increasingly aware that in different cultures as well as different periods (including our own) the body, and more precisely the particular condition of the individual's body, has served as medium of reflection on, and metaphor for, the condition of the body politic. As soon as the body politic, or the state, is thought of in spatial terms as a stable entity in need of intact boundaries, the body as another 'bounded' entity readily suggests itself as a point of comparison and expression of the condition of the body politic. In this way, the integrity of the body and its boundaries may stand for the integrity of the state. Inversely, violations of bodily boundaries may reflect the state's (perceived) disintegration.[126]

In the case of classical Athens, such an approach seems not out of place. We have already above that the *polis* was conceived of not least in terms of its various, ideally stable, boundaries. Importantly, there also existed a close relation between that *polis* and the body. On the one hand, at least from the fourth century onwards the *polis* could be referred to as a body. Both Hyperides and Dinarchus speak of τὸ τῆς πόλεως σῶμα in contexts where what is arguably emphasised is that the city is (like) a living organism, fragile and potentially subject to corruption.[127] (Heinrich von Staden also notes the importance, in ancient Greece, of skin as 'a magical symbol of... the integrity of individual or collective organisms that might become susceptible to disintegration or fragmentation'; in several foundation myths, we find skins signifying 'the integrity, oneness, and inviolability of the new city.')[128] On the other hand, throughout the classical period (and beyond) physical integrity was immensely 'political', an essential aspect of the ideal

---

[125] For an important contribution within the field of Classics, see Bartsch (1997) 10–47 on Lucan's *Civil War*.

[126] Bartsch (1997) 10: 'The analogic role of the body seems to span cultures and times, surfacing repeatedly as a metaphor that suggests the organic unity of anything perceived as bounded, whether it be the political state or the human psyche; similarly, the body's vulnerabilities can reflect the susceptibility to wounding or dismemberment of the other "bodies" at stake.'

[127] Hyperides 5 fr. 6 (v col. 25; ἐπ' αὐτῷ τῷ σώματι τῆς πόλεως); Dinarchus 1.110 (ὑμεῖς εἰς τὸ τῆς πόλεως σῶμ' ἀποβλέψαντες) sets the body of the *polis* in opposition to (the body of) Demosthenes; the background is the Harpalus affair of 324 BC in which Demosthenes was accused of having acted against the interests of the city by accepting bribes from Harpalus, imperial treasurer of Alexander and a central figure in a delicate diplomatic affair between Athens and Alexander, for facilitating his escape from Athenian imprisonment. The prescribed penalty was either an enormous fine or even death. The circumstances were such, then, that the city's stood against Demosthenes' well-being. By referring to the *polis* as body Dinarchus suggests that the *polis*'s integrity is just as fragile as Demosthenes'.

[128] Von Staden (1992a) 227–31 (227–8 and 228 for the quotations).

Sophocles' Antigone

image of the citizen who also had to take his stand in the hoplite ranks.[129] One need only think of the muscular bodies depicted on the frieze of the city's most political monument, the Parthenon; or of the fact that as one made one's way to and from the city's gymnasia located to the north-west of the city, outside the Dipylon Gate, to hone one's body (and talk philosophy and politics at the Academy) one also walked along the *dēmosion sēma*, the city's public cemetery, an ideologically charged site, home to the city's war dead and setting for the Athenian democracy's idealising self-projection in the funeral oration.[130] In this cultural context, then, the more specific use of the body as map of the city, the body's condition reflecting the city's condition, would seem to be entirely at home.

The assumption of such a correlation between body and city, while perhaps evident in Sophocles more widely,[131] makes particular sense in *Antigone*. In this play, the connection between body and city is especially strong. Two points stand out. First, the play 'politicises' the body in the sense sketched above. Creon is the key figure here, establishing an analogy of the type we are interested in between bodies and cities. The vehicle is the idea of straightness. Creon, we have seen, is obsessed with this idea, as is suggested not least by his continual use of ὀρθόω and ὀρθός. For him, the sense of stability, of straight lines and clear boundaries, implied in these words constitutes the essence of the *polis*: Oedipus, after a period of internal strain, made the city straight (ὤρθου πόλιν, 167); now it is paramount to sail on a straight ship of state (ταύτης ἔπι | πλέοντες ὀρθῆς, 189–90); yet, for that straightness and stability of the state to be maintained the citizens' *bodies* must be straight and stable, too. Creon advances this view in the encounter with Haemon and in the passage analysed earlier, 661–80. True patriarch and statesman that he is, he turns to his son with a lengthy speech on the many advantages of clear lines and their acceptance by the city's subjects. Anarchy is deviance and horror, laying low many a city (673). Obedience, by contrast, the acceptance of clear lines, is city-saving as the hoplites take their ordered stand in the ranks, body stable, straightened, upright: 'but when men remain put and straight, it is order and obedience which saves the lives of most' (τῶν δ' ὀρθουμένων | σῴζει

---

[129] Stähli (2001) 197: 'An intact virility was seen as a direct precondition for the stability of the *polis* and a virile body perceived as a visible sign of the individual's ability and aptitude to stand up for the good of the *polis* and act in its best interest' (my translation).

[130] On the funeral oration and its role in Athenian self-projection, see Loraux (1986). On the inter-relations between classical Greek ways of carrying the body, Athens' cityscape and democratic ideology, see Sennett (1994) esp. 31–51.

[131] Mitchell-Boyask (2012) 317–23 (his focus is more on the body as physical *system*, whereas mine is on the body as a bounded *entity*).

τὰ πολλὰ σώμαθ' ἡ πειθαρχία, 675–6). For Creon, the body's straightness is a tangible reflection of the desired straightness of the city.

Second, Polyneices' corpse has a close relation to the *polis*. Its placement vis-à-vis the city is carefully controlled, by the city's authority; and it is the site (and sight) upon which the differing visions of the *polis* are visually inscribed – by leaving the corpse exposed, a horrific sight for the citizens to see (αἰκισθέν τ' ἰδεῖν, 206), Creon makes visible his vision of an exclusive *polis*, with clear distinctions between insider and outsider; by covering it with dust, Antigone makes visible her vision of a more inclusive *polis*, one showing greater respect towards family ties. It is in relation to the corpse that the make-up of civic space is defined.

Let us inspect, then, Polyneices' corpse, inasmuch as the play readily encourages us to take a closer look at the condition of the body as a symbolic reflection of the condition in which the city finds itself. Its condition is such that it has entirely lost its boundaries. Instead of decomposing in an 'orderly' and 'bounded' fashion, it has been torn open by dogs and birds (κυνοσπάρακτον σῶμα, 1198; οἰωνῶν τε καὶ κυνῶν βορᾶς, 1017). This scenario may seem troubling enough, the body's innards ripped outwards by scavenging animals. But Polyneices' corpse is even more 'transgressive', its scraps, along with the rotting flesh's 'unholy smell', not remaining in place, in the far reaches of Thebes' territory, but carried off by these scavenging animals into the city and even onto the city's altars and hearths (see 1016–18, quoted above; see also the difficult lines 1082–3 where there is talk of an 'unholy smell' that is carried into the city, φέρων | ἀνόσιον ὀσμὴν ἑστιοῦχον ἐς πόλιν).[132]

We may identify a rich visual metaphor here. Against the background sketched above (Creon's vision of civic space as clearly defined by stable boundaries of various sorts and his politicisation of the citizen's upright body, a clear vertical line in the clear horizontal lines of the hoplite ranks, as analogous expression of the upright *polis*) the loss of the boundaries of Polyneices' body and its inordinate 'transgressiveness' appear pointed. Arguably, it does not merely constitute a rather graphic and very specific illustration of Creon's folly as violator of divine laws as it has tended to be understood;[133] especially in view of Creon's presentation of straightness and stability as the reverse of, and remedy for, internal unrest (162–9), the body's fate of laceration, innards transgressing outwards, may be seen also

---

[132] Rehm (2006) remarks that 'Creon's *Totentheater*... cannot contain its principal set piece... Polyneices' corpse refuses to stay put' (ibid. 191); it 'proves more "expansive" than [Creon] had expected' (ibid. 192).

[133] E.g. Patterson (2006b) 35; see also Rehm (2006) esp. 200.

to provide a comment on the condition of the body politic; to reflect more broadly a community again (or: still) at war with itself and in which, in the aftermath and as the result of Creon's edict, vital boundaries are again being dissolved.

In other words, the corpse's fate of spatial expansion may be understood as a tangible expression not only of a specific transgression against the divine sphere, but also, more comprehensively, of the destabilisation of civic space, the 'dismemberment' of crucial internal boundaries in the hostile encounter between two citizens that results from Creon's refusal to bury a friend turned enemy. It is important in this regard to keep in mind the specifics of the body's spatial expansion: sure enough, transgression vis-à-vis the divine sphere constitutes the end point of the body's journey as parts of it come to a final rest upon the altars of Thebes (1016–18); but on their way to these altars, the corpse's scraps pass through the entire Theban territory, 'transgress', that is, the land's civic space, crossing from its far reaches across the city-walls and towards the city's heart and hearth (ἑστιοῦχον ἐς πόλιν, 1083). Dissolution of the body's boundaries and transgression of civic boundaries go hand in hand here. The image strongly suggests a metaphorical understanding.

CHAPTER 3

Evaluation and stability in Aeschylus' Oresteia

One elementary characteristic of pollution has thus far largely been overlooked: it attaches a label to certain states (and acts), gives them meaning and allows categorisation. Awkward states (and certain acts) are given a name and are in this way drawn from the obscure depths of non-differentiation and meaninglessness into the light of differentiation and meaningfulness. For instance, contact with death 'means' pollution, as Theophrastus' superstitious man memorably reminds us (*Characters* 16.9). So does the shedding of human blood: homicide is not neutral, but entails pollution – that its perpetrator *is polluted*, as tragedy in particular underscores time and again.

Though this seems to be unproblematic and not the stuff tragedy would worry about, at least in the case of homicide, there is considerable critical potential. Unlike, say, childbirth or contact with death, homicide is a (usually) avoidable act of violence that is particularly threatening to the civic community. As such it is not only subject to ritual categorisation along the coordinates provided by the concept of pollution but also readily invites moral censure. More to the point, it is readily subject to non-ritual evaluation along the coordinates provided by the concept of justice (and even legal justice). Thus, like the mother in childbed, the homicide is polluted; unlike the mother in childbed, however, the homicide may also be considered 'bad' or, more importantly, 'unjust'. The critical potential lies in the underlying question of the relation between ritual and non-ritual evaluation: are they to some extent coextensive? Or are they entirely dissociated?

Athens is a case in point. In the classical city, a developed legal system is in place. What we find, at least in the late fifth and certainly in the fourth centuries BC, is at times a near-congruence of ritual and legal categories.[1]

---
[1] See Parker (1983) 366–9; Harris (2010b) esp. 128–9, 133–4. On Athenian homicide law in general, see MacDowell (1963) and Phillips (2008). Where pollution is concerned, both these studies should

A number of passages in Demosthenes indicate that certain types of homicide which were not liable to legal sanctions were also not polluting. For instance, Draco, according to the speaker in Demosthenes 20.158, 'did not take away [from the homicide] the arrangements of justice, [but] defined circumstances that made homicide justifiable and determined the perpetrator in such a case to be pure' (οὐκ ἀφείλετο τὴν τοῦ δικαίου τάξιν, ἀλλ' ἔθηκεν ἐφ' οἷς ἐξεῖναι ἀποκτιννύναι, κἂν οὕτω τις δράσῃ, καθαρὸν διώρισεν εἶναι).[2] As Robert Parker observes, therefore, in Athens '[r]itual and legal status are assimilated to the extent that in contexts of homicide "pure" and "not subject to legal sanctions" are often synonymous.'[3]

Among the extant samples of Greek tragedy, it is Aeschylus' formidable *Oresteia* in which these concerns play an important role.[4] Homicide is certainly ubiquitous, in particular as part of the disconcerting sequence of 'crime and punishment': King Agamemnon kills his daughter to gain favourable winds for his revenge expedition against Troy;[5] Queen Clytemnestra kills the king in return; son Orestes in turn kills the queen; Orestes then is pursued by the Erinyes and escapes death only when finally acquitted before the law court of the Areopagus. In the intervals between 'crime' and 'punishment', processes of attaching meaning to these acts of violence are paramount. The ritual category of pollution occupies a conspicuous place, from Agamemnon's anticipation of pollution resulting from the sacrifice of his daughter, to Clytemnestra, the 'pollution of the land and the local gods' (*Ag.* 1645), to Orestes, contracting 'unenviable pollutions' as the result of the matricide (*Choe.* 1017). But non-ritual evaluation has its conspicuous place, too; after all, in the words of Reginald

---

be read alongside Parker (1983) esp. 104–30. Phillips has little to say on the subject of pollution (see Phillips (2008) 62–3); MacDowell (1963) 141–50 has a few useful (and appropriately cautious) concluding pages on the role of pollution in legal trials but does not comment on the relation between legal and ritual categories. On homicide law and pollution, see also Arnaoutoglou (1993) and Eck (2012) 216–25, 299–310 (the latter underlining that pollution is largely absent from Greek homicide laws).

[2] See also Dem. 9.44, 23.53–5; Lycurgus, *Against Leocrates* 125; Plato, *Euthyphro* 4b–c (with McPherran (2002)), *Laws* 874b–c (and 868bc, 869c–d); RO 79, 7–11 (dating from 337/6 BC).

[3] Parker (1983) 114; see also Harris (2010b) 128–9.

[4] 'Formidable' in various senses: one of them relates to the 'formidable' difficulty the trilogy presents for interpreters, not least because of its 'unassailable and inexhaustible richness': Goward (2005) 9 on *Ag.* For certain aspects of this 'richness' (such as linguistic richness as well as a peculiar 'indeterminacy of voices'), see Griffith (2009), Raeburn and Thomas (2011) lxi–lxix. Lebeck (1971) is fundamental on the *Oresteia*'s language and structure.

[5] Agamemnon's predicament on Aulis received considerable attention in particular in the mid-twentieth century. Classic studies of Agamemnon's guilt, double motivation and related issues are Lloyd-Jones (1962) and Lesky (1966). (Examples of a similar type of scholarship in French in these years include Rivier (1966) and (1968).)

P. Winnington-Ingram, the *Oresteia* is a 'vast exploration of justice'.[6] This is certainly true, in view of the trilogy's ubiquitous references to both (personified) Justice and (the concept of) justice and its movement from the μέγας ἀντίδικος (*Ag.* 41), Menelaus and Agamemnon, advancing upon Troy, to Justice which 'cries out loud: expiation of bloodshed through bloodshed' (*Choe.* 311–13), to Orestes' exasperated declaration at the end of *Choephori* that he has killed his mother 'not without justice' (οὐκ ἄνευ δίκης, *Choe.* 1027), to the δίκη of the legal trial in *Eumenides*.[7]

The present chapter takes its starting point here, exploring, in Part I, the *Oresteia*'s concern with Justice/justice as well as the relation of pollution to such Justice/justice. Analysed within this framework, we shall see, pollution is not the vehicle of commentary: comparable in this respect to the scenario of *Oedipus tyrannus*, it is rather the object of commentary. I build on traditional lines of argument. Justice is bifurcated in the *Oresteia*: on one view, justice cares only for the act and the murderer is automatically on the wrong side of justice – he is 'unjust'; on another view, justice is more nuanced, taking into account factors that are external to the act – the murderer is not necessarily 'unjust'. Pollution, by contrast, is not bifurcated in the *Oresteia*: it cares only for the act of murder, not for its circumstances, and attaches automatically to the homicide. Therefore, it may serve as a stand-in to express 'injustice', but only when justice is understood in the first, narrow, sense. If the *Oresteia* is understood as a 'vast exploration of justice', therefore, pollution is the jetsam of the movement of the trilogy away from the narrow conception of justice to the legal trial by which the justice of Orestes' matricide is determined in wider terms and upon which pollution, because of its automatic and 'external' character, no longer impinges.

In a second part I shall look at the same ingredients from a slightly different angle, harking back to the previous chapter's key concept. In Sophocles' *Antigone* the patently obvious concern with law is embedded within a less obvious concern with stability; similarly, in the *Oresteia* the concern with justice is framed by a concern with stability. (It is for this reason that the present chapter is placed as it is, subsequent to the discussion of *Antigone*.) In the *Oresteia*, however, the concern with stability circles very specifically around the two systems of justice outlined above, which are each

---

[6] Winnington-Ingram (1983) 75; see id. (1985) 288; Goldhill (2000) 41 speaks of an 'obsessive thematic focus on justice'; similarly Zeitlin (1996a) 100; for explorations of justice in the *Oresteia*, see e.g. Goldhill (1986) 33–56 (with references to Kitto (1961)), Euben (1990) 67–95 (esp. 81–3). On Athena's justice (in *Eumenides*) and Athenian imperial ideology, see Futo Kennedy (2009) 19–45.
[7] On the trial and the legal background of the *Oresteia* (and esp. of *Eumenides*), see Leão (2010) and Sommerstein (2010a).

associated with different kinds of stability. Pollution comes into the picture by way of its close association with revenge justice: it may be understood to reflect the particular instability on the level of meaning which this type of justice brings with it.

As befits the discussion of a trilogy, these two parts are followed by a third, an appendix, which briefly considers the other side of the coin, purification. Famously, purification fails to bring ultimate release to the matricide Orestes. Against the background of the points raised in parts I and II, we shall better understand why this may be so.

Part I: evaluation, justice, pollution

The Atreid myth's obsessive focus on cycles of retributive violence in the *Oresteia* results in an equally obsessive concern with the kinds of meaning that may be attached to this violence: it provokes continual processes of categorisation and evaluation. Most prominently, these proceed along the coordinates provided by the concept of δίκη. To begin with, let us merely establish the wider framework, the ubiquity of the concept of justice in processes of evaluation.

Agamemnon sets the tone. In the early stages of the Greeks' revenge expedition against Troy, led by the μέγας ἀντίδικος (*Ag.* 41) Menelaus and Agamemnon, the latter sacrifices his daughter: the act provokes the first attribution of meaning, on the part of the chorus, who consider the deed 'impious, unholy and unhallowed' (δυσσεβῆ... ἄναγνον ἀνίερον, *Ag.* 219–20). Justice, too, is invoked, in personalised form: the chorus is sure that Justice will not remain disengaged, but 'lower its scales and teach people "learning through suffering"' (Δίκα δὲ τοῖς μὲν παθοῦ-|σιν μαθεῖν ἐπιρρέπει, *Ag.* 250–1). The implication is that Agamemnon is conceived of as putting himself on the wrong side of Justice/justice, turning out 'unjust'. Later in the play, processes in which acts of violence are evaluated are more expressly formed within the mould provided by the concept of justice. After Δίκη (as Clytemnestra claims) has led Agamemnon into the house there to meet his end (ἐς δῶμ' ἄελπτον ὡς ἂν ἡγῆται Δίκη, 911), the evaluation of Clytemnestra's murder of her husband becomes central. Upon the murder, the queen, blood-splattered, enters the stage and expounds her view of the murder. According to her, that murder was 'just, nay more than just' (τάδ' ἂν δικαίως ἦν, ὑπερδίκως μὲν οὖν, 1396)[8]

---

[8] That in 1396 it is the murder that is referred to as 'just, nay more than just' depends on a particular reading of the line: see Fraenkel (1950) ad loc., Collard (2002) 39, Raeburn and Thomas (2011) ad 1395–6.

and the hand which dealt the fatal blow a 'just workman' (δικαίας τέκτονος, 1406).[9]

In *Choephori* the characters likewise evaluate in terms of δίκη. In the scenes leading up to the matricide, it is assumed, or hoped, that it will be 'just', or perpetrated 'in justice'. For instance, when Electra, upon the instruction of the chorus, pours libation at her father's tomb, she bids her father's avenger appear and prays that 'those dealing out death be dealt out death with justice' (τοὺς κτανόντας ἀντικατθανεῖν δίκῃ, 144). In the *kommos*, Electra, again, prays that the gods bring things [or 'prayers', if we accept Newman's supplement] to pass 'in a just way' (ἰὼ θεοί, κραίνετ' ἐνδίκως <λιτὰς>, 462). As in the *Agamemnon*, evaluation in terms of δίκη becomes a particularly pressing issue after the deed. Again, the killer defends his action in terms of δίκη: after the matricide, Orestes appears upon the stage and appeals to the sun to be a 'witness in justice' or 'in the trial', testifying that he 'went after this business of matricide justly' (ὡς ἂν παρῇ μοι μάρτυς ἐν δίκῃ ποτὲ | ὡς τόνδ' ἐγὼ μετῆλθον ἐνδίκως φόνον | τὸν μητρός, 987–9).[10] Slightly later, a note of doubt may be felt to enter into this evaluation. As Orestes begins to feel the first symptoms of pursuit by the Erinyes, he emphasises that he killed his mother 'not without justice' (κτανεῖν τέ φημι μητέρ' οὐκ ἄνευ δίκης, 1027).

Eumenides, finally, requires little comment: the problem that is so urgent at the end of *Choephori* becomes the nub of the play. The question that was implicit there is now explicitly formulated and put, for evaluation, before the jury of the Areopagus, established for this purpose by Athena. Their task is precisely to evaluate whether or not Orestes acted 'justly' in killing his mother (εἰ δικαίως εἴτε μὴ κρῖνον δίκην, 468; εἰ δικαίως εἴτε μὴ τῇ σῇ φρενὶ | δοκεῖ, τόδ' αἷμα κρῖνον, 612–13).[11] And as in *Agamemnon*, the process

---

[9] Importantly, too, the chorus react to the queen's claims to justice with 'harsh judgment' (δικαστὴς τραχὺς εἶ, *Ag.* 1421; see also δικάζεις, *Ag.* 1412), considering her an 'object of hate for the citizens' (μῖσος... ἀστοῖς, 1411).

[10] On δίκη in this passage, see Goldhill (1986) 45.

[11] Sommerstein (2010a) 26 points out that Orestes' case would not have been judged before the Areopagus in fifth-century Athens. Homicide cases in which the defendant does not deny the act but claims to have acted 'with justice' were dealt with by the *ephetai* in the Delphinium. See ibid. *passim* for further remarks on Orestes' trial and Athenian homicide procedure. His conclusion is (ibid. 31–2) that 'the trial of Orestes bears a much closer resemblance to an ordinary Athenian trial before a heliastic jury than to a homicide trial on the Areopagus... Aeschylus is... encouraging his audience to see the members of this 'council of *dikastai*' as performing the same function which they themselves had performed, or... would one day be performing, as *dikastai* in the regular Athenian courts.' (The members of the historical Areopagus were not drawn by lot, but were ex-archons: see MacDowell (1963) 40.) On the different courts dealing with (different types of) homicide in classical Athens, see Leão (2010) 46; on the various circumstances in which the homicide was justifiable, see Harris (2010b) 132. On the Areopagus in general, see MacDowell (1963) 39–47; on the Palladium and the Delphinium, see ibid. 58–81.

itself of evaluation is referred to in the language of δίκη, in the technical sense of 'legal process'.[12] It has been observed that the *Oresteia* is built around a proleptical, 'teleological' structuring principle by which certain central themes are first developed obliquely to come into full and 'obvious' bloom later.[13] This is certainly so in the case of the trilogy's preoccupation with evaluation. Already very important in the earlier two plays, with the trial in the *Eumenides* it becomes clear that evaluation, in particular in the form of the determination of δίκη, is among the central concerns – is perhaps *the* central concern – of the play.

The evaluation of murder along the coordinates of justice is problematic, however, and is presented as such in the trilogy. It is a 'thrice-old story' that in the *Oresteia* the meaning of δίκη veers between a narrow retributive conception according to which it is justice that 'the doer suffers' ('the killer pays: as long as Zeus remains on his throne, it remains [valid] that the doer suffers', ἐκτίνει δ' ὁ καίνων· | μίμνει δὲ μίμνοντος ἐν θρόνῳ Διὸς | παθεῖν τὸν ἔρξαντα, *Ag.* 1562–4) and a wider conception which takes into account factors that are external to the act of homicide and which figures most prominently in the final play, where the determination of justice becomes a matter of legal trial.[14] As Simon Goldhill has shown, however, we are not dealing with a neat and clear-cut development by which the narrow conception prevails to the complete exclusion of wider conceptions until it is replaced by the wider, and indeed legal, conception when the Areopagus is founded.[15] Rather, because δίκη has complex semantic affiliations in the contemporary city – where it is 'one of the dominant terms in the public discourse'[16] and in no way delimited to the notion of 'eye for an eye', instead constituting a far-reaching moral, political and religious concept as well as 'social metaphor for the whole, and for the health of that whole'[17] – even

---

[12] See esp. *Eum.* 752, ἀνὴρ ὅδ' ἐκπέφευγεν αἵματος δίκην. On legal expressions in the *Oresteia*, see Robertson (1939); Harris (2010a) 16–17 also offers a list of words for law and justice in Aeschylus.

[13] Lebeck (1971) 2 (on prolepsis, the gradual development of recurrent imagery and the movement 'from riddle to solution'); see also Gagné (2013) 394–5. This teleological structuring principle mirrors, on the level of poetic design, the character's preoccupation with progression towards 'fulfilment' (τέλος) within the trilogy. On τέλος in the *Oresteia*, see Goldhill (1984c). On the *Oresteia*'s imagery, see (besides Lebeck's comprehensive study) e.g. Goheen (1955) 115–26, Peradotto (1964), Zeitlin (1965) and ead. (1966). See also Vidal-Naquet (1972) on hunting imagery; Rabinowitz (1981) on cosmogonic imagery; Seaford (1984) on the imagery invoked in the description of Agamemnon's 'last bath' in *Ag.*

[14] For the 'thrice-old story', see e.g. Kitto (1961) 67–95; MacLeod (1982) 134–5. Gagarin (1976) 66–79 and esp. 68 rightly points out that the movement towards legal justice does not necessarily imply a movement towards deliberative justice.

[15] Goldhill (1986) 37–47; see also Goldhill (1984b) esp. 233–61.   [16] Goldhill (1986) 34.

[17] Rosenmeyer (1982) 293. On the far-reaching connotations of *Dikē* in classical Athens, see also Goldhill (1986) 33–7. See Gagarin (1976) 66–79 on the complexity of *dikē* within as well as outside the *Oresteia*.

before the third play we find a number of passages in which different semantic affiliations of δίκη provocatively sound together.

Such complex soundings are present already in the first play. Throughout the idea of revenge justice looms large since the chorus' reference, in the parodos, to the μέγας ἀντίδικος (*Ag.* 41), Menelaus and Agamemnon, leaders of the (revenge) expedition against Troy; it looms even larger as the chorus later invoke such pieces of wisdom as 'blow for a blow' (τύμμα τύμματι τεῖσαι, *Ag.* 1430) inferring from this that in consequence of Clytemnestra's murder Justice is 'whetted for other deeds' (see *Ag.* 1535). One may build a case that Clytemnestra conceives of justice in just such retributive terms, in particular when she rejoices that Δίκη has led Agamemnon into the palace there to perish (ἐς δῶμ' ἄελπτον ὡς ἂν ἡγῆται Δίκη, 911). Similarly, when Clytemnestra later speaks of the murder of Agamemnon as 'just, nay more than just' (τάδ' ἂν δικαίως ἦν, ὑπερδίκως μὲν οὖν, 1396), one may argue that the queen herself has retributive justice in mind.[18] Even at this point, however, there lurks, at least in the background and as provocation, the question whether the murder is 'just' in a wider, say moral, sense as well – and perhaps even whether the queen does not lay claim to such justice, too.

This polyphony of different semantic mappings of δίκη becomes more striking in the second play. On the one hand, the concept of retributive justice is here advocated most explicitly, as well as most fiercely. In particular the chorus is a vociferous champion of such retributive justice (perhaps as Trojan 'agents provocateurs', driven by a strong – retributive – interest in the destruction of the House of Atreus?),[19] invoking the 'law that drops of blood fallen to the ground demand further blood' (*Choe.* 400–2) and proclaiming (*Choe.* 310–14):

> τοὐφειλόμενον
> πράσσουσα Δίκη μέγ' αὐτεῖ·
> ἀντὶ δὲ πληγῆς φονίας φονίαν
> πληγὴν τινέτω. δράσαντι παθεῖν,
> τριγέρων μῦθος τάδε φωνεῖ.

> As she exacts the debt, Justice shouts out loud: 'for a murderous stroke let a murderous stroke be paid in return'. 'The doer suffers', the thrice-old story says so.

---

[18] Of importance is not least her formulation at 1432–3 that she sacrificed Agamemnon to *Dikē*, *Atē* and the Erinys. See Thiel (1993) 363–412 for a detailed discussion of Clytemnestra's self-justification.

[19] I owe this suggestion as well as the expression 'agents provocateurs' to Renate Schlesier (conversation).

Evaluation, justice, pollution

But the concept of justice can be much wider, and when the protagonists, rather than the chorus, attribute meaning to murder in terms of the evaluative vocabulary of justice, the semantic affiliations of their evaluative categories is sometimes ambiguous. The frame is set early in the play, in the first dialogue between Electra and the chorus. Electra, unsure what she should pray for when pouring the libation at her father's tomb, wonders in particular whether she should ask for a 'judge' or a 'justice-bringer' to come (δικαστὴν ἢ δικηφόρον, *Choe.* 120).[20] With this, two very different semantic affiliations of δίκη, between wider 'judgment' and simple retribution, are thrown into high relief, henceforth to reverberate through the play. To pick out but one example, in the case of Electra's ensuing prayer that 'those dealing out death be dealt out death with justice' (τοὺς κτανόντας ἀντικατθανεῖν δίκῃ, 144), 'the precise sense of *dikē*... remains uncertain' and '[i]t is in the uncertainty of choice between... different semantic areas, or rather in the combination of suggestive connotations, that the uncertain status of the act of matricide is formed.'[21] As we shall see in greater detail below, much the same is true of Orestes' assertion to have carried out the matricide 'justly' (ἐνδίκως, *Choe.* 988) or 'not without justice' (οὐκ ἄνευ δίκης, *Choe.* 1027).

Pollution is intimately bound up with this concern with evaluation and in particular the trilogy's preoccupation with justice, in which it crystallises. The general point to be made is that pollution, along with the concept of justice, is arguably the central category by which meaning is attached to the act of murder, as each such act unfailingly provokes diagnoses of pollution and predications of the murderer as polluted (or indeed as 'pollution'). Thus, in *Agamemnon*, the king anticipates pollution as the result of the sacrifice of his daughter (μιαίνων παρθενοσφάγοισιν | ῥείθροις πατρῴους χέρας, *Ag.* 209–10). The queen later confirms the king's contraction of pollution (*Ag.* 1419–20); and as the result of her own murderous act she is herself considered a 'pollution of the land' (χώρας μίασμα καὶ θεῶν ἐγχωρίων, *Ag.* 1645) by the outraged chorus. In *Choephori*, bloodshed is one with pollution (*Choe.* 646–52); Clytemnestra and Aegisthus, as the twin murderers of Agamemnon, are therefore disqualified, in the eyes of the chorus, as 'two polluters' (δυοῖν μιαστόροιν, *Choe.* 944); upon the matricide, however, it is Orestes who is seen to have contracted pollution, 'having the unenviable pollutions of this victory [the matricide]' (ἄζηλα

---

[20] On the distinction in this passage between retribution and 'the glimmer of something less crude' (mediation through a judge deciding upon justice), see Kitto (1961) 79; see also Goldhilll (1984b) 115.
[21] Goldhill (1986) 43; see ibid. 23.

νίκης τῆσδ' ἔχων μιάσματα, *Choe.* 1017), much like the 'father-slaying pollution and abomination to the gods' that is Clytemnestra (πατροκτόνον μίασμα καὶ θεῶν στύγος, *Choe.* 1028). In *Eumenides*, too, pollution is repeatedly invoked as the one central (ritual) meaning of the act of murder: the Erinyes severally fall back upon the concept (e.g. at *Eum.* 312–20 and 607); and Orestes, too, in the trial, points to Clytemnestra's twin pollution which the murder of Agamemnon 'means' (δυοῖν γὰρ εἶχε προσβολὰς μιασμάτοιν, *Eum.* 600).[22]

The more specific point is that pollution is indeed in close relation, and to some extent overlaps, with non-ritual evaluation and in particular the concept of justice. To this point there is an important twist, however, which is the result of the particular version of pollution which we encounter in the *Oresteia*: as is not necessarily the case in the contemporary Athenian *polis*, where under certain circumstances the homicide remained pure,[23] in the *Oresteia* murder unfailingly results in pollution, in conformity, as it were, with Eric R. Dodds' famous formulation, in *The Greeks and the irrational*, that 'pollution is the automatic consequence of an action, belongs to the world of external events, and operates with the same ruthless indifference to motive as a typhoid germ.'[24] As we have seen, Agamemnon, Clytemnestra and Orestes are each severally referred to as polluted in the aftermath of their respective acts of murder.[25] This, however, means that being on the wrong side of the kind of Δίκη which requires retribution (and is certainly indifferent to motive) and pollution are two sides of the same coin: murder implies both. Consequently, pollution may easily serve as a stand-in to express the fact of a contravention of the tenets of (revenge) Justice, but sits ill with a more widely conceived justice.

The point is underscored as the trilogy progresses and in particular in the second play, where wider conceptions of justice move into the foreground with increasing emphasis (preparing for the δίκη of legal trial in the third play). In *Agamemnon*, pollution and the charged vocabulary of justice are not explicitly correlated. In *Choephori*, by contrast, the first reference to pollution is already pointed and in immediate dialogue with (revenge) Justice: shortly before Orestes turns to murder, the chorus of

---

[22] The pollution is twofold because by killing Agamemnon Clytemnestra had committed a 'double murder', killing her husband as well as Orestes' father: see Sommerstein (1989) ad 602.

[23] See e.g. Demosthenes 20.158, 23.53–5; see Harris (2010b) 133–4 on the different ritual consequences of different types of homicide (from intentional homicide to unwilling homicide to justifiable homicide).

[24] Dodds (1951) 36.

[25] Agamemnon: *Ag.* 209–10, *Ag.* 1420. Clytemnestra: e.g. *Ag.* 1645, *Choe.* 1028. Orestes: e.g. *Choe.* 1017, *Eum.* 281.

libation bearers sing a strophe about Justice whose 'anvil is firmly planted'. The development of the strophe implies that this Justice requires that 'the pollution of blood shed long ago' be avenged through further bloodshed (*Choe.* 646–52):

> Δίκας δ' ἐρείδεται πυθμήν,
> προχαλκεύει δ' Αἶσα φασγανουργός·
> τέκνον δ' ἐπεισφέρει δόμοις
> αἱμάτων παλαιτέρων
> τίνειν μύσος χρόνῳ κλυτὰ
> βυσσόφρων Ἐρινύς.

> The anvil of Justice is firmly planted, and the swordsmith Destiny is preparing the weapon; and a child is being imported into the house, to pay at last for the pollution of older deeds of blood, by the far-famed, deep-thinking Erinys.[26]

Further references underscore the connection between pollution and revenge justice. Let us take these in order of importance. In *Choephori*, when Orestes is inside the palace to carry out the matricide, the chorus once more hail (revenge) Justice who in the past has come to the House of Priam (*Choe.* 935–41), 'heavy and just in punishment' (βαρύδικος ποινά, *Choe.* 936; Collard's translation), and presently comes to the House of Atreus (946–52); framed by these acclamations of Justice, they raise a cry of joy at the imminent deliverance of the house from the 'two polluters' Clytemnestra and Aegisthus (*Choe.* 942–5; δυοῖν μιαστόροιν, 944).

In *Eumenides*, the connection is established in particular through the Erinyes. Outside the play, the Erinyes were complex and multifaceted creatures whose functions are not easily defined.[27] They were associated with curses and vengeance; with (the punishment of) transgression and familial disruption; with implacable pursuit, at times avenging wrongs of an earlier generation in a later one; they were upholders of *Dikē* in the broad sense, signifying order in 'the natural as well as social universe.'[28] Heraclitus fr. 44 (Kahn) may serve as an apt, if idiosyncratic, example. The philosopher here proposes that 'the sun will not transgress his measures; if he does, the Erinyes, ministers of Justice (Δίκης ἐπίκουροι), will find him out' (translation adapted from Kahn). In *Eumenides*, their function is much more

---

[26] Trans. adapted from A. Sommerstein, Loeb Classical Libary (Cambridge, MA, 2009). On the idea of ancestral fault in the passage, see Gagné (2013) 410–11; ibid. 394–416 on ancestral fault in the trilogy (esp. *Ag.*).
[27] The brief remarks here are indebted esp. to Sommerstein (1989) 7–10. For a recent account of the Erinyes, see Eck (2012) 30–48, 49–55.
[28] Sommerstein (1989) 9.

precise,[29] and in a way that impinges on our present concerns: they are both avengers of pollution and the agents of a retributive type of justice (this latter function becoming most explicit at *Eum.* 490–565). *Eumenides* 312–20, for instance, indicates that to the Erinyes, being of 'straight justice' means that they spare the pure but relentlessly hunt those 'hiding murderous hands'. Pollution is not spelt out but is undoubtedly implied in view of the reference to 'pure hands' in juxtaposition to these 'murderous hands' and the Erinyes' reference to Orestes as polluted elsewhere in the play (at *Eum.* 169–70, but see also *Eum.* 607). The Erinyes assert (312–20):

> εὐθυδίκαιοι δ' οἰόμεθ' εἶναι·
> τὸν μὲν καθαρὰς χεῖρας προνέμοντ'
> οὔτις ἐφέρπει μῆνις ἀφ' ἡμῶν,
> ἀσινὴς δ' αἰῶνα διοιχνεῖ·
> ὅστις δ' ἀλιτὼν ὥσπερ ὅδ' ἀνὴρ
> χεῖρας φονίας ἐπικρύπτει,
> μάρτυρες ὀρθαὶ τοῖσι θανοῦσιν
> παραγιγνόμεναι πράκτορες αἵματος
> αὐτῷ τελέως ἐφάνημεν.

> We claim to be straight in our justice: to whosoever holds out pure hands none of that inexorable wrath of ours will come; he will go through life unharmed. But who commits an offence, as this man here, and hides his murderous hands, to him we appear as avengers of blood to the end, seconding as upright witnesses for the dead.

A central passage at the end of *Choephori*, finally, intimates both sides of the coin, that such pollution as we find in the *Oresteia* is largely congruent with revenge justice, but dissociated from a wider conception of justice. After the matricide, Orestes exits the palace and becomes increasingly doubtful about the matricide. He calls upon the sun 'to be his witness ἐν δίκῃ that [he] went after the business of matricide justly' (μάρτυς ἐν δίκῃ ποτὲ | ὡς τόνδ' ἐγὼ μετῆλθον ἐνδίκως φόνον | τὸν μητρός, *Choe.* 987–9); he parades the blood-stained robe in which Agamemnon's body was wrapped in the first play; and finally he declares (*Choe.* 1027–8):[30]

> κτανεῖν τέ φημι μητέρ' οὐκ ἄνευ δίκης,
> πατροκτόνον μίασμα καὶ θεῶν στύγος.

---

[29] On the Erinyes in the *Oresteia* (and esp. *Eumenides*), see also Brown (1983), Winnington-Ingram (1983) 154–74, Lardinois (1992) 315–22, Föllinger (2003) 105–10 and Eck (2012) 36–9. See also Bacon (2001). Gagné (2013) 413 notes that *Eumenides*' Erinyes do *not* present themselves as avengers of ancestral crime.

[30] The 'father-slaying pollution' is Clytemnestra. We witness here once more the elision of pollution and person to which I have drawn attention in the discussion of Sophocles' *OT*.

I say that it is not without justice that I have killed my mother, the father-slaying pollution and object of hate for the gods.

As Simon Goldhill has argued, the challenge of the passage lies in the ambiguity of the term δίκη at this point.[31] In view of the play's continued focus on revenge justice, adumbrated by Orestes himself in the *kommos*, when he declares that 'Justice will meet with Justice' ("Ἄρης Ἄρει ξυμβαλεῖ, Δίκα Δίκα, *Choe.* 461), the reference to justice surely calls to mind such revenge justice. Yet, we are dealing here with one of those instances where 'the precise sense of *dikē* . . . remains uncertain.'[32] In this particular instance, such overdeterminacy of the evaluative vocabulary of δίκη is particularly urgent because at 987–9 that vocabulary is subjected to a striking widening. As again Goldhill has shown, 987–9 provocatively juxtaposes different semantic areas of δίκη,[33] raising in particular the question whether the matricide would be considered 'just' also in legal terms, at trial, ἐν δίκῃ, and not only within the logic of revenge justice. Not least in view of this, δίκη at 1027 cannot easily be reduced to the idea of revenge justice.[34] In the face of this complexity, pollution is firmly located in the realm of revenge justice: Orestes enlists pollution in his project of justification, thereby approximating the concept of pollution to the idea of 'guilt'. But the passage challenges us to recognise that pollution can stand in for such 'guilt' only when the frame of reference is revenge justice. If justice is conceived in wider terms, pollution and (such) justice become dissociated and pollution can no longer serve to designate the 'guilt' of the homicide.

That is indeed the one central point the *Oresteia* makes *about* pollution, the one adumbrated in the introductory section to this discussion: that in the movement of the trilogy towards a wider concept of justice pollution, blind as it is to motivation and circumstances or other external factors, is jettisoned, or else exposed as squarely at home in the system of revenge justice, but an alien element in a system where the act itself is not wholly determinative of its 'justice'.

This 'externality' of the category of pollution as the automatic result of murder, not indicating anything about the polluted murderer's motivation and legal (or even moral) guilt, may be seen to be implied by the

---

[31] Goldhill (1986) 46; see 37–47 generally on the complexity of the vocabulary of justice in the *Oresteia*.
[32] Goldhill (1986) 43; id. (1984b) 102.   [33] Goldhill (1986) 45; id. (1984b) 101.
[34] For Goldhill (1986) 46 *dikē* at 1027 'recalls all the senses of "retribution", "penalty" and "justice" that have been at play, as well as the legal implications of the forthcoming trial'.

visualisation of pollution through its marker 'blood' in the trilogy.[35] Such blood indicates first and foremost the act of murder itself and may serve as metonymical stand-in for murder (as for instance at *Choe.* 400–2).[36] By the same token, however, it also indicates pollution as the automatic consequence of murder, as is underlined, for instance, when Agamemnon anticipates pollution resulting from the streams of maiden blood (*Ag.* 209–10); or when the chorus of *Choephori* speak of the 'pollution of blood shed long ago' (αἱμάτων παλαιτέρων... μύσος, *Choe.* 649–50).

That such blood expresses something about the externality of the category of pollution as the automatic consequence of murder may be seen to be suggested by the very conspicuity of blood, which is itself a matter of its (literal) externality. The question is: may we take this conspicuity as a consequence of its literal externality to be an expression also of the externality of pollution as evaluative category? I argued above that in Sophocles' *Oedipus tyrannus* the 'conspicuous' invisibility of pollution suggests that it is not extrinsic but intrinsic, not external and detachable but inextricably bound up with the protagonist's very being, his very essence in a Delphic 'Know thyself!' fashion. May the striking *visibility* of pollution in the *Oresteia* then be understood as the visual expression of its *exteriority* as nothing more than the automatic consequence of murder, allowing but the most superficial grasp of such murder and failing to indicate anything about its meaning in a wider (say, legal or even moral) sense? A number of striking statements about conspicuity in particular in the first play should at least give us reason to pause and reflect along these lines.

In agreement with the logic of revenge justice, according to which the murderer is necessarily 'unjust' (or even 'guilty'), for the trilogy's choruses (all of which champion revenge justice) blood would seem to indicate such 'injustice' along with pollution. It is arguably against this background that we are invited to understand two interconnected statements of the chorus of *Agamemnon*: early in the play, they proclaim their conviction that 'mischief does not remain hidden, but *shines forth*, a baneful light' (οὐκ ἐκρύφθη, | πρέπει δέ, φῶς αἰνολαμπές, σίνος, *Ag.* 388–9); as a blood-covered Clytemnestra returns onstage after the murder of Agamemnon, they take up the vocabulary of conspicuity, pointing to the drops of blood which

---

[35] Blood-related imagery is ever-present in the trilogy. Lebeck (1971) fittingly entitles one of her chapters on the *Oresteia*'s imagery 'The endless flow of blood' (80–91). For her (ibid.), the purple-red cloth on the ground (which Agamemnon is made to tread on in *Ag.*) forms part of this network of images (see also Goheen (1955) 115–26). For a reinterpretation of the cloth as bridal cloth, see McNeil (2005).

[36] *Choe.* 400–02: ἀλλὰ νόμος μὲν φονίας σταγόνας | χυμένας ἐς πέδον ἄλλο προσαιτεῖν | αἷμα; see also e.g. *Choe.* 649–50: αἱμάτων παλαιτέρων | τίνειν μύσος.

'shine forth' in the queen's eyes (λίβος ἐπ' ὀμμάτων αἵματος ἐμπρέπει, *Ag.* 1428). The impression created here is that for the chorus 'mischief' (σίνος) now 'shines forth', in the form of blood, i.e. blood indicates 'injustice' as a matter of indicating the perpetration of homicide.[37]

There is a third statement, however, which is also concerned with conspicuity but may be taken as a provocation. Just before Agamemnon's entry at midpoint, the chorus, preoccupied once more with Justice, express their view that Justice is able to see through the exterior of 'gold-sprinkled mansions' to recognise 'filthy hands' within (τὰ χρυσόπαστα δ' ἔδεθλα σὺν | πίνῳ χερῶν παλιντρόποις | ὄμμασι λιποῦσ' ὅσια †προσέβα, *Ag.* 776–8). Applying the gist of the passage to the case of Clytemnestra at 1428, we may interpret as follows: the queen has long harboured 'mischief' within, hidden underneath an innocent, and indeed splendid exterior, not only literally clean in aspect, but also feigning adoration and loyalty to the king. Agamemnon's blood on her hands finally makes visible the filth that has (invisibly) clung to her hands all along: 'mischief' formerly hidden now shines forth.[38] But the passage's focus on the rift between reality and appearance, inside and outside, may be taken to lead us in a very different direction. In particular as the play progresses and the rift between 'mischief' that is simply the violent act itself and 'mischief' that would need to be defined in wider terms, are we not entitled to draw our own conclusions? The suggested split between (inner) reality and (outward) appearance implied in the chorus' reference to 'gold-sprinkled mansions' hiding 'filthy hands' within is intriguing: for the blood on the murderer's hands is eventually only outward, too, 'appearance' but not indicative of a 'reality' beyond the act itself.

Part II: stability and justice

Let us now adopt a slightly different perspective on these concerns, one which widens our understanding of the particular crisis of justice which underlies the *Oresteia*, but which in the process will also shed further light on the integration of the ritual nexus of pollution and purification into the trilogy. In particular, the frame will be different: in the above, attention

---

[37] Importantly, the chorus subsequently draws attention to the logic of revenge justice at *Ag.* 1430, pointing out that 'a blow is to pay for a blow' (τύμμα τύμματι τεῖσαι, *Ag.* 1430; Collard's translation Collard (2002)).

[38] Clytemnestra is a bit like the lion cub of *Ag.* 717–36, which eventually shows its real character, wreaking havoc in the house. On the lion-cub simile, see Knox (1952b). On related issues of ἦθος in the *Oresteia*, see e.g. Peradotto (1969) 255–63.

was drawn to the basic concern of the *Oresteia* with evaluation and the fact that this concern crystallised in an insistent preoccupation with the concept of justice and its different semantic mappings. We may integrate this concern with a further preoccupation of the trilogy. From early on, the *Oresteia* betrays an interest in stability. This interest, I suggest, is intimately connected to the trilogy's concern with two different types of justice, as these may be understood to stand for two different types of stability, both of which are problematic. In this sense, the *Oresteia*, like *Antigone*, may be seen to revolve around a crisis of stability (albeit one that is very different from *Antigone*'s). The ritual nexus of pollution and purification comes into the picture by way of its close association with revenge justice: it expresses in ritual terms the particular instability associated with this type of justice.

Stability is a central concern in the *Oresteia*. It manifests itself in two forms: first, in the repeated invocation of divinely sanctioned principles which allow the imposition of a sense of order on the flow of events over time; second, in the frequent use of the language and imagery of stability (in reference precisely to these principles or the authority on which the validity of these principles depends). Stability therefore matters both as the product of principles which afford a sense of (stable) order; and as the frame for these principles which themselves need to be stable and fixed.

The concern with stability is most expressly formulated by the trilogy's choruses. Faced with the violent acts of the protagonists on stage, they feel encouraged to impose fixed patterns and, in the words of Simon Goldhill, exert 'explanatory control over the passage of events'.[39] We are dealing here in the main with the first of the above-outlined manifestations of the concern with stability, the assumption of divinely sanctioned principles, although the language of fixity (as well as permanence over time) already creeps in to suggest that these principles provide stability only because they are themselves firmly established. When recalling the happenings on Aulis, for instance, the chorus of *Agamemnon* turn to reflections on the 'fixed' tenet, guaranteed by the authority of Zeus, that 'learning comes through suffering' (τὸν πάθει μάθος | θέντα κυρίως ἔχειν, *Ag.* 177–8);[40] more importantly, upon Clytemnestra's murder of Agamemnon they invoke the principle by which 'as long as Zeus remains on the throne it remains [valid] that the doer suffers; for this is laid down' (μίμνει δὲ μίμνοντος ἐν θρόνῳ Διὸς | παθεῖν τὸν ἔρξαντα· θέσμιον γάρ, *Ag.* 1563–4).

---

[39] Goldhill (1984c) 171.
[40] On this maxim and in particular on *pathos* as 'condition de réflexion et de savoir', see Schlesier (2009) 89.

Stability and justice

In *Choephori* we encounter, again, a concern with sanctioned principles, but also concrete spatial imagery. The chorus of *Choephori* return to the idea that 'the doer suffers', albeit now in connection with Justice (for, while Zeus is seen as their ultimate authority,[41] more immediately these principles are taken to be under the aegis of Justice). According to them, 'Justice cries out loud: expiation for bloodshed through bloodshed. The doer suffers; the thrice-old story says so' (Δίκη μέγ' αὐτεῖ· ἀντὶ δὲ πληγῆς φονίας φονίαν | πληγὴν τινέτω. δράσαντα παθεῖν, τριγέρων μῦθος τάδε φωνεῖ, *Choe.* 311–14); similarly, 'there is a law (νόμος) that murderous drops spilt on the ground call for further blood' (*Choe.* 400–2). Significantly, the idea of fixity implicit in the recourse, in *Agamemnon*, to the vocabulary of τίθημι/θεσμός is now translated, at an important juncture, into a concrete image of spatial fixation: as Orestes enters the Argive palace, there eventually to kill Aegisthus, the chorus suggest that Justice, as the upholder of the tenet that 'the doer suffers' by which to impose order and to connect past (murderous act) to future (murderous act), is to be conceived of as an 'anvil fixed firmly' (Δίκας δ' ἐρείδεται πυθμήν, *Choe.* 646), guaranteeing in this way the validity ('fixity') of the principle that bloodshed is paid back with bloodshed. We are invited to think of the immovable marble *stelai* with their fixed legal prescriptions often planted firmly in the Greek *poleis'* public spaces.

The Erinyes in *Eumenides* continue this train of thought, but make more explicit its implications for the civic community. In their view, holding fast to the tenets of Justice – which for them, by and large, means retributive justice, too – is paramount for the stability of the community. In their famous choral song before the trial, in any case, they stress that τὸ δεινόν, fear in the face of certainty of severe punishment, is profitable for the *polis* and therefore needs to 'remain seated' (ἔσθ' ὅπου τὸ δεινὸν εὖ | καὶ φρενῶν ἐπίσκοπον | δεῖ μένειν καθήμενον, *Eum.* 517–19);[42] by contrast, it is a vision of horror to see 'the house of Justice fall' (πίτνει δόμος Δίκας, *Eum.* 516), which they presumably take to imply a falling to pieces of every kind of order, too. But Justice provides stability not only as a (firmly established) house for the Erinyes; it also offers the fixed reference point of an altar planted in the earth (βωμὸν ... Δίκας, *Eum.* 539)[43] or of a reef against which the wrongdoer will inevitably be smashed (ἕρματι προσβαλὼν Δίκας | ὤλετ', *Eum.* 564–5).

---

[41] On the relation of Zeus to the principles of retribution, see e.g. Gagarin (1976) 141–2. On Zeus in Aeschylus, see (slightly dated but still interesting) Lloyd-Jones (1956) (and see also id. (1983)).
[42] On these famous lines (and the entire sequence *Eum.* 517–65), see e.g. Dover (1957) 231–2.
[43] The 'altar of Justice' appears already in the first play, at *Ag.* 381–4.

This preoccupation with stability is not confined to the choruses, however. *Eumenides'* Athena is the most important point in case. Confronted with the affair of Orestes, the goddess founds the law court of the Areopagus. The words by which the foundation act is performed reflect, once more, the idea of firm fixation in space resonating in the language of τίθημι/θεσμός: she selects judges revering the θεσμός she will presently 'lay down' for all time (θεσμόν, τὸν εἰς ἅπαντ' ἐγὼ θήσω χρόνον, 484).[44]

But the name itself of the locale of the law court expresses this desire for stability. It consists of two elements, Ares and πάγος, the latter deriving from the verb πήγνυμι and designating that which has become fixed and permanently planted and more specifically a 'rock', 'hill' or 'crack'. The Areopagus is therefore the 'rock of Ares'. Within this trilogy, the word πάγος as part of the etymology seems readily paramount. Arguably, the play itself invites us not to lose sight of the word in view of its prominent position at the beginning of line 685, at the very beginning also of Athena's etymological excursus on the 'hill of Ares' at *Eum.* 685–90.[45] If we take the play's invitation as well as the connection with the trilogy's earlier concern with fixed points of reference (such as firmly planted anvils, altars and reefs) seriously, Athena's references appear in a new light. The play seems to suggest that the Areopagus is not simply the hill of Ares but, as a πάγος, something become solid, a place that affords firm anchorage, a place of stability.[46] As the Areopagus is associated with the safeguarding of justice and the implementation of law, we are reminded once more of Athens' law codes on rock-solid marble *stelai* and the city's established laws, οἱ προκείμενοι νόμοι – the society's need for '*pillars* of justice'.

---

[44] The word θεσμός recurs in the play, at times in reference to the institution of the Areopagus itself: see e.g. *Eum.* 614–15. On the presentation of the Areopagus in *Eumenides* and the old question of Aeschylean 'politics', see Braun (1998). (Older discussions of 'Aeschylean politics' include Smertenko (1932), Forbes (1948), Dover (1957), Dodds (1960), Meier (1980) 144–222; see also Schaps (1993), Samons II (1998/9) and Mitchell-Boyask (2009) 102–7.)

[45] Scholars have mostly concentrated on general reflections on Aeschylus' innovation of the myth which underlies the etymology. The traditional explanation of the name harks back to the trial of Ares on that hill, held before a jury of gods and in the matter of Ares' killing of Halirrothius, son of Poseidon, who had raped or attempted to rape Ares' daughter. Not least because of the premise of the play, that it is for Orestes' trial that the Areopagus is established, Aeschylus replaces this myth by another: the Amazons, in the course of their invasion of Attica to rescue an Amazonian princess Theseus had captured, were encamped on that hill and made sacrifice to Ares there. See Zeitlin (1996a) 93–4; also Sommerstein (1989) 2–3 ad ad 685–90; and Braun (1998) 89–91. On the possibility of corruption at *Eum.* 685 (Ἄρειον may be a later gloss on πάγον; there may have been a verb in place of Ἄρειον originally), see e.g. Braun (1998) 90.

[46] Lebeck (1971) 165 already points in this direction: she suggests that the play here (as well as earlier, with its references for instance to the 'throne of the Erinyes' (*Eum.* 512) or the 'reef of justice'; *Eum.* 564) expresses the need for firm foundation.

Stability and justice

More immediately, though, the πάγος of Ares, by way of pointed verbal reminiscence, harks back to the solid principles of revenge justice, in this way intimating a continuity between the stabilities that are (hoped to be) provided by the fixity of the principle that murder will be repaid through murder, on the one hand, and by the institution of the law court, on the other. For, earlier in the trilogy we find the verb πήγνυμι (πάγ-) embedded in a passage concerned with revenge justice and expressing the particular stability this justice affords. The passage in question occurs in the parodos of *Choephori*. The chorus, at this point, is preoccupied with gloomy thoughts about the queen's murder of Agamemnon and the general inevitability of punishment. This inevitability, dictated by revenge justice, is given expression by the image of blood of the victim (Agamemnon, in this case) which is fixed ('clotted') on the ground and cannot be removed, in this way adamantly calling for further blood: 'Because of blood drunk up by the nurturing earth the avenging gore lies solid [clotted] and does not flow away' (*Choe*. 66–7; the translation is Garvie's):

> δι' αἵματ' ἐκποθένθ' ὑπὸ χθονὸς τροφοῦ
> τίτας φόνος πέπηγεν οὐ διαρρύδαν.[47]

This observation brings us to the hub of the matter: one may conceive of the development of the trilogy in terms of a search for the right kind of stability, the right kind of πάγος between 'clotted blood' and the 'solid rock of Ares'.[48] In particular the trilogy's choruses champion 'clotted blood' and with this the idea of retributive justice – Justice which demands that bloodshed be expiated through bloodshed. The Areopagus, by contrast, represents legal justice, the δίκη of the legal trial. That the *Oresteia* veers between different kinds of justice was outlined above; my point here is that we are dealing also with a dynamic between different kinds of stability.

Revenge justice offers one kind of stability, but one which implies instability on another level. It allows control over the flow of events over time, from (murderous) act to (murderous) act: the image of clotted blood expresses this type of stability. Especially from the vantage point of the final play, however, the trilogy suggests that this type of stability entails an impasse. As Athena founds the Areopagus, she explains that its function

---

[47] See Goldhill (1984b) 108–09 on 'avenging gore': '"avenger", when we might have expected "needing to be avenged"... This confusion of subject and object, acted on and acting, suggests the complexity of cause and effect.' We encounter clotted blood again later, in the chorus's account of Clytemnestra's dream, in which a serpent, to which she offered her breast, drew in clotted blood with the milk (ὥστ' ἐν γάλακτι θρόμβον αἵματος σπάσαι, *Choe*. 533).

[48] Alternatively, one may conceive of the trilogy as a search for the right kind of θεσμός between the tenets of retribution which are θέσμιον (*Ag*. 1564) and the θεσμός of the Areopagus (*Eum*. 615).

is to 'dissect justice' (διαιρεῖν ... δίκας, 472) and to 'dissect this matter [the matricide] truly' (διαιρεῖν τοῦτο πρᾶγμ' ἐτητύμως, 488); the goal is to 'recognise justice well' (ὅπως ἂν εὖ καταγνωσθῇ δίκη, 573; διαγνῶναι δίκην, 709). These formulations underscore that the system of justice provided by 'blood for blood' does not allow attributing stable (and 'true', ἐτήτυμος) meaning to the act of revenge murder. One and the same act is in line with Δίκη and τὸ δίκαιον (see e.g. *Choe.* 308) and constitutes an act of 'kicking against the altar of Justice' (see e.g. *Eum.* 538–41). Hence such striking formulations – such as we find in particular in the *kommos* in *Choephori* – as Orestes', declaring that 'Ares meets with Ares, Justice with Justice' (Ἄρης Ἄρει ξυμβαλεῖ, Δίκᾳ Δίκα, *Choe.* 461). Equally intriguing is Electra's earlier demand for 'justice out of injustice' (δίκαν δ' ἐξ ἀδίκων ἀπαιτῶ, *Choe.* 398). Electra's intended meaning may well be that justice arise '*in place of* (earlier) injustice', as Garvie suggests;[49] but the preposition ἐξ is ambiguous and may be taken to indicate the necessarily contradictory nature of the impending matricide, by which, according to the logic of revenge justice, justice comes about '*as the result of* unjust acts'.

The institution of the *dikē* of legal process before the Areopagus may be seen as an attempt to restore stability on the level of meaning. Before the '(solid) rock of Ares', it is no longer the act alone which counts for the 'recognition of justice', but external factors, too. It is perhaps the tragedy of the *Oresteia* that in *Eumenides*, with its human jurors divided over the question of Orestes' guilt and its goddess (Athena) deciding the case in favour of Orestes on such dubious grounds as her preference for the male over the female principle, stability in the form of the establishment of unambiguous, self-evident meaning is not achieved.[50] In fact, one could easily make the argument that by making the decision dependent upon Athena's introduction of a criterion which obviously reflects the personal preferences of the goddess it is eventually the arbitrariness of the final decision which is foregrounded.[51] A decisive problem is nonetheless overcome: the inherent instability in the form of endlessly self-contradictory meaning that the system of revenge justice implies for the judgment of revenge

---

[49] Garvie (1986) ad 398–9: "'out of (instead of) injustice'".
[50] For Athena's preference of the male principle, see *Eum.* 736–8 (esp. 737, τὸ δ' ἄρσεν αἰνῶ πάντα). On Athena's vote and her 'explicit absence of sympathy for the opposite cause', see Winnington-Ingram (1983) 119–31 (quote ibid. 131). The vote has invited discussion as to whether Athena breaks or produces a tie vote: see esp. Gagarin (1975), Hester (1981) and Seaford (1995); see also Meier (1980) 191–2 on the problematic aspects of the (tie) vote more generally. For a good overview over the various scholarly opinions of the last decades on the trilogy's ending (and the question whether or not it moves towards resolution), see Porter (2005) 301–5.
[51] This arbitrariness is underlined by Cohen (1986) esp. 139.

Stability and justice

murder. In this sense, the πάγος of Ares is perhaps preferable to the πάγος of clotted blood.[52]

The ritual nexus of pollution and purification comes into the picture, not by way of any inherent associations with (in-)stability, but because of its close connection with the conception of justice as revenge justice, propagated most outspokenly by the chorus. In the case of pollution, we have outlined this connection in the first section and need not repeat the argument here: suffice it to point out (once more) that in view of pollution's indifference to motive and circumstances, this connection readily suggests itself and is therefore unsurprising. What is more surprising is that, as the reverse of this connection, purification too is drawn into the logic of revenge justice.

The basis for this rapprochement is the conviction, propagated by the choruses of *Choephori* and *Eumenides* and in agreement with the logic of revenge justice, that pollution cannot be removed by conventional means of purification. This conviction is made explicit at *Choe.* 71–4. Upon pointing out that 'the avenging gore lies clotted and does not flow away', the chorus hold that it is impossible for the murderer to wash away his pollution:

> θιγόντι δ' οὔτι νυμφικῶν ἑδωλίων
> ἄκος, πόροι τε πάντες ἐκ μιᾶς ὁδοῦ
> διαίνοντες τὸν χερομυσῆ φόνον καθαί-
> ροντες ἴθυσαν μάταν.

For the one who touches the bridal chamber there is no cure; and all streams flowing together in one rush in vain to cleanse the bloodshed which pollutes the hand.

This does not mean that no purification is available, however. Rather remarkably, murder is seen as purification. At the climax of the play, at the point when Orestes is inside the palace to kill Clytemnestra, the chorus are explicit about this. In their view, the present act of murder is the purification by which 'all pollution is driven out' (*Choe.* 965–8):

> τάχα δὲ παντελὴς χρόνος ἀμείψεται
> πρόθυρα δωμάτων, ὅταν ἀφ' ἑστίας
> μύσος ἅπαν ἐλαθῇ
> καθαρμοῖσιν ἀτᾶν ἐλατηρίοις.

---

[52] One may still be hesitant to agree that 'by any account, the ending of the *Eumenides* represents a ringing endorsement of Athens and its political system' (the 'standard' reading in the words of Griffith (1995) 64).

But soon will (that) time, all-completed, pass out of the front door of the house, when all the pollution is driven from the hearth through purifications that expel ruin (Garvie's translation for 965–6).[53]

Similarly, the Erinyes demand Orestes as 'a proper sacrifice to cleanse a mother's murder' (ματρῷον ἅ-|γνισμα κύριον φόνου, *Eum*. 326–7; Sommerstein's translation), indicating, through the use of the adjective κύριος, 'proper', 'valid', that only death purifies the murderer. It should be pointed out that this assimilation of murder to purification is perhaps adumbrated already in the first play. According to Froma Zeitlin, at least, Clytemnestra's reference to her murder of Agamemnon as σφαγή to Δίκη, Ἄτη and the Erinys (*Ag*. 1431–3) may imply a purificatory sacrifice.[54]

Through this rapprochement the ritual nexus of pollution and purification is assimilated to revenge justice to such an extent that it can serve as its stand-in and, as such, express the particular stability afforded by revenge justice as well as the particular instability it necessarily comes with. The sequence of events is set in stone: pollution is incurred (through murder); just as 'clotted blood' does not flow away, it cannot be washed away; as the only valid means of purification, revenge murder necessarily ensues. At the same time, as soon as the ritual nexus of pollution and purification (and in particular purification) is manipulated in such a way as to become congruent with the *lex talionis*, as is the case at important points in the *Oresteia*, it also reflects this system's circularity. Just as revenge justice entails that one and the same act is both in line with the requirements of (revenge) Justice and a contravention of it, is both 'just' and 'unjust', so retributive murder constitutes an act of purification, but also incurs pollution.

In particular in *Choephori*, this contradiction is an important element of the play. Orestes' murder of Clytemnestra, we have seen, is welcomed by the highly partial chorus as purification, driving out 'all pollution' (μύσος ἅπαν ἐλαθῇ | καθαρμοῖσιν ἀτᾶν ἐλατηρίοις, *Choe*. 967–8): the idea clearly is that this murder is something 'good' and 'necessary' and indeed required by (revenge) Justice to 'avenge the pollution of blood shed long ago' (*Choe*. 651). However, but a few lines later Orestes, utterly dejected, diagnoses his own pollution, ἄζηλα νίκης τῆσδ' ἔχων μιάσματα (1017). Although Orestes does not at this point make it explicit, in view of the earlier close association of pollution with 'guilt' (in the sense of a contravention of Δίκη as revenge justice), it is clear that the reference to pollution throws into high relief the point that on the terms of (revenge) Justice, his

---

[53] Garvie (1986) ad loc. [54] Zeitlin (1965) 475–80, esp. 479.

act is not only a purification, but also a pollution, is not only 'just', but also 'unjust'.

Appendix: pollution, purification and release

These remarks feed into another problem of the trilogy to which we should briefly turn our attention in the conclusion to this discussion, not least in anticipation of the subsequent excursus on Euripides' *Iphigenia among the Taurians*: the *Oresteia*'s concern with 'release' and the concomitant question why purification cannot afford such release.

The trilogy's concern with release is present from the first line, as the worn-out watchman longs for release from toils (ἀπαλλαγὴν πόνων), but becomes pointed in the second and third play when the need for release becomes more pressing in the face of endless cycles of 'crime and punishment'. In *Choephori*, desire for 'release' is expressed by the chorus. Resentful of the murderous queen, they are certain that the libations she had enjoined them to offer at the king's tomb will be in vain; for, they ask, 'what release can there be, once blood has fallen to the ground?' (τί γὰρ λύτρον πεσόντος αἵματος πέδοι; *Choe.* 48). The chorus itself suggests an answer some hundred lines below, when they express the desire that 'some man mighty with the spear come, a deliverer of the house' (ἴτω τις δορυσθενὴς ἀνὴρ | ἀναλυτὴρ δόμων, *Choe.* 160–1). As the man duly arrives, the expected 'deliverance' is repeatedly invoked. In the choral song before the arrival of Aegisthus, when Orestes is already inside, the chorus looks forward in excitement to the impending λύσις of the 'blood of ancient deeds' (τῶν πάλαι πεπραγμένων | λύσασθ' αἷμα προσφάτοις δίκαις, *Choe.* 804–5) as the resolution and end of the clan's fixation to disaster:[55] soon, they hope, the house will see the 'light of freedom' (ἐλευθερίας φῶς, *Choe.* 809) again. In this elated mood, they also anticipate the 'song of deliverance for the palace' they will sing as the deed is done (*Choe.* 819–22). *Eumenides* requires little comment: the deliverance of Orestes from his toils is the central concern of the play (ἀπαλλάξαι πόνων, *Eum.* 83).[56]

---

[55] For Garvie (1986) ad 803–05, 'λύσασθ' suggests not so much "atonement" (LSJ) or "expiation", as the ... annulling of the former deeds and the solving of the problem of the endless chain of crime and punishment.'

[56] The centrality, in the *Oresteia*, of 'striving for release', is underscored by the allusions to initiatory experience (esp. the Eleusinian mysteries) that have been diagnosed in the trilogy: see Bowie (1993b) 24–6 with further references, especially to Thomson (1935). The watchman's (and Orestes') wish for 'release from toil' fits into this pattern, as do the references to 'ends', 'safety' and in particular the recurring motif of the 'light' that is (soon) to be seen: *Ag.*'s beacon signal; the *Choe.*'s chorus's hopes that Orestes' deed bring light to present darkness (see *Choe.* 808–11, 863–4, 961; see Peradotto (1964)

Initially, purification is suggested as central to Orestes' 'release', annulling such miasma as clings to Orestes (and had clung to other 'doers' before); but expectations are eventually frustrated. The end of *Choephori* certainly gives prominence to Orestes' pollution (*Choe.* 1017) and, correspondingly, proposes purification as the means of choice for Orestes to achieve release (*Choe.* 1059–60). The opening sequence of *Eumenides* in Delphi may even have included an onstage purification of Orestes by Apollo in a 'stumme Szene'.[57] But if so, this purification is not sufficient for the matricide to achieve release; instead, Apollo sends his protégé to Athens there to find release by means which no longer seem to have anything to do with conventional purification (*Eum.* 81–3). The Athenian conclusion of the *Oresteia* bears this out. The question of Orestes' ritual status at first remains central. Orestes emphasises on several occasions that he has received (multiple?) purification (*Eum.* 236–9, 280–3, 445–52). The Erinyes do not seem to acknowledge that purification has altered Orestes' ritual status and demand the death of the matricide as 'proper sacrifice to cleanse a mother's murder' (ματρῷον ἄ-|γνισμα κύριον φόνου, *Eum.* 326–7; Sommerstein's translation). The Erinyes therefore deny that conventional purification brings release and continue to think along the lines of the assertion that death is the only valid 'purification' for the matricide. Orestes' toils are eventually ended, however, not by convincing the Erinyes that Orestes is pure, but through legal trial.[58]

In fact, Orestes himself does not seem to consider purification the ultimate solution, but only as a precondition to approach Athena. The idea is implicit at 236–9. It is made explicit at 280–9, when Orestes offers an account of a purification by blood he has received at the hands of Apollo as foundation for the claim that he now calls upon Athena 'from a ἁγνός mouth and in all ritual propriety' to come to his help (280–9):

388–93 on light imagery in the *Oresteia*). The quest for release was arguably the nub of mystery initiations, which Pindar in fact refers to as λυσίπονοι τελεταί: see Pindar fr. 131a. See also Plutarch, *Moralia* 47a on the mystic progress from terror and anxiety to wonder and clarity; and Plutarch fr. 178 (Sandbach) on the progression from confused and frightening wandering in the dark to panic, sweat and finally to amazement, quoted by Parker (2005) 352. Relevant to the *Oresteia*'s concern with release is also its preoccupation with 'ends' and the vocabulary of τέλος: see Goldhill (1984c).

[57] For discussions of this contested issue, see Dyer (1969) 39 n. 5; Taplin (1977) 381–4; Kossatz-Deissmann (1978) 107–10; Brown (1982) 30–2; Parker (1983) 386–7; Sidwell (1996), 52–6; Revermann (2006) 56–9.

[58] The Erinyes seem to accept the verdict as such, even if they feel that they have been dishonoured in the process. It is true that after the trial the Erinyes need to be persuaded by Athena to remain in Athens; but a continued pursuit of Orestes is no longer an issue at this point. What is at stake is that they threaten to direct their anger against Athens. It is this threat against Athens that Athena averts.

> βρίζει γὰρ αἷμα καὶ μαραίνεται χερός,
> μητροκτόνον μίασμα δ' ἔκπλυτον πέλει·
> ποταίνιον γὰρ ὂν πρὸς ἑστίᾳ θεοῦ
> Φοίβου καθαρμοῖς ἠλάθη χοιροκτόνοις.
> πολὺς δέ μοι γένοιτ' ἂν ἐξ ἀρχῆς λόγος,
> ὅσοις προσῆλθον ἀβλαβεῖ ξυνουσίᾳ.
> χρόνος καθαιρεῖ πάντα γηράσκων ὁμοῦ.
> καὶ νῦν ἀφ' ἁγνοῦ στόματος εὐφήμως καλῶ
> χώρας ἄνασσαν τῆσδ' Ἀθηναίαν ἐμοὶ
> μολεῖν ἀρωγόν.

For the blood is slumbering and dies away from my hand; the pollution of matricide is washed away: for when it was still fresh, it was removed at the hearth of god Phoebus; the blood of a slaughtered piglet provided purification. It would be a long story to tell from the beginning, the number of the people I have visited and spent time with without doing them any harm. Time purifies all things, as it ages with them. So now it is with a pure mouth and with auspicious speech that I call upon Athena, the mistress of this land, to come to my aid.

Athena, in turn, passes over the question of Orestes' ritual status quickly. She declares him to be a 'pure suppliant' (ἱκέτης προσῆλθες καθαρὸς ἀβλαβὴς δόμοις, *Eum.* 474) and proceeds to solve the question of 'release from toils' in non-ritual terms, convening the Areopagus to decide the issue.

It is noteworthy that the rejection of purification as sufficient means of release is given implicit emphasis. Important in this respect is the fact that the scenario of Orestes as suppliant before Athena, like the earlier scenario of Orestes as suppliant of Apollo at Delphi, recalls the 'host (abroad) receives polluted suppliant' schema we occasionally encounter in the historical record. Herodotus 1.35 and the last paragraph of the Cyrene cathartic law are good examples. In the former, Croesus receives Phrygian Adrastus, who had accidentally killed his brother, and purifies him.[59] In the latter, there is talk of a (polluted) 'suppliant' (ἱκέσιος τρίτος, αὐτοφόνος) who appears to have a 'sponsor' by whom he is presented to 'the city' and the 'three tribes'; who is then seated on a white fleece, (washed?) and anointed; and who finally seems to offer sacrifices – comparable perhaps to the sacrifice on the public altar specified on Side B of the *lex sacra* from Selinous which in that law constitutes the end point and climax of the

---

[59] Hdt. 1.35: ἀπικνέεται ἐς τὰς Σάρδις ἀνὴρ συμφορῇ ἐχόμενος καὶ οὐ καθαρὸς χεῖρας ... παρελθὼν δὲ οὗτος ἐς τὰ οἰκία κατὰ νόμους τοὺς ἐγχωρίους καθαρσίου ἐδέετο ἐπικυρῆσαι, Κροῖσος δέ μιν ἐκάθηρε.

purificatory process.⁶⁰ By invoking this schema, *Eumenides* calls attention to the procedure of purification as means of release only to discard it as Orestes is declared pure by Athena, but not by this act 'released from toils'.

Attractively but not entirely convincingly, it has been proposed by Keith Sidwell that the issue of Orestes' purity is obliquely underlying the trial. Since the Erinyes are still able to pursue their victim, there is a suggestion that purification has not been 'wholly effective' – yet effective enough to allow Orestes to escape from the sleeping Erinyes to Athens. The argument is that the question whether or not Orestes is 'really pure' is resolved only in and through the trial, the proof being that by the end of that trial the Erinyes for the first time let go of their victim.⁶¹ The idea seems appealing but it is at odds with Athena's declaration of Orestes' purity before the trial: the question of purity is precisely *not* at stake in the trial. It seems to me, therefore, that the emphasis is after all on the legal trial as superseding ritual purification as the ultimate means for Orestes to achieve ἀπαλλαγὴ πόνων, with ritual purity – and therefore purification, too – constituting but a precondition for that legal trial.⁶²

One of the reasons why this should be so, why purification eventually proves insufficient for Orestes to achieve release, is a matter of the logic of the play, which intimates that for an 'end' to be achieved, the particular 'justice' of the act needs to be determined, not in the terms of a blind revenge justice, but in wider terms, factors which are external to the act itself. One set of passages in *Choephori*, which has been discussed before, is particularly relevant: Orestes' twofold assertion, after the matricide, that he killed his mother 'justly'/'not without justice' (τόνδ' ἐγὼ μετῆλθον ἐνδίκως φόνον | τὸν μητρός, *Choe.* 988–9; οὐκ ἄνευ δίκης, *Choe.* 1027). These urgent appeals underscore that the question of justice needs to be resolved once and for all. But this cannot be done on the terms of revenge justice, which is circular and self-defeating, suggesting that the same act is in line with

---

⁶⁰ For the Cyrene cathartic law, see *SEG* ix 72 B §20 (= RO 97 B §20). For the sacred law from Selinous, see Jameson et al. (1993). The sacrifice is specified at B 10–11: hιαρεῖον τέλεον ἐπὶ τôι βομôι τôι δαμασίοι θύσας καθαρὸ | ς ἔστο. On the Selinuntine law, see Burkert (2000). On Greek sacrificial practices generally, see recently Parker (2011) 124–70.

⁶¹ Sidwell (1996) esp. 45–6, 54 on the sleeping Erinyes. Akin to this argument would be the suggestion (not explicitly made by Sidwell) that, just as sacrifice may follow upon conventional washing in this way to complete purification, so in *Eumenides* the trial before the Areopagus is a type of ultimate purification following upon conventional rites.

⁶² See MacDowell (1963) 150: for him, purification is 'distinct from the legal procedure'; 'Aiskhylos keeps it quite separate in the *Eumenides*'. Sidwell (1996) does not comment on Athena's declaration of Orestes as pure. One could of course argue, with Vellacott (1984) 37–50 (esp. 40–1) that Orestes is not pure and that Athena by declaring Orestes to be pure merely betrays her partiality; but this stretches the text (too) far.

justice, but also a contravention of it – is both just and unjust. Instead it needs to be resolved in the terms of a wider justice. Purification does not address these issues, but constitutes a mechanical solution to a problem – pollution – which has no bearing upon such a wider understanding of justice.[63]

[63] For related views, see e.g. Delcourt (1981) 269 (who finds that A. perhaps considered purification from matricide 'childish' in view of the magnitude of the crime) and Meier (1980) 160 (viewing the failure of the purification before the split of the 'new' – Olympian – and the 'old' – chthonian – order: purification belongs to the old order and can no longer satisfy the new one). For Lesky (1931) 211 the sequence 'purification–legal trial' signals a development 'vom starren Ritus zum heiligen Recht'.

Excursus
Rereading the Oresteia: *Euripides'* Iphigenia among the Taurians

Aeschylus seems to have been something of a star in fifth-century Athens. According to a scholion to Aristophanes' *Acharnians*, 'Aeschylus received the highest honours from the Athenians and by popular decree his plays continued to be produced even after his death, an honour granted to his dramas alone.'[1] The third century AD sophist Philostratus indeed informs us that 'the Athenians considered [Aeschylus] the father of tragedy.'[2] It is not unlikely that the *Oresteia*, which in the eyes of posterity (at least those of Wagner and Nietzsche) has seemed one-of-a-kind,[3] was one of the mainstays of Aeschylean stardom. The scanty remains of post-Aeschylean Attic tragedy, at any rate, suggest that the trilogy quickly acquired authoritative status and, for the city's tragic poets, soon became something of a yardstick against which to measure, and prove, their own dramatic qualities and to showcase their divergent concerns and perspectives. If it is ultimately beyond proof whether or not the Athenians 'really' regarded Aeschylus as the 'father of tragedy', it is certainly true, and demonstrable, that the *Oresteia* 'fathered' tragedy.

Of the two later poets whose dramatic work has in part survived it is Euripides who seems to show greater 'anxiety of influence' vis-à-vis his 'tragic father'. Again, this would seem to be so at least in regard to the *Oresteia*. There can be little doubt that Euripides 'read' and 're-read' Aeschylus' imposing trilogy and that he wrote his own 'Oresteian' tragedies, and in particular *Electra, Iphigenia among the Taurians* and *Orestes* (but also

---

[1] Σ Ar. *Ach.* 10 (the translation is that of Csapo and Slater (1995) nr. I.17b). In the passage in question, Dicaeopolis recalls the 'tragic pain' he once felt when, sitting in the theatre, he expected an Aeschylean tragedy only to hear announced a play by Theognis. The passage implies that at least by the 420s (*Acharnians* dates from 425 BC) Aeschylean tragedies were reperformed. For further notes, see Olson (2002) ad loc. Biles (2006–7) questions the reality of reperformance of Aeschylean tragedy in fifth-century Athens, at least as part of the City Dionysia.
[2] Philostratus, *Life of Apollonius* 6.11 (= Csapo and Slater (1995) nr. I.17c).
[3] See Silk and Stern (1981) 252–7; for Wagner's reception of the *Oresteia* in the *Ring*, see Ewans (1982).

Iphigenia in Aulis), against the backdrop of, and in engagement with, the Aeschylean paradigm.[4]

Arguably the earliest of the three, *Electra* is already a case in point. An Aeschylean overtone is difficult to deny. Clytemnestra's arrival in a chariot at the rough-and-ready hut of the poor but noble farmer to whom Electra has been betrothed seems oddly reminiscent of Agamemnon's arrival in a chariot at the rather grander Argive palace in *Agamemnon*.[5] Both enter the respective dwellings and presently meet with death.[6] It is a staple of Euripidean criticism, too, to regard *Electra*'s recognition scene between brother and sister as clear evidence of engagement with the corresponding scene in *Choephori*.[7] Euripides uses the exact same recognition tokens that were eagerly accepted by Aeschylus' Electra: lock, footprints and piece of clothing. Only in this play, these tokens are rejected out of hand by a rather sharp-minded Electra and emphatically replaced by another – very Odyssean – recognition token: the scar Orestes had once acquired when chasing a fawn.[8]

If we take this engagement with tradition, and with Aeschylean tradition in particular, seriously, this cannot but influence our reading of particular issues which were prominent in the *Oresteia* and reappear in Euripides' 'Oresteian' plays. Pollution and purification arguably form a particularly prominent, and certainly visually spectacular and memorable, part of Aeschylus' dramatisation of Atreid legend, taking a central role in the trilogy's dramatisation, and negotiation, of urgent problems. It is *a priori* likely, therefore, that Euripides, when inserting these ritual issues into his own Atreid dramas, did so with an eye to his predecessor and the problems negotiated by him through the nexus of pollution and purification. Consequently, it is worth asking to what extent and in what ways Euripides represents his own version of pollution and purification, and

---

[4] For the most recent treatment of Euripides' engagement with the *Oresteia*, see Torrance (2013) 13–62.
[5] Goldhill (1986) 250.
[6] Cropp (1988) ad 998–9 notes that Clytemnestra's command to her Trojan servants to 'get down from the carriage' (ἔκβητ' ἀπήνης) echoes the Aeschylean Clytemnestra's command to another Trojan captive, Cassandra, to get down from the carriage (ἔκβαιν' ἀπήνης τῆσδε, A. *Ag.* 1039) – only this time, it is the one who gives commands who dies, not the one who receives them.
[7] See e.g. Gellie (1981) esp. 3–4, Halporn (1983), Hammond (1984) esp. 382, Goldhill (1986) 247–50, Torrance (2013) 14–31.
[8] See Goff (1991) on the scar as alternative recognition token and the significant difference between Odysseus' scar as the result of a fight with a wild boar and Orestes' scar as the result of a fall when chasing a fawn. Torrance (2013) 30 suggests that in chasing a fawn Orestes is also cast in the role of the *Oresteian* Erinyes, who are said (*Eum.* 246) to track Orestes 'as a hound would a wounded fawn'.

renegotiates the issues (or 'crises') connected with pollution and purification, in dialogue with the Aeschylean paradigm in this way to nuance his own dramatic concerns. Two slightly different scenarios are possible.

The first is that Euripides rewrites Aeschylean pollution and purification. Both *Electra* and *Orestes* would perhaps seem to betray this type of rewriting. In the case of *Electra* it is interesting to observe, for instance, that pollution and purity are each presented at different points in the drama in ways that mark their potential fictionality. Orestes, upon Aegisthus' invitation to 'stand round the altar by the lustral water' in preparation for the sacrifice to the nymphs (ἀμφὶ βωμὸν στῶσι χερνίβων πέλας, *El.* 792; incidentally a potential allusion to *Ag.* 1036–8, where Clytemnestra urges Cassandra to be κοινωνὸν ... χερνίβων ... βωμοῦ πέλας), declares that he and his entourage 'have recently purified [themselves] by washing with pure water from a flowing stream' (ἀρτίως ἡγνίσμεθα | λουτροῖσι καθαροῖς ποταμίων ῥείθρων ἄπο, *El.* 793–4). This is non-verifiable. There is no indication in the play that such purification has taken place. It may or may not be true. Elsewhere in the play we encounter a pollution that is clearly make-believe. Electra lures Clytemnestra to, and into, her rural hut with the story of her recent delivery of a child and the tenth-day sacrifices which need to be offered (652–6, 1124–33). The story implies the fiction of birth-pollution on Electra's part, a kind of pollution whose worst stage was terminated by the offer of the tenth-day sacrifice (we may remember here Theophrastus' superstitious man who will not go anywhere near a corpse or a woman in childbed for fear of pollution, μιαίνεσθαι, *Characters* 16.9).[9]

Because both the potential fiction of Orestes' purity and the obvious fiction of Electra's impurity intimate that purity and pollution can be a matter of make-believe, an external show put on, there is perhaps a sense that Euripides here picks up on the idea that can be derived from Aeschylus, that pollution and purity are somehow external, divorced from a person's moral being, reworking it into the typically Euripidean notion of a potential split between reality and appearance (while also translating the high-flown into the everyday by transforming at this point the gory blood-pollution of Aeschylus into the rather profane notion of birth-pollution).[10] Incidentally, this presentation of pollution and purity sits well with a play which in general is intensely interested in rifts between reality and appearance and the difficulty of judging, for instance, character by appearance (and which

---

[9] Parker (1983) 48–52.
[10] The note of the everyday and 'realistic' in *Electra* has been a matter of fervent debate. See e.g. Gellie (1981), Goldhill (1986) 251–2, Lloyd (1986), Goff (1999/2000).

in this way, too, would seem to be strikingly reminiscent of the *Oresteia* and its concern with evaluation).[11]

Orestes, on the other hand, could be seen to respond to the vision offered at the end of *Choephori* of polluted Orestes driven mad by invisible Erinyes. In that play, the blood on the murderer's hands seems to affect his mind, causing it to be 'assailed by disturbances' (ταραγμὸς ἐς φρένας πίτνει, *Choe.* 1056), and the Erinyes for the moment appear to be but phantasms, at least to the chorus (τίνες σε δόξαι... στροβοῦσιν; *Choe.* 1051–2).[12] This strikingly elusive scenario, involving invisible presences (the Erinyes) and some kind of inner, mental disturbance as the result of murder (and murder-pollution), would seem to invite the kind of playfulness Euripides appears to be so fond of. We are not disappointed. As the result of the matricide, Orestes is afflicted by fits of madness (μανίαι... μητρὸς αἵματος τιμωρίαι, *Or.* 400). In these fits, Orestes has visions of Erinyes (e.g. *Or.* 255–7), much like the Aeschylean Orestes, but now more markedly hallucinatory (Electra remarks that Orestes 'sees none of the things he thinks he is sure of', ὁρᾷς γὰρ οὐδὲν ὧν δοκεῖς σάφ' εἰδέναι, *Or.* 259. This arguably harks back to *Choe.* 1061 where Orestes observes vis-à-vis the chorus, 'You don't see them [the Erinyes], but I do', ὑμεῖς μὲν οὐχ ὁρᾶτε τάσδ', ἐγὼ δ' ὁρῶ). Whatever we make of the end of *Choephori*, *Orestes* uses invisible Erinyes to suggest, obliquely, that Orestes' sickness may be, not externally imposed by objective Erinyes, but internal, entirely in his mind, the result of auto-suggestion.[13] In response to Orestes' seizure, Electra, for instance, remarks that 'even if one is not ill, but fancies one is (ἀλλὰ δοξάζῃ νοσεῖν), the effect is fatigue and despair' (*Or.* 314–15; the translation is that of West (1987)). Orestes famously pursues this line of thought, and makes explicit the assumption underlying it, when he later declares that he suffers from 'bad conscience' because he is 'conscious of the terrible things he has done' (ἡ σύνεσις, ὅτι σύνοιδα δείν' εἰργασμένος, *Or.* 396).[14]

Where pollution is to be placed in this is difficult to pinpoint. For one, pollution is itself strikingly elusive in application to matricidal Orestes, much like the Erinyes attacking him. For some characters Orestes would seem to be polluted: when Tyndareus at one point bemoans the insanity

---

[11] See e.g. Eur. *El.* 367–400, 550–1, 558–9; Goldhill (1986) 258.
[12] See Garvie (1986) 317 on the invisibility of the Erinyes to chorus and audience alike; he points out that some have (unconvincingly, I think, not least in view of *Choe.* 1061) argued that the Erinyes are visible, but that the chorus is turned away from them.
[13] See West (1987) ad 314 from whom I borrow the term 'auto-suggestion'.
[14] The word σύνεσις at this time usually refers to 'understanding'. But here 'conscience' seems implied. See West (1987) ad 396: 'Greek did not yet have a word for "conscience" (*syneidēsis* is Hellenistic), but the concept was beginning to be familiar'; see also Parker (1983) 252–4.

of revenge murder, pointing out that on its terms 'there would always be one person guilty of homicide, taking over the latest pollution on his hands' (τὸ λοίσθιον μίασμα λαμβάνων χεροῖν, *Or.* 517; West's translation), the implication is clearly that Orestes, as the latest revenge murderer, is assumed to be polluted;[15] Menelaus intimates much the same by pointing to the αἷμα μητρὸς μυσαρὸν (lit. 'polluting blood of the mother', 1624) bound up with the matricide. Then again, such statements as Helen's, that she is not polluted by speaking to Electra because the fault is Apollo's, not hers and Orestes' (προσφθέγμασιν γὰρ οὐ μιαίνομαι σέθεν, | εἰς Φοῖβον ἀναφέρουσα τὴν ἁμαρτίαν, *Or.* 75–6), and Orestes' similarly pointed question whether, because of Apollo's ultimate responsibility for the matricide, 'the god is not credit-worthy for me to refer to him to clear my pollution?' (ἢ οὐκ ἀξιόχρεως ὁ θεὸς ἀναφέροντί μοι | μίασμα λῦσαι, *Or.* 597–8; West's translation), introduce at least some degree of doubt as to the actual nature of Orestes' ritual status. The second problem is that, on the assumption that Orestes is polluted, it is still hard to judge to what extent pollution is responsible for Orestes' present state as it is juxtaposed with diagnoses of 'imagined illnesses' (Electra) and 'bad conscience' (Orestes).

It is arguably in line with this overall elusiveness of pollution, as well as with the suggested movement towards an internalised conception of Orestes' affliction that comes with Erinyes which may be merely the product of a hallucinating mind, that pollution is itself internalised; such is the case late in the play, when Orestes declares that Menelaus, because supposedly wronging him, is of 'impure mind' (Menelaus: ἁγνὸς γάρ εἰμι χεῖρας·, 'My hands are clean', Orestes: ἀλλ' οὐ τὰς φρένας, 'But not your mind', 1604).[16]

The second scenario is this: in rewriting pollution and purification in dialogue with the Aeschylean paradigm Euripides focuses, not on the various characteristics of Aeschylean pollution and purification, but on the problems with which this ritual nexus was prominently associated in Aeschylus. In particular the example of *Electra* shows that these two scenarios are by no means mutually exclusive. In the play whose discussion

---

[15] A few lines later, at 524, Tyndareus speaks of ruthless (revenge) murder as τὸ θηριῶδες τοῦτο καὶ μιαιφόνον.

[16] We are reminded of Phaedra and her 'polluted mind' in *Hippolytus* (v. 317). In view of my discussion of the *Hippolytus* passage in chapter 1 (and even the brief remarks here), it should be clear that it is not enough merely to point out, as commentators are wont to do (see e.g. Willink (1986) ad 1604), that it is rare to extend the idea of pollution 'to cover moral guilt incurred without positive action' (Willink's formulation). Both these 'polluted minds' fit their dramatic contexts well, and in ways specific to each play. For the development of ideas of a 'purity of the mind' esp. in the post-classical period, see Chaniotis (1997), (2012); see also Graf (2007b) 113–15.

will occupy the remainder of this chapter, *Iphigenia among the Taurians*, it is however largely this second scenario that applies. Although in this play, too, certain qualities of pollution and its effects are rewritten – we shall meet once more a hallucinating Orestes arguably mirroring Aeschylus' of *Choephori* – the overall significance of *Iphigenia*'s adaption of pollution and purification seems to lie, not so much in any one quality, but in the association of the ritual nexus, in Aeschylus, with the idea of 'release from toil' (discussed earlier), the ἀπαλλαγή πόνων that is central from the very first line of the trilogy and is then, at the end of *Choephori*, adapted to Orestes' toils as polluted matricide. The chorus at this point envisage purification as adequate means to free Orestes from his suffering (εἷς σοι καθαρμός· Λοξίας δὲ προσθιγὼν | ἐλεύθερόν σε τῶνδε πημάτων κτίσει, 'There's only one purification for you: Apollo, by his touch, shall set you free you from your troubles', *Choe.* 1059–60). *Iphigenia among the Taurians* picks up on this. Markedly post-*Oresteian*, it renegotiates Orestes' ἀπαλλαγή πόνων, using the ritual nexus prominently associated in Aeschylus with the problem of ἀπαλλαγή πόνων. The central question accordingly is not so much how Euripides rewrites Aeschylean pollution and purification, but how he uses pollution and purification, prominently associated in Aeschylus with the question of release, to dramatise his own version of Orestes' release.[17]

Perhaps the central upshot of this examination of the role of pollution and purification in Euripides' reconsideration of Orestes' release is the advancement of a particular view of *Iphigenia*'s 'tragic' quality, which takes issue with a prominent critical tradition. Euripides' play has frequently been called a 'melodrama' or, alternatively, a 'romance', a sort of comedy of innocence. The notion persisted, for a considerable time, and probably still persists in some quarters, that *Iphigenia* was somehow not 'tragedy'; that it was a far cry from, and simply could not belong to the same 'category' as, Aeschylus' dramas of violent bleakness, most notably the formidable and relentless *Oresteia*, or Sophocles' claustrophobic visions of uncompromising, self-destructive individuals such as Oedipus, Antigone and Ajax; a far cry even from Euripides' own masterful dramas of utter destruction, among them *Medea*, *Hippolytus*, and the much-admired *Bacchae*. *Iphigenia among the Taurians*, along with *Ion* and *Helen* (*Alcestis*, because of its curious position as fourth play in the tetralogy in the place of a satyr-play, is a different beast altogether), has seemed beyond the 'genre' of 'true' tragedy

---

[17] The term 'release' will frequently occur in the following discussion. Each time, the reference is to the idea of ἀπαλλαγή πόνων or ἐλευθέρωσις πημάτων and must be understood before the Aeschylean (and more specifically *Choephorean*) background that purification can bring such release.

and, anyway, of debatable quality, a self-serving comedy of ideas at best and a decadent frivolity at worst, not suited, in any case, to the refined tastes of serious and tragically minded scholars.[18] Not all, to be sure, have taken such a condemnatory stance, but the assumption of a certain levity of *Iphigenia* has underlain many a study of the play, up to today.

A few examples of this view of the play will suffice. In the 1960s, D. J. Conacher dismissed *Iphigenia* as a 'play of little depth'.[19] In the early 1970s, Anne P. Burnett diagnosed an 'uncloying sweetness' in what she considered the 'most humane and good-tempered of the classical tragedies' and a 'poetic redemption of the House of Atreus'.[20] A few years later, Richard Caldwell felt the need to categorise *Iphigenia* as 'romance', emphasising in particular its nostalgic, dream-like, and wish-fulfilling quality.[21] As recently as the late 1980s, Michael O'Brien tried to demonstrate how Euripides transforms Tantalid history into a tale of success by muting its sinister aspects to create a 'cheering sequel' to the *Oresteia*.[22]

In the 1990s, at last, when the emphasis placed by post-structuralist criticism on loose ends and self-contradictions began to take effect even on those venturing to explore the seemingly unrewarding world of Iphigenia in Taurian lands, a note of ambiguity began to enter. Strikingly, though, such diagnoses of ambiguity were restricted almost entirely to the play's prominent cult aetiologies, not to the actual *mythos*, the story of Orestes. *Iphigenia*, in those days, tended to be read as an allegory, almost, of Artemisian cult and scholars homed in on the intrinsic double-sidedness of a cult whose rites, in the play's denouement, are transformed from human sacrifice into symbolically re-enacted bloodshed.[23]

---

[18] An early and notable exception to most scholars' dismissive attitude to *IT* is Zuntz (1933). His dithyrambic enthusiasm, Nietzschean in style but utterly un-Nietzschean in its admiration for Euripides, deserves to be quoted at some length: 'Und welche Kunst! Zu jeder Zeile, jedem Wort wäre ein Kommentar nötig, wollte man Rechenschaft geben von diesem eigentlich frevelhaften Alleskönnen' (ibid. 252; I suspect young Zuntz was an ardent admirer of *Faust*); 'Auf dem schmalen Grat zwischen Zweifel und Verzweiflung hält und leitet den Dichter sein Genius; sein Werk aber schwebt unangreifbar über toddrohendem Abgrund, von Flammen der Unterwelt angestrahlt nicht verbrannt, und geschwellt nicht gesprengt vom zerstörerischen Geist einer neuen Zeit' (ibid. 254).

[19] Conacher (1967) 305.

[20] Burnett (1971) 54, 47, 64. Hall (2010) 275 also speaks of a 'moving, atmospheric, and humane drama'.

[21] Caldwell (1974) 31–4. The label 'romantic tragedy' has also been applied to *Helen* (see Dunn (1996) 133–57 on '*Helen* and romance'); see also Mastronarde (2010) 59–60 (with reference to Fusillo [1992]). Whitman (1974) 34 speaks of 'a tense, confident melodrama'; but he acknowledges that 'more solemn notes are always present, constantly reverberating through the plot, and keeping it in tune with Euripides' life-long concern for the meaning of divinity as it enters the human scene'.

[22] O'Brien (1988) 115: 'As a tragedy with a happy ending, I.T. contains more than it might seem to at first sight: not only a cheering sequel to the Orestes and Iphigenia legends, but also an alternative history of the Pelopids, one that begins and ends with a tale of success.'

[23] Notable examples are Wolff (1992), Goff (1999), Tzanetou (1999/2000), Papadopoulou (2005a); also Zeitlin (2011). On Euripidean cult aetiologies (of which *IT* offers a striking example), see the

While this is not to deny that (especially since the 1990s) many scholars have evidently taken *Iphigenia* seriously and identified various weighty issues it negotiates, a radical reappraisal of the play and its overall 'tragic' outlook and 'tone' was formulated (and from a less narrowly ritualistic perspective) only fairly recently, by Matthew Wright, in his monograph on Euripides' so-called escape tragedies. For Wright, *Iphigenia*, along with *Helen*, is no longer cheerful, but 'horribly bleak' and 'radically negative' because full of 'epistemological nihilism'; for him, it presents a 'view of the world [which] is absolutely comfortless and terrifying'.[24]

The present analysis of pollution and purification in the play will suggest taking this latter position seriously. I do not want, nor do I see the need, to engage in a discussion about 'the tragic'.[25] However, the subsequent remarks will suggest that *Iphigenia* is indeed 'tragic' in the unspecific, colloquial sense of the word: it is pessimistic. In the following discussion, I shall first sketch the play's engagement with the *Oresteia* and its presentation of pollution and purification in terms of 'rewriting': how, that is, the play, in its own version of Orestes' ἀπαλλαγὴ πόνων, echoes and reconfigures specific aspects of Aeschylean pollution and purification. In the second section we shall see that, for all its surface cheerfulness and its apparently successful outcome, release is not unproblematic and purification not unequivocal; tensions remain. In a third step, I will explore the implications of the decidedly metatheatrical quality of the play's infamous mock-purification in relation to other metatheatrical elements in the play. I will argue that what the *Oresteia* strove for and finally, if tentatively, achieved – a solution for matricide and internecine killing – in *Iphigenia* is exposed as a poetic manipulation of tradition.

Release and purification in *Iphigenia among the Taurians* and the *Oresteia*

There can be little doubt that Euripides' reconsideration of Atreid myth in *Iphigenia* also constitutes a reconsideration of, and critical engagement with, Aeschylus' *Eumenides* and the version of (ab)solution offered therein for the matricide Orestes and, by extension, the 'diseased' House

---

sceptic remarks by Scullion (1999/2000) (these aetiologies or the cults they refer to could be entirely a matter of fiction) with the (less sceptic) response by Seaford (2009) (close correspondence between these aetiologies and Athenian reality).

[24] Wright (2005) 387.
[25] For extended discussions of this question, see Silk (1996); Judet de la Combe (2010). For discussions of genre in reference to Euripidean tragedy, see Goff (1999/2000), Mastronarde (1999/2000) and id. (2010) 44–62; see also Knox (1970) on 'Euripidean comedy' and Seidensticker (1982) 89–242 on comic elements.

of Atreus.²⁶ The very premise of the play indicates as much: contrary to what Apollo had promised in *Eumenides*, Orestes has not been 'released from toil' (τῶνδ' ἀπαλλάξαι πόνων, *Eum.* 83); the fact is, some of the Erinyes had not been persuaded by the verdict reached in the trial of the Areopagus, which occupies such a prominent place in Aeschylus' play; consequently, Orestes is back to where he started in *Eumenides*, eager to win release, 'an end of toils' (τέλος πόνων, *Eum.* 83; ἀμπνοὰς... πόνων, *Eum.* 92).²⁷

In view of this, the question how Euripides incorporates the ritual nexus of pollution and purification into his revision of Aeschylus becomes pertinent. After all, in *Eumenides* pollution and purification were central (and spectacularly visualised) elements in the play's negotiation of, and progression towards, release. I have indicated above that the significance of the integration of pollution and purification into *Iphigenia* lies above all in their renewed association with the problem of 'release' that is being reviewed and rewritten. In this first section, and for introductory purposes, I shall nonetheless remain with the rewritings of certain Aeschylean aspects of pollution and purification. I elaborate on three points, the first two concerning details, the third a wider pattern.

First, *Iphigenia*'s Erinyes appear decidedly Aeschylean, bearing witness in this way to the later playwright's indebtedness to the *Oresteian* world of pollution; after all, in the *Oresteia* these horrifying creatures are associated closely with pollution. (As we shall see below, in Euripides the relation between pursuit by the Erinyes and Orestes' ritual status remains conspicuously nebulous. This, however, does not mean that in *Iphigenia* there is no relation between the Erinyes and *miasma*; it means, rather, that this relation is already subject to Euripidean rewriting.) That Euripides' Erinyes hark back to Aeschylus' is true not only in the obvious sense that as former participants in the Areopagus trial they *are* in a sense Aeschylus' Erinyes; it is true also of their actual appearance. As in the later *Orestes*, their presentation at 285–94, if in striking contrast to the tangible nature of the *Eumenides*' Erinyes, is reminiscent of their appearance at the end of the

---

[26] This view is shared by most scholars. See especially Caldwell (1974), Torrance (2013) 33–45; see also Sansone (1975) esp. 292–3. Burnett (1971) 71–2 argues that Euripides intended *IT* as a replacement for Aeschylus' *Proteus* (the satyr-play which concluded the *Oresteia*); contra Seidensticker (1982) 202 who finds that 'in a deeper sense' *IT* is not so much a sequel as an alternative to *Eumenides*.

[27] That we are dealing with a revision in particular of *Eumenides* is indicated by a number of further echoes of that play, recently explored by Torrance (2013) 33–45, 72–5. Even verbal echoes may be detected: for instance, *IT* 621 (αὐτὴ ξίφει θύουσα θῆλυς ἄρσενας;) may be considered an allusion to A. *Ag.* 1231 (θῆλυς ἄρσενος φονεύς) – Orestes' impending sacrifice is thus assimilated to earlier Atreid violence, Clytemnestra's murder of Agamemnon (also noted by Torrance (2013) 42).

Choephori. Not only are they described in similar terms;[28] more importantly, both passages emphasise the nature of their appearance as visions, visible only to the troubled matricide but *not* to bystanders.[29] These observations may appear alarmingly truncated and oversimplified. At this point, however, I merely want to suggest that the presentation of the Erinyes in *Iphigenia* links this play, and its concern with Orestes' suffering, to the Aeschylean world of pollution, purification and release.

The second point is perhaps more intriguing because indicative of an engagement at a deeper level with Aeschylean scenarios of pollution and purification: *Iphigenia*, I propose, alludes to the idea, frequently invoked in the *Oresteia*, of purification through (revenge-) murder, in a passage whose significance, it seems, has thus far been overlooked. I refer to lines 704–5, where Orestes bids Pylades report his death at the hands of the Argive woman (whom he has not yet recognised as Iphigenia) to his dear ones back home:

ἄγγελλε δ' ὡς ὄλωλ' ὑπ' Ἀργείας τινὸς
γυναικὸς ἀμφὶ βωμὸν ἁγνισθεὶς φόνῳ.

Report that I perished at the hands of an Argive woman, consecrated for slaughter at the altar.

Consider the formulation ἁγνισθεὶς φόνῳ. Poulheria Kyriakou, author of the most recent commentary on the play, proposes to translate this as 'consecrated for slaughter', taking the dative φόνῳ as dative proper; her explanation that the word ἁγνίζω here refers to 'consecration' and defines Iphigenia's role in the human sacrifices – as the one who carries out the preliminary lustrations (ἁγνίσματα) of the sacrificial victim *for the slaughter* (φόνῳ) – makes perfect sense.[30]

There are other ways to understand the formulation, however. For instance, according to Mark Griffith, ἁγνισθεὶς φόνῳ could be translated as 'sacrificed (in/through murder)'.[31] Kyriakou discards this 'because the dat. φόνῳ would then be superfluous.'[32] But there is also an intriguing third

---

[28] In both descriptions, 'dogs' and 'serpents' figure large (which, of course, may have been conventional).
[29] Of particular relevance is the emphasis on the absence of sight in both *IT* 291–2, παρῆν δ' ὁρᾶν | οὐ ταῦτα μορφῆς σχήματ', and *Choe*. 1061, ὑμεῖς μὲν οὐχ ὁρᾶτε τάσδ', ἐγὼ δ' ὁρῶ. The question of the chorus at A. *Choe*. 1051, τίνες σε δόξαι ... στροβοῦσιν is relevant to the entire passage in *IT* 281–94.
[30] Kyriakou (2006) ad 702–5. The line is understood similarly by Whitman (1974) 34 and Cropp (2000) who translates 'purified *for* slaughter', taking the dative, like Kyriakou, as dative proper.
[31] Griffith (1999) ad 196–7 (commenting on the use of ἐφαγνίζω in *Antigone*).
[32] Kyriakou (2006) ad 702–5.

possibility, which, significantly, throws the question of release and purification into high relief – in terms reminiscent, again, of the *Oresteia*. The verb ἁγνίζω may refer, not only to preliminary lustrations, consecrations or the mere sacrificial act, but to actual purification from pollution;[33] as Robert Parker points out, this is indeed the verb's primary sense.[34] If one understands the dative φόνῳ as instrumental, the line could be taken to express the idea that Orestes is 'purified *through* slaughter'. Later in the play it is in fact precisely in this sense, and in the framework of such a construction, with the instrumental dative indicating the medium of purification, that ἁγνίζω appears again, when Iphigenia instructs the Taurian king Thoas to 'purify the [goddess's] chamber with sulphur' (ἄγνισον πυρσῷ μέλαθρον, 1216).

Of the three above-given possibilities, the first (Kyriakou's), it is true, readily suggests itself to be primary, for two reasons. First, there has been much talk in the preceding sections about Iphigenia's role in preparing the victims for slaughter, most recently at 621–4. Second, in that passage (621–4; but also at 40, if the line is not spurious) some emphasis is placed on the fact that Iphigenia is not responsible for the actual killing, which indeed 'concerns those within' (ἔσω δόμων τῶνδ' εἰσὶν οἷς μέλει τάδε, 624). Therefore, it would be desirable to take the sentence in such a way as to comply with this scenario, involving Iphigenia, not as sacrificer, but as officiant in charge of the preparations. The easiest solution is in fact to construe ὑπ' Ἀργείας τινὸς γυναικὸς with the passive ἁγνισθείς and to understand that word in the sense suggested by Kyriakou: 'tell [those back home] that I perished having been consecrated for slaughter near the altar by some Argive woman'. On these terms, the two other options would seem immediately to be ruled out as valid alternatives.

And yet, while Griffith's understanding of the passage would indeed appear to be an unlikely rendering, the idea of 'purification through slaughter', I suggest, is playfully engaged with and present at least in the background. Importantly, just before lines 704–5, attention is obliquely drawn to the issue of pollution, when Orestes remarks, vis-à-vis Pylades, that his (Pylades') house is 'pure and not afflicted by sickness' (καθαρά τ', οὐ νοσοῦντ', ἔχεις | μέλαθρ', 693–4; the obliqueness, we shall see below, is important). With the issue of pollution thus (obliquely) highlighted, a good case can be made that Euripides' audience would have been likely to detect in 704–5 a significant surplus of meaning, hinting at a scenario wherein death is the ultimate purification for the matricide.

---

[33] See LSJ ἁγνίζω 2; see esp. Eur. *HF* 1324 ἁγνίσας μιάσματος. [34] Parker (1983) 329.

This significant surplus and the scenario it implies are appropriate in, and indicative of, a rewriting of Aeschylus' *Oresteia*, in which revenge-murders are referred to, and justified, as acts of purification. One might wish to go even further and diagnose a specific allusion to *Eumenides*. In the famous 'binding-song', the Erinyes demand Orestes as expiatory sacrifice in terms strikingly similar to the Euripidean Orestes' turn of phrase. They envisage Orestes as 'valid purificatory sacrifice for the matricide', ματρῷον ἅ-|γνισμα κύριον φόνου (*Eum.* 326–7).

If one detects in this an engagement with the Aeschylean notion of purification through (sacrificial) death or even an intertextual allusion, a number of further observations suggest themselves. In addition to revisiting Aulis and the ensuing revenge killings all of which were framed in one way or another as sacrificial,[35] *Iphigenia* here arguably plays with the idea that for Orestes expiation may take exactly the form that in *Eumenides* was demanded but finally averted. But then in this play, too, this type of expiation and death is finally averted. That is, 704–5 not only suggest *Iphigenia*'s indebtedness to *Eumenides* and more specifically the Erinyes' vision of purification through murder. Insofar as it casts, albeit obliquely, Orestes' sacrifice as a form of purification, it toys with the idea of enacting what in the *Eumenides* remained on the level of language; and insofar as this purification is eventually not enacted, it reproduces the *Eumenides*' movement towards release.

I mention in passing here that the rite which, at the end of the play, Athena bids Orestes institute at Halae may be seen to invoke, and replace, 'the valid purificatory sacrifice for the matricide' (and therefore be understood as another sign of Euripides' engagement with the Aeschylean world of pollution and purification). The point has recently been made by Isabelle Torrance.[36] She draws attention in particular to the formulation τῆς σῆς σφαγῆς ἄποιν' (1459) which may be taken to imply a 'compensation', not only 'for Orestes' (escape from) slaughter' (which is its primary meaning), but also 'for the slaughter (of his mother)'. Taken in this second sense, the rite is not an appeasement intended for Artemis, who is denied the human sacrifice of Orestes, but an appeasement intended for the Erinyes, who have precisely demanded Orestes' blood as ματρῷον ἅγνισμα φόνου.

My third point is that *Iphigenia*'s vision of Orestes' (supposed) release, and the place of purification therein, seems to be fashioned after the structure of release envisioned in *Eumenides*. In the *Oresteia*, pollution is

---

[35] On the relation of Orestes' near-sacrifice to Aulis, see O'Brien (1988) 109–12; see also Caldwell (1974) 24–5. On the motif of the corrupted sacrifice in the *Oresteia*, see Zeitlin (1965).
[36] Torrance (2013) 37–8.

continually insisted on, from Agamemnon who fears the pollution resulting from the shedding of maiden blood (*Ag.* 209–10), to Clytemnestra, the 'pollution of the land and the local gods' (*Ag.* 1645) to Orestes polluted as a result of the matricide (see e.g. *Choe.* 1017). In particular when the chorus, at the end of the second play, excitedly proclaims 'There's only one purification for you!' (εἷς σοι καθαρμός, *Choe.* 1059) expectations are raised that the eventual solution, for Orestes, will involve ritual purification. In *Eumenides*, however, purification is no longer an ultimately valid means of release. Purification is still important. But it is important, it would seem, only as a precondition for standing trial, for the legal solution, that is, which supersedes a purely ritual one: something of the sort is indicated at least in Athena's assertion, just before she declares her intention to summon jurors to decide Orestes' case (at *Eum.* 482–4), that Orestes 'has come as a pure suppliant, not harmful to our houses' (ἱκέτης προσῆλθες καθαρὸς ἀβλαβὴς δόμοις, *Eum.* 474). The important point is that rites of purification, of which Orestes had undergone several prior to his arrival in Athens, allow no escape from post-matricidal toils. *Iphigenia* echoes this Aeschylean sequence of purification as a precondition for, but not the ultimate means of, release. A rite of purification, albeit a fake one, makes possible escape towards Greece; in this way, it is the 'precondition' for the instalment, by Orestes, of the statue of Taurian Artemis in Attica, which Apollo had promised as the ultimate means for the matricide 'to win respite from toils' (85–92; ἀμπνοὰς ἕξειν πόνων, 92).

We must not overlook crucial differences, though. If *structurally* purification in each play occupies the same position, there appears to be a great difference between the two plays as to the *symbolical* weight of the rite. In *Eumenides*, purification is reduced to a formality with no impact on the question of release itself; the play essentially devalues purification. In *Iphigenia*, by contrast, the attention given to the successful outcome of Iphigenia's contrivance – to the success, that is, of the ruse of the purification – as well as the extended space allowed to its description, seem to place in the foreground the relevance of the rite to the release of the matricide.

This first exploration confirms that Euripides uses Aeschylus' earlier treatment of pollution and purification in relation to the question of release as a point of reference (and of departure) for his own (re)presentation of the problem. The specific nature of Euripides' engagement with his predecessor delineated above also begs two important questions, however. The first concerns, more generally, the 'agenda' of rewriting. If Euripides recycles Aeschylus 'with an "ironic" difference' (the Erinyes regress to their Choephorean form; Orestes unwittingly evokes the schema of revenge-killing which underlies the *Oresteia*; purification appears as a 'fake' version of Aeschylus' blood-reeking rites), this may suggest conceiving of the play merely in terms of playful literary re-enactment with ultimately no serious concern of its own. But would this be an appropriate view of the play? The second question is related but more specific: if, at first sight at least, Euripides seems to portray purification and its role in the play's progression towards Orestes' release in a decidedly more positive light, does this mean that *Iphigenia among the Taurians* presents release of the matricide as unproblematic?

These two questions are central to the following more detailed analysis of pollution and purification in the play. As I hope to show, release is not unproblematic; by implication, the play does have a serious concern of its own.

Pollution, purification and release

If the above observations seem to suggest that *Iphigenia* reproduces the *Oresteia*'s solution and positively re-evaluates the role of purification to work towards a positive outcome, in the following discussion I want to draw attention to certain tensions in the play's engagement with pollution and purification, which intimate that release for matricidal Orestes must remain illusionary, tentative, incomplete. I shall argue, first, that the play's promise of release is highly ambivalent and eventually unsatisfactory; then, I will focus more directly on pollution and purification. I shall argue that their particular integration into *Iphigenia*'s plot reflect the problematic nature of Orestes' release.

The question whether Orestes is finally released upon return home to Attica, whether, that is, the matricide's expiation through exile and recovery of Artemis' Taurian image (itself a form of 'purification', if in the broader sense)[37] will bring the successful outcome which Apollo had promised Orestes, has received very little scholarly attention. For the most part, this is due to the view outlined above, that the tone of *Iphigenia among the Taurians* is playful and light, and that it 'intends' to present a trouble-free happy ending. We need not rehearse these views here again. But it is noteworthy that neither Christian Wolff's thoughtful analysis of the play nor Matthew Wright's radically pessimistic reinterpretation seriously call into question the success of Orestes' release.[38] Though the

---

[37] And one which aptly (in view of the crime) involves the saving of a female Atreid: Zeitlin (2005) 201–2.
[38] Wolff (1992) 319–20 notes the darker aspects of Iphigenia's future, though: she ends up in Brauron, when she wanted to go to Argos; and as patron of mothers who die in childbirth she is 'drawn

latter finds the end frustrating, this is not because it leaves questions about Orestes' salvation unanswered but because questions are answered in such a perfunctory, theologically shallow, manner.[39] Voices of dissent are few and far between. Thalia Papadopoulou, for example, remarks (if only in passing) that the play does not answer the question why bringing the statue of Artemis to Attica would end Orestes' suffering.[40]

This observation is valuable because it draws our attention to the peculiarly open-ended nature of *Iphigenia*'s ending. *Iphigenia* defers resolution to the future. In the here and now of the play, the audience is offered merely the prediction of Orestes' release by Athena as *dea ex machina*. This stands in glaring contrast to the *Eumenides*' vision. In Aeschylus' play, Orestes' release is beyond doubt: he is declared 'pure' by Athena (ἱκέτης . . . καθαρός, 'a pure suppliant', *Eum.* 474); he is acquitted on the authority of Athena; and by the end of the play, the Erinyes-turned-Eumenides have accepted the verdict.

But *Iphigenia*'s vision of release is precarious not only because of a lack of certainty through enactment; the very premise upon which Euripides' play is built calls into question the promise of release.[41] The authorities on whom Orestes' ultimate release depends in *Iphigenia* are Apollo, who had ordained that Orestes recover the statue of Artemis from Taurian lands to win 'respite from toils' (85–92; ἀμπνοὰς . . . πόνων, 92), and Athena, who confirms this course of action as a means to bring 'relief from present misery' (1438–41b, 1441: τῶν νῦν παρόντων πημάτων ἀναψυχάς) and further specifies its minutiae (1446–61). But must we believe them? Other Euripidean tragedies do not invite the audience to question divine predictions for the future.[42] This is dramatically different in *Iphigenia*. After all, the play starts on the assumption that Apollo's advice to seek release at Athens was somehow not good enough and that Athena's intervention, at the trial, in favour of Orestes was ineffectual. Because it entails in this way that 'release' and 'resolution', even if divinely sanctioned, may be called into question,

---

into that realm of the goddess's fearful ambivalence, which she had earlier sought to deny (380–91)' (ibid. 320).

[39] For Wright (2005) 382 *Helen* and *IT* 'end on a note of emptiness'; there is no 'theological profundity'.
[40] Papadopoulou (2005a) 116.
[41] See Zeitlin (2005) 201 on the *Oresteia*'s solutions which 'the premises of this play have refused to honor'.
[42] When placed in prologue-speeches, divine prophecies are consistently proven accurate by the ensuing action, most notably (and cruelly) perhaps in *Hippolytus*. Further, in those cases where predictions for the future are placed at the end of the play, as, for instance, in *Electra* (where Castor predicts Orestes' future release from matricide through acquittal by the Areopagus), no encouragement is given to question these predictions nor any textual clue on whose authority one could justifiably do so. On the gods in Euripidean tragedy, see Mastronarde (2010) 153–206; see ibid. 174–81 for gods and their predictions in Euripidean prologues.

Iphigenia encourages rather than discourages the audience to view critically divine pronouncements which intimate the new solution as valid and successful. More specifically, it is bitterly ironic that, in a particularly striking *déjà vu*, it is again Apollo and Athena who sanction release. To accept Orestes' ultimate release as successful thus becomes a matter of accepting the authority of precisely those two gods the instability of whose authority is the premise of the present play.

Significantly, the play draws attention to the shortcomings of these gods. In the case of Apollo, the sense of a certain deficiency of the god's oracles is not unheard of in tragic presentations of the matricide and its aftermath.[43] Here, too, such a notion is present from the beginning. Orestes, in his first *rhēsis* (77–103), begins by criticising Apollo for his oracular pronouncements: 'Which entrapment is it this time, Apollo', asks an exasperated Orestes, 'that you have driven me into with your prophecies?' (ὦ Φοῖβε, ποῖ μ' αὖ τήνδ' ἐς ἄρκυν ἤγαγες | χρήσας, 77–8). At this early point, the reference is unspecific and most naturally associated with Apollo's encouragement of the matricide. But when it becomes clear that *Iphigenia* takes place in a post-*Eumenidean* world in which the trial at Athens has failed to afford ultimate release, Orestes' criticism of Apollo appears more pointed. There is not only Apollo's (perhaps unwise) encouragement of matricide. There is also his oracular advice to seek release at Athens (ἐς τὰς Ἀθήνας... ἔπεμψε Λοξίας, 'Loxias sent me... to Athens', 943), which time has proven deficient. Apollo is simply not reliable.

Athena seems similarly questionable. When the goddess appears as *dea ex machina* to announce Orestes' escape and, by implication, the successful progression towards the matricide's release, the audience has already encountered the goddess as one whose authority was insufficient, in the past, entirely to convince the Erinyes to let go of their pursuit of matricidal Orestes. Half the Erinyes still haunt the matricide, unconvinced by the verdict reached under the presidency of Athens' patron goddess (οὐκ ἐπείσθησαν νόμῳ, 970). Significantly, the end of *Iphigenia* highlights rather than mutes the problematic nature of Athena's authority. In conclusion to her proclamation of salvation, the goddess self-confidently points out to the absent Orestes that she had saved him before, on the occasion of the trial (1469–71):

ἐξέσωσα δὲ
καὶ πρίν σ' Ἀρείοις ἐν πάγοις ψήφους ἴσας
κρίνασ', Ὀρέστα·

---

[43] The locus classicus is Castor's famous line in *Electra* that 'wise though he is, he gave you unwise oracles' (σοφὸς δ' ὢν οὐκ ἔχρησέ σοι σοφά, *El.* 1246).

> I saved you once before, Orestes: on the hill of Ares, when I judged the votes to be equal.

But this is not true: she *tried* to save him and failed. By drawing attention to this incongruence at such a prominent point, *Iphigenia* invites the audience to take note of the essential open-endedness of a play whose happy outcome in matters pertaining to release depends entirely on the authority of gods whose infallibility has already been disproved.[44]

This frustrating circularity severely undermines any certainty about Orestes' release. In that it leaves the tension between the play's premise, that release sanctioned by Apollo and Athena may not be ultimately valid, and its solution as one based on the authority of these very gods suggestively unresolved, *Iphigenia* undercuts its ostensibly happy ending and suggests, rather, the irresolvable nature of Orestes' matricide. Σωτηρία, for Orestes, remains strikingly intangible: a never-ending story.

This open-endedness is borne out by the play's engagement with pollution and purification in their function as vehicles of renegotiation of release. Pollution and purification are strikingly elusive in this play. As we shall see below, this elusiveness is itself part of their significance. But it also allows us to infer various scenarios. I discuss two. The first is hypothetical; the aim of its presentation is largely to discuss the 'successfulness' of Iphigenia's purification, on the assumption that it actually takes place. The second will give due weight to the vagueness itself which surrounds pollution and purification in *Iphigenia*.

The first scenario is that *Orestes is polluted and the purification as part of the escape-plot takes place*. I engage with this scenario only briefly because of the two it seems the less significant. Certainly, the audience is invited to view Orestes as polluted. The matricide is still pursued by Erinyes; the text obliquely suggests the need for purification in the passage discussed above (ἁγνισθεὶς φόνῳ, 705); matricide is viewed as one of the most polluting crimes by Thoas (1174, 1178); Iphigenia expresses the wish that 'the purification have the outcome [she] desires' (εἰ γὰρ ὡς θέλω καθαρμὸς ὅδε πέσοι, 1221; cf. ἢν νίψω φόνον, 'if I wash away the blood-guilt', 1230). One could go on.

On the assumption, then, that Orestes is polluted, is this pollution successfully removed? We shall see below that the play leaves it suggestively

---

[44] Mastronarde (2010) 162–3 is generally more optimistic about the two gods. For him, assertions such as Orestes' that Apollo has again led him into a trap are mostly signs of the characters' limited knowledge and concomitant misapprehensions; the outcome is after all a happy one. Not that it is entirely unproblematic: 'the near failure of the escape... may be viewed as evidence that even with the favour of the gods (or *some* of the gods) human efforts are not assured of success' (ibid. 165).

open whether a rite of purification is carried out. On the further assumption that it is, is it successful?

The overriding impression is that it is, but tension remains. The larger picture is that the contrived ritual allows escape; as was seen above, purification, in comparison with Aeschylus, is given a vastly increased importance in the matricide's progression towards release. Tension enters by way of close-up. Despite its central position, it is in the end not Iphigenia's contrived rite alone which allows escape: Athena's intervention is required to ensure the Argive ship's *bon voyage* (see 1444–5).[45] It seems therefore that purification both is and is not decisive for Orestes' escape. In combination with the play's open-ended ending, analysed in the previous section, this tension exacerbates the notion of ambiguity surrounding Orestes' release.

The second scenario implies that *pollution and purification come to stand for the illusionary nature of Orestes' release*. Significantly, both pollution and purification in this play appear not as matters of fact but as 'illusionary', if in different senses. If it was noted above that the play intimates, obliquely, that Orestes is polluted, what is remarkable about *miasma* in this play is its decided vagueness. Despite the above-noted intimations of pollution, the play (strikingly similar in this respect to *Orestes*) nowhere states, positively and unambiguously, that Orestes' troubles are intrinsically associated with a ritual state of 'having contracted *miasma*'. The first half of the play remains entirely silent about the ritual status of Orestes. Until the deception-scene, there is only one instance where *Iphigenia* seems to suggest that Orestes is polluted. When Pylades offers to die in the place of Orestes, the latter rejects on the grounds that (693–4):

> σὺ δ' ὄλβιός τ' εἶ καθαρά τ', οὐ νοσοῦντ', ἔχεις
> μέλαθρ', ἐγὼ δὲ δυσσεβῆ καὶ δυστυχῆ.
>
> You are prospering; your house is clean and not afflicted with sickness; my house, however, is godless and ill-starred.

But the passage remains suggestively vague. The reference to Pylades' home as 'clean' may imply that Orestes' own home is 'polluted', but this is not made explicit. Instead, we find the unspecific adjectives 'sick' (νοσοῦντα), 'godless' (δυσσεβῆ) and 'ill-starred' (δυστυχῆ).[46]

---

[45] Papadopoulou (2005a) 120 observes that this also makes it uncertain whether or not Artemis really wants to be 'rescued', which in turn raises important questions about the nature of the goddess. Caldwell (1974) 28 points out that *IT* in this way reproduces *Eumenides*: 'His desperate plight and the final reprieve in the IT replicate the events of the *Eumenides*, and thus it is completely appropriate that Athena should once again appear to rescue him.'

[46] νόσος is at times associated with pollution, not least in S.'s *OT*. But this association is never direct. Note that νοσέω is used in a clearly metaphorical context (which also refers to an 'ailing home')

Arguably in dialogue with this surprising silence on the question of Orestes' ritual status stand Iphigenia's sceptical views on concepts of pollution, first stated as a theoretical position, then translated into action in the deception-scene. The theoretical position is formulated in what is perhaps the play's most famous passage, Iphigenia's criticism of an Artemisian cult which demands human sacrifice.[47] Implicitly, the heroine calls into question the validity of concepts of pollution (380–4):

> τὰ τῆς θεοῦ δὲ μέμφομαι σοφίσματα,
> ἥτις βροτῶν μὲν ἤν τις ἅψηται φόνου
> ἢ καὶ λοχείας ἢ νεκροῦ θίγῃ χεροῖν
> βωμῶν ἀπείργει, μυσαρὸν ὡς ἡγουμένη,
> αὐτὴ δὲ θυσίαις ἥδεται βροτοκτόνοις.

> As for the goddess' clever wisdom, I find fault with it: any mortal who has come into contact with bloodshed or has touched a woman in childbirth or a corpse she bars from her altars, considering him polluted. But she herself delights in human sacrifice.

In her view, pollution – including that of murder (381) – is not an objective reality, the 'natural' result of a certain course of action, but a matter of subjective perspective (μυσαρὸν ὡς ἡγουμένη; note especially the conjunction ὡς with its emphasis on subjective perception of reality): Iphigenia dissociates 'act' from ritual categorisation, 'reality' from 'language'.

This 'sophistic' view of pollution seems to inform *Iphigenia*'s particular engagement with the issue of Orestes' pollution in the second half, which further undercuts any certainty about Orestes' ritual status. Again, Orestes' pollution is nowhere stated as unambiguous fact. Instead, it becomes part of a trick, the infamous mock-purification, to deceive the barbarian king and escape. As part of this ruse, pollution becomes but a word which is 'used' and 'said' to deceive Thoas. As Iphigenia points out, 'I will make use of your troubles (note that she does not speak of pollution!) as clever devices!' (ταῖς σαῖς ἀνίαις χρήσομαι σοφίσμασιν, 1031).[48] In the ensuing passage in which Iphigenia expounds her plan (to convince Thoas that both victims and the cult statue need to be cleaned at far-off shores, the latter from the pollution exuding from the matricidal stranger), pollution appears,

---

elsewhere in *Iphigenia*: in reference to Odysseus' plight, Orestes remarks that 'all his affairs are diseased', πάντα τἀκείνου νοσεῖ (536).

[47] On this scene, see e.g. Wolff (1992) 311; Papadopoulou (2005a) 119; Wright (2005) 145; see also the comments by Cropp (2000) ad 380–91, with references to other occurrences of the idea that stories attributing unworthy qualities and actions to the gods ought to be rejected as human inventions.

[48] Zeitlin (2011) 452 notes a parallel between Iphigenia and Artemis: both wield σοφίσματα; but the one relates to human sacrifice, the other to mock-purification and aversion of human sacrifice.

emphatically, as a matter of words. Iphigenia will '*say* that it is not right to sacrifice [Orestes] to the goddess because of his pollution' (ὡς οὐ θέμις σε λέξομεν θύειν θεᾷ... οὐ καθαρόν ὄντα, 1035, 1037). Likewise, Pylades 'will be *said* to have the same pollution on his hands' (ταὐτὸν χεροῖν σοὶ λέξεται μίασμ' ἔχων, 1047). As a result, the later protestations, on the part of Iphigenia, of Orestes' pollution vis-à-vis Thoas in the actual deception-scene (1153–1233) also appear as mere fictions. This is significant. There is no scene in Greek tragedy in which references to pollution appear with comparable frequency: Orestes is not καθαρός (1163); he has contracted a μύσος (1168, 1229) and a μίασμα (1178); his blood-guilt must be washed off (ὡς φόνῳ φόνον | μυσαρὸν ἐκνίψω, 1223–4); and so forth. However, integrated into Iphigenia's strategy of deception they appear but as words, possibly but not necessarily corresponding to any reality.[49]

In this dynamic interplay between the play's reticence about Orestes' ritual status and the implication of the terminology of ritual pollution in a discourse wherein objective reality is pitted against subjective human perception which can be manipulated, the category of pollution is emptied entirely of meaning. At the same time, Orestes' pollution, like the Erinyes who appear but as visions, as μιμήματα ('imitations', 294) of reality rather than reality, seems peculiarly 'illusionary'.[50]

It is fitting, then, that ritual purification appears no less illusionary, on two levels. First, *Iphigenia* remains decidedly vague on the question whether purification ever takes place. The audience is told much about this purification; the combined explanations of Iphigenia vis-à-vis Orestes and Thoas and later those of the messenger add up to the most insistent invocation of ritual purification in all of Greek tragedy. But for all these words, by the end of the play the audience has not been told that the rite has really taken place. Iphigenia's purification is twice distanced from the audience: not only is it *not* seen by the audience; it is also *not* seen by the messenger who reports the Atreids' δόλια καθάρματα ('counterfeit purifications', 1316; for the messenger not seeing the rites, see 1329–44). This purification takes place (or not) off-stage in an off-stage scenario.

Second, purification is also 'illusionary' in the sense that it is an 'illusion' created for an audience (the Taurian guards) through imposture. Important

---

[49] This aspect is underestimated by Torrance (2013) 156; for her, Iphigenia's 'fictions will exploit the true *logos* of Orestes' pollution caused by matricide'.

[50] See Wolff (1992) 333–4 on the herdsman's report of Orestes' visions. He emphasises the metatheatrical implications of the scene; for such a reading, the reference to mimesis is obviously important. Some prefer to read μυκήματα at 294. Diggle's OCT keeps μιμήματα; Kyriakou (2006) ad loc. also defends this reading.

here is the level on which the ritual is 'really' carried out by Iphigenia: the vocal one. 'She raised a ritual cry', the messenger informs the audience, 'and started reciting barbarian chants, playing the magician, as though she were cleansing the blood-guilt' (ἀνωλόλυξε καὶ κατῇδε βάρβαρα | μέλη μαγεύουσ', ὡς φόνον νίζουσα δή, 1337–8).[51] Through the use of her voice, she makes an absence present. In this, the notion of imposture is underlined through the word ὡς: the reality of the performance of this purification is relegated to the realm of the 'as though'.[52] In this way, Orestes' purification appears as the illusion of an illusion. It is an illusion of the 'first order', that is, because even if carried out before witnesses, in view of the preceding plotting it would have retained the strong notion of a show put on for an audience.[53] It is an illusion of an illusion because, as we have just seen, even this first-order illusion is 'illusionary' in the sense that the performance itself remains intangible, a matter of words conjuring up reality.

The illusionary character of both pollution and purification strike a problematic note. Surely, one may be tempted to consider the ensuing ironies in a positive light: in a sense, if Orestes' pollution remains so frustratingly intangible and illusionary, an equally intangible and illusionary rite of purification may be seen to constitute the most adequate means of release. But this seems a superficial reading, which blots out the more worrying implications. The intangibility of pollution would appear to indicate that *miasma* no longer constitutes a category of any relevance for Orestes' suffering. His πόνοι seem of a different order, exceeding the concreteness of ritual categorisation (and approaching the inwardness of *Orestes*). Something of this sort is indeed expressed by this play's peculiar Erinyes, now visions rather than tangible beings. What Orestes is troubled by is madness (μανία, 83), something within the culprit and beyond immediate grasp. But because of this, it appears also less easily removable.[54]

The mock-purification, too, gives cause for concern. If Orestes' troubles exceed ritual categorisation, it is perhaps no coincidence that a rite of purification is not envisaged, by Apollo, as a solution to the problem. It is ironic, then, that purification acquires such a central place in the

---

[51] Charlatanism rather than 'illusionism' is diagnosed here by Kyriakou (2006) ad loc. See ibid. 425: 'The messenger...may use μαγεύουσα with hindsight to scornfully point out that Iphigenia's chanting was no more effective than the hocus-pocus of a charlatan.'

[52] Belfiore (2000) 36 registers this element of make-believe but relates it mainly to the avoidance of bloodshed in the purification (Iphigenia does not cleanse 'blood with blood' as she had stated vis-à-vis Thoas at 1223–4). She seems to hold that a purification takes place nonetheless, Iphigenia's purification being a part of a wider 'new purification' in which bloodshed is avoided (ibid. 36–7).

[53] On the metatheatrical dimension of these 'illusions', see my discussion below.

[54] In this way, the play intimates a view of Orestes' *miasma* which is spelt out in the later *Orestes*, where the matricide's main problem seems to be his guilty conscience (see *Or*. 396).

matricide's progression towards release. However, a purification which is but the illusion of an illusion appears less than straightforward as a means of release. Starting from the assumption that release at the end of the play is beyond question, scholars have tended to consider this mock-purification as symbolically successful.[55] But if Iphigenia's mock-purification seems successful in that it allows the most important first step towards escape to Greece and thus to final σωτηρία, its illusionary character, which the play parades so ostensibly, at the same time suggests that release from matricide can only be itself an illusion.[56]

Metatheatre, rewriting and the question of release

We must now widen the perspective and give due weight to the 'theatrical' character of Iphigenia's contrived purification by placing it within the play's omnipresent concern with 'tradition' and 'metatheatre'. I will suggest that the play encourages us to read the scenes circling around the deceptive purification as a commentary on the poetic manipulation of a poetic tradition. Such manipulation is foregrounded, in the deception-scene but elsewhere, too, in relation to the issue of salvation. In this way, the play emphasises that its solution for Orestes' salvation is but a matter of poetic manipulation and (re)writing. This reinforces the impression that Orestes' release is but an illusion, albeit now one dependent not on a contrived ritual but on the aesthetic product itself which is *Iphigenia among the Taurians*. The aim of this section is to place the mock-purification scenes within the wider concerns of the play; this entails that the following will take detours through material which has little to do with pollution and purification but much with the fictional character of Iphigenia's purification, a consideration of which will conclude this excursus.

Iphigenia is eminently 'theatrical': so much so that (if Oliver Taplin's interpretation is correct) a vase painter in the fourth century might reproduce, not any particular scene of the play, but 'the sense of theater and the

---

[55] Whitman (1974) 28 may be taken as representative of the majority opinion when he writes that the 'pretended ritual of purification... will in fact bring about true purification'. Even Wolff, in his admirably perceptive article, is convinced that we are to view the fake purification positively: id. (1992) 317, 'The invented, "false" ritual in fact achieves an actual, "true" final purification and release of Orestes as well as the recovery of Artemis' image.'

[56] I find myself in partial agreement with Tzanetou (1999/2000) 212. She notes that the 'successful resolution is... set against the backdrop of Orestes' banishment from Argos and his failed trial in Athens, a reminder that matricide itself can never be overridden. The symbolic language of ritual conveys at the same time the success of Orestes' return and the illusion of such an outcome.' She does not note the illusionistic nature of *this* ritual, however.

general excitement of Euripides' play'.⁵⁷ *Iphigenia* is also eminently aware of its place in a tradition.⁵⁸ This means that *Iphigenia* is not only replete with more or less overt references to Aeschylus' earlier treatment of the Atreid myths;⁵⁹ more poignantly, the play displays an acute awareness of the status of its myth as but another version of the myths surrounding the House of Atreus and repeatedly points to itself as theatre-play among other theatre-plays. In other words, *Iphigenia* exposes itself as an aesthetic product subordinated to a creative, order-imposing mastermind.

The first point, that through reference to mythical tradition *Iphigenia* parades an awareness of its *logos* as just another version of Atreid myth, must be prefaced with a *caveat*: evidently, reference to a tradition of mythical narratives need not necessarily imply an awareness of this type. Pindar frequently makes a point of explicitly 'improving' on, or disavowing, certain (dominant) versions of myths he considers improper or improbable.⁶⁰ Famously, too, Stesichorus, in his *Palinode*, emphatically declares the dominant version of the Helen myth to be false: 'the story is not true, you did not sail aboard well-oared ships, you did not come to the citadel of Troy' (οὐκ ἔστ' ἔτυμος λόγος οὗτος, | οὐδ' ἔβας ἐν νηυσὶν εὐσέλμοις | οὐδ' ἵκεο πέργαμα Τροίας).⁶¹ What is arguably at stake in these references to the mythical tradition is not the status of the presently narrated version as 'but another version' of the mythical material, but the authority of the presently narrated version as against other versions and, by extension, the poetic *sophia* of the *sophos* poet presently at work.⁶² One may therefore suspect that when a dramatic play draws attention to mythical narratives in dialogue with the one presently enacted on stage, it is the foregrounding, and display, of authority and poetic *sophia* that is at stake (or else, as Matthew Wright has it, 'a desultory throwing-round of witty ideas, aiming for a certain "piquant intellectual novelty"'),⁶³ and not any self-awareness about the particular status of its myth as just the latest version.

---

[57] Taplin (2007) 51 (vase depicted ibid. 155; a Campanian neck amphora attributed to the Ixion Painter, *c.* 330s BC, Saint Petersburg, State Hermitage Museum B2080).
[58] Goff (1999) 110: 'As a relatively late play, dealing with the hoary legends of the Atreid house, the *Iphigenia in Tauris* is necessarily charged with a weight of self-consciousness.'
[59] See Caldwell (1974) and Torrance (2013) 33–45 on *Iphigenia* and the *Oresteia*.
[60] The most famous example is *Ol.* 1.53, where the poet disavows the dominant version of the Pelops myth.
[61] *PMG* 192 (= Plato *Phaedrus* 243a–b).
[62] On such references to poetic tradition before the background of the agonistic nature of Greek poetry, see the illuminating account of Griffith (1990). Griffith distinguishes between three different types of poetic *sophia*: knowledge and factual accuracy; moral and educational integrity; technical skill (ibid. 188–9); in Pindar's 'myth corrections' it is mostly the second type of *sophia* which is at stake.
[63] Wright (2005) 156.

In *Iphigenia* (as well as *Helen*, Euripides' other surviving 'escape-tragedy' concerned with the elaboration of a 'counterfactual' version of a certain myth),[64] such self-awareness would nonetheless seem to be at stake (too). The issue has received ample attention in Matthew Wright's monograph on Euripides' escape-tragedies.[65] Wright introduces the term 'metamythology' to get hold of the particular sense in which *Iphigenia* and *Helen* are as much about myth as they are about the tribulations of their respective mythical characters. In his definition, metamythology is 'a type of discourse which arises when mythical characters... are made to talk about themselves and their own myths, or when myths are otherwise presented, in a deliberate and self-conscious manner; it is a type of discourse which seems to be designed to emphasize the fictionality of myth, as well as to signal that the myth is being discussed *qua* myth.'[66] Wright's careful examination of the plays shows that:

> Ostensibly, the counter-factual myths of *Helen* and *Iphigenia* are presented as the re-examined, true versions of these stories, in contrast to those false myths which were previously the basis of our 'knowledge'. But the manner of presentation makes it progressively more plain that there is no more justification for believing the new than the old version, and that there is, ultimately, no way at all of deciding which myths are true and which false. That is, all myths are nothing more than substitutable fictions.[67]

I do not wish to retrace Wright's entire argument nor the detailed evidence he adduces. Two points may be raised, however. As Wright observes, *Iphigenia* and *Helen* stand out in that characters continually refer to their own life-stories as well as contemporary events 'in such a way as to suggest that these were already well known',[68] with a frequency and insistence not found outside these escape-tragedies. Second, family affairs, the details of these characters' own myths, are treated in a 'strangely disinterested way':[69] for instance, Iphigenia responds to Orestes' question whether she knows about the quarrel between Atreus and Thyestes that she has 'heard about it' (813). Any one of the passages discussed by Wright may well be taken as a reference to tradition as part of a strategy to showcase poetic *sophia* and establish the authority of the present account. Cumulatively, however, they add up to a sense that 'myths stand out with unusual clarity and emphasis' and a tone which I think Wright is correct in describing as one of 'complete artificiality'.[70]

---

[64] 'Counterfactual': Iphigenia did *not* die; Helen did *not* go to Troy. I borrow the term 'counterfactual' from Wright (2005) e.g. 135.
[65] Ibid. 133–57.   [66] Ibid. 135.   [67] Ibid. 156.   [68] Ibid. 136.   [69] Ibid. 144.
[70] Both quotations: ibid. 154.

This tone of artificiality is best discernible in the curious scene in which Iphigenia interrogates Orestes about the return from Troy of the Iliadic heroes (517–75) and in which references to mythical tradition abound to a remarkable extent. The heroine, in her opening remark, does not simply ask whether Orestes knows about Troy; rather, she inquires about Troy, 'of which there is talk everywhere' (Τροίαν ἴσως οἶσθ', ἧς ἁπανταχοῦ λόγος, 517). The ensuing question-and-answer scene continues in this mould: Troy, 'they say' (φασίν, 519), no longer exists; the Achaeans have returned home, 'as is reported' (ὡς κηρύσσεται; 527); Calchas is dead, 'so the story goes in Mycenae' (ὄλωλεν, ὡς ἦν ἐν Μυκηναίοις λόγος, 532); Odysseus has not yet returned home 'as the story goes', ὡς λόγος (534). It is only in the case of the story closest to home that what Iphigenia knows from hearsay needs updating: 'what of the general', she asks, 'who, *they say*, fares well?' (τί δ' ὁ στρατηγός, ὃν λέγουσ' εὐδαιμονεῖν; 543). *Iphigenia* itself is another of these *logoi*. Two points stand out. First, the play moves from these *logoi* to *logoi* with an immediate bearing on the *logos* presently enacted onstage, the troubles of the House of Atreus (543–75), so that the present action is made dependent upon, and thus inserted into, this *traditio* of mythical stories. Second, the heroine actually refers to the 'reality' which the present play is based on in terms of storytelling: 'Now what?', she asks, 'What's the story about the other daughter, the one who was slaughtered?' (τί δέ; σφαγείσης θυγατρὸς ἔστι τις λόγος; 563). Arguably, the cumulative effect of these references to mythical material as disseminated through *logoi* is a distancing of the 'reality' behind these *logoi* and a concomitant foregrounding of these *logoi* as *logoi*. That such *logoi*, including the one about Iphigenia, smack of fiction is unavoidable.

The play's awareness of itself as part of a mythical tradition, its metamythological dimension, goes hand in hand with a decided interest in itself as part of a poetic and, more specifically, theatrical tradition. This should not come as a surprise: after all, it is not least through concrete poetic traditions, including theatrical ones, that mythical narratives are disseminated.[71]

---

[71] Boundaries between 'metamythological' and 'metapoetic'/'metatheatrical' are therefore fluent. Within the frame of poetry/theatre, any 'metamythological' point has by necessity implications for that frame. If a play points to (its) myth as fiction, it necessarily exposes itself as fiction, too. Wright's term 'metamythology' is extremely useful in that it helps to differentiate nuances. Certain passages in *Iphigenia*, for instance, are arguably primarily concerned with the status of myth as crafted fiction and the art of myth-making: these are 'metamythological'; the inevitable implications of these passages about the crafted nature of the frame within which such myth is presented (i.e. the play) may be seen as secondary.

To detect allusions to a general poetic tradition, therefore, we do not need to look far beyond the material presented above. Consider, for instance, Iphigenia's remark about Troy at 517 ('of which there is talk everywhere'). For the audience, too, this talk is everywhere. Certainly, this may be taken as an unspecific reference to the ubiquitous presence of mythical lore in the classical city;[72] but it may also be taken to imply something more specific, in that such talk is a matter not least of, say, rhapsodic performances of Homeric epic or theatre plays, where Trojan themes are very much *en vogue* (this is true, in particular, for Euripides' own oeuvre).

Metapoetic in much the same (unspecific) way is Pylades' reaction, some 150 lines later, to Orestes' expression of surprise at the priestess' detailed knowledge of Greek (and not least Argive) 'history': 'everybody', he observes, 'knows about the afflictions of the royal household, if they have contact with others' (τὰ γάρ τοι βασιλέων παθήματα | ἴσασι πάντες ὧν ἐπιστροφή τις ᾖ, 670–1). Athenians, too, provided they 'have contact with others', know about the afflictions of the Atreid household. Again, this may be understood as an unspecific hint, not necessarily concerned with poetic traditions; but it may also be taken to imply that Athenians, provided they participate in the life of the *polis*, acquire such knowledge precisely through epic and lyric traditions (Stesichorus springs to mind) as well as through attendance of the theatre, where, not long before, Aeschylus' *Oresteia* had perhaps received the unique honour of reperformance.[73]

One passage in *Iphigenia*, however, seems after all to imply a reference to the play as part of a tradition specifically of theatrical performances. In reaction to Iphigenia's inquiries about his fit of madness on Taurian shores, witnessed earlier by local herdsmen, Orestes observes that 'it wasn't the first time that people have seen me suffer' (ὤφθημεν οὐ νῦν πρῶτον ὄντες ἄθλιοι, 933). The fact that in the late fifth century seeing a tragedy concerned with the hoary legends of the House of Atreus is necessarily a matter of *déjà vu* could hardly be given more literal expression. Since, in addition, Orestes' words are placed just before his account of the trial in Athens, this rewriting of Aeschylus with a difference, one would be hard pressed indeed to find another line in the corpus of (Greek) tragedy which formulates similarly explicitly, and succinctly, the status of the present enactment as theatrical performance in a history of theatrical performances.

---

[72] Plato, for instance, indicates that nurses and mothers are wont to tell their children mythical stories (*Republic* 377c). One imagines that Trojan tales were among the children's favourites.
[73] See Σ Ar. *Ach.* 10 (= Csapo and Slater (1995) nr. I.17b) with the further notes by Olson (2002) ad *Ach.* 10 and the *caveat* by Biles (2006–7). The point that lines 670–1 may be taken to imply a specifically metatheatrical quality is also made by Wright (2005) 140.

Significantly, this awareness of itself as a piece of 'literature' and, by implication, an aesthetic product tied to the authority of the poet, which *Iphigenia* parades so ostensibly, is intertwined closely with the play's concern with salvation. As we shall see, the scenes most ostensibly interested in 'meta'-aspects, and in particular in scripted and pre-composed performance, those involving Iphigenia's curious letter and the deception-scene, revolve around the question of σωτηρία. Both eventually intimate that for Orestes such σωτηρία is a matter of a theatrical performance tied to a script. In this, the scenes involving Iphigenia's tablet (δέλτος), with their combined interest in scripts, scripted performance and release, seem to anticipate, and prepare for, the deception-scenes, which, we shall see, take further (for instance in the direction of explicitly metatheatrical concerns) the issues raised here.[74]

The scenes involving Iphigenia's δέλτος evolve in two stages. First, the existence of the letter is announced and it is suggested that it should be brought to Argos (esp. 578–96, 636–42); in the second scene, the letter has been fetched and recognition eventually ensues (727–94ff.; this scene (let's conveniently say: for its theatrical excitement) seems to have been particularly popular with vase painters and their customers).[75] The letter is doubly concerned with σωτηρία, therefore: the initial plan entails Pylades' σωτηρία as bearer of the letter sent off to Argos; its actual effect is recognition and thus the first step towards the σωτηρία of the matricide, along with Iphigenia and Pylades.

The conditions of this release appear as 'scripted', in intriguing ways. Pylades' σωτηρία as messenger to Argos is strikingly presented as a matter of writing. When Iphigenia, in the first scene, expounds her idea that one of the prisoners be released in order to deliver the letter, she points out the profitability of a deal in which σωτηρία is acquired 'thanks to light writing' (κούφων ἕκατι γραμμάτων σωτηρίαν, 594). It is tempting, already at this point, to understand Iphigenia's reference to scripts upon which release depends as a comment on the dependence of release on literary scripts; and therefore eventually as a comment on the play itself, in which release, too, depends on a pre-composed script.

The second scene would seem retroactively to validate such an interpretation. For what is put on stage in this second scene is the interplay

---

[74] The scenes involving the letter have received surprisingly little attention. Goff (1999) 119–20 offers a few valuable insights. Wolff (1992) 332 lists the letter as one of the play's metatheatrical passages and notes (ibid. 332–3) that the 'audience will be drawn into... the process of interpretation, or at least they must notice the conditions and choices of interpretation.'

[75] Taplin (2007) 150–4 (nos. 47–9).

between a prefabricated script and the oral delivery of this script: poetic recitation. The nature of the letter as a prefabricated piece of writing is strongly emphasised. In the first scene, Iphigenia had insisted that the letter had been 'written' (by a captive: ἔγραψεν αἰχμάλωτος, 585). Significantly, in the second scene, this nature of the letter as a piece of writing is set in opposition to speech: upon Pylades' observation, at 755–8, that the tablet, because it is a material object, may get lost at sea and that therefore successful delivery to Argos cannot be guaranteed, Iphigenia suggests she will 'say in *speech* what is contained and *written* in the folds of the tablet' (τἀνόντα κἀγγεγραμμέν' ἐν δέλτου πτυχαῖς | λόγῳ φράσω, 760–1). This dichotomy between pre-composed script and oral delivery seems startlingly reminiscent of (non-oral) poetic traditions; and as Iphigenia proceeds to recite (from memory) what is written down, moving from *grammata* to *logoi*, tablet (presumably) in hand, the sense that the heroine here takes on the role of the performer of a poetic script becomes difficult to ignore. I do not wish to press the point. For present purposes, suffice it to add that this scripted performance leads to salvation (σωτηρία) and may therefore be understood as the enactment of Iphigenia's earlier remark that such salvation will ensue 'thanks to writing'.

Importantly, even if the scene is not taken as necessarily *theatrical* (not in the strict sense, at any rate; Iphigenia seems reminiscent of a rhapsode rather than of an actor), it nonetheless has striking self-referential, metatheatrical implications: after all, *Iphigenia*, too, is a scripted performance in which salvation ensues 'thanks to writing'. It would seem that attention is drawn to the scripted nature of the play's progression towards salvation. In this curious interplay between a plot which unfolds in the direction of σωτηρία and a meta-plot in which such a denouement is exposed as scripted, the scene implies that Orestes (along, in this case, with Iphigenia and Pylades) can be saved and thus 'released' only because the playwright has so scripted his plot.

This is the backdrop against which the scenes circling around the mock-purification must be placed. Anything but 'unrelated' to the play's earlier parts, as D. J. Conacher regretted some forty years ago,[76] it is at this crucial point that *Iphigenia*'s ever-present concern with fictionality and theatre is drawn into a final, culminating enactment of salvation as *theatrical* act bound to fiction and the authority of the playwright. I noted above that

---

[76] Conacher (1967) 310 notes that, whereas in *Helen* the second half, with its mock funeral designed to delude Theoclymenus as Helen's ghost had deluded Menelaus, repeats the theme of 'reality vs. illusion', the escape-ruse in *IT* is unrelated to what has happened before and, in this way, illustrative of the play's essentially episodic character (for the latter point of criticism, see ibid. 305).

the mock-purification, because it allows progression towards release and salvation, comes to stand for 'release'; but because this purification is fake and perhaps not even enacted, it comes to stand for a release which is open-ended, problematic, and in a sense 'fake' and 'illusionary'. What I wish to draw attention to now is that the scenes revolving around Iphigenia's mock-purification, more pointedly than all preceding scenes, put theatre itself onstage and suggest the dependence of the matricide's progression towards release on the rewriting by the poet of the mythical tradition.

It has been noted by previous scholars, among them in particular Wolff and Tzanetou, that Iphigenia's mock-purification is, in a vague sense, 'theatrical': make-believe, illusionary, and self-consciously symbolic.[77] But what is more emphatically 'theatrical' than the rite itself, and the 'reality' (of a purified Orestes) which it purports to create, is the *talk* about the purification prior to its (supposed) enactment and, in particular, the scene in which Iphigenia, in *stichomythia* with Orestes, develops the idea of a fake purification as a means of escape (1029–51). In this dialogue, Iphigenia appears as a poet-figure;[78] what is presented is a plot *in statu nascendi*. The relevant passage begins with Iphigenia's excited '*Eureka*!', 'It seems I may have a novel discovery' (ἔχειν δοκῶ μοι καινὸν ἐξεύρημά τι, 1029), and the subsequent specification that she 'will make use of (Orestes') troubles as clever devices' (ταῖς σαῖς ἀνίαις χρήσομαι σοφίσμασιν, 1031). In particular, the play's insistence on the verb λέγω, already noted above, seems significant. 'I will say (φήσω, 1033) you come from Argos as a matricide'; 'we will say (λέξομεν, 1035) it is not right to sacrifice you to the gods because you are not pure'; 'I will say (ἐρῶ, 1041) that the statue needs to be washed, too, because you touched it'; 'I will say (lit. 'it will be said', λέξεται, 1047) that he (Pylades) has the same *miasma* on his hand as you'. Like the playwright, Iphigenia produces lines to be spoken, a script, a verbal choreography, which 'uses' mythical tradition (ἀνίαις χρήσομαι σοφίσμασιν).

The subsequent implementation of this choreography vis-à-vis the barbarian king further underlines that what is put on stage here is theatre itself. In the light of the plotting-scene, that is, Iphigenia's deception of Thoas appears emphatically as a 'play within the play', in which the heroine performs a scripted role. Through this juxtaposition of 'composition' and

---

[77] Wolff (1992) 317–18: 'This play, within the drama, of deceptive contrivance and "real" effect, involved with ritual material, runs parallel to the way the drama itself may be seen to work: as a fictional construction (performed on the ritual occasion of the festival of Dionysus) that produces meanings that are symbolically or psychologically "true", that engage in some sense with the audience's sense of reality'; Tzanetou (1999/2000) 211.

[78] This is noted also by Torrance (2013) 152–7.

'performance', the theatrical character of both is accentuated. Iphigenia appears as both actress and, more importantly for my present purposes, playwright.

This metatheatrical streak has important implications. First, *Iphigenia* in this way draws attention to its own status as theatre-play, as a mimesis of reality subordinated to the authority of the playwright, and in such a way as to suggest that release is scripted, too. In that the heroine appears so emphatically as 'composer', as the producer of a plot, and, subsequently, as an 'actress' who creates an illusion for Thoas by performing her pre-composed script, the play lays open its own mechanisms. It focuses attention on its own nature as a pre-composed script performed by actors to create an illusion for the audience. Because this self-referential dimension is brought to the attention of the audience precisely at the point when Orestes' release is most emphatically in question (note that the plotting-scene is introduced by Orestes' call for help at 979–80, ἥνπερ ἡμῖν ὥρισεν σωτηρίαν | σύμπραξον, 'help me achieve the salvation he [Apollo] set out for me!', and Iphigenia's enthusiastic assent at 994–5, σφαγῆς τε γὰρ σῆς χεῖρ᾽ ἀπαλλάξαιμεν ἄν | σώσαιμί τ᾽ οἴκους, 'I would keep my hand from shedding your blood in sacrifice and also save our house'),[79] the play intimates that Orestes' release itself, too, is but a matter of 'theatre', of poetic recomposition, that is, of a mythical tradition by the playwright.

But there is a second important nuance which, in conclusion to the present chapter, brings us back to the role of pollution and purification in the play: the plotting-scene not only intimates the dependence of the plot on the poet; more precisely, it suggests that the escape-plot is the product of the manipulation, by the creative poet, of the existing tradition of Orestes' pollution and purification. Attention is drawn to (this) tradition at the outset of the scene, when Iphigenia proposes to 'make use of Orestes' troubles as clever devices' (1031). In view of the play's heightened awareness of its place in a tradition and specifically Orestes' earlier remark that people have seen him suffer before (ὤφθημεν οὐ νῦν πρῶτον ὄντες ἄθλιοι, 933), Iphigenia's striking line readily betrays a metatheatrical concern. The 'troubles' (ἀνίαι) the heroine speaks of are precisely those which people have not seen for the first time: in the form of gruesome Erinyes, for instance, they were spectacularly staged in Aeschylus' *Eumenides*. Iphigenia's formulation χρήσομαι σοφίσμασιν may therefore be taken to point to the manipulation, by the 'clever' poet, of this existing tradition in the act of writing a

---

[79] Wolff (1992) 314 rightly notes the suggestive ambiguity of 994. While Iphigenia will arguably have in mind her near-fratricide ('the sacrificial slaughter of you'), Orestes' matricide ('your sacrificial slaughter' of Clytemnestra) and release from it loom large as a secondary level of meaning.

'cleverly' novel play on the matricide Orestes' fate and final release.[80] The tradition of Orestes' pollution has been recycled; the process has resulted in a plot which has incorporated, in a 'cleverly' novel way, the Aeschylean tradition of Orestes' purification. (From this perspective, it makes eminent sense that Iphigenia's 'script' ultimately fails and that Athena's intervention is required to ensure escape.[81] Mythical tradition, in the form of the Aeschylean version of Orestes' send-off into freedom, delimits the scope of poetic innovation: Iphigenia's σοφίσματα as a 'poet' go only so far, just like Euripides', who writes within the parameters set by Aeschylus; eventually, the Aeschylean plot, wherein Athena saves the day, takes over.)

We are in a position, finally, to situate more precisely the role of pollution and purification in Euripides' play. As was noted above, the ritual terminology of pollution and purification appears almost exclusively in the scenes revolving around Orestes' mock-purification. There is not a single (explicit) reference to ritual purity and/or purification (καθαρμός) outside these scenes and only one to pollution; but in this one instance, the reference is to 'certain people' whom Artemis excludes from worship 'deeming them impure' (μυσαρός, 383), not to Orestes' ritual status. This means that pollution and purification, in reference to Orestes, appear exclusively in a context in which what is at stake is their transfer from an existing tradition of Orestes' ἀπαλλαγὴ πόνων to a novel plot. Not least when it comes to Greek theatre, such reassembling of tradition to produce a new play is of course natural. But it is significant that the play so emphatically draws attention to the mechanics of this poetic process. What is intimated in this way is that pollution and purification are not present, at this point, because the clarification of his ritual status is somehow vital for Orestes' final release or because their incorporation allows Euripides to have Orestes 'symbolically' purified; rather, pollution and purification are present because the poet renegotiates 'release' within, and in terms of, a tradition in which pollution and purification occupy a conspicuous place and because he does so by rewriting, and thus also renegotiating, that tradition.

In the framework of a play which writes the matricide Orestes out of the secure haven of Aeschylean release and into renewed 'troubles' and in this way foregrounds the question of release, the resulting notion of emptiness

---

[80] Just how 'novel' *Iphigenia*'s plot is has been a matter of debate. Wright (2005) 113–15 points out that Euripides' innovation lay in the fusion of precise details and the unusual combination of (not necessarily newly invented) elements. See also ibid. 56–133.

[81] Torrance (2013) 152–7 places great weight on Iphigenia's failure as a creator of fictions. She sees that failure in the context of her being a skilled weaver, but unable to write and in fact completely illiterate.

is not without significance. One is tempted to conclude that *Iphigenia*'s vision of release, because scripted in terms of a tradition in which release is achieved, is but a matter of rewriting that tradition; that there is nothing intrinsically 'natural' or 'logical' or 'cogent' about Orestes' release; that it is but the result of a clever engagement, conducted by the latter-born poet, with the Aeschylean paradigm.

CHAPTER 4

Pollution, purity and civic identity

In this final chapter, we turn to an aspect which has been in the background of some of the preceding discussions, but requires explicit and extended comment: the associations of the ritual nexus of pollution and purification with civic identity.

If one takes but a cursory look at tragedy, pollution quickly, and unsurprisingly, turns out to be connected with scenarios that would seem to betray a certain anti-civic dimension and, to adopt the parlance of tragedy itself, is often bound up with acts which, literally and/or metaphorically, propel the individual 'beyond the *dēmos*' (ἔκδημος, see Eur. *Hipp*. 37). One need only think of Orestes' worrisome matricide and the unsettling flight of the polluted murderer from the civic community which ensues. The disturbing pollutions haunting the Labdacid family, too, are a case in point: in the discussion of *Antigone* we have already seen that the anti-civic dimension for instance of the pollution resulting from the two enemy brothers' mutual fratricide is given emphasis; in Euripides' *Phoenissae*, the incestuous union of Oedipus and Jocasta results in children which are not only 'their mother's birth-pang, their father's pollution' (παῖδες ματρὶ λόχευμα μίασμα πατρός, 816), but also unlawful, μὴ νόμιμοι (815), sired against the civic community's norms and conventions.

Purification and the maintenance of purity, by contrast, often seem to be eminently civic pursuits. In the *Oresteia*, purification is complex; but despite its inadequacies it is thought of as a first step towards ending matricidal Orestes' state of being ἔκδημος.[1] In *Oedipus tyrannus*, purification is assumed to restore order to a community suffering from 'woes beyond [the ordering powers of] measure' (ἀνάριθμα ... πήματα, *OT* 168–9). More to the point, purifications, albeit metaphorical rather than ritual, appear as civilising acts. The culture hero Heracles is particularly closely associated with such purifications: at the end of Sophocles' *Trachiniae*, pain-stricken

---

[1] See e.g. A. *Eum*. 236–9, 445–52 and *passim*.

Pollution, purity and civic identity

Heracles reproaches those around him for not assisting him in ending his suffering, seeing as he had 'purified for [the Greeks] much that roams at sea and all that roams the thickets' (1012):

πολλὰ μὲν ἐν πόντῳ, κατά τε δρία πάντα καθαίρων.[2]

Not much later, he returns to the issue. None of the many monsters and barbarians he faced in the past, he asserts, nor Hellas, nor any land in which he carried out his purifying activities (οὔθ' ὅσην ἐγὼ | γαῖαν καθαίρων ἱκόμην, 1060–1) has ever inflicted comparable suffering on him. The Heracles of Euripides' play of the same name likewise appears as such a 'purifier': as his family is threatened by Lycus, Amphitryon, reminiscent of Heracles in Sophocles' play, deplores the lack of assistance given to the hero's family, 'in requital for [Heracles'] purifications of sea and land' (ποντίων καθαρμάτων | χέρσου τ' ἀμοιβάς, 225–6).[3] In that they render the land inhabitable for human communities, ridding it of monsters and other threats, these Heraclean purifications are intimately bound up with the very foundations of culture and, by extension, the civic community. It is consistent with these observations that in Euripides' *Ion* the maintenance of ritual purity is cast as the condition for entering the civic community of Athens. As Ion is about to drag Creusa away to her appointed death, the Delphic Pythia intervenes and enjoins him to forego pollution instead to 'go pure to Athens, with good omens' (καθαρὸς Ἀθήνας ἔλθ' ὑπ' οἰωνῶν καλῶν, 1333).

That pollution and purity would seem to be readily associated with civic identity may not come as a surprise. After all, if we consult one of the most widely read handbooks on Greek religion on matters of purification, we encounter what is at base the same idea right at the beginning of the relevant discussion. According to Walter Burkert, '[p]urification is a social process. To belong to a group is to conform to its standard of purity; the reprobate, the outsider, and the rebel are unclean.'[4]

But if the rapprochement of the ritual nexus of pollution and purity with civic identity seems unsurprising, it is surprising that its implications for our reading of tragedy have thus far largely been neglected. For a

---

[2] Heracles is cast here as another Odysseus as the line's first half alludes to the *Odyssey*'s πολλὰ δ' ὅ γ' ἐν πόντῳ πάθεν ἄλγεα ὃν κατὰ θυμόν (*Od.* 1.4).

[3] For a reading of Euripides' play taking into account Heracles' associations with purification and his incurrence of pollution in the process of carrying out purificatory sacrifices, see Papadopoulou (2005b) 10–34. It is striking that it is this 'radical purifier' who incurs the most 'monstrous' pollution, so that he may be seen to turn into something as (or even more?) monstrous than the monsters from which he freed ('purified') land and sea.

[4] Burkert (1985a) 76.

considerable time now, after all, the nature of tragedy as a civic discourse negotiating the identity of the self (above all as full member of the – Greek; Athenian – civic community) vis-à-vis various others (non-Greeks; non-Athenians; but also socio-culturally others, i.e. marginal figures that are not (yet) full members of the civic community but are instead in one way or another 'ἔκδημοι') has been a hot topic.[5] And indeed, in a number of tragedies in which such negotiation of civic identity seems to be an obvious concern, concepts of pollution and purity occupy a strikingly prominent place. I refer above all to certain tragedies which revolve around figures which embody foreignness or marginality and which seek to, or are about to, enter a civic collective: Aeschylus' *Suppliants*, Sophocles' *Oedipus at Colonus* and Euripides' *Ion*.

In this chapter, I shall attempt to fill the gap. I shall trace how concepts of purity and pollution, not least in the form of pure and impure space, become vehicles in these plays for (re-)negotiations of civic identity.[6] Before turning to the plays themselves, however, I shall take another detour, and this time in particular through classical Athens. This will help us to set the present inquiry within a wider framework and gauge its significance within the context of the classical *polis*. It will also help us to acquire a better sense of the ways in which purity and pollution were bound up with civic identity. This, in turn, will contribute to a better understanding of the issues at stake in the tragic texts. These historical preliminaries will concentrate on two aspects in particular. First, I shall outline the specific

---

[5] Classic (if not uncontested) studies which are interested especially in negotiations of self and other in tragedy include Hall (1989) and Zeitlin (1990); see also Grethlein (2003) and Bernek (2005). See e.g. Mills (1997) and Tzanetou (2012) on tragedy's projection of the Athenian imperial self. The construction of identity along the coordinates of 'self' and 'other' has been a hot topic outside literary studies, too. See e.g. Cartledge (1993) for a general historical account; Cohen (2000) on Greek art. Explicitly or implicitly, these studies are often based on the assumption that the Greeks were fond of polarisation and binary oppositions; the classic study here is Lloyd (1966). On such polarisation, see now Osborne (2011) 19–21. For general reflections on the relation of Greek drama to 'civic ideology', see Goldhill (1990) and (2000). Goldhill's focus on tragedy as *democratic* discourse has elicited a number of responses: see e.g. Griffin (1998), Rhodes (2003); see also Carter (2004) and Burian (2011). For a recent reappraisal of the Athenian character of Greek tragedy (and its 'politics'), see the essays in Carter (2011); Osborne (2012).

[6] A word on my understanding of 'civic identity': one may understand the concept in a narrow legalistic sense, in reference to the free adult male with political capacities. By and large, my understanding is wider, denoting a broader sense of 'belonging to a community'. In the historical introduction we shall see that this may extend to a wide range of people, including women and at times even girls and metics (as when they participate in religious processions). In my analyses of the tragedies, it is clearly this sense of 'belonging to the community' which is used unless otherwise specified. We may note already that this makes for many ironies, especially in *Ion*: here the (marginal) youth is decidedly outside the community and therefore in need of a civic identity; but the representatives of the civic community are women and (in the form of the chorus) even female slaves. The definition of the 'citizen' was complex already in antiquity: Osborne (2011) 88–102.

importance of purity and purification in the definition of civic space and, by extension, the civic self. Second, I shall draw attention to the importance of the concept of ethnic purity in the contemporary discourse about (civic) identity.

Purity, space and civic identity

As has often been remarked, the social and the religious were in many respects inextricably intertwined in classical Athens. The point need not be elaborated at great length here, in view of many excellent discussions.[7] Two observations will suffice.

First, certain civic offices were articulated in religious terms. Aeschines informs us, for instance, that the archonship is 'crown-wearing'; it is in this way marked as sacred in character and therefore readily set in parallel to the sacred office of the priesthood (Aeschin. 1.19: ἄν τις Ἀθηναίων . . . ἑταιρήσῃ, μὴ ἐξέστω αὐτῷ τῶν ἐννέα ἀρχόντων γενέσθαι, ὅτι οἶμαι στεφανηφόρος ἡ ἀρχή, μηδ' ἱερωσύνην ἱερώσασθαι, '"if any Athenian . . . has prostituted his person, he shall not be permitted to become one of the nine archons", because, I believe, that office is crown-wearing, "nor to discharge the office of priest"', trans. adapted from C. D. Adams).

Second, as Demosthenes proposes, being part of the civic community amounted to 'sharing in religious rites and common privileges' (ἱερῶν καὶ κοινῶν μετέχειν, see Dem. 57.3).[8] Of ἱερά there were many in the classical city: according to Paul Cartledge, '[i]t would scarcely be an exaggeration to say that . . . festivals were the single most important feature of classical Greek religion in its public aspect.'[9] In Athens, indeed, 120 days of the year were devoted to festivals of some type.[10] Because these festivals constituted so prominent a part of the public life of the *polis*, it is certainly not far-fetched to claim that the specific make-up and character of these festivals significantly contributed to a given *polis*' identity. Something of the sort is arguably intimated by the chorus in Aristophanes' *Clouds* who refer to Athens not least in terms of its abundance of splendid festivals,

---

[7] The work of Jean-Pierre Vernant has been foundational in this regard: see e.g. id. (1974). But see also e.g. Connor (1988); Sourvinou-Inwood (1990); Blok (2007) and (2009).
[8] See also Dem. 39.35 (τῶν πατρῴων ἔχεις τὸ μέρος μετὰ τὴν τοῦ πατρὸς τελευτήν· ἱερῶν, ὁσίων μετέχεις· ἀπάγει σ' οὐδεὶς ἀπὸ τούτων). On the idea that 'the core business of the *polis*' was 'participation in cult and in human practices', see Blok (2009) 159–62 (the quote is from ibid. 160); see also ead. (2007) 317.
[9] Cartledge (1985) 98.
[10] Ibid. 99. On these festivals, and the problems involved in studying them, see Parker (2005) 155–77 and id. (2011) 171–223.

including the Dionysia with its melodious choruses and the deep-sounding flute-music.[11] *Mutatis mutandis*, participating in these festivals and sacrifices was one prominent way of performing one's identity as part of the civic community.

Xenophon (*Hellenica* 2.4.20) offers apt illustration of Demosthenes' proposition. After the battle of 403 BC between the proponents of Athenian democracy and the forces of the infamous Thirty, Cleocritus, 'herald of the initiated' (the reference is to the Eleusinian Mysteries) and according to Xenophon 'a man of very fine voice' (μάλ' εὔφωνος), appeals to the opponents' shared religious identity:

> Fellow citizens, why do you drive us out? Why do you want to kill us? We have never done you any harm, but have shared with you in the most august rites, in sacrifices and in the finest festivals; we have joined in dances with you... (μετεσχήκαμεν δὲ ὑμῖν καὶ ἱερῶν τῶν σεμνοτάτων καὶ θυσιῶν καὶ ἑορτῶν τῶν καλλίστων, καὶ συγχορευταί... γεγενήμεθα).

I begin with this well-known point on the interrelation of sacred and secular in classical Athens in order to suggest that in such an environment, in which the religious is an intrinsic part of the civic and in which civic identity is therefore also 'religious identity' (which is one reason why it is apt to take civic identity to extend not only to the free adult male but to other members of the community as well, who share in a 'sense of belonging'),[12] a ritual nexus that is concerned with inclusions and exclusions from the realm of the religious – from communication with the divine – easily acquires wider socio-political connotations.

The evidence from ancient Greece supports this suggestion. Consider purification-related activities first. In Aeschylus' *Agamemnon*, when Clytemnestra refers to Cassandra's newly won affiliation with the house of Atreus, she does so invoking the image of 'shared lustral water': 'Zeus', she comments, 'has appointed [Cassandra] to be a companion of the lustral water' (σ' ἔθηκε Ζεὺς ἀμηνίτως δόμοις | κοινωνὸν εἶναι χερνίβων,

---

[11] Ar. *Nu.* 308–13: εὐστέφανοί τε θεῶν θυσίαι θαλίαι τε | παντοδαπαῖσιν ὥραις, | ἦρί τ' ἐπερχομένῳ Βρομία χάρις | εὐκελάδων τε χορῶν ἐρεθίσματα | καὶ μοῦσα βαρύβρομος αὐλῶν. Important from this perspective is also Dem. 21.51–2, where the specific set-up of Athenian festivals turns out to be a matter of particular customs, πατρίοισι νόμοις ἰθύνεθ' ἑορτάς (21.52).

[12] On the concept of 'religious citizenship', see Borgers (2008), Blok (2007) and ead. (2009) 161–2; for recent approaches to the concept of citizenship, see Blok (2005), Osborne (2011) 85–123. Manville's chapter entitled 'Who was an Athenian citizen?' also still has much to commend it: a clear effort is made here to move away from purely legalistic conceptions of the citizen to include the performative aspects of citizenships which cannot be grasped through a narrow legalistic definition: Manville (1990) 3–34. On the terminology of citizenship in tragedy (esp. *astos* and *politēs*), see Brock (2010).

Ag. 1036–7). In this passage, it is only the group of the *oikos* that is referred to in such terms. In Aristophanes' *Lysistrata*, however, we encounter the same concept again; this time it refers to a shared Hellenic identity. Lysistrata, addressing the war-mongering Athenians and Spartans, reproaches them for continued warfare and bloodshed: in her view, such behaviour is unseemly, seeing as in Olympia, Pylae and Pytho Athenians and Spartans sprinkle water 'from one lustral basin on the altars as though of common descent' (μιᾶς ἐκ χέρνιβος | βωμοὺς περιρραίνοντες ὥσπερ ξυγγενεῖς, 1129–30). 'Sharing lustral water' here seems to express a wider socio-political community.

Full-blown purifications carry similar socio-political significance. As in particular Walter Burkert has emphasised, purification rituals include elements connoting social incorporation: for instance, in fifth-century Selinous the restoration of the homicide's purity involves sacrifice at the public altar at (and as) its climax (hιαρεῖον τέλεον ἐπὶ τῶι βομῶι τῶι δαμασίοι θύσας καθαρὸ | ς ἔστο, B 10–11).[13] Therefore, purification not only restores the homicide's purity but implies at the same time 'an act of social recognition'[14] by the civic community.

Pollution, correspondingly, is markedly 'un-civic'. For one, it sits ill with civic space; concomitantly, its removal is a public and civic concern. We need only think of the law quoted by Demosthenes and which we encountered in the earlier discussion of *Antigone*, enjoining the demarch to take care that the deme be purified in the event of death in a public place (Dem. 43.57–8).

More to the point, our sources specify time and again that the homicides or other polluted individuals must be excluded from the social community, religious activity and public places (until purification is received). Demosthenes 20.158, for instance, records the official declaration against the homicide, the *prorrhēsis*, barring him from lustral water, mixing bowls, libations and the *agora*.[15] Though pollution is not explicitly mentioned, the parallel passage in Demosthenes 24.60, speaking of 'those whose hands are not clean' (οἱ μὴ καθαρὰς τὰς χεῖρας) who are not allowed to enter the *agora*, intimates that pollution is implied. Oedipus' edict of excommunication at *Oedipus tyrannus* harks back to the practice (at *OT* 238–42) underpinning its wider social implications: here, the culprit (whether murderer or non-forthcoming informant) is excluded from any kind of social contact,

---

[13] I quote from the edition of Jameson et al. (1993). [14] Burkert (2000) 213.
[15] [Draco laid down:] χέρνιβος εἴργεσθαι τὸν ἀνδροφόνον, σπονδῶν, κρατήρων, ἱερῶν, ἀγορᾶς.

even including conversation (μήτ' εἰσδέχεσθαι μήτε προσφωνεῖν τινα, *OT* 238). Because of certain grammatical difficulties in the *OT* passage, the connection with pollution may only be indirect.[16] Euripides' *Orestes*, however, also connects such complete social isolation with pollution: the Argive people have decreed that the matricides Electra and Orestes are not to be received nor to be spoken to (μήθ' ἡμᾶς στέγαις, | μὴ πυρὶ δέχεσθαι, μηδὲ προσφωνεῖν τινα | μητροκτονοῦντας, *Or.* 46–8); Helen's remark a few lines later that she 'is not polluted by [Electra's] speech' (because Apollo is to blame; προσφθέγμασιν γὰρ οὐ μιαίνομαι σέθεν | ἐς Φοῖβον ἀναφέρουσα τὴν ἁμαρτίαν, *Or.* 75–6) intimates that for the Argive people it is in part pollution that is at issue in this comprehensive social exclusion.[17]

If we want to go further and understand better the importance of notions of pollution and purity in the ancient *polis*' construction of civic identity, we need to return once more to the city's spaces. In the discussion of *Antigone*, space already played an important role, but primarily in the form of the association of civic space with fixity and stability. By contrast, at present the concern is with the arrangement of different spaces and the relations between them – with what may be called the 'civic topography' or '(ritual) geography' of the ancient *polis*.[18] Let us review a few basics first.

Providing a concrete backdrop for the insight afforded by *Antigone*, that '[c]ivilisation is a function of boundaries',[19] scholars have increasingly come to hold that the 'invention of the *polis* was the invention of its space'.[20] It has been recognised that the evolution of the *polis* and of a concomitant civic consciousness was less a matter of the refinement of abstract definitions of the 'citizen' (such as we find in Aristotle's *Politics*, for instance)[21] than of spatial demarcation (another reason why the concept of civic identity is best not restricted to the free adult male with political capacities).[22] The point

---

[16] On these problems, see Carawan (1999).
[17] But see my earlier remarks on *Orestes* in the opening part of the excursus on Eur.'s *IT* on the elusiveness of pollution in the play.
[18] Discussions of civic topography have been central to both historical and literary classical studies for a long time. See e.g. de Polignac (1984); Loraux (1993) 42–6; Alcock and Osborne (1994); von Reden (1998); Cole (2004); Vlassopoulos (2007); see Scott (2013) on 'space and society'. Some would perhaps argue that 'space' *tout court* has gone out of style and that the 'spatial turn' has been followed (and/or supplemented) by the 'performative turn'. For theoretical accounts of the concept of space and the human perception of (as well as 'human practices' in) space, see de Certeau (1980) 139–91 and Soja (1996).
[19] Carson (1999) 77.   [20] Croally (1994) 163.
[21] On Aristotle's concept of the citizen, see Osborne (2011) 88–90.
[22] Walls matter, then, even if for Nicias 'men are the city, not walls or ships without men' (ἄνδρες γὰρ πόλις, καὶ οὐ τείχη οὐδὲ νῆες ἀνδρῶν κεναί, Thuc. 7.77.7).

Purity, space and civic identity 179

emerges already in Homer.²³ Take for instance Nausithous' establishment of the Phaeacian *polis* on Scheria (*Od.* 6.9–10):

ἀμφὶ δὲ τεῖχος ἔλασσε πόλει καὶ ἐδείματο οἴκους
καὶ νηοὺς ποίησε θεῶν καὶ ἐδάσσατ' ἀρούρας.

He drew up a wall to encircle the city, he built houses,
made temples for the gods and divided up the fields.

The act of founding a city is equated here with the building of walls;²⁴ and further definition of the civic space thus marked is afforded through the building of houses and sanctuaries as well as the staking out of arable land. But archaeological evidence, too, bears witness to the rise of the *polis* as an increasingly nuanced definition in space, of the separation not only of *astu* and *chōra*, but also, for instance, of private and public, and of places for the living, the dead, and the gods.²⁵

What is established here, along with walls, houses, sanctuaries, *agorai* and cemeteries, is a rich symbolic topography, which provides the *polis* inhabitants with a system of classification and hierarchisation (and 'semiotic control').²⁶ The erection of walls, for example, creates insides and outsides, which in turn may become associated with 'civilisation' and 'wilderness', (civic) self and other.²⁷ Similarly, the demarcation of a central space reserved for political purposes creates a sense of centeredness, a hierarchical grid wherein authority, power and entitlement radiate outwards from the centre and wherein the a-political is associated with de-centeredness and the margins.²⁸

To see how this 'ideology' of space functions in the classical city, we need only think of the various initiatory rites and the geographical marginality of the sites where these rites were carried out, such as Brauron or Halae.²⁹ Spatial marginality in these cases may be taken to express socio-political marginality. At the same time, the location of the relevant sanctuaries on the 'threshold' of Attic territory allows the return from these marginal spaces to the centre to become the acting out in spatial terms of a socio-political reality: the crossing of the threshold into the heart, geographically

---

[23] On the 'rich symbolic topography' in Homer and the Homeric *polis* as marked-out space, see Hölkeskamp (2002).
[24] On the importance of walls in Homer, see Scully (1990) 41–53 (45–6 on the Scheria example).
[25] Hölscher (1999); Hölkeskamp (2002) esp. 330–1.
[26] Ober (2005) 191. See Croally (1994) 163–72; Hölkeskamp (2002).
[27] On the significance of walls, from Berlin to tragic Thebes, see Goldhill (2007).
[28] Croally (1994) 165: 'In Athens... the civic order itself was based on the spatial and hierarchical model of centre and margin... Athenian political space was centred space, where authority and power stood at the centre and radiated outwards to the margins.'
[29] On the *arkteia* at Brauron, see Sourvinou-Inwood (1988).

as well as socially, of the Athenian *polis*. This spatial acting out of a sociopolitical reality in turn bears eloquent witness to the interdependence of the organisation of space and civic identity.[30]

In this process of creating a civic map through the semantisation of space, purity and purification played an important role. Obviously, sacred space, whether permanent (sanctuaries) or temporary (procession routes), was 'pure space': sacred *temenē* were marked off by lustral basins so that the individual worshipper entering the precinct could ensure ritual purity as the precondition for entertaining proper relations with the divine.[31] For analogous reasons, procession routes were purified.[32] In this way, a protected (permanent or temporary) ritual space was created. This space, in turn, had an important socio-political dimension. For one, it made possible the maintenance of a reciprocal communication with the divine, which, in turn, ensured the community's well-being. In addition, in particular the procession routes had socio-political significance because it was on these that members of the community (free adult males, but also often women, children and at times even metics),[33] by participating in the festival processions, performed an important aspect of their identity as part of the civic collective. In this roundabout way, the purity of these routes may be seen to become obliquely associated with civic identity.[34]

Intriguingly, certain public spaces where the community flocked together, not primarily to conduct religious worship, but to participate in the social and political life of the *polis*, were closely associated with ritual purity, too. It is here that the connection between such purity, space and civic identity can be most readily grasped.

One such place was the *agora*, the heart of the civic life of the *polis*. All but identified with the *polis* in Pindar's Athenian dithyramb,[35] it was the centre of Athenian democracy, where the greater part of the city's commercial, juridical and political business was conducted.[36] Though primarily a social

---

[30] The interdependence of social and spatial marginality is also stressed e.g. in Vidal-Naquet's discussion of the *ephebeia*. See id. (1986a) 106–28.
[31] See Cole (1988) 162 and *passim*.
[32] See Cole (2004) 49–50. There is evidence for this in the case of the Piraeus processions for Dionysus and Zeus Sōter (*IG* II² 380; early fourth century BC). See also Delos where a piglet was used to purify the parade route of the Dionysia (*IG* XI.2 203A.38; 269 BC); see Cole (2004) 50.
[33] On festivals and their celebrants, see Parker (2005) 155–77; on the (citizen) girls participating in the Panathenaia procession as *kanēphoroi*, see ibid. 223–6; on the question of the exceptionality of the participation of metics in the Panathenaia procession, see ibid. 170.
[34] See Blok (2007) esp. 318–19 on the participation of metics in (some of) the city's processions and the resulting integration of these metics into the cultic and social make-up of the city.
[35] Pindar fr. 75 SM, 5 (where Pindar speaks of the πανδαίδαλόν τ' εὐκλέ' ἀγοράν).
[36] Martin (1951) 298–308.

and political space in view of the quotidian uses to which it was put, it too had religious connotations and was associated with purity. It was marked out not only by inscribed *horoi*, which, as Josiah Ober argued so eloquently, enjoined the visitor to the *agora* to behave in a certain way acceptable to the civic community,[37] but also, like sacred precincts, by lustral basins (περιρραντήρια). Within these, purity was required.[38] It is not entirely clear whether or not the area marked off by these περιρραντήρια included the entire *agora* or specific areas within the *agora*.[39] It seems nonetheless evident that these basins designated an area whose significance was, not narrowly religious, but more widely civic and social; and that the ritual space thus created was coextensive with a 'privileged space associated with the responsibilities of citizenship'.[40]

In line with my earlier remarks it should be emphasised, however, that the *agora* was not restricted to free adult males ('citizens' in the narrow sense) and that it was not the free adult male's political business only that was conducted in the *agora*. Therefore, the civic identity associated with purity here is not only that of the free adult male, but that of a wider group sharing a sense of belonging and participation in the life of the *polis*.[41]

Civic identity in the narrow sense of the identity of the free adult male participating in the political affairs of the *polis* is associated with purity in the case of the Pnyx. This is where the central organ of the Athenian democracy, the *ekklēsia*, met. The ancient evidence indicates that at the beginning of every meeting special officials, the so-called *peristiarchoi*,[42] sacrificed piglets and carried them around the meeting-place to 'purify the assembly' (τὴν μὲν ἐκκλησίαν καθαίρετε, Aeschin. 2.158).[43] According to

---

[37] Ober (2005).
[38] Pl. *Laws* 868a alludes to this purity requirement, speaking about murderers unlawfully entering the *agora* without prior purification: ὅστις δ' ἂν τῶν ἀποκτεινάντων πάντων μὴ πείθηται τῷ νόμῳ, ἀλλ' ἀκάθαρτος ὢν ἀγοράν τε καὶ ἆθλα καὶ τὰ ἄλλα ἱερὰ μιαίνῃ κτλ.
[39] The ancient evidence is inconclusive on this point. Aeschin. 1.21 (ἐντὸς τῶν τῆς ἀγορᾶς περιρραντηρίων) and 3.176 (ἔξω τῶν περιρραντηρίων τῆς ἀγορᾶς) allow for both interpretations. The scholiast on the latter passage is certain that the entire *agora* is thus marked (πρὸ τῆς εἰσόδου τῆς ἀγορᾶς ἦν περιρραντήρια παρ' ἑκάτερα, τοῦτ' ἔστι λουτῆρες ὕδωρ ἔχοντες).
[40] Cole (2004) 47.
[41] On the complexities of the *agora* as a space where civic identity is laid out, see Vlassopoulos (2007) 39–47.
[42] According to Σ Aeschin. 1.23 and the *Suda* (s.v. καθάρσιον) these officials were responsible also for purifying the city, the sanctuaries, public buildings and the theatre of Dionysus.
[43] For the fifth century, Aristophanes is our main source; see Ar. *Ach*. 44, *Ec*. 128–30. For the fourth century, see Aeschin. 1.23, Dem. 54.39. The Aeschines passage is particularly illuminating: ἐπειδὰν τὸ καθάρσιον περιενεχθῇ καὶ ὁ κῆρυξ τὰς πατρίους εὐχὰς εὔξηται, προχειροτονεῖν κελεύει τοὺς προέδρους περὶ ἱερῶν τῶν πατρίων καὶ κήρυξι καὶ πρεσβείαις καὶ ὁσίων, καὶ μετὰ ταῦτα ἐπερωτᾷ ὁ κῆρυξ· "τίς ἀγορεύειν βούλεται τῶν ὑπὲρ πεντήκοντα ἔτη γεγονότων;" ἐπειδὰν δὲ οὗτοι πάντες εἴπωσι, τότ' ἤδη κελεύει λέγειν τῶν ἄλλων Ἀθηναίων τὸν βουλόμενον, οἷς ἔξεστιν.

the scholiast on Aeschines, this was done to prevent demons and spirits from interfering with the *dianoia* of the participants so that deliberation and decision-making could be conducted in a 'pure way' (ἵνα καθαρῶς βουλεύσωνται).[44] But what seems important from the present perspective is that in this way a 'pure space' was created which was associated with heightened civic responsibility.

The language used by the ancient writers to refer to these purifications is particularly revealing. In each case, the spatial dimension is underlined. The lustral basins of the *agora* as well as the 'sacred enclosure' of the assembly create insides and outsides: Aeschines, in reference to the lustral basins of the *agora*, emphatically distinguishes between space within and outside these basins (ἐντὸς τῶν τῆς ἀγορᾶς περιρραντηρίων, 1.21; ἔξω τῶν περιρραντηρίων τῆς ἀγορᾶς, 3.176). In the case of the *ekklēsia*, the same author stresses the aspect of circambulation (τὸ καθάρσιον περιενεχθῇ, 1.23). In this way, an inside was created and participation in the activity carried out there could be referred to in terms of 'being inside the purification' (πάριθ', ὡς ἂν ἐντὸς ἦτε τοῦ καθάρματος, Ar. *Ach.* 44). Demosthenes' use of εἰσιέναι to refer to the convention of the assembly seems to point in the same direction:[45] to take part in the civic activity of decision-making was also a matter of being within 'pure space'.

The implications of this are striking. It may well be that the 'original' function of these purification requirements was to ensure the benevolence and protection of the gods for the various important transactions conducted in the *agora* as well as the assembly. The effect, however, of this spatial association of purification with the collective life of the *polis* was that purity became closely associated with certain aspects of civic identity in the form of participation in the socio-political life of the *agora* and the assumption of political responsibility in the assembly. Laying claim to these aspects of civic identity was a matter, not least, of 'being inside' these pure spaces.

Ethnic purity and identity

Before we turn to the tragic texts themselves, another aspect of purity important in the Athenian construction of the civic self needs to be

---

[44] Σ Aeschin. 1.23: ἐκέχρητο δὲ ὁ περιστίαρχος χοίρῳ καὶ τοῖς τοιούτοις ἀκαθάρτοις, διὰ τούτων τοὺς ἀκαθάρτους δαίμονας καὶ τὰ πνεύματα τὰ πολλάκις ἐνοχλοῦντα ταῖς διανοίαις τῶν ἀνθρώπων, ὥστε πολλάκις ἄλλως βουλεύεσθαι, ἕλκων πρὸς τὰ θύματα καὶ ὥσπερ ἀποχωρίζων τῆς ἐκκλησίας, ἵνα καθαρῶς βουλεύσωνται.

[45] Dem. 54.39: τούτους τά θ' Ἑκαταῖα [κατεσθίειν,] καὶ τοὺς ὄρχεις τοὺς ἐκ τῶν χοίρων, οἷς καθαίρουσιν ὅταν εἰσιέναι μέλλωσιν, συλλέγοντας ἑκάστοτε συνδειπνεῖν ἀλλήλοις, καὶ ῥᾷον ὀμνύναι καὶ ἐπιορκεῖν ἢ ὁτιοῦν.

Ethnic purity and identity

briefly laid out: that of 'ethnic purity'. We turn, that is, from the spatial to the discursive practice of the classical *polis*: the civic discourse about who was and who was not properly ('purely') Athenian. Certainly, the notion of 'ethnic purity' is no longer ritual. It is necessary, nonetheless, to explore briefly the non-ritual concept of 'pure identity' in order to appreciate fully the implications, from the perspective of 'civic identity', of notions of purity and pollution as they appear in the tragedies discussed below.

The idea of ethnic purity, which caused so much havoc in more recent times,[46] was not unknown to classical antiquity. Outside of Athens, there is some evidence to suggest that the doctrine of purity constituted an important element of the national identity of the Ionian tribes in Asia Minor. This is perhaps not surprising: Jacques Sémelin notes that the idea of ethnic purity gains particular prominence in times of social crisis.[47] But surely, geographical location must be of paramount importance: ethnic purity must become an attractive concept when a group's identity becomes contested in a multi-ethnic environment. This may have been the case with the Ionian tribes. It is not unlikely that the idea of ethnic purity served to increase the cultural and political cohesion of the Dodecapolis in the face of ethnic 'otherness'.[48] Be that as it may, in his Ionian *logos* Herodotus, in the last quarter of the fifth century (and before an Athenian audience), reports that the Ionians of the Dodecapolis considered themselves 'more Ionian than others' and 'of better descent'. Herodotus finds this quite absurd (1.146):

> But it is quite foolish to say that these Ionians are more Ionian than the others or of better descent (μᾶλλον οὗτοι ῎Ιωνές εἰσι τῶν ἄλλων Ἰώνων ἢ κάλλιόν τι γεγόνασι): not a small fraction of them are actually Abantians from Euboea, who do not even share in the name of Ionia; and Minyans from Orchomenus are mixed in (ἀναμεμείχαται) ... as well as many others. Even those who set out from the prytaneion in Athens and who consider themselves the noblest of the Ionians (νομίζοντες γενναιότατοι εἶναι Ἰώνων) took no women with them to their colony but married Carian girls, whose parents they had killed.

In the next passage, Herodotus returns to the issue. Only this time he refers to the idea no longer in the language of 'beauty' or 'nobility', but in terms of 'purity'. The historian holds that if these Ionians set such great store by their 'pure descent', then let them (1.147):

---

[46] For a comprehensive account of the political uses of the concept of ethnic purity in twentieth-century genocides, see Sémelin (2005); see also Mann (2005).
[47] Sémelin (2005) 46–7.   [48] Asheri et al. (2007) 176.

But since they cling to the name more than the other Ionians: well, let them be the pure-bred ones (ἔστωσαν δὴ καὶ οἱ καθαρῶς γεγονότες Ἴωνες).

It is not unlikely that the idea of ethnic purity will have struck familiar notes with an Athenian audience.[49] There is evidence, if admittedly only from the fourth century, which intimates that in Athens, too, identity could be conceived of in terms of ethnic purity.

To begin with, the idea of such purity is never far in Athens' myth of autochthony. This is true in particular for one specific version of the myth (among several versions recently identified by Josine Blok)[50] which gained wide currency at least in the fourth century (and perhaps before). It held that the Athenians were born *en masse* from the earth; that they had continually inhabited their Attic homeland; and that they were therefore 'unmixed'.[51] The idea of purity is clearly present in the idea of an absence of (ethnic) admixture, even if it is usually not expressed in the corresponding terminology in the strict sense.[52]

We encounter such terminology *sensu stricto* to denote ethnic purity outside the world of myth, in contexts where civic rights are at issue. The most relevant passage occurs in Ps.-Aristotle's *Constitution of the Athenians*. The author comments on the politically charged situation of the first half of the sixth century BC. Three factions stood against each other, one of them led by Pisistratus. This faction included men who were not 'of pure descent' (οἱ τῷ γένει μὴ καθαροί, 13.5) and therefore not entitled to taking a share in political rights (πολλῶν κοινωνούντων τῆς πολιτείας οὐ προσῆκον, 13.5). Another passage occurs in Demosthenes. In one of the cases of contested citizenship we find in Demosthenes, *Against Eubulides* (Dem. 57), the defendant sets out to prove that he rightfully 'shares in the *polis*' (57.1). At 57.17, he points out that he is born of two Athenian parents, in accordance with the requirements of the Periclean citizenship

---

[49] For a recent study of the interrelation of ethnic affiliation and citizen identity in Athens, see Lape (2010).
[50] Blok (2009) 150–4.
[51] Connor (1994) 37 points out that this vision is indeed a 'myth': in particular, it may be seen as 'a reflection of the anxiety of a people who knew that they were of very diverse origins and preferred not to look too closely at the descent lines of the fellow citizens'.
[52] See for instance Pl. *Menexenos* 245cd: οὕτω δή τοι τό γε τῆς πόλεως γενναῖον καὶ ἐλεύθερον βέβαιόν τε καὶ ὑγιές ἐστιν καὶ φύσει μισοβάρβαρον, διὰ τὸ εἰλικρινῶς εἶναι Ἕλληνας καὶ ἀμιγεῖς βαρβάρων. οὐ γὰρ Πέλοπες οὐδὲ Κάδμοι οὐδὲ Αἰγύπτιοί τε καὶ Δαναοὶ οὐδὲ ἄλλοι πολλοὶ φύσει μὲν βάρβαροι ὄντες, νόμῳ δὲ Ἕλληνες, συνοικοῦσιν ἡμῖν, ἀλλ' αὐτοὶ Ἕλληνες, οὐ μειξοβάρβαροι οἰκοῦμεν, ὅθεν καθαρὸν τὸ μῖσος ἐντέτηκε τῇ πόλει τῆς ἀλλοτρίας φύσεως; Isocrates *Panegyricus* 24–5: οὐδ' ἐκ πολλῶν ἐθνῶν μιγάδες συλλεγέντες, ἀλλ' οὕτω καλῶς καὶ γνησίως γεγόναμεν, ὥστ' ἐξ ἧσπερ ἔφυμεν, ταύτην ἔχοντες ἅπαντα τὸν χρόνον διατελοῦμεν.

law of 451/50 BC.⁵³ At 57.54, again, he sets forth that when he was still a child his father had sworn the customary oath and introduced him to the phratry-members, in the knowledge that his son (the defendant) was an Athenian citizen born of an Athenian mother who had been betrothed to him according to custom (ἀστὸν ἐξ ἀστῆς ἐγγυητῆς αὐτῷ γεγενημένον εἰδώς). The defendant concludes, therefore, that he is no foreigner (57.55):

> Am I, then, a foreigner (ξένος)? Where have I paid the metics' tax? Or who from amongst my family has ever paid it? Have I ever gone to the members of another deme and, because I was unable to convince them [to accept me], registered myself here? Have I done any of the things which those who are not pure citizens [literally, 'citizens in a pure way'] have been revealed to have done (ποῦ τί ποιήσας ὧν ὅσοι μὴ καθαρῶς ἦσαν πολῖται πεποιηκότες φαίνονται;)?⁵⁴

It is not entirely clear what the defendant means by the striking formulation according to which one can be 'a citizen in a pure way'. In particular, the adverbial form καθαρῶς is irritating. It would seem perhaps that the defendant refers to the entire process by which one becomes a citizen, starting from birth from two Athenian parents, but including also introduction to the phratry as well as deme-registration. I think we are nonetheless invited to think prominently along the lines of ethnic identity (and, in the event, connect this type of ethnic purity with the Periclean citizenship law).⁵⁵ After all, seeing as 'pure Athenian birth' is the defendant's central concern and the *sine qua non* of citizenship, being a citizen 'in a pure way' must prominently imply 'pure' Athenian birth.

To sum up, then, pollution and purity were important to civic identity in manifold ways. That the ritual nexus of pollution and purity was bound up with acts carrying important socio-political connotations is the most mundane aspect of this. More importantly, purity as an element of the city's ritual as well as imaginary ideological space emerged as a category through which inside and outside could be negotiated. The city's geography of pure

---

⁵³ See [Aristotle] Ath. Pol. 26.4: καὶ τρίτῳ μετὰ τοῦτον ἐπὶ Ἀντιδότου διὰ τὸ πλῆθος τῶν πολιτῶν Περικλέους εἰπόντος ἔγνωσαν μὴ μετέχειν τῆς πόλεως, ὃς ἂν μὴ ἐξ ἀμφοῖν ἀστοῖν ᾖ γεγονώς; Plutarch *Pericles* 37.3: νόμον ἔγραψε μόνους Ἀθηναίους εἶναι τοὺς ἐκ δυοῖν Ἀθηναίων γεγονότας. See also Ael. *VH* 13.24; *Suda* s.v. δημοποίητος. The 'why' of this citizenship law at this particular point in time is contested. For the most recent account of the potential reasons for the introduction of the law in the mid fifth-century, see Blok (2009).

⁵⁴ Trans. adapted from Norman W. DeWitt and Norman J. DeWitt, Loeb Classical Library (Cambridge, MA, 1949).

⁵⁵ It is, I think, not unlikely that this law, from which resulted a convergence of the ethnic with the civic of a type which (despite Ps.-Aristotle's intimations about worries concerning ethnic purity and civic rights in the sixth century) the city had arguably not seen before, invited talk about purity.

space emerged as a map of the civic self; and the citizen's 'pure' identity, expressed at times in language overlapping with ritual terminology, as the touchstone of an ideological ideal. With these remarks in mind, let us turn to the tragic dramas themselves.

Aeschylus' *Suppliants*

The *Suppliants* of Aeschylus, staged in all likelihood in the second half of the 460s BC (conceivably in 463),[56] is the earliest surviving example of what in modern scholarship has come to be called 'suppliant drama', to which, along with Aeschylus' *Eumenides* and the two Euripidean plays *Children of Heracles* and *Suppliants*, Sophocles' *Oedipus at Colonus* also belongs and to which some thought will be given subsequent to this analysis of *Suppliants*.[57]

It is no coincidence that it is two representatives of this 'sub-genre' of suppliant drama that have been chosen for discussion within the framework of the present study on pollution and purification from the specific viewpoint of civic identity and its presentation, definition and redefinition in Greek tragedy. It is in this 'sub-genre' that the issue of civic identity becomes most pressing and is addressed most explicitly.[58] Suppliant drama enacts the entry of the outsider and foreigner into the city; the encroachment of the other, in the form of the suppliant as well as the pursuer from whom the suppliant seeks protection, upon the territory of the self. In the process, the question of identity is thrown into high relief. In accordance with the basic psychological insight that the identity of the self is constituted only in the encounter with the non-self, that without the *tu* an awareness of the *ego* would not exist, it is in this encounter with the outsider and non-citizen that the citizen is made acutely aware of his own identity and called upon to redefine that identity in the face of the intruder.[59]

---

[56] On the dating of *Suppliants*, see Friis Johansen and Whittle (1980) vol. 1, 21–5; see also Papadopoulou (2011) 15–17.
[57] On suppliant drama in general, see Bernek (2005); on the Athenian suppliant plays, see Tzanetou (2012); on Aeschylus' *Suppliants*, see Gödde (2000a); on the Euripidean plays, see Mendelsohn (2002); see also Grethlein (2003).
[58] On suppliant drama and civic identity (and ideology), see in particular Grethlein (2003) (for whom suppliant dramas placed in Athens are largely affirmative of a positive image of Athens) and Bernek (2005); on Athenian *imperial* ideology and the portrayal of the relation between Athens and her allies in the Athenian suppliant plays, see Tzanetou (2011) and (2012).
[59] Bernek (2005) 13 considers suppliant dramas as paradigmatic cases of plays in which Athenian society reasserts its identity in opposition to other groups. The process of self-definition need not of course be entirely negative ('I am what the other is not'); the other may also bear traits of the self. This is true, for instance, of the opposition in Greek tragedy between Athens and Thebes; since

As holds true in particular, but not exclusively, for Aeschylus' *Suppliants*, purity and pollution play an important role in the ensuing redefinitions, and not least through their 'spatial mappings'.[60]

Suppliants is characterised by a twofold dynamic. The suppliants in this play are the daughters of Danaus, their pursuers the sons of Aegyptus.[61] Both are descendants of Argive Io, the famous paramour of Zeus who, transformed into a cow and driven wild by a gadfly sent by jealous Hera, fled to Egypt. There, touched by Zeus' divine breath, she gave birth to Epaphus, great-grandfather of Danaus and Aegyptus. In the present of the play, the Danaids have returned to their ancestral land as suppliants because, chosen as wives for their cousins quite against their will, they have fled from Egypt to escape the conjugal yoke of (this) marriage.[62] As a result of this particular constellation, the intruder here is both ethnically and socio-politically other. The Argives are faced not only with non- (or half-) Greeks;[63] more importantly for the following discussion, they are faced also with virgins who by virtue of their unmarried state stand at the margins of the social system.[64] These are virgins, moreover, who present as the essential reference point of their identity the asexual union between a mortal (Io) and an immortal (Zeus) and in this way distance themselves further from human society.[65] In this encounter with a complex other, the redefinition of civic identity becomes the central concern of the play.

I shall argue below that this redefinition is conducted through the intermediary of a negotiation of the purity of three spaces: the sanctuary where the action of the play is set; the territory of the political community of Argos; and the 'space' of the female body. Obviously, these spaces are different in kind. Accordingly, different kinds of purity and impurity are brought into play: the ritual pollution of human transgression and the sanctity ('purity', *hagneia*) of the sanctuary; the (metaphorical?) purity of the Argive territory from which all foreign elements have been eradicated; and the 'purity' and chastity (*hagneia*) of the virginal Danaids. But these forms of purity, as well as the three spaces with which each is associated, do

---

Zeitlin's famous article (ead. (1990)), which argues for a definition of self vs. other in oppositional terms, scholars have repeatedly pointed out that Thebes also bears many traits of the Athenian self: see e.g. Blundell (1993) esp. 303.

[60] See Tzanetou (2012) 26 and 110 on the importance of (the threat of) pollution in suppliant plays.
[61] The Danaids' appearance as suppliants may have been Aeschylean innovation: Papadopoulou (2011) 34–8.
[62] The question whether the Danaids shun this specific marriage or marriage in general is an important one, but never entirely resolved; see my discussion below.
[63] On the degree of the Danaids 'otherness', between Greek and Egyptian, see Mitchell (2006).
[64] See Zeitlin (1996c) esp. 125, 131; see also Murnaghan (2005) 184–5.
[65] See e.g. 40–56; 526–8; 536; see Murnaghan (2005) 187; Zeitlin (1996c) 157 (and 151–2).

not remain separate and distinct. Rather, the different spaces and types of purity intertwine, reinforce and enrich each other in the play's redefinitions of identity.[66] Inasmuch as 'purity', albeit in different forms, serves as the common denominator of the spaces onto which identity is mapped, it is also the central category through which the play negotiates civic identity.

I shall first outline the importance of the concept of space in the *Suppliants'* negotiation of identity. Then, I shall analyse the ways in which purity, through the intermediary of pure and/or sacred space, comes to define the identity of both Argives and Danaids. Finally, I shall move towards a discussion, more specifically, of the significance of the interconnection of these spaces through the category of purity. We shall find that the idea of 'pure identity' is drawn into complex negotiations.

Suppliants' *spaces*

As we have seen during our tour through the classical city's places of purity, space constitutes a prime category through which identity can be expressed. As we have seen, too, this is mainly so because the existence of a circumscribed space also implies the existence of boundaries and, as a result, of categories of 'inside' and 'outside'. These spatial categories, in turn, may easily be appropriated to provide the coordinates for a civic map of 'insider' and 'outsider', 'self' and 'other'. Certainly, other important categories exist through which identity can be constructed and reflected upon; word ('discourse') and action ('performance') readily spring to mind. But in *Suppliants*, a play in which the violation of physical boundaries of various sorts is central, the category of 'space' is arguably the most important. Three spaces are staked out.

There is, first, the female body, which in this play is time and again presented as a space whose boundaries, through transgressions of various sorts, can be infringed. For the Danaids, such spatial notions are of prime importance. They constitute the reference point of an identity which is conceived of largely in terms of the paradigmatic 'gentle touch' by which Zeus, without (it seems) penetrating the boundaries of Io's body, engendered their great-great-grandfather Epaphus (ἔφαψιν ἐπωνυμίαν, 45; Ζεύς γ' ἐφάπτωρ χειρὶ φιτύει γόνον, 313; see 535).[67] As a result of the Danaids' conception of

---

[66] On similar spatial negotiations in Euripides' *Children of Heracles*, see Mendelsohn (2002); ibid. 50: 'Throughout the play we can detect a dramatic symbiosis between those overlapping categories of space – sacred, political, gendered, geographical – with each serving at different moments as a metonymical stand-in for the others, expanding and enriching their dramatic meaning.'

[67] See Zeitlin (1996c) 157 and Murnaghan (2005) 187. Both imply that there is (presumably) a sexual element to the union between Io and Zeus, but that this element is suppressed: see esp. Murnaghan

their identity in terms of non-penetration, their bodies appear like 'walled' spaces. In a much-discussed passage in the first choral song, for instance, they appeal to Artemis to 'keep safe the solemn façades' (ἔχουσα σέμν' ἐνώπι' ἀσφαλές, 146). The passage is ambiguous about the precise nature of these 'façades';[68] arguably, the Danaids refer to temple walls; in an appeal by virgins to virginal Artemis for protection of virginity, however, one may well be reminded of the 'façades' of the Danaids' virginal bodies. We shall see in greater detail below that the Danaids' conception of their identity indeed suggests an assimilation of their bodies to sacred space. For now, let us simply note that the Danaids' identity is mapped spatially and that it is intimately bound up with the female body's boundaries.

Second is the space of the Argive territory, conceived as the territory of the *polis* of Argos. This qualification is important because at 254–9 Pelasgus sketches out a wider territory under his rule that is not coextensive with, but exceeds, the territory of the *polis* of Argos.[69] This wider territory under Pelasgus' rule is irrelevant to the remainder of this discussion. Nonetheless, it provides an apt starting point since it is here that spatial definition begins to be important. Thus, when Pelasgus introduces himself upon first contact with the protection-seeking virgins from Egypt, he first refers to 'this land' (Argos) and its inhabitants (the 'Pelasgians'/Argives), then sketches the wider territory over which he also rules, delineating boundaries which 'cut' through the landscape (250–9):[70]

> τοῦ γηγενοῦς γάρ εἰμ' ἐγὼ Παλαίχθονος
> ἶνις Πελασγός, τῆσδε γῆς ἀρχηγέτης,
> ἐμοῦ δ' ἄνακτος εὐλόγως ἐπώνυμον
> γένος Πελασγῶν τήνδε καρποῦται χθόνα·
> καὶ πᾶσαν αἶαν, ἧς δί' ἁγνὸς ἔρχεται
> Στρυμών, τὸ πρὸς δύνοντος ἡλίου, κρατῶ·
> ὁρίζομαι δὲ τήν τε Περραιβῶν χθόνα
> Πίνδου τε τἀπέκεινα Παιόνων πέλας
> ὄρη τε Δωδωναῖα· συντέμνει δ' ὄρος
> ὑγρᾶς θαλάσσης. τῶνδε τἀπὶ τάδε κρατῶ.

I am Pelasgus, son of earthborn Palaechthon and the ruler of this land; its crops are reaped by the race of the Pelasgians, appropriately named after me,

---

(2005) 187, but also Zeitlin (1996c) 151–2. See also Brill (2009) 172–5 (who stresses the notion of violence lurking beneath Zeus' gentle touch).
[68] On the line and the various interpretations of ἐνώπια, see Friis Johansen and Whittle (1980) vol. 2 ad loc.
[69] See Friis Johansen and Whittle (1980), vol. 2, pp. 210–11 (wider 'empire': 250–9; Argos: 260–70). Arguably, though, Pelasgus speaks of Argos in 250–3 and of the wider empire only in 254–9: note the καί in 254 (I thank Alan Sommerstein for drawing my attention to this).
[70] On these boundaries, see also Gödde (2000a) 239.

their ruler. I am also master of all the land through which flows the holy Strymon, that part which lies to the side of the setting sun. As my boundary I take the land of the Perrhaebeans and the parts beyond Pindus, near the Paeonians, and the mountains of Dodona. The limit that terminates my realm is the watery sea. What lies within these boundaries I rule.

What is at stake in this emphasis on boundaries is the marking out of identity: Pelasgus moves from identification in terms of name and descent (εἴμ' ἐγὼ Παλαίχθονος | ἶνις Πελασγός) to an elaborate identification in terms of a nameable, because demarcated, territory. Argive territory itself – the reference point of Argive identity – is laid out by Pelasgus subsequently, at 260–70, and is also called Apian land. We shall see below that Argive territory has a particularly distinct identity as well as marked boundaries as the result of a purification of that land carried out by the healer-seer Apis that serves Argos as something of a foundation myth.

Third, there is sacred space, that of the sanctuary in which the Danaids take refuge. The character of the sanctuary as well-defined space is strongly emphasised in the play. This is not least a matter of stage-setting and the movements of the characters in that setting. The acting space of *Suppliants* will have been separated into two areas, the *orchestra*-floor representing profane grounds and the *skēnē* representing the altar-mound. In spatial terms, the drama essentially enacts significant crossings (and non-crossings) of the boundary between these two spaces.[71] But the importance of the sanctuary as defined space is also reflected in language. For instance, when Danaus advises his daughters to climb the altar-mound, he compares the space of the sanctuary to the protected space of the walled city, taking the altar-mound to be 'stronger than a tower, an unbreakable shield' (κρεῖσσον δὲ πύργου βωμός, ἄρρηκτον σάκος, 190).

For the subsequent discussion, it is important to note, however, that in the play's negotiation of identities this sacred space occupies an intermediary position. It is a place apart, with its specific assemblage of gods receiving worship (the κοινοβωμία [222] of ἀγώνιοι θεοί [355]) and therefore its own identity; a place apart also because of its greater protective power, 'stronger than a tower' (190). At the same time, the spaces of female body and Argive territory overlap with (this) sacred space. In the case of the Danaids, we have touched upon a general rapprochement of inviolable body and sacred space; we shall have to say more about a rapprochement to this specific sacred space below. In the case of Argive territory, the κοινοβωμία of divine images assembled on the altar-mound defines the identity not only of this

---

[71] See Sommerstein (1996) 158–162 on these and other movements (and 'spectacle') in *Suppliants*.

specific *temenos* but also of the Argive *polis*. In the encounter between Argive king and Egyptian herald, for instance, the κοινοβωμία becomes the reference point of the Argive self in a discourse about self and other according to religious affiliation.[72] And the sanctuary is seen as part, even representative part, of the *polis* proper: the Danaids view it as 'stern' of the *polis* (αἰδοῦ σὺ πρύμναν πόλεος ὧδ' ἐστεμμένην, 345) and, slightly later, as the hearth itself, and thus essential element, of the Argive territory (κρατύνεις βωμόν, ἑστίαν χθονός, 372).

Three spaces, then, are laid out in *Suppliants*, at least two of them well-defined and equipped with their distinctive identity. Sacred space, even at this early point, suggests itself as a third space onto which the other two spaces can be mapped. This observation will be important for the subsequent discussion. As Argive territory is conceived of as 'pure' space, the assimilation of the *polis*' space to sacred space, albeit now a different type of sacred space, becomes more pronounced; and as the female body is likewise mapped onto inviolable sacred space, sacred ('pure') space becomes the point of comparison, 'sacredness', or 'purity', the category through which civic identity and the Danaids' identity can be set in dialogue.

Purity, territory, identity

Let us examine this assimilation of Argos' territory to sacred space by way of its purity first.[73] We remain with Pelasgus' words of introduction in the first encounter with the foreigners from Egypt. Upon sketching the contours of his wider empire (254–9), he returns to Argos, providing an account of one of the city's foundational myths, the purification of Argive territory by the healer-seer Apis (260–70):

> αὐτῆς δὲ χώρας Ἀπίας πέδον τόδε
> πάλαι κέκληται φωτὸς ἰατροῦ χάριν·
> Ἆπις γὰρ ἐλθὼν ἐκ πέρας Ναυπακτίας
> ἰατρόμαντις παῖς Ἀπόλλωνος χθόνα
> τήνδ' ἐκκαθαίρει κνωδάλων βροτοφθόρων,
> τὰ δὴ παλαιῶν αἱμάτων μιάσμασιν
> χρανθεῖσ' ἀνῆκε γαῖα †μηνεῖται ἄκη†,
> δρακονθόμιλον δυσμενῆ ξυνοικίαν·
> τούτων ἄκη τομαῖα καὶ λυτήρια

---

[72] See 922–3: [Egyptian herald] τοὺς ἀμφὶ Νεῖλον δαίμονας σεβίζομαι. | [Pelasgus] οἱ δ' ἐνθάδ' οὐδέν, ὡς ἐγὼ σέθεν κλύω.
[73] The following remarks borrow from, and elaborate upon, Susanne Gödde's insightful observations on Pelasgus' definition of Argive identity in terms of purity and pollution: Gödde (2000a) 238–44.

πράξας ἀμέμπτως Ἆπις Ἀργείᾳ χθονὶ
μνήμην ποτ' ἀντίμισθον ηὕρετ' ἐν λιταῖς.

The ground of this land itself has long been called Apia, in honour of the healer. For the healer and seer Apis, the son of Apollo, came from Naupactus beyond the sea and purified this land of the man-eating monsters which the earth, defiled by the pollution of blood shed long ago, had sent up in anger, a hostile brood of serpents living with us. From these Apis, beyond all reproach, devised an incisive and liberating cure for the Argive land; as a reward he won remembrance in prayers.

Pelasgus' words of identification suggest that Argive identity is intimately bound up with the purity of Argive territory (χθόνα | τήνδ' ἐκκαθαίρει κνωδάλων βροτοφθόρων, 263–4).[74] As part of one of the city's foundational myths, that purity acquires paradigmatic force and appears as the very basis and hallmark of Argive identity.

This identity constructed around the notion of purity has two important aspects. First, as the result of Apis' purification it is the result also of a drawing of boundaries between inside and outside. Territorial boundaries had presumably existed before. But the act of purification by which Argive purity is established marks afresh a particular quality of the territory within these boundaries and in this way constitutes a redefinition by which the distinction between inside and outside is reinforced: the inside is henceforth markedly pure. This idea of reinforcement, and redefinition, of boundaries is emphasised by Pelasgus' use of the prefix ἐκ- in reference to the act of purification (χθόνα | τήνδ' ἐκκαθαίρει, 263–4). This prefix, on one hand, brings with it a notion of thoroughness and completion,[75] suggesting in this way that the territory's inside is 'particularly' ('completely') marked, not only pure but 'thoroughly' so. On the other hand, in the light of the preceding emphasis on boundaries, the primary spatial connotation of the prefix ἐκ- arguably remains important. From this perspective, the specific importance of this purification is the banishment of pollution 'from within' (ἐκ), its relegation from inside to outside, which also implies a redrawing of boundaries.

Second, as the result of the particular nature of Apis' purification Argive identity is bound up with conceptual boundaries in addition to territorial ones. It is important that purification does not refer to the elimination of some ill-defined ritual pollution, but that the object of purification are

---

[74] See also 254–5: καὶ πᾶσαν αἶαν, ἧς δὶ ἁγνὸς ἔρχεται | Στρυμών, τὸ πρὸς δύνοντος ἡλίου, κρατῶ. On Pelasgus as political figure (between 'proud autocrat' and 'constitutional monarch'), see Burian (1974); see also Sommerstein (1997) 75–7 (on the more problematic aspects of Pelasgus as 'crafty politician').
[75] See Smyth, § 1688.2.

monstrous, men-devouring intruders that the earth had sent forth 'defiled by a pollution resulting from blood shed long ago' (παλαιῶν αἱμάτων μιάσμασιν | χρανθεῖσ[α], 265–6).[76] That the land regains purity through their elimination implies that these monsters constitute themselves, in some sense, a pollution.[77] At the same time, these κνώδαλα βροτοφθόρα represent the totally other, the opposite of the civic self. As a result, pollution acquires socio-political overtones. It is associated with the alien and anti-civic, which transgresses boundaries marking the territory of the self, confounding in this way insides and outsides. Inversely, purification of the land becomes an effort not only to demarcate those insides and outsides anew, but also a redefinition and clarification of the identity of self and other.

The first *rhēsis* of the Argive ruler, then, focuses our attention on the importance, in general, of identity and (self-)definition in terms of self and other;[78] but it also establishes a paradigm according to which purity and pollution provide the determinants to distinguish self from other, sharply.

Purity, sanctity, virginity

The paradigm is taken up by the intruders presently carrying the threat of pollution into the Argives' land of purity. Theirs is another identity that is distinguished by its 'purity' and attention to boundaries.

Oddly, in the eyes of Pelasgus as well as, presumably, the Athenian theatre audience, the Danaids shun marriage in preference for the socially awkward status of maidenhood; and whether their φυξανορία implies a general aversion to marriage or a specific rejection of marriage in the case of their cousins,[79] in the dramatic present the Danaids' choices result in

---

[76] The reason for this pollution is obscure. The scholiast's laconic ὡς τῶν πολιτῶν αὐτοκτονησάντων does not help much to clarify things; as Friis Johansen and Whittle (1980) vol. 2 ad loc. point out, the scholiast's note may reflect a local tradition which has left no trace in the mythographical tradition known to us.

[77] The point is made by Gödde (2000a) 239.   [78] Ibid.

[79] The issue is contested: see e.g. Zeitlin (1996c) 125; see also Papadopoulou (2011) 51–64 on gender conflict and the question why the Danaids reject marriage. Two reasons may be adduced to suggest that this φυξανορία is the result not specifically of the prospect of an undesirable marriage with their cousins, but of an aversion to marriage in general. First, even though the text is frustratingly inconclusive on this point, certain passages may be taken to point in this direction. While at times it seems that marriage to a specific husband is shunned (e.g. 790), both Danaus' exhortation of his daughters to be on the lookout against Argive male desire (996–1013) and the emphasis which the mysterious half-chorus who chants the concluding stanzas in exchange with the Danaids puts (presumably in reaction to the Danaids' stance) on the necessity of marriage (1034–42; 1050–1) suggest otherwise. Second, in the early 1990s an attractive (if speculative) case was made, by Wolfgang Rösler (following Martin Sicherl), for a reconstruction of the trilogy in which the Danaids' aversion to marriage results from an oracle given to Danaus that he would be killed by

an identification of the Danaids with inviolability – with the maintenance, that is, of the integrity of their bodies' boundaries.

Female inviolacy in fact appears as an integral part of the Danaids' identity. Others point to it: their father seems to exhort them forever to guard their sexual integrity (τὸ σωφρονεῖν τιμῶσα τοῦ βίου πλέον, 1013); and the mysterious half-chorus at the end bows to the power, and works, of Aphrodite (1034–42) in obvious contrast to the Danaids' preference for chaste Artemis (1030). More importantly, the Danaids themselves time and again identify themselves, if obliquely, with female inviolability. Attention was drawn already to the Danaids' prayer to Artemis, asking the goddess to 'keep safe the solemn façades', which, I suggested, may be seen to imply the inviolacy of their virginal bodies. Beyond this, the Danaids constantly seem to assimilate their identity as untouched and untouchable virgins to the curiously (and supposedly) asexual encounter between their forebears and *genos*-founders Zeus and Io, in which, as the Danaids are ever quick to point out, all-too-human penetration of the female body was apparently replaced by a gentle touch and divine breath (ἐξ ἐπαφῆς κἀξ ἐπιπνοίας | Διός, 17–18; see 45, 313, 535, 577).[80]

Although this is not a concern of the present study, this assimilation is perhaps another argument in favour of the view that the Danaids reject marriage in general. For it appears to be so insistent as to suggest that the Danaids identify with the paradigmatic asexual touch not only temporarily, in view of their cousins' attempts at touches of, presumably, quite a different sort (Zeus: Ζεύς γ᾽ ἐφάπτωρ χειρὶ φιτύει γόνον, 313; sons of Aegyptus: ῥυσίων ἐφάπτορες, 728; οὐ μή ... ἡμῶν χεῖρ᾽ ἀπόσχωνται, 756), but that untouched inviolacy seems to them a permanently desirable state.

Be that as it may, this virginal identity invokes the paradigm set up by Pelasgus and his definition of identity in terms of purity and pollution. The Greek term which lends itself most readily to express this virginal identity is *hagneia*, denoting a type of ritual purity which is frequently, though by no means necessarily, bound up with sexual purity and chastity.[81] In Aeschylus' play, this term is never straightforwardly applied to the Danaids.[82] Instead,

---

a future son-in-law: Rösler (1993); Sicherl (1986); both draw attention to the scholion to line 37 (ὧν θέμις εἴργει) ὧν τὸ δίκαιον ἡμᾶς εἴργει διὰ τὸ μὴ θανατωθῆναι τὸν πατέρα). Φυξανορία, in this case, would be the result of the child's reverence towards the parent and ensue from any male's advances, not just those of the sons of Aegyptus.

[80] See Zeitlin (1996c) 151–2, 157; Murnaghan (2005) 187; see also Brill (2009) 172–5.
[81] Parker (1983) 147–50.
[82] Ἁγνός is used of Zeus' sacred abodes (103); Artemis (144–5, 1030); the sanctuary (223); (obliquely) of Aegyptus and his sons (226, 228; cf. 751); the river Strymon (254); Zeus (653); and singers at sacrificial festivals (696).

it is displaced from the inviolate virgins themselves onto the inviolable space which presently serves as their refuge.

The central passage to support this claim is 223–8, in which Danaus compares his daughters, in their position as suppliants at the sacred altar, to doves attempting to escape the attacks of falcons. *Hagneia* and μίασμα figure prominently:

> ἐν ἁγνῷ δ' ἑσμὸς ὣς πελειάδων
> ἵζεσθε κίρκων τῶν ὁμοπτέρων φόβῳ,
> ἐχθρῶν ὁμαίμοις καὶ μιαινόντων γένος.
> ὄρνιθος ὄρνις πῶς ἂν ἁγνεύοι φαγών;
> πῶς δ' ἂν γαμῶν ἄκουσαν ἄκοντος πάρα
> ἁγνὸς γένοιτ' ἄν;

> In this pure place sit like a flock of doves in fear of hawks, their fellow-birds, foes to their kin and defiling their race. How could a bird prey on a bird and remain pure? How could a man marry the unwilling daughter of an unwilling father and be pure?

What is arguably at stake in this passage is sexual encroachment; this much, context as well as the use of the vocabulary of *hagneia* would seem to suggest. On this reading, *miasma* denotes this encroachment and therefore the impairment of the Danaids' virginal identity.[83] Just as the infringement of territorial boundaries impairs the purity of Argive territory, so the infringement of bodily boundaries is seen to pollute the Danaids' sexual integrity. Yet the idea that the Danaids' identity is one of *hagneia*, which could be impaired by polluting transgressions, is expressed only obliquely. What is explicitly impaired is the *hagneia* of the attackers (226–8); more importantly for the present argument, what is impaired, too, is the *hagneia* of the *hagnos* space which Danaus' doves inhabit. Through all this obliqueness, however, there emerges a picture in which the *hagnos* space of the doves is the equivalent of the inviolable, and hence equally *hagnos*, space of the altar-mound; and in which the strikingly vague formulation ἐν ἁγνῷ comes to stand not only for that altar-mound but also for the band by which it is occupied and whose members, one might say, are not only spatially but also physically (and socially) ἐν ἁγνῷ ('in a state of *hagneia*' may be a suitable translation for the latter case).[84]

The passage, then, serves a complex function. Not only does it frame the Danaids' concern to escape the marriage-bed of the sons of Aegyptus

---

[83] The point is made by Zeitlin (1996c) 128.
[84] Zeitlin (1996c) 132 implies something of the sort, that the formulation ἐν ἁγνῷ is expressive also of the Danaids' virginity.

in the language of purity and pollution, in this way to draw together closely the outsider's intrusion into the self's political territory and the male's intrusion into the female body; importantly, even while it intimates, in the appropriate terminology, the Danaids' concern as a concern, not least, about their *hagneia*, it does so through the intermediary of the *hagneia* of sacred space. That is, just as the Argives' identity is mapped onto, and expressed in terms of, their 'pure territory', so the Danaids' identity as inviolate virgins is mapped onto, and expressed in terms of, the specific 'pure' (*hagnos*) space of the sanctuary. The inviolable space of the sanctuary in this way comes to stand for the Danaids' virginal purity (their *hagneia*) and is set up as the intermediary through which this purity can be (and is) negotiated.

Before we inspect the specifics of this negotiation, however, let us briefly observe the ways in which the convergence of the inviolacy of sacred space and the Danaids' virginity which the above passage intimates is played out in the drama.

The general point to emerge is that transgression of the sanctuary's boundaries is correlated to the Danaids' loss of virginity. This is arguably implicit in lines 223–8. It is further underscored by the explicit, and paradigmatic, association, at the beginning of the play, of spatial trangression and loss of virginity: in the prologue, which introduces the audience to the Danaids' plight, their virginity, metonymically expressed in terms of the marriage-bed yet unmounted by specimens of the male sex, appears as something which vanishes along with the spatial transgression of this marriage-bed (λέκτρων... ἐπιβῆναι, 37–9); as a result, any further transgression upon spaces connected with the Danaids, and in particular the Aegyptiads' transgression of the sanctuary (see e.g. 423–4: μηδ' ἴδῃς μ' ἐξ ἑδρᾶν | πολυθέων ῥυσιασθεῖσαν), may be understood to evoke the mounting of the marriage-bed and its implications.

Not least, such transgression is exemplified by the Aegyptiads' inappropriately appetent hands. As we have already seen, *Suppliants* is much concerned with hands. The most important is arguably that of Zeus which, miraculously, engenders Epaphus (Ζεύς γ' ἐφάπτωρ χειρὶ φιτύει γόνον, 313). Its role as paradigm for other hands, and especially the covetous ones of the sons of Aegyptus, is, however, complex. It comes to stand, on the one hand, for the chaste, asexual touch; on the other, because it plays such a prominent role in child-conception and replaces so emphatically the sexual act, it draws all further hands into a negotiation where what is at stake is precisely their relation to sexuality. Such is the case with the second pairs of hands that is important in the play, those of the sons of

Aegyptus. Seen in the light of Zeus' hand, the Aegyptiad hand which, in disrespect of the sanctity of the precinct, reaches across its boundaries to take violent hold of the virgin (ῥυσίων ἐφάπτορες, 728) is the hand, too, which not only violates sacred space but, in contrast to Zeus', which ever so gently touches but does not seem to penetrate, threatens to violate also the virgin's inviolate body.[85]

In this interplay of reaching across the sacred and violation of female virginity, a further point emerges with some force: because the play correlates the sanctity of the virginal body with that of sacred space so intimately, remaining ἐν ἁγνῷ, in the sanctuary, becomes virtually equivalent with remaining ἐν ἁγνῷ, in the state of virginity.[86] The point is borne out by the maidens' desperate outcry 'O chiefs and rulers of the city! Violence I suffer!' (ἰὼ πόλεως ἀγοὶ πρόμοι, δάμναμαι, 905). The violence the virgins suffer here is their violent removal from the sacred space of the altar-mound. But the verb δάμναμαι also has the strong connotation of the sexual subjugation (lit. 'breaking-in') of the female by the male.[87] The use of δάμναμαι at this point, then, makes explicit what has been implicit at least since Danaus' doves fearfully crouching ἐν ἁγνῷ: that removal from the sanctuary is somehow tantamount to the loss of the virgins' ἁγνεία.

Sacred space, virginity and civic space

So far, I have described some of the basic elements which constitute *Danaids*' point of departure. In the remainder of this discussion, I shall explore the dynamics these elements are engaged in as the play unfolds and consider the implications of these dynamics for our understanding of the play's vision of 'pure identity'. The starting point will be the problematic nature of the Danaids' virgin status.[88] I shall then examine the play's negotiation of this problematic identity through the intermediary of the virgin's relation to the pure space of the sanctuary which they occupy. After a brief complementary discussion of the second problematic aspect of the Danaids' identity, their composite ethnic affiliations, I shall return to the significance of the parallel mapping of the Danaids' and the Argives' identity in the terms of pollution and purity.

---

[85] See especially 755–6: οὐ μὴ τριαίνας τάσδε καὶ θεῶν σέβη | δείσαντες ἡμῶν χεῖρ' ἀπόσχωνται, πάτερ. See Zeitlin (1996c) 158 on the contrast between the brutal hands of the Danaids and the gentle hand of Zeus.
[86] The point is adumbrated by Zeitlin (1996c) 132.   [87] See LSJ s.v. δαμάζω II.
[88] Stressed by Zeitlin (1996c) e.g. 125, 131 and Gödde (2000a) 240.

Virginal purity, while demanded by the norms of Greek society in the case of the unwed maiden, becomes problematic if it is kept beyond the age at which the παρθένος becomes marriageable.[89] This attitude is deeply engrained in Greek culture: we may, for instance, consider the Hippocratic treatise *On the diseases of young girls* with its master-remedy of marriage and intercourse in the case of a virgin's suffering from 'hysteria' as a 'scientific' rationalisation of it.[90] In the play, it appears in a different form, with physical necessities replaced by social ones, when Pelasgus draws attention to the (social) necessity of marriage, holding that it is through marriage that 'people increase their strength' (σθένος μὲν οὕτως μεῖζον αὔξεται βροτοῖς, 338).[91]

The play would seem to foreshadow the Danaids' future yielding to this necessity. If, as a result of the convergence of female ἁγνεία and the sacred precinct's sanctity, the movement of the Danaids in relation to that space can be interpreted to imply a statement also about their relation to virginity, it becomes important to observe how in the course of the play the Danaids cross back and forth between sacred and profane space until, finally, they are convinced by a male representative of Argive society to abandon the sanctuary for good and exchange the sacred κοινοβωμία for the civic κοινωνία of the *polis*: the Danaids, once their identity is defined in terms of the pure space of the sanctuary, are reluctant to leave it even upon the bidding of male authority (509); but male authority insists (955–6) so that finally they leave the inviolable altars and make their way to the *exodos*, away from the marginal sanctuary and towards the city proper of Argos. In the play's terms, this spatial movement away from the sanctuary indicates a change of status;[92] and it is only appropriate that the movement is accompanied by hymenaeal stanzas which turn the Danaids' procession towards the city into a bride's procession to a new home as well as (wifely) status.[93]

To be exact, the abandonment of the sanctuary has (at least) three implications regarding the Danaids' status and their stance vis-à-vis the

---

[89] See King (1983); Zeitlin (1996c) 125, 131; Dillon (2002) 234–5.
[90] On this treatise and its socio-cultural significance, see King (1983); Lloyd (1983) esp. 69 (on women in the Hippocratic corpus more generally, see ibid. 62–86). (In Foucauldian terms, we might speak of this scientific rationalisation of a 'discours de vérité' (Foucault (1971) 21).)
[91] On the importance of marriage in the play, see Zeitlin (1996c).
[92] See Zeitlin (1996c) 136 who argues that bringing the virgins into the *polis* functions 'like an initial phase' of the wedding ceremony; incorporation into the city is analogous to incorporation into married life. See also Murnaghan (2005) on the experience of the Danaids as reflecting the initiatory scenario of female choruses in ancient Greece, also pointing to the hints that marriage lies in the future for the Danaids (ibid. 187–8).
[93] On these concluding stanzas as hymenaeal, see Seaford (1987) 114–15, Rösler (1993) 14–15.

civic community. First, it implies the abandonment of their inviolable identity and, by extension, of their virginal purity, which associates them with the divine rather than the human sphere; they join civic life instead.[94] Second, it implies the abandonment of the divine and not-quite-human (the τέρας Io, 570) as reference point for an identity constructed around the idea of keeping aloof from human 'touch' and trafficking in exchange for integration into the rhythms of human reciprocity. Third, it implies that the Danaids finally give up the protection offered by altars which come to stand for their anti-civic virginity and instead trust in the protection of the city-walls which no longer express the virgin's insulated inviolability, but that of the civic κοινωνία as a whole.[95]

Importantly, these concerns with the Danaids' identity may fruitfully be thought together with pollution and in particular the pollution crisis which the Danaids presently carry into the Argive land as suppliants at communal altars whose abandonment to their pursuers would result in pollution (μιαίνεται πόλις, 366). Susanne Gödde has made a strong case for an understanding of this crisis as concerned not only with religious transgressions but also with the challenge posed by the Danaids' marginal identity.[96] The hub of the argument is the marked sense of *déjà vu* that emerges from the expression of the present crisis in terms of the crisis resulting from the intrusion of polluting monstrous others which the Apis-myth describes: monsters and Danaids are referred to in the same or similar terms (monsters: κνώδαλα βροτοφθόρα, 264, δρακονθόμιλον... ξυνοικίαν, 267; Danaids: τὰς ἀνάνδρους κρεοβ[ρ]ότους τ' Ἀμαζόνας, 287; μετοικεῖν, 609, ὅμιλος, 993); and resolution, in the past as well as in the present, involves 'cures', ἄκη (past: ἄκη τομαῖα, 268; present: ξυνῇ μελέσθω λαὸς ἐκπονεῖν ἄκη, 367). The past crisis, we have seen above, revolved around identity. The monsters represented the totally other, and this otherness was coded as pollution. In view of the marked parallels between past and present, the present pollution crisis may be seen to give expression to the challenge posed to Argive civic identity by the problematic identity of the Danaids.

This interpretation has important implications for our understanding of the aversion of the present pollution threat. If that threat is seen to be bound up with the Danaids' problematic identity as virgins, the fact that averting

---

[94] Their ἁγνεία associates them closely with Artemis (144–5; 1030) and Zeus (103); see also Zeitlin (1996c) 132 n. 25.
[95] Significantly, the Danaids first prefer the protection of the altars in preference to the more profane protection of the city's 'towers' (κρεῖσσον δὲ πύργου βωμός, 190); later, it is precisely these 'towers' they are advised to trust in (στείχετ' εὐερκῆ πόλιν | πύργων βαθείᾳ μηχανῇ κεκλημένην, 955–6).
[96] Gödde (2000a) 238–44, esp. 239–40.

it involves the Danaids' abandonment of the sanctuary is significant. The Danaids' abandonment of the sanctuary's ἁγνός space in exchange for the protection of the city-walls is after all the final and most important step towards the prevention of pollution. On the terms of the above interpretations a significant relation between the Danaids' spatial movement and the concomitant prevention of pollution emerges: in that the abandonment of the sanctuary's ἁγνεία under the parameters set by the play suggests a movement towards the abandonment of sexual ἁγνεία, the resolution of the pollution crisis – which, I contend, gives expression to an identity crisis carried into the land by the Danaids' otherness as unwed virgins – consists precisely of the rejection of the Danaids' marginal, 'other' identity as resolute virgins in favour of their integration, ultimately as citizen-wives, into the civic community.[97] In other words, the abandonment of the sanctuary in exchange for the protection offered by the city-walls solves the pollution problem not only on a practical and literal level; it also solves it at a deeper, more significant level in that it suggests the abandonment of that marginal identity as virgins, which is part of the identity crisis of which the pollution crisis may be seen as the tangible expression.

Admittedly, though, things are not as neat as would appear at this point. I have left aside so far the other problematic aspect of the Danaids' identity briefly referred to in the introductory section: the Danaids' composite ethnic affiliations as both Egyptian and Greek;[98] as 'citizen-foreigners' (ἀστόξενοι, 356), as Pelasgus famously, and paradoxically, has it.[99] This ethnic otherness, too, locates the Danaids on the margins and in this way corresponds to the Danaids' socio-cultural 'otherness' as unwed virgins at marriageable age.[100] In a play centrally concerned with the idea of marriage, one may well understand this ethnic otherness to serve Aeschylus as an apt amplification, or perhaps even as a vehicle, for the Danaids' otherness as virgins. Nonetheless, the matter complicates things.

---

[97] Their role as citizen-wives is foreshadowed in the play's concluding hymenaeal stanzas. For the time being, it seems, they are granted a status that resembles those of metics: see v. 609, with Brock (2010) 97–8.

[98] This ethnic otherness of the Danaids is commented on in most major discussions of the play, including the ones particularly relevant to the present discussion by Zeitlin (1996c) esp. 134 and Gödde (2000a) esp. 240; the Danaids' composite ethnic affiliations are central to the discussion of Mitchell (2006) esp. 210–18.

[99] The term has been remarked upon by various scholars. See Zeitlin (1996c) 125; Gödde (2000a) 240; Mitchell (2006) 216. The LSJ's gloss ('public guest of a city') falls rather flat. Not unfittingly (in view of their identity betwixt and between), the suppliant maidens appear to Pelasgus as people who occupy no fixed space but forever cross boundaries, like nomads who forever remain only in the 'neighbourhood' of the central spaces of civic life (νομάδας . . . ἀστυγειτονουμένας, 284–6).

[100] Zeitlin (1996c) 125, 131.

To begin with, if the present threat of pollution is seen to be bound up with the Danaids' problematic identity, their composite ethnic affiliations must be part of this threat. Arguably, the claim is supported by the text. The pollution which Pelasgus fears is in one striking formulation referred to as ξενικὸν ἀστικόν θ' ἅμα . . . μίασμα (618). On one reading, at least, the strange twofoldness of this pollution is a matter precisely of the Danaids' twofold identity as foreigners (ξενικόν) of Argive descent (ἀστικόν).[101] While Pelasgus surely does not mean that it is from this complex identity itself that pollution results, it is precisely in this sense that we are invited to understand his striking words. (It so happens that the syntax – the direct juxtaposition of ξενικόν and ἀστικόν which the construction with the postpositive enclitic τε permits – also suggests this pollution to be specifically a matter of the 'unity' of ξενικόν and ἀστικόν.[102])

Second, unlike the Danaids' otherness as virgins, their ethnic otherness is not, and cannot be, entirely resolved. The Danaids may turn from *astoxenoi* into '*asto*-metics', as it were, when Pelasgus invites them to 'live with' the Argives as free inhabitants of the land (ἡμᾶς μετοικεῖν τῆσδε γῆς ἐλευθέρους, 609);[103] but their complex ethnic affiliation as both Greeks and Egyptians is not thereby removed.

Following the pattern of the above interpretation, which contends that the present pollution crisis is in part an expression of the present identity crisis, we must therefore attest a tension. On the one hand, the resolution of the crisis depends on the Danaids' (foreshadowed) abandonment of their problematic virginity: Argive standards, we may say, are maintained; the Danaids comply. On the other hand, the preservation of purity also depends on the admittance of those who are (still) ethnically other into the city. But this implies that the preservation of purity – the resolution of the pollution crisis – also depends on a redefinition of Argive standards: the standards of purity that define the Argive self since Apis' purificatory 'cutting-out' of monstrous 'others'.

---

[101] The pollution would be 'foreign' and 'belonging to the city' because the Danaids are both 'foreign' and 'belonging to the city': see Bernek (2005) 61 and Mitchell (2006) 216.

[102] The *Suppliants*' crisis, then, is not a matter of the encounter of the self with the other as complete other; it arises in the encounter between self and another that is other because at the same time self *and* other. On the latter point see Mitchell (2006) 210–18; she notes (218), 'In the context of this play, a simple categorisation of "Greeks and barbarians" or "self and other" is not adequate.' (Earlier views on this topic could be markedly different; e.g. Burian (1974) 9 holds that the Danaids 'remain, despite their Argive ancestry, profoundly barbarian.')

[103] Taking our cue from Zeitlin (1996c) 125 on the term *astoxenos*, one may consider the term '*asto*-metic' 'an excellent metaphor for the general ambiguities of women's social status in the community'.

In concluding this analysis of Aeschylus' *Suppliants*, we need to return to where we began. It was claimed that identity is negotiated through the intermediary of a negotiation of the purity of three spaces: the political territory, sacred space and the female body. The preceding analyses have provided the framework within which to reflect upon the interrelation of these spaces in terms of their purity and what this means for the play's meditations on civic identity.

For the sake of clarity, let us recapitulate: 'purity' has emerged as the common denominator of both the civic identity of the Argive community and the Danaids' self-conception in terms of inviolable, virginal integrity. The purities in terms of which each identity is constructed may not, as a general rule, be expressed through the same vocabulary (Argive identity: ἐκκαθαίρει, μιαίνεται; Danaid identity: ἁγνός; but note that the language of *miasma* is used in both cases; see 225); but the similarities and overlaps are brought out clearly through the spatial associations of these purities. In both cases, sacred space is involved. That sacred space is, in the case of the Danaids, the sacred space of the sanctuary; and, in the case of the Argives, the quasi-sacred space created through Apis' cleansing act of the *polis*-territory (and, in the present of the play, the sacred space of the altars the preservation of whose purity comes to stand for the integrity of the entire *polis*-space; see 366: τὸ κοινὸν δ' εἰ μιαίνεται πόλις).[104]

This allows us better to grasp the interrelation of the spaces of female body, political territory, and sacred space. The virginal body, upon which the Danaids' identity depends, and the political territory, upon which Argive identity depends, converge in their assimilation to related forms of sacred space. What is brought out along with these convergences and overlaps is the fact that both Argive and Danaid identities are conceived of in terms of a demarcated space the transgression of whose boundaries impairs that space's integrity ('purity'), in this way posing a threat to the identity thus demarcated.

---

[104] As the play progresses, the entire *polis*-territory is cast as a space whose purity needs to be preserved. In order that the Danaids' suppliant status be clear, Pelasgus instructs Danaus to deposit their suppliant branches on the city-altars (βωμοὺς ἀστικούς, 501). Danaus thus carries the suppliant conflict into the political heart of Argos, along with the threat of pollution; but he also connects margins with centre and demarcates the entirety of Argos' political territory as religious space whose sanctity must not be defiled. When the Danaids, upon receiving the news of the *dēmos*' acceptance of their role as protectors of suppliants, sing in praise of this decision to keep the altars pure (τοιγάρ τοι καθαροῖσι βω-|μοῖς θεοὺς ἀρέσονται, 654–5), these unspecified altars consequently comprise both margins and centre (the sanctuary where the play is set and the city-altars) and stand for the entire civic topography of the *polis* as sacred and pure topography.

Considering in particular the close juxtaposition of the key passages which in each case establish the paradigm for an identity defined in terms of sacred and/or 'pure' space from which pollution is excluded (223–8; 250–70), it seems clear that these overlaps are important to the play and that the audience is invited to take note of them. But what, then, are the implications of these overlaps?

Above all, *Danaids* invites us to conceive of Argive identity as 'guilty by association'. For if the Danaids' assimilation to, and identification in terms of, the inviolable purity of sacred space appears problematic because it gives expression to the problematic 'exclusiveness' of their identity as virgins, their removal of their bodies from the exchanges necessary to the preservation of the *polis*-community, this necessarily throws a problematic light also on the exclusiveness which underlies the construction of Argive civic identity in terms of inviolable, pure space.

At first sight, the play would seem not only to respond to, but neatly to resolve the dilemma: in accepting the Danaids into the city the Argives, after all, jettison absolute exclusiveness in favour of a greater permeability between self and other. On the play's terms, we have seen, the Danaids are as much 'other' as the man-eating monsters of the past.[105] Their entry into the city, to be sure, may be taken to imply the resolution of their 'otherness' as unwed virgins at marriageable age. But since their composite ethnic affiliations cannot be similarly removed, admitting the Danaids amounts to the acceptance, on the part of the Argives, of a certain degree of otherness.

In the process, Argive 'purity' is perhaps redefined. This is so at least if we allow the maintenance of ritual purity, which goes hand in hand with the admittance of the Danaids into Argos, to indicate that Argive purity in the wider socio-political sense is maintained, too. If we accept the above interpretation of the present pollution crisis as another identity crisis then surely such a reading suggests itself. The striking inverse parallelism between past and present further underscores it: then, purity – ritual as well as socio-political – was established through Apis' 'cutting-out' of the monsters, their total *ex*clusion; now, (ritual) purity is maintained, not by exclusion, but by inclusion of the other. We may say that 'purity', as a determinant in the definition of self and other, becomes more flexible and adapted, one might add, to the exigencies of a reality (not least a contemporary Athenian reality perhaps) in which it is impossible simply

---

[105] Pelasgus' comparison of the Danaids to man-devouring Amazons at 287 underscores the point that for Argives the Danaids are hardly less 'monstrous' than the monsters of the past.

to exclude the other (or to bypass the problem through turning the other into the self).[106]

Importantly, this redefinition of what one might call 'civic purity' is in parallel to the redefinition of *hagneia* for the Danaids. According to the above interpretation, their safety depends on their abandonment of the *hagneia* of the sanctuary, which foreshadows, symbolically, their abandonment of virginal *hagneia*. Yet, the trilogy seems to underline that such an abandonment of virginal *hagneia* does not amount to an abandonment of *hagneia* altogether but merely its exchange for a different kind of *hagneia*. In an important fragment which presumably belongs to the final play of the Danaid trilogy, and whose speaker has been identified as Aphrodite, it is precisely sexual intercourse which is associated with ἁγνεία.[107] Everything we say about the fragment necessarily remains pure conjecture. Nonetheless, it seems plausible that Aphrodite here, presumably at a late point in the trilogy and in the context perhaps of the Danaids' impending marriage to Argive citizens, praises the bliss of conjugal life.[108] Redefinitions of 'purity' in the direction of less exclusiveness and greater flexibility thus apply to the terms according to which Argive identity is constructed as well as those according to which Danaid identity is constructed; combined they seem to lead to an end where tensions are resolved and where all involved live happily ever after.

But in tragedy, if sometimes things turn out for the good, they are never easy, clear-cut or unproblematic. In *Suppliants* and the Danaid trilogy, I am afraid, the good comes with the bad; and if there is a happy end, it is achieved at great costs. For the Argives, inclusion of the other may prevent a '*miasma* which cannot be overtopped' (μίασμ' ἔλεξας οὐχ ὑπερτοξεύσιμον, 473); but it also means war with Aegyptus and his sons; and with this, corpses and the spilling of blood.[109] Nor is the Danaids' exchange of sanctuary for city an entirely happy affair: after all, myth has it that the

---

[106] On the importance of Athenian reality to the play, see e.g. Mitchell (2006) who underlines the importance of the fact that ten years after the Persian wars 'Aeschylus in the *Suppliants* explores the inextricable intertwining of Greekness and barbarity' (ibid. 205).

[107] *TrGF*, vol. 3, fr. 44: ἐρᾷ μὲν ἁγνὸς οὐρανὸς τρῶσαι χθόνα, | ἔρως δὲ γαῖαν λαμβάνει γάμου τυχεῖν· | ὄμβρος δ' ἀπ' εὐνάεντος οὐρανοῦ πεσών | ἔκυσε γαῖαν· ἡ δὲ τίκτεται βροτοῖς | μήλων τε βοσκὰς καὶ βίον Δημήτριον | δένδρων τ' ὀπώραν· ἐκ νοτίζοντος γάμου | τελεῖθ' ὅσ' ἔστι. τῶν δ' ἐγὼ παραίτιος. On the fragment and its positive portrayal of sexual union, see Zeitlin (1996c) 159.

[108] See Zeitlin (1996c) 159. Marriage at the end: see Sommerstein (1996) 148, 150; Latacz (2003²) 146.

[109] The impending encounter with the sons of Aegyptus may have been the subject of the second play (on the assumption that *Suppliants* is the first play of the trilogy) or narrated at the beginning of the third play (if *Suppliants* is taken to be the second play of the trilogy). In this encounter, the Argives will have been defeated and Pelasgus killed; see e.g. Sommerstein (1996) 149–50, id. (1997) 75–6, Latacz (2003²) 145–6. For a discussion of the reconstruction of the trilogy, see also Garvie

Danaids do not escape their Aegyptiad pursuers so easily, but are (probably in the wake of Argos' defeat in the war) forced into marriage with their cousins whom they famously kill on their wedding night; worrisomely, too, it is not unlikely that the trilogy involved their father's demise as part and parcel of this (forced) marriage.[110] Therefore, if Alan Sommerstein is correct in assuming that the trilogy's grand finale, following upon these multiple disasters, involved the prediction of a blissful marriage between Danaids and Argives,[111] their abandonment of the sanctuary may ultimately lead to marital bliss and the happy exchange of virginal *hagneia* for Aphrodite's conjugal *hagneia*; but along the way there is spilled blood for them, too.

Thus, if the Danaids' occupancy of the sanctuary is problematic, not least as an expression of their problematic identity as virgins, so is their leaving this sanctuary; and if the Argives' mythically anchored vision of a territory strictly kept free from the pollution incurred through the presence of foreign elements appears problematic in view of the exigencies of a complex present, so does their newly won inclusiveness. Danaids and Argives may eventually leave the tragic stage in marital bliss, very likely disinclined to ask further questions. The audience will feel differently.

Sophoclean variations: excursus to Colonus

We may expect to find much the same in *Oedipus at Colonus*. After all, Sophocles' late play would seem to provide the ideal framework within which to re-enact an encounter between self and other in terms reminiscent of the initial scenario of Aeschylus' *Suppliants*. As in *Suppliants*, the civic self is faced with the intrusion of an outsider. In this case, the civic self is represented by the inhabitants of the rural deme of Colonus, about a mile north-east of the Athenian city, and their king;[112] and the outsider by an aged and frail Oedipus who, after long years of exile, has come to an end, both of his nomadic existence and of his life.[113] The divide between insider and outsider, moreover, appears wider even than in Aeschylus: the Coloneans, after all, are pious deme-men who show a respectful care for

---

(1969) 163–233. (He takes *Suppliants* as the first play; I tend to prefer Rösler's reconstruction: Rösler (1993)).

[110] See Rösler (1993), Sommerstein (1996) 141–51.   [111] Sommerstein (1996) 149–50.

[112] According to some, this king, moreover, stands for an entire city; see e.g. Wallace (1979) 46–7; Knox (1964) 152.

[113] See 89–91. For Oedipus, Colonus is the χώρα τερμία (89), the place where he will exchange his existence as restless exile for permanent fixedness (90) and die (91). Knox (1964) 144 suggests that this frail, but eventually powerful, Oedipus may be understood to be the embodiment of a hopeful vision of Athens in the final years of the Peloponnesian War.

the integrity of their shrines; Oedipus, by contrast, is the potentially totally other, the transgressor of all civic norms, the incestuous parricide, polluted (or so it would seem) beyond purification.

But Sophocles' *Oedipus at Colonus* is different. It provides an excellent counter-example to the scenario we initially find in Aeschylus' play. In *Suppliants*, the conceptual world of the characters is, at first at least, closely mapped onto the classical city's geography of pure and impure space. When we first encounter these characters, purity and impurity provide categories which allow clearly demarcated spaces of self and other to be laid out. *Oedipus at Colonus*, on the other hand, has (almost) none of this. Instead, the play offers a vision of a world in which categories of 'pure' and 'impure' are not laid out later to be redefined, but largely abandoned altogether; and with them, well-defined territories of self and other. In contrast to Aeschylus' *Suppliants*, *Oedipus at Colonus* does not struggle towards, but more easily opens up, what one might call in-between spaces of identity.

In *Oedipus at Colonus*, identity, not least one mapped in terms of space, plays no less important a role than in Aeschylus' *Suppliants*. Faced with the outsider Oedipus who intrudes upon their Attic homeland, the Coloneans are encouraged to reassert their sense of self and place. There is no need to elaborate the point at length. Many scholars have commented on the strong sense of locale and the ubiquity of references to territory (in the form of words such as γῆ, χώρα, χθών, χῶρος, τόπος).[114] Attention also has been drawn to the stranger's words before the arrival of the chorus of Colonean elders which establish, with some emphasis, Colonean identity in terms of the local cultic system (54–61).[115] Not a few, finally, have remarked upon the serene beauty of the first two choral odes in which an insistence on Colonus' natural wonders (a *locus amoenus* par excellence), religious affiliation, Attic cult-places, and spatial demarcation in terms of these cult-places stakes out the deme-men's Colonean as well as Attic identity.[116]

In view of Oedipus' identity as incestuous parricide, confounder of distinctions most vital to the orderly functioning of the civic community, one would expect this identity to be negotiated in terms of polarities and

---

[114] Allison (1984) 69 and *passim*; Bernek (2005) 134; Kelly (2009) 98–103; Rodighiero (2012) 57–8 and *passim*; Saïd (2012) 84–8; Tzanetou (2012) 107–9. For further references, see Markantonatos (2002) 171 n. 8.
[115] Krummen (1993) 195–6; Bernek (2005) 135, 166, 197.
[116] E.g. Segal (1981) 371; Krummen (1993) 200–1. Segal (1981) 371 points out that the second stasimon lists the sacred boundaries of Attica. He finds (ibid. 404–5) that with 'its use of the cults and topography of the Colonus, the play is among the most parochial of Greek tragedies'. Allison (1984) 69 stresses that the deme-men are never called Ἀθηναῖοι; instead, their Colonean (or at most Attic) identity is prime. See also Saïd (2012).

well-defined boundaries, derived, not least, from the categories of 'pure' and 'impure'. These expectations are raised by the opening sections of the play; subsequently they are largely frustrated.

In the first instance, it is Oedipus himself who suggests an encounter of the expected type. Barely on stage, he identifies himself as the quintessential wanderer, τὸν πλανήτην Οἰδίπουν (3), forever outside the civic community[117] and indeed by his own confession ἀπόπολις (208), who is presently about to encounter those who are very unlike himself, 'men of the city' (see line 2), whose sense of self, as we have seen, is bound up precisely with rootedness in space, not with passing, transit, restlessness. Such permanent wandering, to be sure, is not a citizen's activity; additionally, in Oedipus' case wandering indicates, perhaps, more than a general, unspecific loss of anchorage in the civic community (like that of Iolaus and the children of Heracles in Euripides' play of that name).[118] Not least for an Athenian audience, familiar with Sophocles' memorable presentation of the king who sets out to discover the 'pollution of the land' and finds only himself, and whose exile is a paramount concern, this hero's wandering will have suggested notions of pollution as the result of transgression. Hence, when Oedipus ends his first *rhēsis* in anticipation of the encounter between the two distinct parties of outsiders and insiders (ξένοι πρὸς ἀστῶν, 12), there arguably lingers a notion that this *xenos* is 'foreign' not only as non-citizen but also as polluted transgressor; and with this notion the expectation that lines between self and other will be drawn in terms of pollution and purity.

The chorus' terms of welcome, at first, continue this pattern. This is initially the case before they identify the stranger as Oedipus, the incestuous parricide. Their continued reference to the foreigner's 'out-of-place-ness' (ἐκτόπιος, 119) and their emphatic differentiation between 'wanderer' and 'local' (πλανάτας, | πλανάτας τις ὁ πρέσβυς, οὐδ' | ἔγχωρος, 123–5) point in this direction, that boundaries between self and other are rigid and set in stone.[119] Further, their identification of the intruder as transgressor of sacred space (περᾷς γάρ, | περᾷς, 155–6)[120] invites the audience to abstract the spatial and literal and conceive of the Coloneans' differentiation between self and other in terms of 'transgression' and 'non-transgression'. The formulation of the idea of pollution and purity as central coordinate in the Coloneans' grid of differentiation seems apposite and imminent, and is

---

[117] Segal (1981) 365.
[118] On dislocation in Euripides' *Children of Heracles*, see Mendelsohn (2002) 74–89.
[119] On the weight given to Oedipus' foreignness, see e.g. Tzanetou (2012) 109.
[120] Segal (1981) 365 on περᾷς: 'It sums up the hero's tragic road of life.'

indeed approximated upon the play's first climax, Oedipus' self-revelation. The chorus envisages complete (spatial) separation, the re-establishment of an inside of the 'pure' and an outside of the (somehow) impure. 'Out! Out!', they say (ἔξω πόρσω, 226); and again, 'Out! Begone!', from the shrine as well as from Attic territory (σὺ δὲ τῶνδ' ἑδράνων πάλιν ἔκτοπος | αὖθις ἄφορμος ἐμᾶς χθονὸς ἔκθορε, 233–4). For they fear that Oedipus' infectious presence might be incompatible with the civic life of their *polis*, possibly 'fixing some heavier burden' on it (μή τι πέρα χρέος | ἐμᾷ πόλει προσάψῃς, 235–6). Inside and outside, or so this climactic passage would seem to intimate, are clear; and they promise to be associated, respectively, with purity and pollution.

Expectations are confounded, however. For one, in the remainder of the play Oedipus comes, and is allowed, to occupy a place that is inside as well as outside, a 'third space' that is, not either/or, but both/and. The claim can again be dealt with briefly, in view of a number of excellent studies which have set out to prove exactly this point.[121] I confine myself to one paradigmatic observation. Oedipus, on one hand, becomes closely associated with the city of Athens, in terms reminiscent, almost, of citizenship; on the other, he remains a foreigner, a *xenos*, throughout.[122] At 637, Theseus declares Oedipus to be part of the city (χώρᾳ δ' ἔμπολιν κατοικιῶ; ἔμπολιν is Musgrave's – widely accepted – emendation for the manuscript's ἔμπαλιν). The exact meaning of ἔμπολις (if accepted) at this point has been a matter of debate;[123] what is clear, however, is that Oedipus, henceforth, is in some sense 'in the city'.[124] But Oedipus' relation to the city remains ambiguous. On the one hand, the hero demonstrates this newly won attachment to Athens: in the face of Creon's outrageous kidnapping of his daughters, Oedipus gives voice to his distress in the form of an appeal to the city (ἰὼ πόλις, 833), as though it were his own. On the other, not least in the eyes of the chorus, Oedipus remains the 'foreign wanderer' (ὦ ξεῖν' ἀλῆτα, 1096), in opposition to proper citizens (πολίταις, 1095).[125]

---

[121] See in particular Segal (1981) 362–408; Vidal-Naquet (1986b). See also Travis (1999); Tzanetou (2012) 105–26, esp. 109.
[122] Vidal-Naquet (1986b) 191–204; in his view, Oedipus becomes a metic with special privileges (ibid. 204).
[123] Vidal-Naquet (1986b) 191–204 engaging with Knox's claim (id. (1983) esp. 21) that Oedipus becomes an Athenian citizen; Tzanetou (2012) 116, 127–8 (for whom the term denotes physical belonging rather than active participation, which underscores Oedipus' marginal position).
[124] This is true even if one rejects Musgrave's emendation: Vidal-Naquet (1986b) 191–204.
[125] Vidal-Naquet (1986b) 196–7 arguing against Knox (1983) 24 on *OC* 833 as evidence that Oedipus has acquired Athenian citizen status. In subsequent passages, the chorus speaks of Oedipus as a ξένος also at 1014, 1449 and (indirectly) at 1705.

At the same time, categories of pure and impure are by and large abandoned. Scholars have often, and rather carelessly, spoken of Oedipus' 'pollution' without making clear what precisely they mean by it.[126] But as was the case in *Oedipus tyrannus* some twenty-five years before (not to forget *Antigone*), the play sets great store by differentiation and by pointed terminological imprecision and significant silences. This applies to Oedipus as well as to his hosts.

Oedipus seems to consider himself neither pure nor polluted, but between, or beyond, these ritual categories. The two statements Oedipus makes in the play about his ritual state point in this direction. At 548, Oedipus asserts that since in killing his father he acted unintentionally (ἄιδρις) he is 'pure by law' (νόμῳ δὲ καθαρός). Oedipus is confident, then, that he is not polluted in the sense that he has contracted ritual *miasma*. Perhaps rightly so: Edward Harris observes that this play's Oedipus, unlike *OT*'s, claims to have killed his father in self-defence (992–6), so that in Athens he may indeed have been considered 'pure'.[127] At the same time, the formulation suggests that he does not regard himself as unambiguously pure either. The qualification 'by law' is significant. We may take the dative νόμῳ to denote the particular perspective from which Oedipus thinks he is pure.[128] Thus, Oedipus regards himself to be 'pure by law' because he acted unintentionally, but in some complex sense, the phrasing suggests, he does not think he is pure in every respect; pure 'enough', that is, as to be καθαρός without further qualification.[129]

Oedipus' later reference to a certain 'stain of evils' which attaches to him may be taken as 548's counterpart, implying much the same, but from the opposite perspective. Rejoicing at the reunion with his daughters, recovered from the clutches of Creon's henchmen, Oedipus turns to Theseus, intending to shake hands with, and kiss, his daughters' saviour. No sooner said than recanted: for how could one such as he, 'wretched' (ἄθλιος γεγώς, 1132) and afflicted with a 'stain of evils' (κηλὶς κακῶν, 1134), dare touch the Athenian king? By evoking the idea of a transmissible 'stain', Oedipus certainly adumbrates pollution. The point is perhaps underscored by

---

[126] E.g. Segal (1981) 363, 364, 366; Winnington-Ingram (1980) 254; Dhuga (2011) 17–18, 24.
[127] Harris (2010b) 138.   [128] See Smyth, § 1516.
[129] Tzanetou (2012) 111–13 also notes an ambiguity surrounding Oedipus' pollution, but locates the ambiguity differently: she dissociates ritual and legal status and holds that Oedipus is ritually polluted and legally ('civically') pure. But Tzanetou seems too quick to attach specific labels and not attentive enough to the play's striking terminological imprecisions and silences in the matter, which discourage an inference quite as precise as hers (that said, Tzanetou's interpretation is easily approximated to mine if her 'ritually' is taken to imply a 'somehow', i.e. the world of the not quite definable and tangible as opposed to the definable and tangible 'civic').

external evidence: in Euripides' *Heracles*, a play which predates Sophocles', a similar scenario is explicitly associated with pollution: there, Heracles, after infanticide, is reluctant to talk to, or even uncover his head in the presence of, Theseus, for fear of transmitting pollution (Eur. *HF* 1219–21, 1232–4). Nonetheless, if by reference to the 'stain' Oedipus indicates that something is amiss with him, that he is 'not entirely pure', the opacity of his terminology – quite apart from the earlier explicit statement that he is 'pure by law' – suggests that he does not conceive of his affliction as a straightforward ritual pollution.[130]

His hosts do not contradict him, allowing in this way for the existence of this indeterminate space beyond ritual categories and permitting Oedipus to occupy it. The Colonean elders, for one, seem to adopt Oedipus' view. Their initial fear that Oedipus might somehow infect, and affect, the city surely implies the identification of an affliction resembling pollution; but (perhaps in reponse to Oedipus' claim to be 'pure by law')[131] they never take the significant next step, to equate this affliction with pollution. Throughout, they refrain from using the language of *miasma* or indeed any clear-cut qualification relating to the protagonist's ritual state. Instead, they find that Oedipus is 'accursed' (ἄλαστον ἄνδρ', 1483). This may be taken as a (in itself significant) lack of concern for precise terminology; but it may also be taken to indicate that the Colonean elders, although acknowledging the existence of an affliction, do not consider this affliction to be quite a ritual pollution. Corroboration for the latter conclusion is perhaps provided by the chorus' instruction, in their description of the required purification of the shrine, that Oedipus fetch water from the near-by stream with hands that are ὅσια (470).[132] It seems that while they consider the man 'accursed', they hold that his hands are easily enough rendered ὅσια – which surely involves ritual purity? – for carrying out intricate ritual purifications. The casualness of the reference to these ὅσια hands may be seen to indicate that the chorus does not, at this point, regard Oedipus as technically polluted, requiring elaborate purification.[133]

---

[130] See also Markantonatos (2007) 100 n. 41 who notes that 'Oedipus' consciousness of his "stain of evils" (1134) should not be interpreted as evidence of defilement.'

[131] Harris (2010b) 138; see also Edmunds (1996) 134–8. Harris does not acknowledge, though, that despite his 'purity by law' there is something amiss with Oedipus.

[132] On the meaning of this purification within the dramatic denouement, see Burkert (1985b) 8–14; see also Cole (2004) 42.

[133] Harris (2010b) 138 more generally argues that the chorus would not have allowed Oedipus to carry out these rites had they considered him properly polluted. It should be noted that some scholars have felt that the purification of the Eumenides purifies the hero also: see e.g. Knox (1964) 152; Segal (1981) 385; Kamerbeek (1984) ad 465–7. See Markantonatos (2007) 128–9 on the points of contact between the (description of the) purification and Oedipus' later heroisation.

A lack of interest in (determining and labelling) the precise nature of Oedipus' affliction is more fittingly attributed to Theseus. To be sure, Theseus, too, may be seen to acknowledge the existence of an affliction: in contrast to the Theseus of Euripides' *Heracles*, who has nothing but disregard for Heracles' fear of infection, Sophocles' Theseus seems to comply with Oedipus' instruction to keep his distance, in this way seemingly endorsing the notion that there is something problematic about the man who killed his father and slept with his mother. But such acknowledgement remains tacit: if the chorus finds few and imprecise words for this 'evil', the Athenian king finds none at all.[134] The point here is, I think, that he does not in fact seem to care at all for finding them. We may infer from this that, whatever his 'real' assessment of Oedipus' ritual state, to Theseus (ritual) labels mean very little. The Athenian king, that is, also allows Oedipus to occupy an indeterminate space between, or beyond, ritual categories; but he does so, not by attaching indeterminate predications to the protagonist's 'evil', but by not bothering to predicate – define, determine – at all.[135]

The picture that emerges here is that *Oedipus at Colonus* portrays a world which, unlike the one we initially find in Aeschylus' Argos, allows for complexity and indeterminacy, identities 'in between'. I suggest that the position Oedipus comes to take up as both insider and outsider, citizen of sorts as well as stranger, and the indeterminate space between, or beyond, ritual categories he is permitted to occupy may fruitfully be seen as coterminous: Colonus accommodates an Oedipus whose position vis-à-vis the city is as vague as his ritual status.

In view of the play's great interest in boundaries, ὅροι,[136] which surpasses even that of Aeschylus' *Suppliants*, the point is perhaps best formulated in terms of 'liminality'. In contrast to Aeschylus' Argos, where what is initially negotiated is on which side of the boundary a particular individual is placed, Sophocles' Colonean world does not require the hero to be on any one side, but allows him to be on the *limen* itself.[137] This is so very literally: for the greater part of the play, the hero is seated on the boundary between two distinct spaces, the sacred space of the shrine and the profane ground

---

[134] Mills (1997) 171 also notes that only the chorus verbalises fears about Oedipus' pollution and concludes that 'Theseus is left as the epitome of Athenian kindness and daring, by accepting Oedipus straightaway'. See Calame (1996a) for Theseus and the 'Athenian imaginary'.

[135] It is significant that the one character in the play most outspokenly concerned with, and perhaps certain about, Oedipus' ritual state is hostile-minded Creon, who thinks that Oedipus is an 'unholy' (or 'unclean') parricide (ἄνδρα καὶ πατροκτόνον | κἄναγνον, 944–5).

[136] Segal (1981) 369; Vidal-Naquet (1986b) esp. 204–7.

[137] On Oedipus' liminal position and the importance of boundaries, see Segal (1981) 364, 369 and generally 362–408; Vidal-Naquet (1986a) 204–11; on Colonus as place of transition, see also Bernek (2005) 135–6.

outside it – in contrast to the Danaids who are *either* inside *or* outside sacred space.¹³⁸ To be sure, the Danaids, as *astoxenoi*, are also 'in-between', on the *limen*. But at least until redefinitions set in and matters become more complex, in *Suppliants* this in-between space (of 'self-and-other') tends to be assimilated to the space of the 'other' in a binary opposition between self and other. Argos' initial conceptual world, in which identity is largely a matter of either/or, of purity (self) *or* impurity (other), does not allow for the *limen* itself to exist as a third space between inside and outside. Being on the *limen* is to be other and is bound up with impurity. Sophocles' Colonus more easily accepts such a third space; liminal identities are accommodated without struggle.

Euripides' *Ion*

Euripides' *Ion* is not, at least not primarily, a suppliant drama.¹³⁹ It does not pit, in the overtly political framework which that genre provides, easily identifiable groups of self and other against each other. On the face of it, what we are confronted with is a family drama full of tender, private emotions. A mother, once raped by a god, finds, by divine providence, the child born of that union, which she had earlier exposed, reluctantly. A child finds its mother (and father, though an absent one). In the process, the god is vindicated and, in the exuberant joy of mother–son reunification, all's well that ends well.

But *Ion* is not just family business.¹⁴⁰ Though it seems to anticipate the (supposedly) apolitical world of family intrigues and happy reunifications generally associated with New Comedy,¹⁴¹ it is in a sense the most overtly political play of Euripides and certainly a no less serious contribution to the negotiation of civic identity than Aeschylus' *Suppliants* with its austere interest in the politics of the community at large so characteristic of that earlier playwright. For the family that is put on stage here is not just any family but the Athenian family par excellence. The mother is Creusa,

---

[138] On spatial configurations in *Oedipus at Colonus*, see Seale (1982) 113–43; on Oedipus seated on the boundary see ibid. 122. On theatrical space in the play, see Edmunds (1996) 39–83.
[139] The play, however, includes a suppliant crisis: Creusa's taking refuge, before Ion, at Apollo's altars. See Thorburn (2001) for the mix of 'genres' in the play.
[140] This arguably holds true for Euripides' family reunion plays in general: see Karamanou (2012).
[141] For the relations between the *Ion* and (new) comedy, see Knox (1970) 77–91; on comic elements in *Ion*, see also Seidensticker (1982) 211–41. For Knox (1970) 77 *Ion* 'is fully-fledged comedy – a work of genius in which the theater of Menander, almost a hundred years in the future, stands before us in firm outline'. Seidensticker considers *Ion* (because it comprises both cheerful and serious/bitter moments) a 'tragic-comedy'. For criticism especially of Knox, see Mastronarde (2010) 58 (esp. n. 38 with references).

Euripides' Ion

noble daughter sprung from the line of earthborn Erichthonius, ruler of the Athenian race of autochthons; and the son is Ion, eponymous hero of the Ionian tribe of which the Athenians are the most illustrious representatives. This family is Athens itself, and a lens through which Athenian origins and in particular the city's infamous autochthony – which suggests the artificial *political* unit of the city-state as *natural* unit by common descent and aligns the civic with the ethnic – can be examined.[142] Its appearance on stage necessarily brings with it a reflection on what it means to be Athenian.

Euripides' specific dramatisation makes the question of identity particularly urgent. This is a matter, not least, of *Ion*'s plot, which seems to differ markedly from earlier versions of the myth. Notably, in earlier versions Ion's parentage does not seem to have been a matter of debate. In Hesiod and Herodotus, for example, he is identified, unambiguously, as Xuthus' son.[143] This means that it may well have been Euripides' invention to present the integration of Ion into Athens in the framework of a foundling/reunification story.[144] Significantly, through this innovation the myth which explains to the Athenians the primordial essence of their being is brought on stage in terms of a story-pattern whose essential feature is the 'quest for identity'. In *Ion*, that is, Euripides transforms into a plot-pattern what in a sense a dramatisation of stories pertaining to the Athenians' autochthonous ancestors necessarily brings with it for an Athenian audience.[145] If in one way or another Athenian identity must be at stake in any treatment of the Ion myth, it is so especially in this one: by displacing Creusa's son as foundling from his Athenian home to Delphi and then setting out on a path of rediscovery ('re-placement'),[146] the play invites the audience to join the protagonist in tracing Athenian identity.

---

[142] The classic discussion of autochthony is Loraux (1993); equally classic is her treatment of the autochthony theme in the *Ion* (Loraux (1990); reprinted in ead. (1993) 184–236). For the political implications of autochthony and their negotiation in the play, see also Saxonhouse (1986). A recent study of *Ion* in (such) political terms (focusing in particular on 'racial ideology') is Lape (2010) 95–136.

[143] Hesiod fr. 10a, 20–4 MW; Hdt. 7.94, 8.44; there is no definite evidence for Apollo as Ion's father before Euripides' play. It has, however, been suggested that the long-standing cult of Apollo *patrōios* indicates that this was already part of a mythical tradition. See Conacher (1967) 271; Lee (1997) 39.

[144] Since our knowledge of the Sophoclean plays treating the same myth (*Ion* and *Creusa* – perhaps a single play) is limited, however, we cannot make any definitive statement. On the related theme of 'abandonment' in *Ion*, see Pedrick (2007) who reads *Ion* alongside Freud's 'From the history of an infantile neurosis'.

[145] Katerina Zacharia's monograph on *Ion* bears the fitting title *Converging truths. Euripides' Ion and the Athenian quest for self-definition*: Zacharia (2003).

[146] For Burnett (1971) 103 the shift of the setting to Delphi is 'a central, overwhelming innovation'.

Answering to, and further emphasising, the particular thrust of this plot-pattern, the play explicitly and insistently lays out the ingredients of Athenian identity. In particular, Ion's displacement from Athens also entails that he appears, to those of established Athenian identity, as non-Athenian and 'other'.[147] As the play twists and turns its way towards final reunification, the challenge that his impending integration into the Athenian ruler-house poses to these Athenians elicits strong statements of Athenian reassertion vis-à-vis this supposed 'intruder'. Creusa, the chorus of her maidservants, and the old man (formerly tutor of Erechtheus) all feel encouraged repeatedly to spell out what it means to be Athenian.

In this negotiation of civic identity, purity figures large.[148] The central aspect of this is the positioning of purity as perhaps the pivotal characteristic of Athenian identity. The purity in question here is ethnic, not ritual, homing in on birth and descent, in this way recalling Herodotus' 'purebred' Ionians (Hdt. 1.147) and foreshadowing Ps.-Aristotle's Athenians 'not pure with respect to their birth' (*Ath. Pol.* 13.5). It constitutes the key concept and summation of the proposition, put forward by various characters and developed in terms of the myth of Athenian autochthony, that 'Athens (is) for the Athenians'[149] and that true Athenians are homebred 'brothers from one mother' (μιᾶς μητρὸς πάντες ἀδελφοὶ φύντες, Pl. *Menex.* 239a), distinguished by their autochthonous origins from 'imported' foreigners such as Xuthus (592), who are citizens in name at best and looked upon with suspicion (673–5).[150]

If in *Ion*, then, purity and identity enter into a particularly close relation, this relation is more complex than may appear at first sight. As we shall see, the (non-ritual) notion of genealogical Athenian purity is embedded within a web of further explorations of different kinds of purity, which reflect back on Athenian purity. There is the story of the foundling whose identity as chaste temple-servant and 'adopted son' of the chaste Pythia and the god of purification is defined in terms of ritual purity; and the story of Apollo, Athens' divine ancestor, whose ambiguous role as both rapist and divine benefactor finds expression in the god's oracular shrine whose purity is under constant attack by the droppings of indecent birds.

---

[147] We shall see below that the use of the term 'other' is not simply fashionable parlance. In particular the chorus time and again refers to Ion as ἄλλος (see e.g. 693).

[148] The centrality of the theme of purity in the play has been emphasised by many scholars. Particularly important contributions on the topic include Whitman (1974) 69–103; Hoffer (1996); see also Thorburn (2000).

[149] Loraux (1990) 184.

[150] The themes raised here have been explored in a number of publications on the play. For the rhetoric of birthright, see Walsh (1978); for explorations of autochthony, see Saxonhouse (1986) and especially the wide-ranging discussion of Loraux (1990); see also the recent monographs by Zacharia (2003) and Lape (2010) 95–136.

As in Aeschylus' *Suppliants*, the various 'purities' are of different kinds. For instance, foundling Ion's purity is at a surface level merely ritual purity; Athenian ethnic purity, on the other hand, has no ritual implications. But since both are not only expressed in the same vocabulary (καθαρός), but – as in *Suppliants* again – also constructed in the same spatial terms, the play invites us to consider these purities, and the identities constructed around these purities, alongside each other.

The central point of the following discussion is that the quest for Athenian identity in this way becomes a (re-)location of that identity's 'purity'. I shall first explore in greater detail the 'web of purities' into which Athenian identity is woven and analyse the parallel laying out of 'pure identities'. This will provide the background for a discussion of the significance of these parallel 'pure identities'. We shall see that the concept of a 'pure' identity is drawn once more into complex negotiations, with ironic twists and turns. But *Ion* perhaps allows us to go further. According to one (strikingly Aristotelian) reading of *Ion*, we may derive from the play the suggestion that 'pure' identity may also be understood as 'clarified identity'. If this is accepted, the play may be taken to imply that, as it reproduces for the audience the quest for identity which Ion embarks on, a type of 'purified' identity is provided for the audience as well. In this way, if *Ion* is a quest for identity not only for the mythical figures within the play, but also for the Athenian audience watching the play, the 'purity' of Athenian identity is relocated in the theatre of Dionysus itself.

Identity, boundaries, purity: Athens

Though not a suppliant drama (with its typical scenario of asylum-seekers confronting citizen-insiders on their home territory) and very different in terms of plot-structure and 'tone', Euripides' *Ion* strongly resembles Aeschylus' *Suppliants* in some respects. Notably, both plays share a common 'grammar' and underlying constellation. Representatives of a civic collective – of Argos in the case of *Suppliants*, of Athens in the case of *Ion* – encounter individuals – or an individual – on the margins and about to enter that civic collective; in each case, a god plays a role as the point of reference for the marginal individual; sacred space constitutes the backdrop of the action and is occupied by the marginal individual(s); and identities are defined in terms of purity and mapped upon spaces with carefully guarded boundaries.

In this complex constellation, the particular identity of the Athenian civic collective constitutes the play's central reference point. In the prologue spoken by Hermes, it certainly occupies a privileged place.[151] Even before we are introduced to the plot proper, we encounter Pallas' 'famous city' (8–10):

> ἔστιν γὰρ οὐκ ἄσημος Ἑλλήνων πόλις,
> τῆς χρυσολόγχου Παλλάδος κεκλημένη,
> οὗ παῖδ᾽ Ἐρεχθέως Φοῖβος ἔζευξεν γάμοις
> βίᾳ Κρέουσαν...

> There is a well-known Greek city which is named after Pallas, the goddess of the golden spear, where Phoebus forced a violent union on Creusa, the child of Erechtheus...

Though spoken about by many, including Hermes and Ion, the 'famous city' has three primary representatives: Creusa, the chorus of Creusa's maidservants and the former tutor of Erechtheus. Creusa's husband Xuthus, who married into the Athenian royal house from the outside, is from the beginning treated as not quite Athenian, of noble birth but not 'born within', as Hermes informs us (οὐκ ἐγγενής, 63). This constellation implies an irony: the civic collective here is represented by a multitude of voices, not by a single authoritative voice as in Aeschylus' *Suppliants*; but none of these is the voice of a (proper) male citizen.

From the beginning, the elementary ingredient of the city's identity, the idea of autochthony, is in the spotlight. As Hermes proceeds to lay out the specifics of the story of Creusa and her exposed child, he refers to the idea twice, in two different forms, suggesting its centrality to the city's self-understanding. First it is the particular autochthony of the Athenian ruling house that is in question; alluding to a 'certain custom of earthborn Erichthonius' (νόμον... τοῦ... γηγενοῦς | Ἐριχθονίου, 20–1), Hermes reminds us that the Athenian royal line descends from ancestry that, having sprung from the earth, is as autochthonous as it gets, supplying the original and rightful inhabitants of Attica. Only a few lines later, a more democratic version of the myth is invoked, conferring the glory of autochthony (and its vision of original unity) upon the Athenian people as a whole.[152] After

---

[151] Hence Wolff (1965) 173: 'The setting of the play is, of course, Delphi. But the story is an Athenian one.' Vogt (1998) 45: 'Das Stück ist damit also auch... ein athenisches Drama vor delphischer Kulisse.'

[152] It has been suggested that the Athenian people, too, must be earthborn, but the play does not make this explicit; what matters more is that they are a unified group of insiders. For the suggestion that a birth of the Athenians *en masse* from the earth is implied here, see Ogden (1996) 167. While it does not contradict this view, the play does not pay great attention to the idea. As Blok (2009) 150–4 has shown, the term 'autochthonous' has various meanings and may imply no more than that the Athenians had never migrated. Though strict logic would lead us to the conclusion that

Creusa's exposal of the infant, Hermes tells us, Apollo bade him to 'go to the autochthonous people of famous Athens' to fetch the newborn (29–30):

ὦ σύγγονον', ἐλθὼν λαὸν εἰς αὐτόχθονα
κλεινῶν Ἀθηνῶν (οἶσθα γὰρ θεᾶς πόλιν) ...

The centrality of autochthony (in both its forms) for Athenian identity is confirmed as the play unfolds; in the process, the fact that exclusivity and xenophobic classifications in terms of insiders and outsiders are part and parcel of this identity becomes more and more apparent.

At first, it is primarily Delphi-bred Ion who comments on the matter. In his first encounter with Creusa, for instance, the youth (at this point not yet revealed as Creusa's son) refers to the 'in-born' quality of Erechtheid Creusa (οὖσαν ἐγγενῆ, 293) and wonders how the foreigner Xuthus, whom Creusa, with an arguably uneasy undertone, designates as 'brought in from another land' (ἐπακτὸς ἐξ ἄλλης χθονός, 290),[153] can possibly be married to her. Later, the autochthonous Athenian people come into focus. Thus, when Xuthus (wrongly) identifies Ion as his son and offers him wealth and power in Athens, Ion worries about the dubious position he would occupy in the autochthonous city as the child of a non-Athenian father and bastard (589–92):

εἶναί φασι τὰς αὐτόχθονας
κλεινὰς Ἀθήνας οὐκ ἐπείσακτον γένος,
ἵν' ἐσπεσοῦμαι δύο νόσω κεκτημένος,
πατρός τ' ἐπακτοῦ καὐτὸς ὢν νοθαγενής.

They say that the famous autochthonous Athenians are not an immigrant race. Were I to intrude there, I would be afflicted with two ills: descent from an immigrant father and my own bastardy.

The representatives of Athens largely validate Ion's idea of their city. Among them, Creusa is the least vocal. Though herself distinguishing between insiders and outsiders 'brought in from another land' (290) and not immune to prejudice vis-à-vis such outsiders,[154] she shows remarkably little interest in autochthony and the make-up of Athenian identity. The chorus and the old man, by contrast, display a veritable obsession in this

---

Ion implies that the entire Athenian people are earthborn, birth from the earth is emphasised only in the case of the royal line.

[153] Saxonhouse (1986) 265 draws attention to Creusa's apologetic tone as she goes on to present her marriage as the unavoidable result of military alliances.

[154] We have already noted her uneasy and apologetic tone at 289–98. But see also her remarks at 1295–9 to the effect that a son of Xuthus and a non-Athenian mother would never inherit the Athenian throne.

respect.[155] In particular the chorus is much preoccupied with the royal line's descent from earthborn ancestry and emerges as aggressively xenophobic.[156] Upon the 'brought-in foreigner' Xuthus they look with suspicion; and the introduction of that foreigner's son, born, not from Creusa, but from a non-Erechtheid (and quite possibly even non-Athenian) mother, into the noble line of earthborn Erichthonius is perceived as an affront to, and seen to be incompatible with, the desired Erechtheid exclusivity. In the chorus' view, Athens is 'their city' (ἐμὰν πόλιν, 719) that 'others' from the outside must never rule. They assume that Creusa is of the same opinion, sharing their dislike of 'others' (1069–73):

> οὐ γὰρ δόμων γ' ἑτέρους
> ἄρχοντας ἀλλοδαποὺς
> ζῶσά ποτ' <ἐν> φαεν-
> ναῖς ἀνέχοιτ' ἂν αὐγαῖς
> ἁ τῶν εὐπατριδᾶν γεγῶσ' οἴκων.

For never, while she lives, would she endure that others from the outside rule over her house, and in bright daylight; she is, after all, of noble descent.

Importantly, this desired Athenian exclusivity is expressed in spatial terms. 'Bringing in', ἐπάγειν, we have seen, is seen as potentially problematic by Ion (and presumably Creusa). The chorus affirm Ion's suspicions as they declare that they would rather see the youth die than intrude upon the carefully guarded space of their Athenian *polis* (μή <τί> ποτ' εἰς ἐμὰν πόλιν ἵκοιθ' ὁ παῖς, | νέαν δ' ἁμέραν ἀπολιπὼν θάνοι, 719–20). The boundaries of this space, it seems, must at all times be defended against transgression. Therefore, 'coming inside' and reaching across these boundaries, and those of the Athenian ruling house, in this way to 'touch' it, appears to be a vision of especial horror.[157] Thus, as Creusa and the old man have left the stage to carry out the murder plot against Ion, the chorus pray that the fatal drops of the Gorgon's blood may be guided towards the one 'touching the house

---

[155] Accordingly, it has been suggested that xenophobia in *Ion* is mostly a matter of the lower classes. See Walsh (1978) 308.

[156] The issue has been a staple of scholarly writing on the play. See especially Walsh (1978) on the rhetoric of birthright and race in the *Ion* and its significance before the contemporary historical background; Saxonhouse (1986) on exclusivity and the autochthony-myth. In the past scholars have read *Ion* as a straightforward piece of racist propaganda; see especially Delebecque (1951) 229: 'La tragédie dégage en effet une véritable théorie du racisme.'

[157] There is perhaps also a suggestion that identification with the virginal patroness Athena plays a role. Her virginity is mentioned at 466 (δύο θεαὶ δύο παρθένοι). If Ion's close association with purity in part aptly reflects his identity constructed in reference to the god of purification and his chaste priestess, Athens' exclusivity may be seen to be connected to identification with a figure that stands for the shutting out of someone other than the self.

of the Erechtheids', because 'no "other" *coming in* [must] ever rule in place of the noble-born Erechtheidai' (1056–60):

> ... τῷ τῶν Ἐρεχθειδᾶν
> δόμων ἐφαπτομένῳ.
> μηδέ ποτ' ἄλλος ἥ-
> κων πόλεως ἀνάσσοι,
> πλὴν τῶν εὐγενετᾶν Ἐρεχθειδᾶν.[158]

The catchword used in the play to describe an Athenian identity conceived of in such exclusive terms, sealed off and inimical to incursions from the outside, is 'purity'; it is delivered by the outsider Ion. We return at this point to the wider perspective that is concerned with the entire Athenian people as λαὸς αὐτόχθων. According to Ion, the notion that Athenians are autochthonous and therefore 'of one stock', much like their Erechtheid rulers, means that Athens is 'pure'. As he leaves the stage to celebrate his partially recovered identity as son of Xuthus, he expresses the wish that his mother be Athenian (ἐκ τῶν Ἀθηνῶν) so that he acquire an acceptable standing in the autochthonous city 'from his mother's side' (μητρόθεν). For 'if a foreigner lands in a pure city, though he be a citizen in theory, he possesses the voice of a slave and does not have freedom of speech' (671–5):

> ἐκ τῶν Ἀθηνῶν μ' ἡ τεκοῦσ' εἴη γυνή,
> ὥς μοι γένηται μητρόθεν παρρησία.
> καθαρὰν γὰρ ἤν τις ἐς πόλιν πέσῃ ξένος,
> κἂν τοῖς λόγοισιν ἀστὸς ᾖ, τό γε στόμα
> δοῦλον πέπαται κοὐκ ἔχει παρρησίαν.

Let us remain with this Athenian purity for a moment in order to clarify just what is meant by it. It does not appear to designate what it at first sight seems to suggest: the kind of absolute (ethnic) purity that comes from two (ethnically) Athenian parents and which is required by Pericles' citizenship law.[159] The view seems to be shared by the chorus and Ion. The chorus, for all their concern with exclusivity and noble birth and despite their aggressive xenophobia, show no sign of disapproval vis-à-vis a child born of Erechtheid Creusa and the 'brought-in' foreigner Xuthus: what matters to them is the unbroken continuity of the royal line as against the usurpation of the Erechtheid throne by a child born of the foreigner Xuthus and 'other', non-Erechtheid blood (ὁ παῖς | ἄλλων τραφεὶς ἐξ αἱμάτων,

---

[158] ἥκων, 'coming in', is Diggle's conjecture for οἴκων. See Diggle (1969) 48–9.
[159] On this law and its relation to the myth of autochthony, see Blok (2009) esp. 150–4.

692–3).¹⁶⁰ Ion's idea of Athenian purity seems to correspond to this. If we take his statements at 589–92 and 671–5 together, the picture that emerges is this: born of the 'brought-in' Xuthus and a non-Athenian mother, he thinks he may acquire the formal status of a citizen, but 'in word' only; in practice, his standing will be low since his father, presumably to be thought of as something of a naturalised Athenian, is not Athenian by blood.¹⁶¹ By contrast, 671–5 seems to say that as the son of a 'brought-in father' and an ethnically Athenian mother, he will not only be a citizen 'in words', with the 'voice of a slave', but a full member of the pure city of Athens.¹⁶² This latter view is never contradicted.¹⁶³ In order to be part of the 'pure city' (as well as, on another level, of the Athenian ruling house) ethnic affiliation on one parental side seems to suffice, therefore.¹⁶⁴

In an (important) aside, it should be pointed out that it is the female parental side which counts in Ion, not the male. One should be wary, though, of deriving from this a triumphal refutation of the misogyny Euripides was credited with already in antiquity:¹⁶⁵ it seems to me that

---

[160] This corresponds to what seems to have been aristocratic ideology. As Lape (2010) 101–2 points out, in order to lay claim to *eugeneia* one noble ancestor was usually seen to be enough; she therefore speaks of the 'aristocratic conception of an inherited essence' (ibid. 105).

[161] It will later turn out (1297), though, that as son of Xuthus and a foreigner Ion will have no access to Erechtheid power and wealth, counting as Aeolian rather than as Erechtheid. Walsh (1978) esp. 302 takes the passage at 589–92 differently, deriving conditions for Athenian citizenship from it that closely parallel those set out in the Periclean citizenship law. For him, Ion implies that while he may acquire citizenship status as the son of a naturalised Athenian (Xuthus) and an Athenian mother, he will not be a citizen as son of a naturalised Athenian and a non-Athenian mother. He points out that the term *nothos* in Athens was a technical term for someone born from an Athenian father and a non-Athenian mother, without citizen status. Two arguments speak against this interpretation. First, it is not at all clear that *nothos* was understood in this technical sense in the fifth century. Arguably, the play itself does not invite us to understand *nothos* in this way. Being a *nothos* is a frequent concern for Ion, but what seems at stake mostly is his bastardy. Second, the subsequent passage seems to imply that he thinks he could be a citizen ('in words') in Athens as the son of a 'brought-in ("naturalised") father' and as *nothos*, albeit looked upon with suspicion. On the contested issue of bastards in ancient Athens, see Ogden (1996) 151–65; see also Lape (2010) 129–36. It is not clear whether or not bastards could be citizens.

[162] If we look for historical parallels, Ion seems to think along the kind of lines that we find in the naturalisation decree of the Plataeans. In the 420s, several hundred Plataeans were granted Athenian citizenship. The decree specifies that the naturalised Athenians (those of the first generation) did not enjoy full citizen rights (for instance, they could not stand for office as *archontes*). Their children, however, if born from a union with an Athenian wife, would be able to enjoy these rights denied to their fathers. See Blok (2009) 166–7.

[163] Except that in order to gain access to Erechtheid power 'some Athenian mother' is presumably not sufficient; at 671–5 Ion's concern is however more with his standing as member of the civic community.

[164] It is symptomatic that Saxonhouse (1986) 265 speaks, cautiously, of 'the purity of noble birth', but never makes it entirely clear just what that really implies.

[165] Famous is the scenario of Aristophanes' *Thesmophoriazusae* in which the outraged women of Athens seek to punish Euripides for badmouthing (κακῶς αὐτὰς λέγω, *Th.* 182) them (as insane

what is in the foreground here is not so much a vindication of 'the female principle', but rather the irony itself of the prominence of 'the marginal' (for instance in the form of females) in a play that is essentially about what it means to be Athenian. It is appropriate that in the form of the chorus it is (slave) women who advocate the view that the 'purity' of the royal line depends on Creusa; and that it is Athena (rather than male Apollo) who predicts the splendid future of the royal Athenian line.[166]

In contrast to Aeschylus' *Suppliants*, in *Ion* we are not presented with a neat exposition of identity in the form of an extended speech by the authoritative representative of the civic community. Nonetheless, the voices that speak loudest construct an identity not unlike Argive identity in *Suppliants*: exclusiveness and boundaries are paramount; and 'purity', though suggested only by an outsider as a term by which one can express Athenian identity, seems to constitute once more a central determinant in the definition of self and other.

Identity, boundaries, purity: Apollo and Ion

As in Aeschylus' play, the civic collective's identity is not the only one that brings into play the notion of purity and a concomitant concern with exclusion, exclusiveness and boundaries. Sacred space, in the form of Apollo's Delphic precinct, is once more important, though in this play it serves a double function: it arguably expresses something about the hoped-for nature of its divine inhabitant Apollo; at the same time, it serves as intermediary through which is expressed, as in *Suppliants*, the 'pure identity' of its immediate occupant, Ion.

Let us first look at the characteristics of the sacred space itself. Much like the Argive sanctuary in *Suppliants*, it is presented as demarcated space. Even more emphatically than in *Suppliants*, it is presented as a type of space whose insides and outsides are defined according to the category of ritual purity. This purity is suggested in visual terms: somewhere on stage, perhaps at the entrance of the *skēnē* building, lustral basins are placed;[167] and (part of) the sanctuary is assiduously cleansed by Ion, who, equipped with broom, bow and (Apollonian) garland, exits from the *skēnē* building

---

and murderous and forever sexually depraved). On Euripides the misogynist, see the remarks by March (1990).
[166] On the importance of the female in the play's presentation of autochthony, see in particular Loraux (1993). This importance of the female could also be seen in the historical framework of the increased importance of Athenian women for citizen identity which resulted from the Periclean citizenship law. On this historical frame, see Osborne (1997b).
[167] These lustral basins are referred to, by Ion, at 434–6 (ἀπορραντήρια, 435).

after the prologue-speech of Hermes to sweep the entrance area of the precinct and chase away the birds which threaten to defile the splendour of the shrine.[168] But its purity is intimated also by Ion's words. By his own indication, he has since childhood cleansed the temple entrance (ἐσόδους Φοίβου | καθαρὰς θήσομεν, 104–5). More importantly, Apollo's temple, not unlike Ion's Athens in this respect, requires the purity, in this case ritual, of those who approach. Ion dutifully instructs the temple-servants (who presumably enter the stage from one of the *parodoi* just after Ion exits from the *skēnē* building) to undergo ritual purification at the Castalian spring and its 'pure drops' (94–7):

> ἀλλ᾿, ὦ Φοίβου Δελφοὶ θέραπες,
> τὰς Κασταλίας ἀργυροειδεῖς
> βαίνετε δίνας, καθαροῖς δὲ δρόσοις
> ἀφυδρανάμενοι στείχετε ναούς.[169]

> Delphian servants of Phoebus, go to the silvery pools of Castalia; and when you have washed yourself with its pure water, return to the temple.

Surely, this sacred space would seem to say something about Apollo.[170] In Aeschylus, sacred space remains anonymous as the κοινοβωμία (*Suppl.* 222) of ἀγώνιοι θεοί (*Suppl.* 355). In *Ion*, by contrast, its association with Apollo is emphasised. It is the 'house of the god' (θεοῦ... δόμον, 45; θεοῦ... δῶμ[α], 315). Further, the two, 'house' and god, even converge as Ion metonymically refers to the temple's entrance as the 'entrances of Phoebus' (ἐσόδους Φοίβου, 104).

The convergence closely associates Apollo with purity. Although temple districts are of course always subject to purity requirements and are demarcated by lustral basins, the insistence on purity and cleansing here seems to constitute a translation into concrete terms of the 'identity' of its inhabitant, incidentally the god particularly closely associated with purity and purification and bestowed with attributes, such as the laurel, that are agents of purification as well as symbols of purity.[171] In addition, there is

---

[168] Incidentally, a number of inscriptions from Delos suggest that this type of defilement (through guano) was perceived as threat to the purity of sanctuaries outside of drama, too: see e.g. *IG* XI.2 147.18 and Cole (2004) 49 n. 104 with further references.

[169] In a related vein Ion later advises the chorus of Athenian maid-servants not to enter the sacred precinct before offering certain sacrifices (219–22; 226–9; note especially the implicit emphasis on boundaries, insides and outsides: ὑπερβῆναι, 220; πρὸ δόμων, 226; πάριτ᾿ ἐς, 228 = 229).

[170] On Apollo in *Ion*, see Zacharia (2003) 103–49.

[171] The point is also made by Zacharia (2003) 129. For Apollo as god of purification, see for instance A. *Eum.* 62–3: ἰατρόμαντις... δωμάτων καθάρσιος; *SEG* IX 72 (the Cyrene cathartic law): [Ἀ]πόλλων ἔχρη[σε· | ἐς ἀ]εὶ καθαρμοῖς καὶ ἁγνήιαις κα[ὶ θε|ραπ]ήιαις χρειμένος τὰν Λεβύαν οἰκ[έν]. For

arguably a sense, too, that the marked purity of the temple expresses some of the mortals' pious hopes about the god, not least in this play: for he is the god who dispenses oracles of which human visitors to the shrine wish that they be 'pure' (καθαροῖς μαντεύμασι, 470–1).

The convergence also intimates an imperfection of Apollo's purity, though. For, just as Athens' purity is not absolute, so the fact that the shrine's purity requires permanent cleansing from dirt and permanent defilement (and indeed the birds' droppings) would seem to reflect an Apollonian purity that is in some sense not quite perfect.[172] We shall return to this latter point below.

Apollo's is an absent presence, however, and the identity more immediately associated with the sacred space of the Delphic temple is that of the foundling Ion. This is another marginal figure yet outside the civic community proper, similar in this respect to the Danaids.[173] It is in the absence of parental affiliation and membership in a civic *oikos* that he occupies, permanently, Apollo's shrine. He has spent his entire life in the sanctuary, ever since the Pythia took pity on the exposed infant and 'took it up' (οἴκτῳ... τρέφει δέ νιν λαβοῦσα, 47–9; see also ἐκ παιδός, 102); the entire precinct seems to have served as his homestead ('all of the god's precinct is my home, wherever sleep overcomes me', ἅπαν θεοῦ μοι δῶμ', ἵν' ἂν λάβῃ μ' ὕπνος, 315);[174] and its altars have centrally contributed to his sustenance ('the altars have nourished me and the strangers who constantly come here', βωμοὶ μ' ἔφερβον καὶ οὑπιών τ' ἀεὶ ξένος, 323).

---

certain reservations about the notion that Apollo is especially concerned with purity and particularly closely associated with purification, see Parker (1983) 393; see also Dyer (1969) 40–4 for doubts at least about Delphic Apollo's role in purification (he holds, however, that Apollo was considered particularly pure: ibid. 43). The god's symbols also appear in Ion's monody, where they are particularly closely associated with purification, for instance in the form of the laurel bow with which Ion cleanses the temple-entrance. For laurel (and gold) as agents of purification, see Parker (1983) 228 n. 118. Inscriptions suggest that there was a 'purification by gold' (whose exact mechanism is nowhere specified). For the association of gold with 'purity', see also Theognis 450–2 and Paus. 8.18.5. For gold imagery in *Ion*, see Thorburn (2000).

[172] The point is made also by Thorburn (2000) 45–6.

[173] On unmarried ('ephebic') males in Euripidean tragedy, see Mastronarde (2010) 285–91. On Ion as liminal figure on the point of transition, see in particular Segal (1999) 75–8 and *passim* and my discussion below.

[174] Ion's remark at 414 that his business is outside, while the oracular dealings inside are the concern of others (ἡμεῖς τά γ' ἔξω, τῶν ἔσω δ' ἄλλοις μέλει), may be taken to indicate that Ion does not inhabit the entire precinct since he is in fact barred from the temple's inside: see Zeitlin (1989) 166. But one needs to be precise: it seems that he is barred from the temple's interior only during the day when the oracle runs its business – in which he is not involved. During the night he appears to be inside: at the beginning of the play, Ion seems to exit from the temple. See e.g. Owen (1939) ad 78; and my remarks below.

More immediately than in *Suppliants*, the sanctuary's purity and that of its immediate inhabitant are coextensive. In one sense, it is simply that the sanctuary's purity requirements and the requirements of his office as temple-servant demand ritual purity and chastity: his instructions to the temple-servants at 94–7 to undergo purification prior to approaching the temple imply that Ion himself, as permanent resident roaming through the entire temple-area (ἅπαν θεοῦ μοι δῶμ', 315), must be perpetually pure. In addition, he explicitly states that he is ritually pure also in the sense of being 'free from the stain of sexual intercourse' and thus fit for his ritual office (ὅσιος ἀπ' εὐνᾶς ὤν, 150).

But if in this sense permanent occupancy conditions Ion's close association with purity, in a roundabout way it also aptly expresses his identity. It is not merely as the result of permanent occupancy of pure space that such purity has become an essential part of Ion's self; as in the case of the Danaids, it also has to do with parental affiliation. The Danaids conceive of their identity largely in terms of the paradigmatic asexual touch of forebear Zeus. Unlike the Danaids, Ion has no forebears known to him. In their stead, he identifies with surrogate parents, each associated in a different way with purity. Among these 'parents' is, first, the 'nurturing' sacred precinct itself with its strict purity regulations (109–11):

> ὡς γὰρ ἀμήτωρ ἀπάτωρ τε γεγώς
> τοὺς θρέψαντας
> Φοίβου ναοὺς θεραπεύω.

Since I have no mother and father I serve the temple of Phoebus, which has given me nurture.

More concretely, he presents as the essential reference point of his identity the god especially concerned with purity and purification,[175] as well as the precinct's chaste priestess.[176] He considers himself as 'belonging to the god' (τοῦ θεοῦ καλοῦμαι, 309; οὐκ οἶδα πλὴν ἕν· Λοξίου κεκλήμεθα, 311) and considers Apollo his surrogate father, quite unaware at this point of the truth of his words (136–40):

> Φοῖβός μοι γενέτωρ πατήρ·
> τὸν βόσκοντα γὰρ εὐλογῶ,

---

[175] See Parker (1983) 393.
[176] See Parker (1983) 93 on the strict chastity required of the Pythia during her tenure of office (noting that the post was usually filled by an old woman who will normally once have been married). Ion's association with Apollo and the Pythia as figures connected with purity is stressed by Hoffer (1996) 295 ('As a virgin son of a virgin mother, with the distant god of purification as his father, both his origin and his way of life are free from sexuality and its pollutions and oppressions').

τὸν δ' ὠφέλιμον ἐμοὶ πατέρος ὄνομα λέγω
Φοῖβον τὸν κατὰ ναόν.

For me, Phoebus is the father who begot me; I praise the one who feeds me and it is to my benefactor that I give the name of father: to Phoebus, lord of this temple.

The Pythia, correspondingly, he views as his surrogate mother (μητέρ' ὡς νομίζομεν, 321).[177]

It is as the result, then, of his permanent occupancy of the sacred precinct with its purity requirements and his identification in terms of that pure precinct as well as its other 'inhabitants', each associated with (different kinds of) purity, that different forms of purity have become an essential part of Ion's identity. Indeed, as Kevin Lee rightly points out, in reference to Ion's instructions to the temple-servants to undergo purification (and his subsequent reflections on appropriate ritual language), '[a]n obsession with ritual purity, both physical and verbal, is clear'.[178]

Ion acts out this identity in several ways. Above all, the cleansing activity he carries out during his monody may be considered as the translation of it into a concrete 'performance'.[179] But we may detect other such 'performances', which may be subsumed under the idea of boundary-obsession. As the result, perhaps, of the internalisation of the kind of duties which the maintenance of the temple district's purity brings with it, Ion worries greatly about boundaries and clear-cut separations. He is greatly dismayed, for instance, by the bird's indecent droppings (he intends to 'put to flight with [his] bow the flocks of birds, which harm the sacred offerings', πτηνῶν τ' ἀγέλας, | αἳ βλάπτουσιν σέμν' ἀναθήματα, | τόξοισιν ἐμοῖς φυγάδας θήσομεν, 106–8), in this way betraying a concern with the boundaries between sacred and profane (and dirt and cleanness).[180] More importantly, Ion carries his body as though it were another (pure) sacred space (although

---

[177] Meltzer (2006) 162 points out that the rearing of Ion by the Pythia as surrogate mother has a parallel in Erichthonius' being taken up by Athena as surrogate mother (mentioned by Creusa at 269–70). On the complex play of parental affiliations in the play, see Pedrick (2007).

[178] Lee (1997) ad 94–101. The importance of purity for Ion is also noted e.g. by Zeitlin (1989) 148, Hoffer (1996) 295–9, Segal (1999) 75–6.

[179] On the idea of 'performed identity', see Zeitlin (1989) 148–9. Such performance of identity includes action, gestures, and speech. Zeitlin (ibid. 172–3) considers important the emphasis on earthly elements in Ion's purificatory activities (he pours water on the earth; at 146–7 the water is specified as 'water from the spring of Gaia'). She connects this to the engendering of Erichthonius through the semen on Hephaestus which fell on the earth.

[180] See Hoffer (1996) esp. 295–99 on Ion's proneness to violence in the execution of his purificatory tasks (evinced in particular in his chasing away of the birds from the roof; but also in the *enforcement* of purity requirements). He emphasises the connection between culture and violence (violence as precondition of culture but masked by it) in the play.

we shall note below a certain imperfection also of Ion's own purity), with limited access across carefully defined boundaries and reminiscent in this respect of the pure city of Athens, which is so apprehensive about 'touches'. This takes two forms.

First, Ion is greatly concerned with the integrity of the physical boundaries of his body. For instance, when Xuthus, upon consultation of the oracle, exits the temple and presently meets Ion, now his 'son' by oracular affirmation, the 'father' tries to embrace his 'son'. Ion, however, attempts to keep his distance in order to preserve the integrity of his laurel wreath, which gives expression to his identity as servant of Apollo ('Stop! Don't touch the god's fillets: your hand could break them', παῦε, μὴ ψαύσας τὰ τοῦ θεοῦ στέμματα ῥήξῃς χερί, 522).[181]

Second, Ion is no less concerned about the abstract boundaries of his body. Justification for this claim comes in an earlier scene between Ion and Creusa. Creusa had just told Ion the troubling story about her 'friend' who was raped by, and gave birth to the child of, Apollo (338–54). Now Creusa has left the stage to pray at the god's altars. Ion is left alone, bewildered by what he just heard. He conceives of this inner turmoil as the effect of a transgression of boundaries: Creusa's words (λόγοι, 429), we may aptly say, 'touch' him. This spatially transgressive nature of Creusa's words is marked in the text. 'But what has the daughter of Erechtheus to do with me?', Ion wonders (ἀτὰρ θυγατρὸς τῆς Ἐρεχθέως τί μοι | μέλει; 433–4). 'Nothing' is his answer, but this 'nothing' is expressed in interesting terms: προσήκει γ᾽ οὐδέν (434), literally 'it does not at all *come* to me'. We have encountered the word ἥκω in the mouth of the xenophobic chorus already, worried that a stranger may 'come' to Athens.[182] Here, the use of the verb ἥκω emphasises the spatial character of the effect of Creusa's words, the intrusion they constitute into Ion's emotional life and inner self.

The scene is particularly revealing because it is closely connected with the idea of ritual purity. Intriguingly, the transgression across the boundaries of Ion's self is juxtaposed with Ion's dutiful care for purification. Immediately upon his assertion that Creusa's story does not 'come' to him, he turns to filling the precinct's lustral basins with water (434–6):

---

[181] Knox (1970) 80 suggests that Ion here sees his chastity endangered. As Xuthus comes out on stage, he addresses Ion as τέκνον, which, unless understood as 'son' (an interpretation not open to Ion at this moment), may have erotic connotations. Therefore, Ion may be taken to think 'that this middle-aged man is making vigorous sexual advances to him.' See also Pedrick (2007) 176 who speaks of a 'nearly erotic physical molestation'. Ion's aversion to Xuthus' touch and his devotion to keeping things separate, in particular by chasing away the birds from the temple, is also noted by Hoffer (1996) 298–9.

[182] 1058–9; as was pointed out above, however, ἥκων is a conjecture (defended by Diggle (1969) 48–9).

ἀλλὰ χρυσέαις
πρόχοισιν ἐλθὼν εἰς ἀπορραντήρια
δρόσον καθήσω.

But I shall go and with my golden pitchers pour water into the lustral basins.

Again, boundaries matter. The abrupt change of focus from inner turmoil to ritual activity marks a conscious effort to turn away, in this way to preserve the integrity of the uninvolved self, keeping at a distance a stranger's troublesome stories. In that the activity Ion turns to (and which marks his inner turning away) eventually implies a concern for boundaries in actual space (the boundaries around sacred space established through purity regulations), Ion's inner space – the 'space' demarcated by his sense of personhood and identity – is implicitly correlated with, and mapped onto, the bounded space of the sanctuary and its access regulations.[183]

At the same time, since this activity is concerned with the paraphernalia of purification, the play strongly suggests that for Ion the preservation of a secure identity is a matter, above all, of purity and purification. The passage, then, not only reinforces the impression that Ion's identity is primarily one defined by a concern with purity, it also lays this identity out in space (the space of the sanctuary) and action (Ion's pouring of water from the Castalian spring), and emphasises that the concern with purity, for Ion, becomes most pressing in the encounter between the supposedly well-defined and sealed-off self and the potential intrusion upon that self by someone, or something, other.

As in the cases of Athens and Apollo we may also detect a certain 'imperfection' of Ion's own purity, however. The cleansing activity itself and the continual battle against the birds' droppings imply at least contact with dirt and perhaps the occasional defilement. A similar, albeit slightly speculative, point may be made from a different perspective: Ion inhabits the 'whole house of the god' and presumably exits from inside the temple at day-break, after Hermes' prologue-speech.[184] During the day, however, when the shrine runs its 'business', Ion, by his own indication, is concerned with what is outside, while the oracular dealings inside are the concern of others (ἡμεῖς τά γ' ἔξω, τῶν ἔσω δ' ἄλλοις μέλει, 414).[185] If the lustral

---

[183] Ion cannot keep this story entirely at a distance, though. After all, it turns out to be his own. He accepts it at a point when he has decided to exchange sanctuary for city.
[184] See e.g. Owen (1939) ad 78.
[185] Zeitlin (1989) 166 – presumably less concerned with the minutiae of Ion's nocturnal whereabouts – seems to infer from 414 continual exclusion from the shrine's interior: 'Exposed at birth on the slopes of the Acropolis and barred at Delphi from the inmost recesses of the sacred shrine, his place has always been on the outside – at the entrance and on the steps of the temple.'

basins referred to at 434–6 were placed at the entrance of the *skēnē*-building (which admittedly we cannot ascertain), what would have been marked would be the especial purity of those within – and, inversely, the fact that being outside, in the area before the temple, implies a somehow less perfect purity. The fact itself of Ion's close association with purity as continual inhabitant of 'the whole house of the god' and chaste temple-servant remains unaffected by this; but its absoluteness at all times and in all places is perhaps called into question.

Intermezzo: purity at play

As in *Suppliants*, the purities with which Athens, Apollo and Ion are respectively associated may be different in kind, from the ethnic purity (and exclusivity) of Athens to the ritual purity of Ion; but since the vocabularies used to express these purities partially overlap and since Ion's and Athens' pure identities in particular are constructed in the same spatial terms, with careful attention being paid to boundaries and their non-transgression, bound up with a particular aversion to touches and intrusions, *Ion* invites us to consider these purities and the 'pure identities' associated with them alongside each other. Let us start quite innocently by looking at the three purities with an eye, not to identity, but to (mere) literary structure.

The first point to emerge from such a survey is *Ion*'s clever compositional play with the purities of Athens, Ion and Apollo. Not least, the play cleverly aligns 'not quite absolute' purities. In particular in the case of Ion's and Athens' purities the alignment is striking: Ion's (*almost* perfect) ritual purity is neatly exchanged for (a not quite absolute) Athenian purity: he abandons the sanctuary and with it his purity as temple-servant eventually to take up his identity as son of an Athenian mother and therefore as full member of the 'pure city' of Athens. As Froma Zeitlin aptly notes, 'Ion brings his "purity of upbringing to merge with the "purity" of the other sort which Athens claims.'[186]

The point is arguably given some emphasis shortly before the recognition scene. Upon Creusa's attempt on Ion's life, the latter returns onstage determined to lead Creusa to her appointed death. The Pythia, exiting from the temple, stops Ion and enjoins him to 'go pure to Athens, with good omens' (καθαρὸς Ἀθήνας ἔλθ' ὑπ' οἰωνῶν καλῶν, 1333). The priestess' intended sense is that Ion must avoid incurring the ritual pollution of bloodshed. Ion's reply confirms that his ritual status is at stake: in his view,

---

[186] Zeitlin (1989) 182.

'whoever kills enemies is pure' (καθαρὸς ἅπας τοι πολεμίους ὃς ἂν κτάνῃ, 1334). But in the context of the scene and in particular Ion's imminent discovery of his true identity as born of an Athenian mother, it is difficult to avoid thinking of the type of purity which Ion earlier referred to as characteristic of the Athenian *polis* and whose criteria, as he will presently find out, he in truth fulfils. If anything, the play seems to suggest, Ion is even 'purer' than he had earlier wished for: instead of being the son of a 'brought-in' foreigner and an Athenian wife, he turns out to be the son of a god and the queen of Athens, daughter of noble Erechtheus.

But clever composition extends to Apollo and his oblique association with purity, too. In fact, he may be taken to provide the paradigm for Ion's abstinence from murder in favour of ritual purity. Inasmuch as the upkeep of his shrine's purity is so central in the earlier parts of the play, it is remarkable that, at least in the eyes of the humans (a view supported by Athena's words at the end), Apollo frustrates the attempt on Ion's life, 'wishing to avoid pollution' (οὐ μιανθῆναι θέλων, 1118).[187] Though we must distinguish sharply between ritual and ethnic purity, it seems appropriate that the god who turns out to be the father of the future ruler of the 'pure city' of Athens should himself remain ritually pure.[188] It seems appropriate, too, that just as the purity of Apollo's shrine is permanently threatened and in fact impaired, so the god's ritual purity is, if not eventually impaired, at least threatened.

Problematic purities: Apollo and Ion

The intimated nexus of the purities of Athens, Apollo and Ion requires a more detailed treatment, however. We need to return, that is, to the idea of identity and we need to give that idea a specific spin: because Athenian identity is so central from the start, *Ion* demands that we look, not so much at the identities of Athens, Apollo and Ion alongside each other, but at Athenian identity alongside, and in the light of, the 'pure identities'

---

[187] The revelation of the murder plot involves 'Dionysus' along with Apollo. See Schlesier (1994) 142–4 on the role of wine and the bird's 'bacchic' death agony (at 1204) in the scene. Apollo may be seen to be present in the form of the doves which flutter in (one dies, thereby revealing the truth): they come in only because they 'live without fear in Phoebus' house' (1197–8). If accepted, this allusion to Apollo throws into stark relief the question of the precise involvement of Apollo in Ion's rescue. It is only at the end of the play that Athena's assertion of Apollo's part in the rescue of Ion and Creusa (μηχαναῖς ἐρρύσατο, 1565) dispels lingering doubts. It is ironic, by the way, that it is one of the 'defilers' of Apollo's temple – a dove – that saves Apollo's ritual purity.

[188] The play with purities and in particular the aspect of repetition with a difference (e.g. ritual purity becomes ethnic purity) may be seen as part of the play's wider structure of repetition and doubling which scholars have identified. See esp. Zeitlin (1989) 150–6.

of Ion and Apollo. This in turn requires that we first consider the wider implications of Apollo's and Ion's pure identities. Both, we shall see, are problematic. In Apollo's case, this is a matter of a certain discrepancy between outward purity and what it covers up; in Ion's case, the problem is, as in *Suppliants*, that the particular identity constructed around purity is problematic from a socio-cultural perspective.

The purity Apollo is associated with is merely an exterior façade. The point emerges, first, on a literal level, as a matter of the play's particular representation of the god's purity. As we have seen, it is constructed indirectly, through the temple which serves as the proxy of the absent god. We have also noted that the defilement of the temple by bird droppings (and other dirt) reflects an Apollonian purity that is somehow not quite perfect and indeed dependent upon continual cleansing. But seeing how this cleansing is presented as a constant occupation of the temple-servant and relates above all to exteriors (the youthful caretaker scrubs the temple's entrance and chases away the birds from its roof), the play seems to suggest that in Apollo's case purity is somehow a surface construct (and one that is forever under construction).[189]

The problem that is alluded to here becomes clear from a consideration of the god's past and in particular the rape of Creusa. Not that because of that rape Apollo is in some actual (ritual) sense impure: rape, though troublesome and in the case of Halirrothius' assault upon Ares' daughter counted among the ἀνόσια,[190] would not seem to result in the god's actual pollution.[191] Rather, the problem is that the purity of the temple is primarily a matter of separation, boundary-drawing, and non-transgression, but that in raping Creusa it is precisely boundaries which the god has not respected. Significantly, Ion's monody and its idyllic image of the sweeping, singing youth joyfully engaged in his safeguarding of purity follow immediately upon the prologue in which Hermes outlined Apollo's violent transgression

---

[189] A similar point is hinted at by Thorburn (2000) 45–6 from a different angle: 'The image of bird droppings on the golden *surface* calls into question Apollo's purity' (italics mine).

[190] See Eur. *El.* 1261. Swift (2008) 95 points out that rape was considered less serious a crime than adultery in classical Athens; still (ibid. 96), 'Euripides makes a point of presenting the rape as something dark and problematic by depicting Creousa's distress.'

[191] In retribution for the rape of his daughter, Ares killed Halirrothius and was tried before the Areopagus. In reference to this incident, Eur. *IT* (945–6) asserts that Ares, by killing Halirrothius in revenge, had incurred pollution. But nothing indicates that Halirrothius had incurred pollution. On a slightly different note, it is worth pointing out that among the gods who incur pollution in the mythical tradition, we also find Apollo. Later sources, at least, tell us that after killing the Python dragon the god had to seek purification in the Tempe valley in Thessaly (Paus. 2.7.7; see Parker (1983) 378). For the killing of the Cyclopes, Eur. *Alc.* 5–7 tells us, Apollo had to serve the mortal Admetus for one year. Pollution is not mentioned here.

of the boundaries of the female body in the form of the god's rape of Creusa (ἔζευξεν γάμους | βίᾳ, 10–11). Disregard for boundaries and 'entrances' which lead to the inner recesses of the female body is therefore fresh in the audience's mind as Ion enters dutifully to purify the temple and to guard and guarantee, more specifically, the purity at, and of, *entry*-points (ἐσόδους... καθαρὰς θήσομεν, 104–5) which give access to other inner recesses (ἐς μυχόν, 228). The contrast between the god's transgression in the past and the present maintenance of the shrine's purity through the safe-keeping of boundaries is therefore poignant. There is not so much a vague notion of discrepancy between violence and purity.[192] Rather, as the result of the inverse parallelism between boundary-transgressing violence and boundary-guarding purity, there is a pointed juxtaposition.

As a result, the idea of purity and its intimations of 'pure' divine splendour appear as a façade, suggesting an outward appearance which mystifies. Beneath the surface care for the integrity of boundaries that comes with the care for purity, there lurks, hidden behind this outward screen, violent transgression (one is tempted to speak of ἐσβολά; see 722) and mixing (μιγῆναι, 338). There is no continuum between outside and inside. The 'truth' about the god's 'inside', his interior 'real' being, is, if not therefore actually impure, at least diametrically opposed to the terms in which the pure outward appearance is constructed. Like the walls of the temple which hide the interior goings-on, purity hides, is superimposed upon, a more complex interiority.

When it comes to Apollo's purity associations, therefore, we should not dig too deeply. Along with the chorus, instructed by Ion not to enter into the inner recesses of the temple without prior sacrifice (ἐπὶ δ' ἀσφάκτοις | μήλοισι δόμων μὴ πάριτ' ἐς μυχόν, 228–9), we should perhaps learn not to intrude too far upon the god's interior and instead feed our eyes upon the beauty of external appearances (230–2):

> ἔχω μαθοῦσα· θεοῦ δὲ νόμον
> οὐ παραβαίνομεν,
> ἃ δ' ἐκτὸς ὄμμα τέρψει.

> I've got it. I do not intend to transgress the god's law. What's outside shall delight my eyes.

Ion's case is different. It brings us back to Aeschylus' *Suppliants*. As was the case with the Danaids in the earlier play, the close association of

---

[192] See Thorburn (2000) 46 and *passim*. In fact, Hoffer (1996) reminds us that the maintenance of purity requires violence, too (albeit a type of violence that keeps things separate rather than forcing them together).

Ion with purity gives expression to a type of identity that is problematic from a socio-cultural perspective. We must distinguish between two levels, however, which we may conceive of as 'tenor' and 'vehicle'.

The tenor is Ion's lack of a proper social identity. The identity outlined above, Ion's self-conception as the foster child of the god of purification, the chaste Pythia and the markedly pure temple district, is one designed to compensate for his lack of identification in terms of proper parental affiliation and an actual social network.[193] The lack of proper parental affiliation is marked in the dramatic text. In what is almost the first reference of Ion to his own fate, the youth foregrounds that he is an orphan, 'mother- and fatherless' (ὡς γὰρ ἀμήτωρ ἀπάτωρ τε γεγώς, 109). His *lack* of social reference points, his identity as foundling upon whom a proper identity yet needs to be inscribed, is therefore primary; his 'Apollonian' identity, of which purity and its maintenance are the central elements, appears as but a stand-in and marker of absence.[194] Problematically, then, from the civic community's perspective Ion's identity is ultimately a 'non-identity'.

Purity is the central element of this compensatory 'non-identity'. The association is arguably emphasised by the immediate juxtaposition of Ion's lack of social identity and Ion's concern for purity. The remark about Ion's mother- and fatherlessness at 109 follows immediately upon the youth's elaborate description of his purifying activities, which are presented as (the) one stable reference-point of his existence, the 'tasks [he] has ever performed since childhood' (πόνους οὓς ἐκ παιδὸς | μοχθοῦμεν ἀεί, 102–3). Through this juxtaposition, the play invites us to think concern for purity and *lack* of social identity together.[195]

But if the idea of purity and the concern for such purity are closely associated with the worrying notion of an identity of absence and distance from the civic community, this is so also because purity and the concern for it are apt *vehicles* of such an identity. First, purity and purification may be seen to have to do with absence rather than presence. This is most tangibly so on the concrete physical level, which is one of the levels on which Ion, as the temple's cleansing staff, is associated with purity – in the form of maintenance of purity. There is in *Ion* arguably a suggestion that ensuring the absence of dirt and suffering the absence of social affiliation are two

---

[193] For Ion's lack of social identity and the complex twists and turns by which he acquires one, see Zeitlin (1989).
[194] Zeitlin (1989) 147 speaks of 'the blank cipher of this temple-servant who has no story of his own'.
[195] See the related remarks by Segal (1999) 75: 'his recurrent concern with purity... set the stage for his childhood innocence... *Ion seems outside of time*' (italics mine).

sides of the same coin, the former expressing the latter.[196] The second point brings us more closely to Aeschylus' Danaids. Ion's permanent occupancy of sacred space is the concrete reason for the centrality of the concern with purity in the make-up of Ion's identity, but it also expresses his distance from civic space;[197] and just as ἁγνεία marked the Danaids' status as socially awkward, so Ion's ritual purity further marks the youth as a marginal figure.[198] It underscores in ritual terms that Ion is permanently shut out from the kind of exchanges that underlie the life of the civic community.

The principle expression of Ion's distance from the properly civic is his problematic relation to boundaries, past and present. Cast beyond the boundaries of the civic community as an infant by Creusa (ἐξόρισεν, 505; ἐκ χερῶν ὁρίζῃ, 1459; see also 46), Ion yet has to find a proper relation to boundaries.[199] His purity observances and their wider implications and associations mark Ion's presently awkward relation to boundaries. As the temple's caretaker, to be sure, Ion to some extent engages with boundaries, chasing away the birds and restoring purity where it is impaired by all sorts of dirt (including guano). As the temple's permanent inhabitant, however, he may cross boundaries between the inside of the temple and its adjacent outside as he presumably does at the opening of the play; but he never seems to cross beyond this *hortus conclusus*, as Charles Segal aptly calls it, preferring instead 'a forever pious life' (ἀεὶ σεμνὸν βίον, 56), which is also one of perpetual (although, as we have seen, not always perfect) purity.[200] The type of boundary-negotiation Ion *does* engage in as the temple's cleansing staff draws attention to the type of boundary-negotiation he *does not* engage in as chaste and in other ways purity-bound youth.

One specific aspect of this is Ion's virginal purity as chaste temple-servant. Unlike his divine father, Ion does not engage in the sort of boundary-negotiation that comes with sexual intimacy. But as such a virginal figure,

---

[196] Such a suggestion is perhaps underlined by the immediate juxtaposition, noted above, of the cleansing activity at 102–8 and the reference to Ion's fate as orphan at 109.
[197] See also Segal (1999) 76 commenting on Ion's *hortus conclusus*, sheltered from the 'violence, sorrow, doubt, and compromise that lie outside this pure enclosure'.
[198] On Ion as marginal figure, see Segal (1999) 75–8 and *passim*. See also Zacharia (2003) 124: 'It is also possible that Ion's preoccupation with purity ... should be connected with his delicate and intermediate status.'
[199] Intriguingly, when Ion announces his decision to find his mother, the journey towards the recovery of identity is cast as a journey along, and in a sense as a search for, boundaries (πᾶσάν γ' ἐπελθὼν Ἀσιάδ' Εὐρώπης θ' ὅρους, 1356). See also 1459–61 (drawn together with v. 46 by Segal (1999) 86) where the earlier separation from the mother is again referred to in the language of ὁρίζω.
[200] Segal (1999) 76.

Ion, like the Danaids, remains outside the social intercourse upon which is based the continuity of the civic community.[201] We may say, therefore, that one socially awkward status – Ion's status as foundling – is translated into, or expressed in terms of (or, if we prefer largely to abandon the idea of tenor and vehicle: reinforced through), another socially awkward status, that of the sexually pure male virgin, whose '[w]ithdrawal from the sexual structure of society brings with it a withdrawal from the social structure'.[202]

The other aspect is less specific and relates to a more general withdrawal from boundary-negotiation which Ion displays and which is bound up with his specific association with purity (and of which sexual abstinence is but one manifestation). We have already noted that Ion carries his body as though it were another sacred space, eager to keep at a distance any kind of intrusion; but he withdraws also from the kind of boundary-negotiation that involvement in community affairs brings with it.[203] Remarkably, Ion initially rejects Xuthus' offer (at 576–81) of the Athenian throne. In his view, the good and wise prefer not to 'rush *into* political involvement' (χρηστοὶ δυναμενοι τ', ὄντες σοφοί, | σιγῶσι κοὐ σπεύδουσιν ἐς τὰ πράγματα, 598–9). Ion, that is, refuses to cross the boundary into political involvement, just as he does not cross the boundary between sacred space and civic space (until, that is, he gives up his 'pure identity' and decides to go to Athens with his 'father' Xuthus).

What allows Ion such non-involvement in social and political affairs is his occupation of, and preference for, a middle-ground. In the management of the shrine's daily business, we have noted, Ion takes care of τὰ ἔξω, leaving τὰ ἔσω to others. But this entails that during the day at least Ion is neither among the ones inside (who remain entirely pure for the duration of their involvement in oracular affairs) nor among those on the outside (who require purification, for instance at the Castalian spring). He is therefore neither among those who dispense the oracle's (ideally καθαρά, but in reality often ambiguous and in *Ion* even deceiving) μαντεύματα, nor among the members of a civic community visiting the oracle. In charge of τὰ ἔξω, he is really in the middle and as such – unlike those (properly) within and those (properly) outside – not engaged in any business of actual (social, political) consequence, requiring social interaction.[204] Importantly,

---

[201] Parker (1983) 86–94 notes that even in the case of priests and priestesses requirements of long periods of chastity were exceptional.
[202] Parker (1983) 93.
[203] On Ion's withdrawal from social interaction, see also Hoffer (1996) 315–16, esp. 316: 'As long as he preserves the purity and chastity of his "continuously pious life" (56 ἀεὶ σεμνὸν βίον), he has no real decisions to make... He is depicted with no strong personal, economic, or political ties that might raise conflicts that might require him to decide on right and wrong action.'
[204] It is in this sense that Ion truly is on the outside, following the dictum of Zeitlin (1989) 166 ('his place has always been on the outside'): by being neither inside nor (properly) outside.

it is just such preference for the middle-ground which Ion makes explicit not long after avowing his aversion to 'rushing into political involvement'. If he were to lead a life in a civic community, Ion muses, his social standing and possessions should be 'in the middle' since this would mean freedom from troubles (εἴη γ' ἐμοὶ <μὲν> μέτρια μὴ λυπουμένῳ, 632): it is from this position – on the boundary – that non-involvement is possible.

This apolitical stance, too, seems problematic from the perspective of the civic – and especially the democratic – community. The Thucydidean Pericles, at any rate, seems to reflect a democratic discourse according to which typical Athenians know their political affairs (τὰ πολιτικά) well and 'regard the one who does not take part in [political affairs] (τόν τε μηδὲν τῶνδε μετέχοντα), not as one who minds his own business, but as good for nothing (οὐκ ἀπράγμονα, ἀλλ' ἀχρεῖον νομίζομεν)'.[205]

First conclusions: dissonances

Let us return, then, to Athenian purity. Does the juxtaposition of Athenian exclusivity (as 'pure city') with the problematic purities of Ion and Apollo throw a problematic light, too, on Athenian purity? The answer to this question must remain inconclusive, for Euripides' play is highly complex, full of ironic play, and open to readings on a variety of levels.[206]

On the level closest to the surface, *Ion* is highly patriotic and affirmative and may be taken to end on a note where all involved live happily ever after. In particular, Athenian purity is reaffirmed as Ion abandons his problematic Delphic identity ('of purity'). By leaving the sanctuary, Ion leaves behind the problematic aspects of that identity and, like the Danaids, takes up a civic identity, complete with parental affiliation, involvement in community affairs[207] and procreative activities, with Ion eventually engendering the eponymous heroes of the Attic tribes.[208] In contrast to what we find in Aeschylus, incorporation into the civic community in *Ion* does not imply a redefinition of that community's 'purity', however. Quite the opposite: whereas the threat of pollution brought into the land of Argos by the Danaids necessitated a renegotiation of 'Argive purity'

---

[205] Thuc. 2.40.2 (trans. adapted from C. F. Smith, Loeb Classical Library, Cambridge, MA, 1919). As Lee (1997) ad 598–601 notes, Ion's preference for not rushing ἐς τὰ πράγματα recalls the term *polypragmosyne* ('busybody-ness') used by conservative politicians as anti-democratic slogan. On this term, see Ehrenberg (1947). On Athenian quietism, see Carter (1986).
[206] See Zeitlin (1989) 145: *Ion* is 'a complex and enigmatic play ... set at Delphi, the very locus of the enigmatic word'.
[207] Athena, as *dea ex machina*, intimates that Ion will take his place on the Athenian throne and rule her land (κἀς θρόνους τυραννικοὺς | ἵδρυσον, 1572–3).
[208] As, again, Athena informs us: 1575–88.

towards a greater degree of inclusiveness (admitting for the integration of the Danaids), Ion is allowed to go to Athens only after the discovery that his parental affiliation corresponds to (what he takes to be) the requirements of Athenian purity. As we have seen earlier, if anything, he heads towards Athens even 'purer' than initially desired, as the son, not of a 'brought-in' foreigner and some Athenian woman, but of a god and the queen of Athens, daughter of noble Erechtheus. From this perspective, then, it seems that the problematic nature of Ion's identity structured around the idea of purity is acknowledged and exchanged for a pure Athenian identity which, unlike Ion's purity (and that of Aeschylus' Argos), is not subject to redefinitions and appears as superior.

Beyond that surface level, we may nonetheless dig up some dirt to sully Athenian purity. The very fact that Athenian identity is brought into parallel with Ion's purity and its manifold problematic associations in the first place surely throws an uncanny light on Athenian purity, too. The idea that Athenian identity is somehow comparable to Ion's purity as temple-servant and the withdrawal from social interaction that comes with it must leave at least some bitter aftertaste.

Another discordant note may be seen to be struck by the very complexity of Athenian purity and the ironies that come with it. Similar in this respect to Apollo's purity hiding dubious interior goings-on, Athenian purity turns out more complex than the idea of purity may lead us to believe. In particular, it is not incompatible with 'otherness'. We have already seen that Athenian purity tolerates one non-Athenian parent. In the play's own striking terms, this means that 'otherness' is tolerated:[209] after the recognition between mother and son and in response to the latter's probing questions about his father, Creusa declares that Ion is 'born other' (ἄλλοθεν γέγονας, ἄλλοθεν, 1471), hinting at Ion's Apollonian parentage. In a different sense otherness may in fact be seen to constitute the very core of what constitutes 'pure' Athenian identity. As *Ion* does not fail to mention, half-bestial Cecrops is a central figure of Athenian lore. But in the description of Ion's tent,[210] Cecrops is obliquely connected to 'otherness': he is suggestively juxtaposed with 'half-bestial heroes' (μιξόθηρας φῶτας, 1161) which appear on 'other barbarian pieces of cloth' (ἄλλα βαρβάρων ὑφάσματα, 1159) and are therefore closely associated with 'barbarian otherness'.[211]

---

[209] See also Zeitlin (1989) 177, commenting on the fact that Ion will in name be Xuthus' child: 'the privileges of autochthony are maintained while the system tolerates the role of the outsider'.

[210] On the significance of the tent for the play's concern with identity, see Goff (1988) and Zeitlin (1989) 166–9. On the tent in general, see Zacharia (2003) 29–39 and Stieber (2011) 302–14.

[211] For a related, but slightly different perspective, see Zeitlin (1989) 167–8: 'the portrayal of Kekrops as a hybrid of mixed form implies that the line between civilization and savagery may have been less

The irony here is that elsewhere in the play 'otherness' gives rise to serious apprehensions on the part of Athenian characters. These apprehensions are ubiquitous, circling around the ἄλλος, the complete stranger not affiliated by blood, who is seen to impair the integrity ('purity') of the royal Athenian line: the chorus in particular are concerned about the one 'born of other blood' (ὁ παῖς | ἄλλων τραφεὶς ἐξ αἱμάτων, 692–3), the 'other coming in' (ἄλλος ἥκων, 1058–9) or the ἀλλοδαπός (1070); but even the otherwise less xenophobic queen seems apologetic about the stranger from an 'other' country (ἐπακτὸς ἐξ ἄλλης χθονός, 290).

The juxtaposition of Athenian tolerance of certain 'othernesses' and Athenian characters' fears of 'others' throws a problematic light on both. Athenian purity, on one hand, emerges as tolerant of, and even based on, elements that in a different guise are seen to threaten it. The irony undermines the very concept of Athenian purity. Perhaps one may even say that *Ion* here plays with an idea not unlike the one we find in the famous passage in Aristotle's *Politics* (1275b25), where the author points out the 'hastiness' of the definition according to which citizenship depends on two citizen parents because at some point in the past there will necessarily be non-citizens in a citizen's ancestry. On the other hand, if Athenian purity tolerates certain types of otherness, fears of other types of otherness appear all the more arbitrary. Eventually, the joke is perhaps on the Athenians in the audience, poised between the glorification of 'pure Athenian-ness' exemplified by Pericles' citizenship law and pride in metropolitan openness, incidentally propagated, in Thucydides' account at least, by the same politician.[212]

Pure identity as clarified identity

So far, owing to the similarity between Aeschylus' and Euripides' play in terms of its underlying 'grammar', the present discussion of *Ion* has largely followed in the footsteps of the earlier discussion of *Suppliants*. We could end at this point, as we did in the case of the Aeschylean play, on a note of complex dissonance. However, there is potential room for (adventurous) further interpretation: the line we have already discussed, the Pythia's injunction to Ion at 1333 to 'go pure to Athens', may invite yet another interpretation, serving in this way as the starting point for

---

solid than one might have supposed.' On the ambiguous nature of Cecrops, see also Mastronarde (1976) 169.

[212] Thuc. 2.39. Although she comes to this conclusion from a different angle, Zeitlin, I think, is right in asserting that the play 'balances out the two sources of national pride: autochthony... and *philoxenia*... two divergent ideals' (ibid. 177).

more far-reaching conclusions about the play's engagement with the issue of purity and pure identity. Caution is certainly required in dealing with this interpretation. In view of its powerful implications, it should however be presented.

The interpretation I am interested in takes 'pure' (at 1333) in an intellectual sense; it goes back to Cedric Whitman's 1974 book *Euripides and the full circle of myth*. Whitman offers a discussion of *Ion* which pays close attention to the play's engagement with the theme of purity, on one hand, and of knowledge, on the other. Commenting on 1333, he points out that the word καθαρός, though ritual in its literal sense, here appears in close proximity to the 'gift of true and long-desired knowledge, knowledge of Ion's real identity'.[213] Just before the Pythia had entered, recognition tokens in hand, 'the dramatic texture is immediately suffused with the coming of something deep, lasting, and true.'[214] Revelation of Ion's *true* identity is upon us. Whitman concludes that we are invited to extend the meaning of purity and allow for an intellectual dimension:

> But in this particular play, as in others too, where the Recognition establishes the truth of the hero's identity, and his final acceptance thereof, the meaning of 'purification' may be implicitly extended, in that in becoming his true self, the hero has finally become really pure (καθαρός).[215]

Although his formulations remain slightly vague, Whitman implies that *Ion* at this point develops a notion of purity which is the result of intellectual clarification and insight; and that Ion goes 'pure to Athens' not only in the ethnic and ritual sense, as an Athenian respectful of ritual decorum, but also as the result of 'clear' insight into the true nature of his identity.

This interpretation is contentious but can, I think, be defended. Certainly, the objection may be raised that Whitman's reading imports too much of a certain view of Aristotle into the notion of purity (Whitman in fact refers to Aristotle's catharsis theory),[216] but that such importation is anachronistic, resulting in a reading not available to the Greeks of the late fifth century. Such an objection is valid, to some extent, and encourages circumspection. However, the vocabulary of purity is used in *Ion* itself in a way which may be seen to support Whitman's suggestion. In the first stasimon, as Creusa has left to pray at the god's altars and Xuthus has disappeared into the temple to consult the oracle, the chorus ask Athena

---

[213] Whitman (1974) 92. [214] Ibid. 92. [215] Ibid. 93.
[216] Whitman refers to Gerald Else's interpretation of catharsis in the latter's *magnum opus* of 1957. The intellectual interpretation of Aristotelian catharsis as 'clarification' has been set out in particular by Golden (1962) and esp. id. (1976); see also id. (1992) 5–39.

Euripides' Ion

and Artemis for support – that they offer prayers, on the Erechtheids' behalf, that 'the ancient race of the Erechtheids meet with pure oracles of long-delayed birth of children' (468–71):

ἱκετεύσατε δ', ὦ κόραι,
τὸ παλαιὸν Ἐρεχθέως
γένος εὐτεκνίας χρονίου καθαροῖς
μαντεύμασι κῦρσαι.

In the immediate context, 'pure' is most naturally taken to mean 'clear, free from ambiguity' or perhaps 'true, free from falsehood'.[217] This is precisely the sense which is required for Whitman's reading of 1333. Therefore, it is not necessarily Aristotelian anachronism to follow Whitman, but may be justified by a close reading of the play itself. Line 1333 may be taken to hark back to 470–1 and its concern with revelation of 'clear truth' to intimate, on a tertiary level of meaning, that in addition to being ritually and ethnically pure Ion will be καθαρός also in the sense of 'clear', or 'free from ambiguity', with respect to his actual identity.[218]

The significance of this interpretation within the wider context of the play and its concern with various pure identities is that an alternative conception may be seen to be developed here wherein purity is the result of a process of recognition of the self's true identity. We are consequently invited to regard as 'pure' also the identity which is put under scrutiny and is in this way clarified.

Second conclusions: relocating Athenian purity

Such an interpretation, if accepted, necessarily entails reflections on the play itself. After all, *Ion* is itself concerned with Athenian identity and may be seen to 'clarify' it. With these reflections, I wish to conclude.

---

[217] Owen (1939) ad loc. prefers 'clear, free from ambiguity'; see also Lee (1997) ad 470–1 ('i.e. devoid of the ambiguity characteristic of oracles'); as Lee observes the word καθαρός appears in this sense also in Ar. *Vesp.* 631.

[218] This interpretation can perhaps be defended on other grounds. A connection between purity and the idea of recognised identity suggests itself not only because the play itself provides clues which intimate such a connection, but also because such a connection is implied in the act of reception. I have suggested that line 1333 constitutes an intratextual allusion to the passage in which Ion speaks of the purity of the Athenian civic body. The acknowledgement of this allusion invites the audience to detect implicit meaning beneath the explicit, to move from the ritual to the ethnic. The allusion, I suggest, is obvious. Not least through the immediate juxtaposition of 'pure' and 'Athens' the play takes the audience almost by its hand. Nonetheless, the allusion emerges only because the audience supplies its knowledge about Ion's true identity as son of an Athenian mother. It is the recognition of this true identity which allows us to make the move from ritual to ethnic, explicit to implicit. The reception-dynamic is such, then, that the audience, through the allusive structure of the text, is implicated in a process of recognition of true identity and that the triggering off of this process is tied to the vocabulary of purity.

Ion is about Athenian identity, and this is not only a detached antiquarian concern, but one which reaches out from the play's past to the present of its (Athenian) enactment. It was pointed out above that a dramatic enactment of myths pertaining to the House of Erechtheus for an Athenian audience, seated on the benches of the theatre of Dionysus on the south slope of the Acropolis, whose most recent addition, at the time of the play's performance, was the Erechtheum,[219] necessarily affords an Athenian focus. Moreover, we have already seen that although the play is set in Delphi the prologue-speech immediately shifts the centre of attention to Athens (from line 8 onwards).[220] In fact, the Delphic setting may be understood, not to detract from, but rather to add to the play's focus on Athens. When Ion at one point in the play remarks that 'things seen from afar appear different than when seen from up close' (585–6),

οὐ ταὐτὸν εἶδος φαίνεται τῶν πραγμάτων
πρόσωθεν ὄντων ἐγγύθεν θ' ὁρωμένων,

we are arguably invited to understand this as a comment on the drama itself to the effect that the transfer of an Athenian narrative into a Delphic context is conducive to the play's Athenian concerns since such distancing affords, along with an outside view on internal affairs, perspective.[221]

An art-historical detail, concerning Apollo's temple, underscores the point. Critics have been worried that the chorus' description of the temple in the parodos does not entirely correspond to Delphic reality.[222] Rather, it inverts that reality by 'wrongly' placing the gigantomachy, which on Apollo's temple at Delphi figured on the west pediment, and not on the east side (of the temple's main entrance) which is the side that the chorus approach and which their description must therefore refer to.[223] Intriguingly, though, the chorus' description splendidly fits the Parthenon at Athens, with its gigantomachy on the eastern façade, above the main entrance, on the metopes.[224] It is therefore tempting to suggest that the

---

[219] The Erechtheum was begun in 421 BC and finished, after a lapse, in 407/6 BC. See Zacharia (2003) 2.
[220] So that *Ion* is (also) an Athenian play despite its Delphic setting: see Wolff (1965) 173; Vogt (1998) 45; also Loraux (1990) 177–8.
[221] See e.g. Zeitlin (1989) 178 ('Distance supplies perspective'); Loraux (1990) 177 ('Distance lends depth').
[222] Stieber (2011) 284–302; Owen (1939) ad 180 with references.
[223] Rosivach (1977) 284; see also Hose (1990) 138.
[224] Also noted by Stieber (2011) 301. The eastern placement of the Gigantomachy on the Parthenon is mentioned only in passing by Stieber, however: the placement of the Gigantomachy the chorus describes is not considered in connection with it. For her, it is the fact that a Gigantomachy is described which matters: for that battle (the most important in which Athena took part, and in a prominent role) had very close Athenian associations, in particular in the Periclean period.

'misrepresentation' of the temple of Apollo at Delphi further emphasises the play's Athenian focus because it implies the presentation of the Delphic temple in terms of the quintessential monument of Athenian national identity. Because this 'misrepresentation' implies a collapse of a mythical Delphic past (the temple of Apollo as element of that past) with the contemporary Athenian present, the quest for Athenian identity is hauled into the audience's presence and made a present concern. The chorus may simply see Delphic temple-decoration; the audience are confronted with an ekphrasis of the monument which perhaps more than any other represents, and negotiates, contemporary Athens and Athenian identity.

These last remarks anticipate the next point: naturally, the Athenian focus implies, for the audience, an *engagement* with Athenian identity. As was noted earlier, because of the peculiar plot-pattern of *Ion*, which recasts the story of Ion as a recovery of identity and therefore makes 'quest for identity' the essential plot-element, the audience is necessarily implicated in Ion's quest for Athenian identity as it watches the play unfold. It is implicated in an exploration of that identity, of what it means to be Athenian. Watching *Ion* means to engage with the various aspects of Athenian identity that the play rehearses. These include not only the aspects at the drama's surface, the laying out of the particular genealogy of the early kings of Athens and the Attic tribes descended from Ion, but also the more subdued – and often problematic – aspects encountered along the way: the potential monstrosity and 'otherness' of Cecrops, for instance; or the ambiguous role of Apollo as Athens' divine ancestor. Watching *Ion*, finally, entails *clarification* of Athenian identity.

As a result, if we accept an interpretation according to which 'pure identity' in *Ion* is also 'clarified identity', we may say that an Athenian identity of this type is also located in the theatre of Dionysus. We may conclude that *Ion* offers an alternative to the ethnic purity which various characters endorse as the benchmark of Athenian identity, but which is not unproblematic.

In conclusion, let us note that the play repeatedly presents processes of clarification of Athenian identity in terms reminiscent of the process of theatre-watching, in this way lending further weight to the above interpretation. Three such instances may be singled out. There is, first, the tent whose decorations the messenger describes in great detail. Within the play, the most important addressee of these depictions is arguably Ion who, inside this tent, celebrates the (mistaken) recovery of identity. As Barbara Goff argues, the tent's scenes, including naval battles between Greeks and non-Greeks as well as the depiction of the mythical Athenian king Cecrops, constitute a negotiation, in visual terms, of what it means to be Greek and, more specifically, of what it means to be Athenian.[225] The passage gives no explicit clue to the effect that the experience of watching *Ion* is at stake. However, the implication is that Ion acquires deeper knowledge about identity, and not least the identity of the city which he is soon to enter, through the contemplation of an artwork, just as the audience acquires such knowledge through the contemplation of the artwork that is the play.[226]

There is, second, the recognition scene between Ion and Creusa, in which a self-reflective streak suggests itself with greater force. Recognition of identity is made dependent upon the contemplation of a piece of weaving depicting the Gorgon and a golden amulet decorated with snakes. For the characters in the play, these recognition tokens ultimately lead towards the discovery of Ion's true identity as son of Athenian Creusa; for the audience, both the Gorgon and the snake reveal aspects of Athenian identity, in particular about their curious nature as earthborns.[227] Since both the recognition within the play and that offered to the audience revolve around Athenian identity and since the artworks within the play, cloth and amulet, parallel the dramatic artwork presently enacted onstage in that what is represented in each case reveals aspects of Athenian identity, the passage is readily understood to imply a point about the experience of the audience presently seated on the benches of the theatre of Dionysus: that watching *Ion* helps them recognise their true self.

Finally, there is the chorus' contemplation of the Delphic temple-decoration in the parodos. This is the most striking instance of an audience contemplating an artwork not only within this play but within all of Greek tragedy.[228] The scenes depicted are again pertinent to Greek, and

---

[225] Goff (1988). The interplay of order and violence figures large in her discussion of the tent's imagery.
[226] See also Hall (2010) 276 on the metatheatrical dimension of the tent-scene and its Athenian affiliations (esp. through the depiction of Cecrops): 'These passages draw attention to the status of theatre, by making the audience contemplate the visual dimension of the dramatic poem they are experiencing, but the myths chosen for visualization also situate the play's master narrative . . . within the tradition of local mythology celebrated in every art form in the Athenians' city.' See also Segal (1999) 102: 'That scene is itself emblematic of the way in which the play invites the Athenians of the present to contemplate their own remote past and to look at personal and collective experience in the mirror of individualizing myth.'
[227] On the recognition tokens, see also Mueller (2010) 391–6. She intimates a metatheatrical dimension, too (ibid. 395): 'Ion orchestrates a theatrical event, directing all gazes to a single point in space. The props become the centerpiece of an intensely personal but also civic collective event. His autopsy . . . becomes a public display of the material history of Athens'.
[228] As Hall (2010) 276 points out, Euripides frequently refers to the visual arts in his plays, but '[i]n no play is this interest more apparent than in *Ion*'. She also notes (ibid. 276) that it is probably because of this interest that Euripides was believed, in post-classical antiquity, to be not only a tragic poet but also a painter and that his paintings were displayed in Megara (see *Life of Euripides*, 5).

specifically Athenian, identity. The chorus see 'their goddess' Athena (λεύσσω Παλλάδ', ἐμὰν θεόν, 211) and other Olympians in the Gigantomachy, fighting 'children of the earth' (Γᾶς τέκνων, 218).[229] This interplay of Olympians and earthborns strikes at the roots of Athenian identity as in particular the prologue intimates, where the Olympian element of Athenian identity is represented by Apollo as Ion's father and Athena as Athens' patron goddess (πόλις... Παλλάδος κεκλημένη, 8–9); and the earthborn element by Creusa's descent from earthborn ancestors (προγόνων νόμον σώζουσα τοῦ τε γηγενοῦς | Ἐριχθονίου, 20–1). The chorus may be dazzled by external appearances (ἃ δ' ἐκτός, ὄμμα τέρψει, 231), unlikely perhaps to ponder on the pediment's implications; nonetheless, the suggestion is that the viewer of the artwork may learn a thing or two about Athenian identity. The experience of the audience presently in the theatre of Dionysus, witnessing *Ion*, is akin. The artwork within the play resembles the artwork that is the play: the temple-decoration presents the battle of earthborns against Olympians; *Ion* presents the encounter between Creusa as the descendant of earthborn Erichthonius and Ion as the descendant of Olympian Apollo (the significant nuance being that in Ion, because he is also the son of Creusa, Olympian and earthborn fuse).[230]

The self-reflective streak, in this last instance, is articulated literally. In particular, the respective audiences, the one contemplating the pediment, the other the play, are set in parallel: implicitly, in that both are Athenian (if not exclusively in the case of the theatre audience) and collectives; explicitly, in that by way of Ion's asking Creusa whether she has come to Delphi 'for sightseeing' (πότερα θεατὴς ἢ χάριν μαντευμάτων; 301) it turns out that both, the sightseeing, pediment-contemplating chorus and the theatre audience, are θεαταί.

---

[229] On the interplay of Olympian and chthonian in the parodos, see Rosivach (1977).

[230] On more specific parallels between the Gigantomachy depicted on the temple pediment and the play, see Hose (1990) 138. He points out that on the pediment earthborns fight against Olympians and lose. Just so Creusa, the earthborn, 'fights' against Apollo's initial plan to introduce Ion to Athens as the son of Xuthus and an unknown woman. She 'loses', however, like the earthborns in the Gigantomachy: her plan to kill Ion is thwarted; Olympian Apollo, by contrast, 'wins' – even though his initial plan requires alterations. Hose therefore concludes: 'The scenes described [by the chorus] can therefore be seen to provide a paradigm for the action' (my translation). See also the related remarks by Segal (1999) 99–100.

Envoi

It is striking: the Dionysia, like other festivals, involved manifold ritual provisions, among them a number of ritual purifications. The procession routes were certainly purified in third-century Delos,[1] and in view of an Athenian inscription from the early fourth century that suggests purifications of Piraeus processions in honour of Dionysus and Zeus Sōtēr,[2] it seems likely that such purifications were carried out in the framework of the Athenian Dionysia, too. At Athens the so-called *peristiarchoi* purified the theatre by circambulation,[3] while on Delos the *skēnē* was purified.[4] And yet, perhaps on the very *skēnē* purified in advance of the dramatic performances, pollution abounded – if only in mimetic form. In the theatre, a public space if ever there were one, and at the very heart of the Athenian *polis*, pollution, in word and action, looms anew with almost every play – if, again, only in mimetic form. Yet in the case of death in public spaces, Athenian demarchs were to see to it that the deme be purified instantly, betraying a fear of pollution there.[5]

This book has suggested one reason for the ubiquity of pollution in tragedy: tragedy as a 'genre' concerns itself with socio-cultural and other 'crises'; pollution and its counterparts, purity and purification, powerfully express and negotiate these 'crises'. 'Crisis', here, is not to be understood as an isolated 'critical' event, but as a complex problem. Pollution designates not only isolated events, which it flags up as difficult, such as deaths or births or acts of violence, but is frequently associated with the wider questions (or 'complex problems') in which tragedy is interested. The qualities and associations of pollution that have proven particularly significant are its aetiological potential, its capacity to provide narratives of cause and effect (to neutralise the worrying suspicion that, in the words of Clifford

---

[1] *IG* XI.2 203A.38 (dating from 269 BC).   [2] *IG* II² 380.
[3] See Σ Aeschin. 1.23, Σ Ar. *Ach*. 44; Harpocrotion s. v. καθάρσιον.   [4] *IG* XI.2 203A.38.
[5] Dem. 43.57.

Geertz, 'one may be adrift in an absurd world');[6] its spatial transgressiveness which sits uneasily with the *polis*' desire for stability; its connection with categorisation and evaluation, in combination with its curious relation to law; and, finally, its associations with civic identity.

Two overarching points may be retained from this. First, pollution (together with its counterparts, purity and purification) is multifaceted. This much may be clear already from a brief look at the table of contents in Robert Parker's book on the topic. This study has suggested in addition that for a full understanding of the significance of pollution it is worth looking not only at the events which result in pollution, but also at the wider context in which pollution is embedded and the functions pollution assumes in that context and why. This perspective yields insights about the qualities and associations of pollution mentioned above and in doing so neatly complements the perspective offered in Robert Parker's study.[7] At the same time, my particular perspective on the various attributes and functions of pollution in different contexts results in a picture of pollution that is not only less abstract, but also broader than that of Mary Douglas and her tenet that pollution designates the confusion of categories.

Second, tragedy is and is not like pollution. Tragedy is like pollution because it, too, negotiates problems and indeed the kind of problems pollution negotiates. I take pollution as primary here to emphasise that historically pollution comes before tragedy. With this in mind, we may say that tragedy assumes the function of pollution as a 'tool of negotiation' and at the same time widens the scope of that function. In the process, pollution is integrated as an essential (though not obligatory) plot-element.

Tragedy is not like pollution in that it is much more. In one sense, this is self-evident: pollution is a ritual concept; tragedy is a full-blown theatrical performance (as part of a religious festival). I refer to something more substantial: in integrating pollution (and its counterparts) into its plots, tragedy plays with pollution. At times, it uses pollution as a vehicle through which to comment on the crises it negotiates. In *Antigone*, for instance, it provides a pointed comment on the failure of Creon's particular vision of a strictly defined and inflexible civic space. At other times, however, tragedy comments on pollution and its qualities and associations. Such would seem to be the case in Aeschylus' *Suppliants* and Euripides' *Ion*, for instance, in which the crisis in question centrally revolves around pollution and purity as parameters of civic identity – and in which these parameters are to some extent put under scrutiny. But it is perhaps more clearly the

[6] Geertz (1973) 102.   [7] Parker (1983).

case in Aeschylus' *Oresteia* and Sophocles' *Oedipus tyrannus*. In these plays, the ritual concept of pollution as well as the rite of purification are critically reflected upon and exposed, in distinct ways, as problematic. Tragedy is more, that is, not only because it comprises pollution as part of a larger enterprise revolving around the negotiation of various kinds of crises, but also because it constitutes a critical voice, an 'intervention', pointing out the shortcomings that pollution and its ritual counterparts have as tools to navigate through certain crises.

But even if tragedy is much more than pollution, to note that tragedy resembles pollution because like pollution it negotiates a variety of (socio-cultural and other) problems is significant. For one, it invites us to reflect on the historical conditions – such as the rise of the *polis* and, with it, of questions important to the socio-political community – in which both pollution and tragedy could flourish and occupy an important place. More immediately, it suggests that tragedy has much in common with (this) ritual (nexus), which in turn may feed into our understanding of the close relation between these performances and ritual (and religious festivals) in ancient Greece. Finally, it throws the doors wide open towards a giant topic I have not at all been concerned with in this book: Aristotle and his idea of tragic catharsis. For the claim that tragedy is like pollution necessarily brings the entire ritual nexus of which pollution forms part into the orbit of reflections about what tragedy is and does. In other words, it positions purification in close proximity to questions about the function(s) of tragedy.

Bibliography

Ahl, F. (1991) *Sophocles' Oedipus. Evidence and self-conviction*, Ithaca.
Ahrensdorf, P. J. (2009) *Greek tragedy and political philosophy. Rationalism and religion in Sophocles' Theban plays*, Cambridge and New York.
Alcock, S. E. and Osborne, R. eds. (1994) *Placing the gods. Sanctuaries and sacred space in ancient Greece*, Oxford.
Allison, R. (1984) '"This is the place." Why is Oedipus at Kolonos?', *Prudentia* 16, 67–91.
Arnaoutoglou, I. (1993) 'Pollution in the Athenian homicide law', *RIDA* 40, 109–37.
  (1998) *Ancient Greek laws*, London.
Ashery, D., Lloyd, A, Corcella, A. (2007) *A commentary on Herodotus Books I–IV*, ed. O. Murray and A. Moreno, Oxford.
Augoustakis, A. ed. (2013) *Ritual and religion in Flavian epic*, Oxford.
Avery, H. C. (1968) '"My tongue has sworn, but my mind is unsworn"', *TAPhA* 99, 19–35.
Bacon, H. H. (2001) 'The Furies' homecoming', *CPh* 96, 48–59.
Barchiesi, A., Rüpke, J., Stephens, S. eds. (2004) *Rituals in ink. A conference on religion and literary production held at Stanford University in February 2002*, Stuttgart.
Barrett, W. S. (1964) *Euripides. Hippolytus*, Oxford.
Bartsch, S. (1997) *Ideology in cold blood. A reading of Lucan's* Civil War, Cambridge, MA.
Belfiore, E. (1992) *Tragic pleasures. Aristotle on plot and emotion*, Princeton.
  (2000) *Murder among friends. Violation of* philia *in Greek tragedy*, New York.
Bendlin, A. (2007) 'Purity and pollution', in D. Ogden (ed.) *A companion to Greek religion*, Oxford, 178–89.
Bernays, J. (1880) *Zwei Abhandlungen über die aristotelische Theorie des Drama*, Berlin.
Bernek, R. (2005) *Dramaturgie und Ideologie. Der politische Mythos in den Hikesiedramen des Aischylos, Sophokles und Euripides*, Munich.
Berressen, H. (2007) 'On the matter of abjection', in K. Kutzbach and M. Müller (eds.) *The abject of desire. The aestheticization of the unaesthetic in contemporary literature and culture*, Amsterdam, 19–48.

Bierl, A. F. H. (1991) *Dionysos und die griechische Tragödie. Politische und 'metatheatralische' Aspekte im Text*, Tübingen.
  (2007) 'Literatur und Religion als Rito- und Mythopoetik. Überblicksartikel zu einem neuen Ansatz in der Klassischen Philologie', in A. Bierl, R. Lämmle, K. Wesselmann eds. (2007) vol. 1, 1–76.
Bierl, A. F. H., Lämmle, R., Wesselmann, K. eds. (2007) *Literatur und Religion vols. 1 and 2. Wege zu einer mythisch-rituellen Poetik bei den Griechen*, Berlin.
Biggs, P. (1966) 'The disease theme in Sophocles' *Ajax, Philoctetes* and *Trachiniae*', *CPh* 61, 223–35.
Biles, Z. P. (2006–7) 'Aeschylus' afterlife. Reperformance by decree in 5th c. Athens?', *ICS* 31–32, 206–42.
Blok, J. H. (2005) 'Becoming citizens. Some notes on the semantics of "citizen" in archaic Greece and classical Athens', *Klio* 87, 7–40.
  (2007) 'Fremde, Bürger und Baupolitik im klassischen Athen', *Historische Anthropologie* 15, 309–326.
  (2009) 'Pericles' citizenship law. A new perspective', *Historia* 58, 141–70.
Blundell, M. W. (1989) *Helping friends and harming enemies. A study in Sophocles and Greek ethics*, Cambridge.
  (1993) 'The ideal of Athens in *Oedipus at Colonus*', in Sommerstein et al. (eds.) 287–306.
Blundell, S. (1995) *Women in ancient Greece*, Cambridge, MA.
Böhme, H. (2002) 'Götter, Gräber und Menschen in der "Antigone" des Sophokles', in G. Greve (ed.) *Sophokles. Antigone*, Tübingen, 93–123.
Bohrer, K.-H. (1991) 'Erwartungsangst und Erscheinungsschrecken. Die griechische Tragödie als Antizipation der modernen Epiphanie', *Merkur* 45, 371–86.
  (2009) *Das Tragische. Erscheinung, Pathos, Klage*, Munich.
Bollack, J. (1990) *L'Œdipe roi de Sophocle. Le texte et ses interprétations. Vols. I–IV*, Lille.
Bond, G. W. (1981) *Euripides. Heracles*, Oxford.
Borgers, O. (2008) 'Religious citizenship in classical Athens. Men and women in religious representations on Athenian vase-painting', *Babesch* 83, 73–97.
Bowie, A. M. (1993a) *Aristophanes. Myth, ritual and comedy*, Cambridge.
  (1993b) 'Religion and politics in Aeschylus' *Oresteia*', *CQ* 43, 10–31.
Bradley, M. (2012a) 'Approaches to pollution and propriety', in M. Bradley ed. (2012b), 11–40.
  ed. (2012b) *Rome, pollution and propriety. Dirt, disease and hygiene in the eternal city from antiquity to modernity*, Cambridge.
Braun, M. (1998) *Die Eumeniden des Aischylos und der Areopag*, Tübingen.
Braungart, W. (1996) *Ritual und Literatur*, Tübingen.
Bremer, J. M. (1975) 'The meadow of love and two passages in Euripides' *Hippolytus*', *Mnemosyne* 28, 268–80.
Brill, S. (2009) 'Violence and vulnerability in Aeschylus' *Suppliants*', in W. Wians ed. *Logos and muthos. Philosophical essays in Greek literature*, Albany, 161–80.
Brock, R. (2010) 'Citizens and non-citizens in Athenian tragedy', in E. M. Harris, D. F. Leão, P. J. Rhodes eds. (2010), 94–107.

Brown, A. L. (1982) 'Some problems in the *Eumenides* of Aeschylus', *JHS* 102, 26–32.
  (1983) 'The Erinyes in the *Oresteia*. Real life, the supernatural, and the stage', *JHS* 103, 13–34.
Budelmann, F. (2000) *The language of Sophocles. Communality, communication and involvement*, Cambridge.
  (2006) 'The mediated ending of Sophocles' *Oedipus tyrannus*', *MD* 57, 43–62.
Burian, P. (1974) 'Pelasgus and politics in Aeschylus' Danaid trilogy', *WS* 8, 5–14.
  (2011) 'Athenian tragedy as democratic discourse', in D. M. Carter ed. (2011), 95–117.
Burkert, W. (1966) 'Greek tragedy and sacrificial ritual', *GRBS* 7, 87–121.
  (1985a) *Greek religion. Archaic and classical*, Oxford.
  (1985b) 'Opferritual bei Sophokles. Pragmatik–Symbolik–Theater', *AU* 28, 5–20.
  (1996) *Creation of the sacred. Tracks of biology in early religions*, Cambridge, MA.
  (2000) 'Private needs and polis acceptance. Purification at Selinous', in P. Flensted-Jensen, T. Heine Nielsen, L. Rubinstein (eds.) *Polis and politics. Studies in ancient Greek history*, Copenhagen, 207–16.
Burnett, A. P. (1971) *Catastrophe survived. Euripides' plays of mixed reversal*, Oxford.
  (1986) 'Hunt and hearth in Hippolytus', in M. Cropp, E. Fantham, S. E. Scully (eds.) *Greek tragedy and its legacy. Essays presented to D. J. Conacher*, Calgary, 167–85.
Bushnell, R. W. (1988) *Prophesying tragedy. Sign and voice in Sophocles' Theban plays*, Ithaca.
Buxton, R. G. A. (1980) 'Blindness and limits. Sophokles and the logic of myth', *JHS* 100, 22–37.
  (1996) 'What can you rely on in *Oedipus Rex*? Response to Calame', in M. S. Silk (ed.) *Tragedy and the tragic. Greek theatre and beyond*, Oxford, 38–48.
Cairns, D. L. (1997) 'The meadow of Artemis and the character of the Euripidean Hippolytus', *QUCC* 57, 51–75.
Calame, C. (1996a) *Thésée et l'imaginaire athénien. Légende et culte en Grèce antique* (second edition), Lausanne.
  (1996b) 'Vision, blindness, and mask. The radicalization of the emotions in Sophocles' *Oedipus Rex*', in M. S. Silk ed. (1996), 17–37.
Caldwell, R. (1974) 'Tragedy romanticized. The *Iphigenia Taurica*, *CJ* 70, 23–40.
Calder III, W. M. (1968) 'Sophokles' political tragedy, *Antigone*', *GRBS* 9, 389–407.
Carawan, E. (1999) 'The edict of Oedipus (*Oedipus tyrannus* 223–51)', *AJPh* 120, 187–222.
Carson, A. (1999) 'Dirt and desire. The phenomenology of female pollution in antiquity', in J. I. Porter (ed.) *Constructions of the classical body*, Ann Arbor, 77–100.
Carter, L. B. (1986) *The quiet Athenian*, Oxford.
  (2004) 'Was Attic tragedy democratic?', *Polis* 21, 1–24.
  (2007) *The politics of Greek tragedy*, Exeter.
  ed. (2011) *Why Athens? A reappraisal of tragic politics*, Oxford.

Cartledge, P. A. (1985) 'The Greek religious festivals', in P. E. Easterling and J. V. Muir (eds.) *Greek religion and society*, Cambridge, 98–127.
  (1993) *The Greeks. A portrait of self and others*, Oxford.
  (1997) '"Deep plays". Theatre as process in Greek civic life', in P. E. Easterling (ed.) *The Cambridge companion to Greek tragedy*, Cambridge, 3–35.
Cawthorn, K. (2008) *Becoming female. The male body in Greek tragedy*, London.
Certeau, M. de (1980) *L'invention du quotidien I. Arts de faire*, Paris.
Chaniotis, A. (1997) 'Reinheit des Körpers – Reinheit des Sinnes in den griechischen Kultgesetzen', in J. Assmann and T. Sundermeier (eds.) *Schuld, Gewissen und Person. Studien zur Geschichte des inneren Menschen*, Gütersloh, 142–79.
  (2012) 'Greek ritual purity. From automatisms to moral distinctions', in P. Rösch and U. Simon (eds.) *How purity is made*, Wiesbaden, 123–39.
Cohen, B. ed. (2000) *Not the classical ideal. Athens and the construction of the other in Greek art*, Leiden.
Cohen, D. (1986) 'The theodicy of Aeschylus. Justice and tyranny in the *Oresteia*', *G&R* 33, 129–41.
  (1991) *Law, sexuality, and society. The enforcement of morals in classical Athens*, Cambridge.
  (1995) *Law, violence and community in classical Athens*, Cambridge.
Cole, S. G. (1988) 'The uses of water in Greek sanctuaries', in R. Hägg, N. Marinatos, G. C. Nordquist (eds.) *Early Greek cult practice. Proceedings of the fifth international symposium at the Swedish Institute at Athens*, Stockholm, 161–5.
  (2004) *Landscapes, gender, and ritual space. The ancient Greek experience*, Berkeley.
Collard, C. (2002) *Aeschylus. Oresteia*, Oxford.
Conacher, D. J. (1967) *Euripidean drama. Myth, theme, and structure*, Toronto.
Connor, W. R. (1988) '"Sacred" and "secular". *Hiera kai hosia* and the classical Athenian concept of the state', *Ancient society* 19, 161–88.
  (1994) 'The problem of Athenian civic identity', in A. L. Boegehold and A. C. Scafuro (eds.) *Athenian identity and civic ideology*, Baltimore, 34–44.
Craik, E. M. (1998) 'Language of sexuality and sexual inversion in Euripides' *Hippolytus*', *Acta Classica* 41, 29–44.
Croally, N. T. (1994) *Euripidean polemic. The* Trojan Women *and the function of tragedy*, Cambridge.
Cropp, M. J. (1988) *Euripides. Electra*, Warminster.
  (2000) *Euripides. Iphigenia in Tauris*, Warminster.
Csapo, E., and Miller, M. C. eds. (2007) *The origins of theater in ancient Greece and beyond. From ritual to drama*, Cambridge.
Csapo, E., Slater, W. J. (1995) *The context of ancient drama*, Ann Arbor.
Dalfen, J. (1977) 'Gesetz ist nicht Gesetz und fromm ist nicht fromm. Die Sprache der Personen in der sophokleischen *Antigone*', *WS* 11, 5–26.
Dawe, R. D. (2001) 'On interpolations in the two Oedipus plays of Sophocles', *RhM* 144, 1–21.

(2006) *Sophocles. Oedipus Rex. Revised edition*, Cambridge.
Dean-Jones, L. (1994) *Women's bodies in classical Greek science*, Oxford.
Decharme, P. (1893/1966) *Euripide et l'esprit de son théâtre*, Brussels (Paris, 1893).
Delcourt, M. (1981) *L'oracle de Delphes*, Paris.
Delebecque, E. (1951) *Euripide et la guerre du Péloponnèse*, Paris.
Demand, N. H. (1994) *Birth, death, and motherhood in ancient Greece*, Baltimore.
Des Bouvrie, S. (1993) 'Creative euphoria. Dionysos and the theatre', *Kernos* 6, 79–112.
Deubner, L. (1932) *Attische Feste*, Berlin.
Devereux, G. (1985) *The character of the Euripidean Hippolytos. An ethno-psychoanalytical study*, Chico, CA.
Dhuga, U. S. (2011) *Choral identity and the chorus of elders in Greek tragedy*, Lanham.
Diggle, J. (1969) 'Marginalia Euripidea', *PCPhS* 15, 30–59.
Diller, H. (1932) 'ΟΨΙΣ ΑΔΗΛΩΝ ΤΑ ΦΑΙΝΟΜΕΝΑ', *Hermes* 67, 14–42.
Dillon, M. (2002) *Girls and women in classical Greek religion*, London.
Dodds, E. R. (1929) 'Euripides the irrationalist', *CR* 43, 97–104.
  (1951) *The Greeks and the irrational*, Berkeley.
  (1960) 'Morals and politics in the *Oresteia*', *PCPhS* 6, 19–31.
  (1966) 'On misunderstanding the *Oedipus Rex*', *G&R* 13, 37–49.
Douglas, M. (1966) *Purity and danger. An analysis of concepts of pollution and taboo*, London.
Dover, K. (1957) 'The political aspect of Aeschylus' *Eumenides*', *JHS* 77, 230–7.
Dubois, P. (2002) 'Ancient tragedy and the metaphor of katharsis', *Theatre Journal* 54, 19–24.
Dunn, F. M. (1996) *Tragedy's end. Closure and innovation in Euripidean drama*, New York.
Dyer, R. R. (1969) 'The evidence for Apolline purification rituals at Delphi and Athens', *JHS* 89.38–56.
Dyson, M. (1973) 'Oracle, edict, and curse in *Oedipus tyrannus*', *CQ* 23, 202–12.
Easterling, P. E. (1982) *Sophocles. Trachiniae*, Cambridge.
  (1988) 'Tragedy and ritual. "Cry 'woe, woe', but may the good prevail"', *Métis* 3, 87–109.
Eck, B. (2012) *La mort rouge. Homicide, guerre et souillure en Grèce ancienne*, Paris.
Edmunds, L. (1981) 'The cults and the legend of Oedipus', *HSPh* 85, 221–38.
  (1996) *Theatrical space and historical place in Sophocles'* Oedipus at Colonus, Lanham.
Ehrenberg, V. (1947) 'Polypragmosyne. A study in Greek politics', *JHS* 67, 46–67.
Else, G. F. (1957) *Aristotle's Poetics. The argument*, Leiden.
  (1977) 'Ritual and drama in Aischyleian tragedy', *ICS* 2, 70–87.
Euben, J. P. (1990) *The tragedy of political theory. The road not taken*, Princeton.
Ewans, M. (1982) *Wagner and Aeschylus. The Ring and the Oresteia*, London.
Faraone, C. A. (2011) 'Magical and medical approaches to the wandering womb in the ancient Greek world', *ClAnt* 30, 1–32.
Fardon, R. (1999) *Mary Douglas. An intellectual biography*, London.

Fartzoff, M. (2010) 'Le "corps" dans la tragédie grecque classique', in M.-H. Garelli and V. Visa-Ondarçuhu eds. (2010) *Corps en jeu. De l'antiquité à nos jours. Actes du colloque international* Corps en jeu, *Université de Toulouse II-Le Mirail, 9–11 octobre 2008*, Rennes, 193–203.

Feeney, D. (2004) 'Interpreting sacrificial ritual in Roman poetry. Disciplines and their models', in A. Barchiesi, J. Rüpke, and S. Stephens eds. (2004), 1–21.

(2007) 'On not forgetting the "Literatur" in "Literatur und Religion". Representing the mythic and the divine in Roman historiography', in A. Bierl, R. Lämmle, and K. Wesselmann eds. (2007), vol. 2, pp. 173–202.

Finglass, P. J. (2009) 'The ending of Sophocles' *Oedipus Rex*', *Philologus* 153, 42–62.

Flashar, H. (2007) 'Die musikalische und die poetische Katharsis', in B. Seidensticker and M. Vöhler eds. (2007), 173–82.

Foley, H. P. (1985) *Ritual irony. Poetry and sacrifice in Euripides*, Ithaca.

(1993) 'Oedipus as pharmakos', in R. M. Rosen and J. Farrell (eds.) *Nomodeiktes. Greek studies in honor of Martin Ostwald*, Ann Arbor, 525–38.

(1995) 'Tragedy and democratic ideology. The case of Sophocles' *Antigone*', in Goff ed. (1995a), 131–50.

(1996) 'Antigone as moral agent', in M. S. Silk ed. (1996), 49–73.

Föllinger, S. (2003) *Genosdependenzen. Studien zur Arbeit am Mythos bei Aischylos*, Göttingen.

(2007) 'Katharsis als "natürlicher" Vorgang', in B. Seidensticker and M. Vöhler eds. (2007), 3–20.

Forbes, P. B. R. (1948) 'Law and politics in the *Oresteia*', *CR* 62, 99–104.

Fornaro, S. (2007) 'Reinigung als religiöser Ritus. Anmerkungen zur Forschungsgeschichte', in B. Seidensticker and M. Vöhler eds. (2007), 83–99.

Foucault, M. (1971) *L'ordre du discours*, Paris.

Fraenkel, E. (1950) *Aeschylus. Agamemnon. Edited with a commentary* (3 vols.), Oxford.

Friis Johansen, H., and Whittle, E. W. (1980) *Aeschylus. The Suppliants, vol. 1–3*, Copenhagen.

Frischer, B. D. (1970) 'Concordia discors and characterization in Euripides' *Hippolytos*', *GRBS* 11, 85–100.

Fusillo, M. (1992) 'Was ist eine romanhafte Tragödie? Überlegungen zu Euripides' Experimentalismus', *Poetica* 24, 270–98.

Futo Kennedy, R. (2009) *Athena's justice. Athena, Athens and the concept of justice in Greek tragedy*, New York.

Gagarin, M. (1975) 'The vote of Athena', *AJPh* 96, 121–7.

(1976) *Aeschylean drama*, Berkeley.

(1992) 'The poetry of justice. Hesiod and the origins of Greek law', *Ramus* 21, 61–78.

(2008) *Writing Greek law*, Cambridge.

Gagné, R. (2013) *Ancestral fault in ancient Greece*, Cambridge.

Garvie, A. F. (1969) *Aeschylus' Supplices. Play and trilogy*, Cambridge.

(1986) *Aeschylus. Choephori*, Oxford.

Geertz, C. (1973) *The interpretation of cultures. Selected essays*, New York.

Bibliography

Gehrke, H.-J. (1985) *Stasis. Untersuchungen zu den inneren Kriegen in den griechischen Staaten des 5. und 4. Jh. v. Chr.*, Munich.

— (1995) 'Der Nomosbegriff der Polis', in O. Behrends and W. Sellert (eds.) *Nomos und Gesetz. Ursprünge und Wirkungen des griechischen Gesetzesdenkens*, Göttingen, 13–35.

Geisser, F. (2002) *Götter, Geister und Dämonen. Unheilsmächte bei Aischylos. Zwischen Aberglauben und Theatralik*, Munich.

Gellie, G. (1981) 'Tragedy and Euripides' *Electra*', *BICS* 28, 1–12.

Gernet, L. (1968) *Anthropologie de la Grèce antique*, Paris.

— (1982) *Droit et institutions en Grèce antique*, Paris.

Ginouvès, R. (1962) *Balaneutikè. Recherches sur le bain dans l'antiquité grecque*, Paris.

Girard, R. (1977) *Violence and the sacred*, Baltimore.

Gödde, S. (2000a) *Das Drama der Hikesie. Ritual und Rhetorik in Aischylos' Hiketiden*, Münster.

— (2000b) 'Zu einer Poetik des Rituals in Aischylos' *Persern*', in S. Gödde and T. Heinze (eds.) *Skenika. Beiträge zum antiken Theater und seiner Rezeption*, Darmstadt, 31–47.

Goff, B. E. (1988) 'Euripides' *Ion* 1132–65. The tent', *PCPhS* 34, 42–54.

— (1990) *The noose of words. Readings of desire, violence, and language in Euripides' Hippolytos*, Cambridge.

— (1991) 'The sign of the fall. The scars of Orestes and Odysseus', *ClAnt* 10, 259–67.

Goff, B. E. ed. (1995a) *History, tragedy, theory. Dialogues on Athenian drama*, Austin.

Goff, B. E. (1995b) 'Introduction. History, tragedy, theory', in ead. ed. (1995b), 1–37.

— (1999) 'The violence of community. Ritual in the *Iphigeneia in Tauris*', in M. W. Padilla ed. (1999), 109–25.

— (1999/2000) 'Try to make it real compared to what? Euripides' *Electra* and the play of genres', *ICS* 24/25, 93–105.

Goheen, R. F. (1951) *The imagery of Sophocles' Antigone. A study of poetic language and structure*, Princeton.

— (1955) 'Aspects of dramatic symbolism. Three studies in the *Oresteia*', *AJPh* 76, 113–37.

Golden, L. (1962) 'Catharsis', *TAPhA* 93, 51–60.

— (1976) 'The clarification theory of "katharsis"', *Hermes* 104, 437–52.

— (1992) *Aristotle on tragic and comic mimesis*, Atlanta.

Goldhill, S. (1984a) 'Exegesis: Oedipus (R)ex', *Arethusa* 17, 177–200.

Goldhill, S. D. (1984b) *Language, sexuality, narrative. The Oresteia*, Cambridge.

Goldhill, S. (1984c) 'Two notes on τέλος and related words in the *Oresteia*', *JHS* 104, 169–76.

— (1986) *Reading Greek tragedy*, Cambridge.

— (1990) 'The Great Dionysia and civic ideology', in J. J. Winkler and F. I. Zeitlin eds. (1990), 97–129.

(1997) 'Modern critical approaches to Greek tragedy', in P. E. Easterling (ed.) *The Cambridge companion to Greek tragedy*, Cambridge, 324–47.
(2000) 'Civic ideology and the problem of difference. The politics of Aeschylean tragedy, once again', *JHS* 120.34–56.
(2007) 'What's in a wall?', in C. Kraus, S. D. Goldhill, H. P. Foley and J. Elsner (eds.) *Visualizing the tragic. Drama, myth, and ritual in Greek art and literature. Essays in honour of Froma Zeitlin*, Oxford, 127–47.
(2012) *Sophocles and the language of tragedy*, Oxford.
Gould, J. (1985) 'On making sense of Greek religion', in P. E. Easterling and J. V. Muir (eds.) *Greek religion and society*, Cambridge, 1–33.
(1994) 'Herodotus and religion', in S. Hornblower (ed.) *Greek historiography*, Oxford, 91–106.
Goward, B. (2005) *Aeschylus. Agamemnon*, London.
Graf, F. (1997) *Magic in the ancient world*, Cambridge, MA.
(2007a) 'Religion and drama', in M. McDonald and J. M. Walton eds. (2007) *The Cambridge companion to Greek and Roman theatre*, Cambridge, 55–71.
(2007b) 'Religiöse Kathartik im Licht der Inschriften', in B. Seidensticker and M. Vöhler eds. (2007), 101–16.
Graffunder, P. L. W. (1885) 'Über den ausgang des "könig Oedipus" von Sophokles', *Neue Jahrbücher für Philologie und Pädagogik. Zweite Abteilung* 132, 389–408.
Gregory, J. (2009) 'A father's curse in Euripides' *Hippolytus*', in J. R. C. Cousland and J. R. Hume (eds.) *The play of texts and fragments. Essays in honour of Martin Cropp*, Leiden, 35–48.
Grethlein, J. (2003) *Asyl und Athen. Die Konstruktion kollektiver Identität in der griechischen Tragödie*, Stuttgart.
(2007) 'Epic narrative and ritual. The case of the funeral games in the *Iliad*', in A. Bierl, R. Lämmle, and K. Wesselmann eds. (2007), vol. 1, 151–77.
Griffin, J. (1998) 'The social function of Attic tragedy', *CQ* 48, 39–61.
Griffith, M. (1990) 'Contest and contradiction in early Greek poetry', in M. Griffith and D. J. Mastronarde (eds.) *Cabinet of the muses. Essays on classical and comparative literature in honor of Thomas G. Rosenmeyer*, Atlanta, 185–207.
(1995) 'Brilliant dynasts. Power and politics in the "Oresteia"', *ClAnt* 14, 62–129.
(1999) *Sophocles. Antigone*, Cambridge.
(2001) 'Antigone and her sister(s). Embodying women in Greek tragedy', in A. Lardinois and L. McClure (eds.) *Making silence speak. Women's voices in Greek literature and society*, Princeton, 117–36.
(2009) 'The poetry of Aeschylus (in its traditional contexts)', *Entretiens sur l'Antiquité Classique* 55, 1–55.
Griffith, R. D. (1996) *The theatre of Apollo. Divine justice and Sophocles' Oedipus the King*, Montreal.
Grube, G. M. A. (1961) *The drama of Euripides*, London.
Guépin, J.-P. (1968) *The tragic paradox. Myth and ritual in Greek tragedy*, Amsterdam.
Hall, E. (1989) *Inventing the barbarian. Greek self-definition through tragedy*, Oxford.

(2010) *Greek tragedy. Suffering under the sun*, Oxford.
Halleran, M. R. (1995) *Euripides. Hippolytus*, Warminster.
Halliwell, S. (2005) 'Learning from suffering. Ancient responses to tragedy', in J. Gregory (ed.) *A companion to Greek tragedy*, Malden, 394–412.
Halporn, J. W. (1983) 'The skeptical Electra', *HSPh* 87, 101–18.
Hame, K. J. (2008) 'Female control of funeral rites in Greek tragedy. Klytaimestra, Medea, Antigone', *CPh* 103, 1–15.
Hammond, N. G. L. (1984) 'Spectacle and parody in Euripides' *Electra*', *GRBS* 25, 373–87.
Hankinson, R. J. (1995) 'Pollution and infection. An hypothesis stillborn', *Apeiron* 28, 25–65.
Hanson, A. E. (1990) 'The medical writer's woman', in D. M. Halperin, J. J. Winkler, and F. I. Zeitlin (eds.) *Before sexuality. The construction of erotic experience in the ancient Greek world*, Princeton, 309–38.
  (1991) 'Continuity and change. Three case studies in Hippocratic gynecological therapy and theory', in S. B. Pomeroy (ed.) *Women's history and ancient history*, North Carolina, 73–110.
Hardie, P. R. (1997) 'Virgil and tragedy', in C. Martindale (ed.) *The Cambridge companion to Virgil*, Cambridge, 312–26.
Harris, E. M. (2006) 'Antigone the lawyer, or the ambiguities of nomos', in eodem, *Democracy and the rule of law in classical Athens. Essays on law, society, and politics*, Cambridge, 41–80.
  (2010a) 'Introduction', in E. M. Harris, D. F. Leão, and P. J. Rhodes eds. (2010), 1–24.
  (2010b) 'Is Oedipus guilty? Sophocles and Athenian homicide law', in E. M. Harris, D. F. Leão, and P. J. Rhodes eds. (2010), 122–46.
Harris, E. M., Leão, D. F., Rhodes, P. J. eds. (2010) *Law and drama in ancient Greece*, London.
Harrison, T. (2000) *Divinity and history. The religion of Herodotus*, Oxford.
Heath, M. (1987) *The poetics of Greek tragedy*, London.
Henrichs, A. (1994/5) '"Why should I dance?" Choral self-referentiality in Greek tragedy', *Arion* 3, 56–111.
  (2004) '"Let the good prevail." Perversions of the ritual process in Greek tragedy', in D. Yatromanolakis and P. Roilos eds. (2004) 189–98.
Hester, D. A. (1971) 'Sophocles the unphilosophical. A study in the *Antigone*', *Mnemosyne* 24, 11–59.
  (1981) 'The casting vote', *AJPh* 102, 265–74.
  (1984) 'The banishment of Oedipus. A neglected theory on the end of *Oedipus Rex*', *Antichthon* 18, 13–23.
Holladay, A. J. (1988) 'New developments in the problem of the Athenian plague', *CQ* 38, 247–50.
Hölkeskamp, K.-J. (1992) 'Written law in archaic Greece', *PCPhS* 38, 87–117.
  (2000) '(In-)Schrift und Monument. Zum Begriff des Gesetzes im archaischen und klassischen Griechenland', *ZPE* 132, 73–96.
  (2002) '*Ptolis* and *agore*. Homer and the archaeology of the city-state', in F. Montanari (ed.) *Omero tremila anni dopo*, Rome, 297–342.

Hölscher, T. (1999) *Öffentliche Räume in frühen griechischen Städten*, 2nd edn, Heidelberg.
Hoessly, F. (2001) *Katharsis. Reinigung als Heilverfahren. Studien zum Ritual der archaischen und klassichen Zeit sowie zum Corpus Hippocraticum*, Göttingen.
Hoffer, S. E. (1996) 'Violence, culture, and the workings of ideology in Euripides' *Ion*', *ClAnt* 15, 289–318.
Holmes, B. (2010) *The symptom and the subject. The emergence of the physical body in ancient Greece*, Princeton.
Hose, M. (1990) *Studien zum Chor bei Euripides. Teil 1*, Stuttgart.
Howe, T. P. (1962) 'Taboo in the Oedipus theme', *TAPhA* 93, 124–43.
Irwin, E. (2005) *Solon and early Greek poetry. The politics of exhortation*, Cambridge.
Jameson, M. H., Jordan, D. R., Kotansky, R. D. (1993) *A 'lex sacra' from Selinous*, Durham.
Janka, M. (2004) *Dialog der Tragiker. Liebe, Wahn und Erkenntnis in Sophokles'* Trachiniai *und Euripides'* Hippolytos, Munich.
Jebb, R. (1897) *Sophocles. The Oedipus tyrannus*, 2nd edn, Cambridge.
Jouanna, J. (2007) *Sophocle*, Paris.
  (2012a) 'Air, miasma and contagion in the time of Hippocrates and the survival of miasmas in post-Hippocratic medicine (Rufus of Ephesus, Galen and Palladius)', in Jouanna (2012b), 121–36.
  (2012b) *Greek medicine from Hippocrates to Galen. Selected papers*, Leiden.
  (2012c) 'Hippocratic medicine and Greek tragedy', in Jouanna (2012a), 55–80.
Judet de la Combe, P. (2010) *Les tragédies grecques sont-elles tragiques? Théâtre et théorie*, Montrouge.
Kahn, C. H. (1979) *The art and thought of Heraclitus. An edition of the fragments with translation and commentary*, Cambridge.
Kamerbeek, J. C. (1967) *The plays of Sophocles. Commentaries. Vol. IV. The Oedipus tyrannus*, Leiden.
  (1978) *The plays of Sophocles. Commentaries. Vol. III. The Antigone*, Leiden.
  (1984) *The plays of Sophocles. Commentaries. Vol. VII. The Oedipus Coloneus*, Leiden.
Kane, R. L. (1975) 'Prophecy and perception in the *Oedipus Rex*', *TAPhA* 105, 189–208.
Karamanou, I. (2012) 'Euripides' family reunion plays and their sociopolitical resonances', in A. Markantonatos and B. Zimmermann eds. (2012), 241–52.
Kelly, A. (2009) *Sophocles. Oedipus at Colonus*, London.
King, H. (1983) 'Bound to bleed. Artemis and Greek women', in A. Cameron and A. Kuhrt (eds.) *Images of women in antiquity*, London, 109–27.
  (1998) *Hippocrates' woman. Reading the female body in ancient Greece*, London.
Kitto, H. D. F. (1961) *Greek tragedy. A literary study*, London.
Kitzinger, M. R. (1993) 'What do you know? The end of Oedipus', in R. M. Rosen and J. Farrell (eds.) *Nomodeiktes. Greek studies in honor of Martin Ostwald*, Ann Arbor, 539–56.
  (2008) *The choruses of Sophokles'* Antigone *and* Philoktetes. *A dance of words*, Leiden.

Knox, B. M. W. (1952a) 'The *Hippolytus* of Euripides', *YCS* 13, 3–31.
  (1952b) 'The lion in the house', *CPh* 47, 17–25.
  (1956) 'The date of the *Oedipus tyrannus* of Sophocles', *AJPh* 77, 133–47.
  (1957) *Oedipus at Thebes*, New Haven.
  (1964) *The heroic temper. Studies in Sophoclean tragedy*, Berkeley.
  (1970) 'Euripidean comedy', in A. Cheuse and R. Koffler (eds.) *The rarer action. Essays in honor of Francis Fergusson*, New Brunswick, NJ, 68–96 (reprinted in B. M. W. Knox *Word and action. Essays on the ancient theater*, Baltimore 1979, 250–74).
  (1983) 'Sophocles and the *polis*', *Entretiens sur l'Antiquité Classique* 29, 1–37.
Kosak, J. C. (2004) *Heroic measures. Hippocratic medicine in the making of Euripidean tragedy*, Leiden.
Kossatz-Deissmann, A. (1978) *Dramen des Aischylos auf westgriechischen Vasen*, Mainz.
Kovacs, P. D. (2009) 'Do we have the end of Sophocles' *Oedipus tyrannus*', *JHS* 129, 53–70.
Kristeva, J. (1982) *Powers of horror. An essay on abjection*, New York.
Krummen, E. (1993) 'Athens and Attica. Polis and countryside in tragedy', in A. H. Sommerstein, S. Halliwell, J. Henderson, B. Zimmermann (eds.) (1993), 191–217.
  (1998) 'Ritual und Katastrophe. Rituelle Handlung und Bildersprache bei Sophokles und Euripides', in F. Graf (ed.) *Ansichten griechischer Rituale. Geburtstags-Symposium für Walter Burkert*, Stuttgart, 296–325.
Kyriakou, P. (2006) *A commentary on Euripides' Iphigenia in Tauris*, Berlin.
LaCourse Munteanu, D. (2012) *Tragic pathos. Pity and fear in Greek philosophy and tragedy*, Cambridge.
Lape, S. (2010) *Race and citizen identity in the classical Athenian democracy*, Cambridge.
Lardinois, A. (1992) 'Greek myths for Athenian rituals. Religion and politics in Aeschylus' *Eumenides* and Sophocles' *Oedipus Coloneus*', *GRBS* 33, 313–27.
Latacz, J. (2003) *Einführung in die griechische Tragödie*, 2nd edn, Göttingen.
Leão, D. F. (2010) 'The legal horizon of the Oresteia. The crime of homicide and the founding of the Areopagus', in E. M. Harris, D. F. Leão, P. J. Rhodes eds. (2010), 39–60.
Lebeck, A. (1971) *The* Oresteia. *A study in language and structure*. Washington, D.C.
Lee, K. H. (1997) *Euripides. Ion*, Warminster.
Lefèvre, E. (2001) *Die Unfähigkeit, sich zu erkennen. Sophokles' Tragödien*, Leiden.
Lefkowitz, M. (1981) *Heroines and hysterics*, London.
  (1989) '"Impiety" and "atheism" in Euripides' dramas', *CQ* 39, 70–82.
Lennon, J. J. (2013) *Pollution and religion in ancient Rome*, Cambridge.
Lesky, A. (1931) 'Die Orestie des Aischylos', *Hermes* 66, 190–214.
  (1966) 'Decision and responsibility in the tragedy of Aeschylus', *JHS* 86, 78–85.
Lewis, R. G. (1989) 'The procedural basis of Sophocles' *Oedipus tyrannus*', *GRBS* 30, 41–66.

Lloyd, G. E. R. (1966) *Polarity and analogy. Two types of argumentation in early Greek thought*, Cambridge.
  (1983) *Science, folklore, and ideology. Studies in the life sciences in ancient Greece*, Cambridge.
Lloyd, M. (1986) 'Realism and character in Euripides' *Electra*', *Phoenix* 40, 1–19.
Lloyd-Jones, H. (1956) 'Zeus in Aeschylus', *JHS* 76, 55–67.
  (1962) 'The guilt of Agamemnon', *CQ* 12, 187–99.
  (1983) *The justice of Zeus*, 2nd edn. Berkeley.
Loraux, N. (1986) *The invention of Athens. The funeral oration in the classical city*, Cambridge, MA.
  (1987) *Tragic ways of killing a woman*, Cambridge, MA.
  (1990) 'Kreousa the autochthon. A study of Euripides' *Ion*', in J. J. Winkler and F. I. Zeitlin (1990), 168–206.
  (1993) *The children of Athena. Athenian ideas about citizenship and the division between the sexes*, Princeton.
  (1995) 'La guerre civile grecque et la représentation anthropologique du monde à l'envers', *Revue de l'histoire des religions* 212, 299–326.
Lurje, M. (2004) *Die Suche nach der Schuld. Sophokles' Oedipus Rex, Aristoteles' Poetik und das Tragödienverständnis der Neuzeit*, Munich.
MacDowell, D. M. (1963) *Athenian homicide law in the age of the orators*, Manchester.
MacLeod, C. W. (1982) 'Politics and the *Oresteia*', *JHS* 102, 124–44.
Mann, M. (2005) *The dark side of democracy. Explaining ethnic cleansing*, Cambridge.
Manuwald, B. (1992) 'Oidipus und Adrastos. Bemerkungen zur neueren Diskussion um die Schuldfrage in Sophokles' "König Oidipus"', *RhM* 135, 1–43.
Manville, P. B. (1990) *The origins of citizenship in ancient Athens*, Princeton.
March, J. R. (1987) *The creative poet. Studies on the treatment of myths in Greek poetry*, London.
  (1990) 'Euripides the misogynist?', in A. Powell (ed.) *Euripides, women, and sexuality*, London, 32–75.
Markantonatos, A. (2002) *Tragic narrative. A narratological study of Sophocles' Oedipus at Colonus*, Berlin.
  (2007) *Oedipus at Colonus. Sophocles, Athens, and the world*, Berlin.
Markantonatos, A., Zimmermann, B. eds. (2012) *Crisis on stage. Tragedy and comedy in late fifth-century Athens*, Berlin.
Martin, R. (1951) *Recherches sur l'agora grecque. Études d'histoire et d'architecture urbaines*, Paris.
Mastronarde, D. (1976) 'Iconography and imagery in Euripides' *Ion*', *CSCA* 8, 163–76.
  (1999/2000) 'Euripidean tragedy and genre. The terminology and its problems', *ICS* 24/25, 23–39.
  (2002) *Euripides. Medea*, Cambridge.
  (2010) *The art of Euripides. Dramatic technique and social context*, Cambridge.
McClure, L. (1999) *Spoken like a woman. Speech and gender in Athenian drama*, Princeton.

McPherran, M. L. (2002) 'Justice and pollution in the *Euthyphro*', *Apeiron* 35, 105–29.
McNeil, L. (2005) 'Bridal cloths, cover-ups and *kharis*. The "carpet-scene" in Aeschylus' *Agamemnon*', *GR* 52.1–17.
Meier, C. (1980) *Die Entstehung des Politischen bei den Griechen*, Frankfurt am Main.
Meltzer, G. S. (1996) 'The "just voice" as paradigmatic metaphor in Euripides' *Hippolytus*', *Helios* 23, 173–90.
Meltzer, G. S. (2006) *Euripides and the poetics of nostalgia*, Cambridge.
Mendelsohn, D. A. (2002) *Gender and the city in Euripides' political plays*, Oxford.
Mikalson, J. D. (2003) *Herodotus and religion in the Persian Wars*, Chapel Hill.
Mills, S. (1997) *Theseus, tragedy, and the Athenian empire*, Oxford.
  (2002) *Euripides. Hippolytus*, London.
Mitchell, L. G. (2006) 'Greeks, barbarians, and Aeschylus' *Suppliants*', *G&R* 53, 205–23.
Mitchell(-Boyask), R. N. (1991) 'Miasma, mimesis, and scapegoating in Euripides' *Hippolytus*', *Cl. Ant.* 10, 97–122.
  (1996) 'Dramatic scapegoating. On the uses and abuses of Girard and Shakespearean criticism', in M. S. Silk ed. (1996) 426–37.
  (1999) 'Euripides' *Hippolytus* and the trials of manhood', in M. W. Padilla ed. (1999), 42–66.
  (2008) *Plague and the Athenian imagination. Drama, history, and the cult of Asclepius*, Cambridge.
  (2009) *Aeschylus. Eumenides*, London.
  (2012) 'Heroic pharmacology. Sophocles and the metaphors of Greek medical thought', in K. Ormand ed. (2012), 316–30.
Molinar, A., and Vöhler, M. eds. (2009) *Un/Reinheit. Konzepte und Praktiken im Kulturvergleich*, Munich.
Moulinier, L. (1952) *Le pur et l'impur dans la pensée des Grecs d'Homère à Aristote*, Paris.
Müller, G. (1967) *Sophokles. Antigone*, Heidelberg.
Mueller, M. (2010) 'Athens in a basket. Naming, objects, and identity in Euripides' *Ion*', *Arethusa* 43, 365–402.
Murnaghan, S. (2005) 'Women in groups. Aeschylus's *Suppliants* and the female choruses of Greek tragedy', in V. Pedrick and S. M. Oberhelman (eds.) *The soul of tragedy. Essays on Athenian drama*, Chicago, 183–98.
Murray, G. (1912) 'Excursus on the ritual forms preserved in Greek tragedy', in J. Harrison, *Themis. A study of the social origins of Greek religion*, Cambridge, 341–69.
Neumann, G. (2000) 'Begriff und Funktion des Rituals im Feld der Literaturwissenschaft', in G. Neumann and S. Weigel (eds.) *Lesbarkeit der Kultur. Literaturwissenschaft zwischen Kulturtechnik und Ethnographie*, Munich, 19–52.
Nussbaum, M. C. (2001) *The fragility of goodness. Luck and ethics in Greek tragedy and philosophy,* rev. edn, Cambridge.

Ober, J. (2005) 'Greek *horoi*. Artifactual texts and the contingency of meaning', in id., *Athenian legacies. Essays on the politics of going on together*, Princeton, 183–211.
O'Brien, M. J. (1988) 'Pelopid history and the plot of *Iphigenia in Tauris*', *CQ* 38, 98–115.
Ogden, D. (1996) *Greek bastardy in the classical and Hellenistic periods*, Oxford.
Olson, S. D. (2002) *Aristophanes. Acharnians*, Oxford.
Ormand, K. ed. (2012) *A companion to Sophocles*, Malden.
Osborne, R. (1997a) 'Law and laws. How do we join up the dots?', in L. G. Mitchell and P. J. Rhodes (eds.) *The development of the polis in archaic Greece*, London, 39–43.
  (1997b) 'Law, the democratic citizen and the representation of women in classical Athens', *Past and present* 155, 3–33.
  (2008) 'Law and religion in classical Athens. The case of the dead', in C. Langenfeld and S. Schneider (eds.) *Recht und Religion in Europa. Zeitgenössische Konflitke und historische Perspektiven*, Göttingen, 46–58.
  ed. (2010) *Debating the Athenian cultural revolution. Art, literature, philosophy, and politics 430–380 BC*, Cambridge.
  (2011) *The history written on the classical Greek body*, Cambridge.
  (2012) 'Sophocles and contemporary politics', in K. Ormand ed. (2012), 270–86.
Oudemans, T. C. W. and Lardinois, A. P. M. H. (1987) *Tragic ambiguity. Anthropology, philosophy and Sophocles' Antigone*, Leiden.
Owen, A. S. (1939) *Euripides. Ion*, Oxford.
Owens, R. (2010) *Solon of Athens. Poet, philosopher, soldier, statesman*, Brighton.
Padel, R. (1974) '"Imagery of the elsewhere". Two choral odes of Euripides', *CQ* 24, 227–41.
  (1983) 'Women. Model for possession by Greek daemons', in A. Cameron and A. Kuhrt (eds.) *Images of women in antiquity*, London, 3–19.
  (1992) *In and out of the mind. Greek images of the tragic self*, Princeton.
Padilla, M. W. ed. (1999) *Rites of passage in ancient Greece. Literature, religion, society*, Lewisburg.
Page, D. L. (1953) 'Thucydides' description of the great plague at Athens', *CQ* 3, 97–119.
Palaver, W. (2004) *René Girards mimetische Theorie im Kontext kulturtheoretischer und gesellschaftspolitischer Fragen*, 2nd edn. Münster.
Papadopoulou, T. (2005a) 'Artemis and constructs of meaning in Euripides' *Iphigenia in Tauris*', *Ariadne* 11, 107–27.
  (2005b) Heracles *and Euripidean tragedy*, Cambridge.
  (2011) *Aeschylus. Suppliants*, London.
Parker, R. (1983) *Miasma. Pollution and purification in early Greek religion*, Oxford.
  (1999) 'Through a glass darkly. Sophocles and the divine', in J. Griffin (ed.) *Sophocles revisited. Essays presented to Sir Hugh Lloyd-Jones*, Oxford, 11–30.
  (2005) *Polytheism and society at Athens*, Oxford.
  (2011) *On Greek religion*, Ithaca.

Patterson, C. B. ed. (2006a) *Antigone's answer. Essays on death and burial, family and state in classical Athens*, Lubbock (*Helios* 33, Special issue).
  (2006b) 'The place and practice of burial in Sophocles' Athens', in ead. (2006a), 9–48.
Pedrick, V. (2007) *Euripides, Freud, and the romance of belonging*, Baltimore.
Pelling, C. ed. (1990) *Characterization and individuality in Greek literature*, Oxford.
Peradotto, J. J. (1964) 'Some patterns of nature imagery in the *Oresteia*', *AJPh* 85, 378–93.
  (1969) 'The omen of the eagles and the ἦθος of Agamemnon', *Phoenix* 23, 137–63.
Phillips, D. D. (2008) *Avengers of blood. Homicide in Athenian law and custom from Draco to Demosthenes*, Stuttgart.
Polignac, F. de (1984) *La naissance de la cité grecque. Cultes, espace et société VIIIe–VIIe siècles avant J.-C.*, Paris.
Poole, J. C. F. and Holladay, A. J. (1979) 'Thucydides and the plague of Athens', *CQ* 29, 282–300.
Porter, D. H. (2005) 'Aeschylus' *Eumenides*. Some contrapuntal lines', *AJPh* 126, 301–31.
Pòrtulas, J. (2006) 'Miasma in Eraclito e in Eschilo. ΑΙΜΑΤΟΣ ΚΑΘΑΡΣΙΟΥ ΣΦΑΓΑΙ', in *Lexis* 24, 23–9.
Pucci, P. (1990) 'The tragic *pharmakos* of the *Oedipus Rex*', *Helios* 17, 41–9.
Rabinowitz, N. S. (1981) 'From force to persuasion. Aeschylus' *Oresteia* as cosmogonic myth', *Ramus* 10, 159–91.
  (1993) *Anxiety veiled. Euripides and the traffic in women*, Ithaca.
Radke(-Uhlmann), G. (2003) *Tragik und Metatragik. Euripides'* Bakchen *und die moderne Literaturwissenschaft*, Berlin.
Raeburn, D., and Thomas, O. (2011) *The Agamemnon of Aeschylus. A commentary for students*, Oxford.
Rechenauer, G. (1991) *Thukydides und die hippokratische Medizin. Naturwissenschaftliche Methodik als Modell für Geschichtsschreibung*, Hildesheim.
Reckford, K. J. (1974) 'Phaedra and Pasiphae: The pull backward', *TAPhA* 104, 307–28.
Reden, S. von (1998) 'The well-ordered polis. Topographies of civic space', in P. Cartledge, P. Millett, and S. von Reden (eds.) *Kosmos. Essays in order, conflict, and community in classical Athens*, Cambridge, 170–90.
Rehm, R. (2006) 'Sophocles' *Antigone* and family values', in C. B. Patterson ed. (2006a), 187–218.
  (2012) 'Ritual in Sophocles', in A. Markantonatos ed. *Brill's companion to Sophocles*, Leiden, 411–27.
Reinhardt, K. (1947) *Sophokles*, Frankfurt.
Revermann, M. (2006) *Comic business. Theatricality, dramatic technique, and performance contexts of Aristophanic comedy*, Oxford.
Rhodes, P. J. (2003) 'Nothing to do with democracy. Athenian drama and the polis', *JHS* 123, 104–19.

Rivier, A. (1966) 'Un débat sur la tragédie grecque. Le héros, le "nécessaire" et les dieux', *RThPh* (ser. 3) 16, 233–54.
  (1968) 'Remarques sur le "nécessaire" et la "nécessité" chez Eschyle', *REG* 81, 5–39.
Robertson, H. G. (1939) 'Legal expressions and ideas of justice in Aeschylus', *CPh* 34, 209–19.
Rodighiero, A. (2012) 'The sense of place. *Oedipus at Colonus*, "political" geography, and the defence of a way of life', in A. Markantonatos and B. Zimmermann eds. (2012), 55–80.
Rösler, W. (1993) 'Der Schluß der *Hiketiden* und die Danaiden-Trilogie', *RhM* 136, 1–22.
Rohdich, H. (1980) Antigone. *Beitrag zu einer Theorie des sophokleischen Helden*, Heidelberg.
Roisman, H. M. (1999) *Nothing is as it seems. The tragedy of the implicit in Euripides' Hippolytus*, Lanham.
Roselli, D. K. (2006) 'Polyneices' body and his monument. Class, social status, and funerary commemoration in Sophocles' *Antigone*', in C. B. Patterson ed. (2006a), 135–77.
Rosenmeyer, T. G. (1982) *The art of Aeschylus*, Berkeley.
Rosivach, V. J. (1977) 'Earthborns and Olympians. The parodos of the *Ion*', *CQ* 27, 284–94.
  (1983) 'On Creon, *Antigone* and not burying the dead', *RhM* 126, 193–211.
Saïd, S. (2012) 'Athens and Athenian space in *Oedipus at Colonus*', in A. Markantonatos and B. Zimmermann eds. (2012), 81–100.
Samons II, L. J. (1998/9) 'Aeschylus, the Alcmeonids and the reform of the Areopagus', *CJ* 94, 221–33.
Sansone, D. (1975) 'The sacrifice-motif in Euripides' *IT*', *TAPhA* 105, 283–95.
Saxonhouse, A. W. (1986) 'Myths and origins of cities. Reflections on the autochthony theme in Euripides' *Ion*', in J. P. Euben (ed.) *Greek tragedy and political theory*, Berkeley, 252–73.
Schaps, D. M. (1993) 'Aeschylus' politics and the theme of the *Oresteia*', in R. M. Rosen and J. Farrell (eds.) *Nomodeiktes. Greek studies in honor of Martin Ostwald*, Ann Arbor, 505–17.
Schadewaldt, W. (1955) 'Furcht und Mitleid? Zur Deutung des Aristotelischen Tragödiensatzes', *Hermes* 83, 129–71.
Schlesier, R. (1993) 'Mixtures of masks. Maenads as tragic models', in T. H. Carpenter and C. A. Faraone (eds.) *Masks of Dionysus*, Ithaca, 89–114.
  (1994) 'Pathos und Wahrheit. Zur Rivalität zwischen Tragödie und Philosophie', in J. Huber and A. M. Müller (eds.) *'Kultur' und 'Gemeinsinn'* (= Interventionen 3), Basle, 127–48.
  (2002a) 'Der Fuß des Dionysos. Zu PMG 871', in H. F. J. Horstmanshoff, H. W. Singor, F. T. van Straten, and J. H. M. Strubbe (eds.) *Kykeon. Studies in honour of H. S. Versnel*, Leiden, 161–91.
  (2002b) 'Heimliche Liebe im Zeichen der Mysterien. Verschleierung und Enthüllung in Euripides' *Hippolytos*', in E. Klinger, S. Böhm and T. Franz

(eds.) *Paare in antiken religiösen Texten und Bildern. Symbole für Geschlechterrollen damals und heute*, Würzburg, 51–91.

(2007) 'Der göttliche Sohn einer menschlichen Mutter. Aspekte des Dionysos in der antiken griechischen Tragödie', in A. Bierl, R. Lämmle and K. Wesselmann eds. (2007) vol. 1, 303–34.

(2009) 'Pathos dans le théâtre grec', in P. Borgeaud and A.-C. Rendu Loisel (eds.) *Violentes émotions. Approches comparatistes*, Geneva, 83–100.

(2010) 'Tragic memories of Dionysus', in L. Foxhall, H.-J. Gehrke, and N. Luraghi (eds.) *Intentional history. Spinning time in ancient Greece*, Stuttgart, 211–24.

Scott, M. (2013) *Space and society in the Greek and Roman worlds*, Cambridge.

Scullion, S. (1998) 'Dionysos and katharsis in *Antigone*', *ClAnt* 17, 96–122.

(1999/2000) 'Tradition and invention in Euripidean aitiology', *ICS* 24–25, 217–33.

(2002) '"Nothing to do with Dionysus". Tragedy misconceived as ritual', *CQ* 52, 102–37.

Scully, S. (1990) *Homer and the sacred city*, Ithaca.

Seaford, R. (1984) 'The last bath of Agamemnon', *CQ* 34, 247–54.

(1987) 'The tragic wedding', *JHS* 107, 106–30.

(1994) *Reciprocity and ritual. Homer and tragedy in the developing city-state*, Oxford.

(1995) 'Historicizing tragic ambivalence. The vote of Athena', in B. Goff ed. (1995a), 202–21.

(2009) 'Aitiologies of cult in Euripides. A response to Scott Scullion', in J. R. C. Cousland and J. Hume (eds.) *The play of texts and fragments. Essays in honour of Martin Cropp*, Leiden, 221–34.

Seale, D. (1982) *Vision and stagecraft in Sophocles*, London.

Segal, C. P. (1970) 'Shame and purity in Euripides' *Hippolytus*', *Hermes* 98, 278–99.

(1981) *Tragedy and civilization. An interpretation of Sophocles*, Cambridge, MA.

(1983) 'Greek myth as a semiotic and structural system and the problem of Greek tragedy', *Arethusa* 16, 173–98 (= Segal (1986), 48–109).

(1988) 'Confusion and concealment in Euripides' *Hippolytus*. Vision, hope, and tragic knowledge', in *Métis* 3, 263–82 (= Segal (1993), 136–53).

(1992) 'Signs, magic and letters in Euripides' *Hippolytus*', in R. Hexter, D. Selden (eds.) *Innovations of antiquity*, New York, 420–56.

(1993) *Euripides and the poetics of sorrow. Art, gender, and commemoration in* Alcestis, Hippolytus, *and* Hecuba, Durham, NC.

(1995) *Sophocles' tragic world. Divnity, nature, society*, Cambridge, MA.

(1996) 'Catharsis, audience, and closure in Greek tragedy', in M. S. Silk ed. (1996), 149–72.

(1999) 'Euripides' *Ion*. Generational passage and civic myth', in M. W. Padilla ed. (1999), 67–108.

(2001) Oedipus tyrannus. *Tragic heroism and the limits of knowledge*, 2nd edn, Oxford.

Seidensticker, B. (1982) *Palintonos harmonia. Studien zu komischen Elementen in der griechischen Tragödie*, Göttingen.
Seidensticker, B., and Vöhler, M. eds. (2007) *Katharsiskonzeptionen vor Aristoteles. Zum kulturellen Hintergrund des Tragödiensatzes*, Berlin.
Sémelin, J. (2005) *Purifier et détruire. Usages politiques des massacres et génocides*, Paris.
Sennett, R. (1994) *Flesh and stone. The body and the city in Western civilization*, New York.
Sewell-Rutter, N. J. (2007) *Guilt by descent. Moral inheritance and decision-making in Greek tragedy*, Oxford.
Shear, J. L. (2007) 'Cultural change, space, and the politics of commemoration in Athens', in R. Osborne (ed.) *Debating the Athenian cultural revolution. Art, literature, philosophy, and politics, 430–380 BC*, Cambridge, 91–115.
Sicherl, M. (1986) 'Die Tragik der Danaiden', *MH* 43, 81–110.
Sickinger, J. P. (1999) *Public records and archives in classical Athens*, Chapel Hill.
Sidwell, K. (1996) 'Purification and pollution in Aeschylus' *Eumenides*', *CQ* 46, 44–57.
Silk, M. S., and Stern, J. P. (1981) *Nietzsche on tragedy*, Cambridge.
 ed. (1996) *Tragedy and the tragic. Greek theatre and beyond*, Oxford.
Smertenko, C. M. (1932) 'Political sympathies of Aeschylus', *JHS* 52, 233–5.
Soja, E. W. (1996) *Thirdspace. Journeys to Los Angeles and other real-and-imagined places*, Cambridge, MA.
Soler, J. (1973) 'Sémiotique de la nourriture dans la Bible', *Annales* 28, 943–55.
Sommerstein, A. H. (1989) *Aeschylus. Eumenides*, Cambridge.
 (1996) *Aeschylean tragedy*, Bari.
 (1997) 'The theatre audience, the Demos, and the *Suppliants* of Aeschylus', in C. B. R. Pelling (ed.) *Greek tragedy and the historian*, Oxford, 63–79.
 (2010a) 'Orestes' trial and Athenian homicide procedure', in E. M. Harris, D. F. Leão and P. J. Rhodes, eds. (2010), 25–38.
 (2010b) '"They all knew how it was going to end": tragedy, myth, and the spectator', in A. H. Sommerstein, *The tangled ways of Zeus and other studies in and around Greek tragedy*, Oxford, 209–223.
 (2011) 'Once more the end of Sophocles' *Oedipus tyrannus*', *JHS* 131, 85–93.
Sommerstein, A. H., Halliwell, S., Henderson, J., and Zimmermann, B. (eds.)
 (1993) *Tragedy, comedy, and the polis*, Bari.
Sourvinou-Inwood, C. (1988) *Studies in girls' transitions. Aspects of the arkteia and age representations in Attic iconography*, Athens.
 (1989) 'Assumptions and the creation of meaning. Reading Sophocles' *Antigone*', *JHS* 109, 134–48.
 (1990) 'What is polis religion', in O. Murray and S. Price (eds.) *The Greek city. From Homer to Alexander*, Oxford, 295–322.
 (1994) 'Something to do with Athens. Tragedy and ritual', in R. Osborne and S. Hornblower (eds.) *Ritual, finance, politics. Athenian democratic accounts presented to David Lewis*, Oxford, 269–90.
 (2003) *Tragedy and Athenian religion*, Lanham.

(2005) 'Tragedy and anthropology', in J. Gregory (ed.) *A companion to Greek tragedy*, Malden, 293–304.
Staden, H. von (1992a) 'The discovery of the body. Human dissection and its cultural contexts in ancient Greece', *The Yale Journal of Biology and Medicine* 65, 223–41.
(1992) 'Women and dirt', in *Helios* 19, 7–30.
(2007) 'Purity, purification, and katharsis in Hippocratic medicine', in B. Seidensticker and M. Vöhler eds. (2007), 21–51.
Stähli, A. (2001) 'Der Körper, das Begehren, die Bilder. Visuelle Strategien der Konstruktion einer homosexuellen Männlichkeit', in R. von den Hoff and S. Schmidt (eds.) *Konstruktionen von Wirklichkeit. Bilder im Griechenland des 5. und 4. Jahrhunderts v. Chr.*, Stuttgart, 197–209.
Steiner, G. (1984) *Antigones*, Oxford.
(1996) 'Tragedy, pure and simple', in M. S. Silk ed. (1996), 534–46.
Stieber, M. (2011) *Euripides and the language of craft*, Leiden.
Swift, L. (2006) 'Mixed choruses and marriage songs. A new interpretation of the third stasimon of the *Hippolytos*', *JHS* 126, 125–40.
(2008) *Euripides. Ion*, London.
Taplin, O. (1977) *The stagecraft of Aeschylus. The dramatic use of exits and entrances in Greek tragedy*, Oxford.
(2007) *Pots and plays. Interactions between tragedy and Greek vase-painting of the fourth century B.C.*, Los Angeles.
Thiel, R. (1993) *Chor und tragische Handlung im 'Agamemnon' des Aischylos*, Stuttgart.
Thomas, R. (2005) 'Writing, law, and written law', in M. Gagarin and D. Cohen (eds.) *The Cambridge companion to ancient Greek law*, Cambridge, 41–60.
Thomson, G. (1935) 'Mystical allusions in the *Oresteia*', *JHS* 55, 20–34.
Thorburn, J. E. (2000) 'Euripides' *Ion*. The gold and the darkness', *CB* 76, 39–49.
(2001) 'Apollo's comedy and the ending of Euripides' *Ion*', *AClass* 44, 221–36.
Torrance, I. (2013) *Metapoetry in Euripides*, Oxford.
Travis, R. (1999) *Allegory and the tragic chorus in Sophocles'* Oedipus at Colonus, Lanham, MD.
Tzanetou, A. (1999/2000) 'Almost dying, dying twice. Ritual and audience in Euripides' *Iphigenia in Tauris*', *ICS* 24/25, 199–216.
(2011) 'Supplication and empire in Athenian tragedy', in D. M. Carter ed. (2011), 305–24.
(2012) *City of Suppliants. Tragedy and the Athenian empire*, Austin.
Utzinger, C. (2003) *Periphrades aner. Untersuchungen zum ersten Stasimon der Sophokleischen 'Antigone' und zu den antiken Kulturentstehungstheorien*, Göttingen.
Valeri, V. (2000) *The forest of taboos. Morality, hunting, and identity among the Huaulu of the Moluccas*, Madison, WI.
Vellacott, P. (1971) *Sophocles and Oedipus. A study of Sophocles'* Oedipus tyrannus *with a new translation*, Ann Arbor.

(1984) *The logic of tragedy. Morals and integrity in Aeschylus' Oresteia*, Durham, NC.
Vernant, J. P. (1974) *Mythe et société en Grèce ancienne*, Paris.
  (1988) 'Ambiguity and reversal. On the enigmatic structure of the Oedipus Rex', in H. Bloom (ed.) *Sophocles' Oedipus Rex*, New York, 103–26 (the English version of the essay also appeared in J. P. Vernant and P. Vidal-Naquet, *Tragedy and myth in ancient Greece*, trans. Janet Lloyd, Brighton 1981, 87–119).
Vernant, J. P., and Vidal-Naquet, P. (1972) *Mythe et tragédie en Grèce ancienne*, Paris.
  (1986) *Mythe et tragédie en Grèce ancienne, Vol. II*, Paris.
Verrall, A. W. (1895) *Euripides, the rationalist. A study in the history of art and religion*, Cambridge.
Vidal-Naquet, P. (1972) 'Chasse et sacrifice dans l' "Orestie" d'Eschyle', in J.-P. Vernant and P. Vidal-Naquet (1972), 133–58.
  (1986a) *The black hunter. Forms of thought and forms of society in the Greek world*, Baltimore.
  (1986b) 'Oedipe entre deux cités. Essai sur l'*Oedipe à Colone*', in J. P. Vernant and P. Vidal-Naquet (1986), 175–211.
Vlassopoulos, K. (2007) 'Free spaces. Identity, experience and democracy in classical Athens', *CQ* 57, 33–52.
Vogt, S. (1998) 'Delphi in der attischen Tragödie', *A&A* 44, 30–48.
Wallace, N. O. (1979) '*Oedipus at Colonus*. The hero in his collective context', *QUCC* 32, 39–52.
Walsh, G. B. (1978) 'The rhetoric of birthright and race in Euripides' *Ion*', *Hermes* 106, 301–15.
West, M. L. (1987) *Euripides. Orestes*, Warminster.
Whitman, C. H. (1974) *Euripides and the full circle of myth*, Cambridge, MA.
Wilamowitz-Moellendorff, U. von (1913[7]) *Griechische Tragödien II*, Berlin.
Willink, C. W. (1986) *Euripides. Orestes*, Oxford.
Winkler, J. J., and Zeitlin, F. I. eds. (1990) *Nothing to do with Dionysos? Athenian drama in its social context*, Princeton.
Winnington-Ingram, R. P. (1948) *Euripides and Dionysus. An interpretation of the Bacchae*, Cambridge.
  (1960) '*Hippolytus*. A study in causation', in J. C. Kamerbeek et al. (eds.) *Euripide. Sept exposés et discussions*, Geneva, 171–91.
  (1980) *Sophocles. An interpretation*, Cambridge.
  (1983) *Studies in Aeschylus*, Cambridge.
  (1985) 'Aeschylus', in P. E. Easterling and B. M. W. Knox (eds.) *The Cambridge history of classical literature I. Greek literature*, Cambridge, 281–95.
Wolff, C. (1965) 'The design and myth in Euripides' *Ion*', *HSPh* 69, 169–94.
  (1992) '*Iphigenia among the Taurians*. Aetiology, ritual, and myth', *ClAnt* 11, 308–34.
Worman, N. (2000) 'Infection in the sentence. The discourse of disease in Sophocles' *Philoctetes*', *Arethusa* 33, 1–36.

(2012) 'Cutting to the bone. Recalcitrant bodies in Sophocles', in K. Ormand ed. (2012), 351–66.
Wright, M. E. (2005) *Euripides' escape-tragedies. A study of* Helen, Andromeda, *and* Iphigenia among the Taurians, Oxford.
Yatromanolakis, D., and Roilos, P. eds. (2004a) *Greek ritual poetics*, Washington.
  (2004b) 'Provisionally structured ideas on a heuristically defined concept. Towards a ritual poetics', in D. Yatromanolakis and P. Roilos eds. (2004b), 3–34.
Zacharia, K. (2003) *Converging Truths. Euripides'* Ion *and the Athenian quest for self-definition*, Leiden.
Zeitlin, F. I. (1965) 'The motif of the corrupted sacrifice in Aeschylus' *Oresteia*', *TAPhA* 96, 463–508.
  (1966) 'Postscript to sacrificial imagery in the *Oresteia*', *TAPhA* 97, 645–53.
  (1982) 'Cultic models of the female. Rites of Dionysus and Demeter', *Arethusa* 15, 129–57.
  (1989) 'Mysteries of identity and designs of the self in Euripides' *Ion*', *PCPhS* 35, 144–97.
  (1990) 'Thebes. Theater of self and society in Athenian drama', in J. J. Winkler and F. I. Zeitlin eds. (1990), 130–67 (an earlier version of this essay appeared in J. P. Euben (ed.) *Greek tragedy and political theory*, Berkeley, 101–41).
  (1996a) 'The dynamics of misogyny. Myth and mythmaking in Aeschylus' *Oresteia*', in Zeitlin (1996b), 87–119. (The original version appeared in *Arethusa* 11 (1978), 149–84.)
  (1996b) *Playing the other. Gender and society in classical Greek literature*, Chicago.
  (1996c) 'The politics of Eros in the Danaid trilogy of Aeschylus', in Zeitlin (1996b) 123–71. (first published in R. Hexter and D. Selden eds. (1992) *Innovations of antiquity*, New York, 203–52.)
  (1996d) 'The power of Aphrodite. Eros and the boundaries of the self in Euripides' *Hippolytos*', in Zeitlin (1996b), 219–84. (The original version appeared in P. Burian ed. [1985] *Directions in Euripidean criticism. A collection of essays*, Durham, NC, 52–111, 189–208.)
  (2005) 'Redeeming matricide? Euripides rereads the *Oresteia*', in V. Pedrick and S. M. Oberhelman (eds.) *The soul of tragedy. Essays on Athenian drama*, Chicago.
  (2011) 'Sacrifices holy and unholy in Euripides' *Iphigenia in Tauris*', in F. Prescendi and Y. Volokhine (eds.) *Dans le laboratoire de l'historien des religions. Mélanges offerts à Philippe Borgeaud*, Geneva, 449–66.
Zuntz, G. (1933) 'Die taurische Iphigenie des Euripides', *Die Antike* 9, 245–54.

Index locorum

Aeschines
  1.19, 175
  1.21, 182
  1.23, 182
  2.158, 181
  3.176, 182
Aeschylus
  Agamemnon
    1, 135
    41, 117, 120
    177–8, 128
    209–10, 121, 126
    219–20, 117
    250–1, 117
    388–9, 126–7
    474, 137
    776–8, 127
    911, 120
    1036–8, 142, 176–7
    1389–90, 106
    1396, 117–18, 120
    1406, 117–18
    1419–20, 121
    1428, 126–7
    1430, 120
    1431–3, 134
    1562–4, 119, 128
    1645, 62, 121
  Choephori
    48, 135
    66–7, 131
    71–4, 133
    120, 121
    144, 118, 121
    160–1, 135
    310–14, 120, 129
    398, 132
    400–2, 126
    461, 132
    462, 118
    646, 129

    646–52, 122–3
    649–50, 126
    804–5, 135
    944, 121, 123
    965–8, 133, 134
    987–9, 118, 125
    988–9, 138
    1017, 62, 121–2, 134–5
    1027, 118, 138
    1027–8, 124–5
    1028, 122
    1051–2, 143
    1056, 143
    1059, 152
    1059–60, 145
    1061, 143
  Eumenides
    83, 135
    280–9, 136–7
    312–20, 124
    326–7, 134, 151
    468, 118
    472, 131–2
    474, 137, 152
    484, 130
    488, 131–2
    516–19, 129
    539, 129
    564–5, 129
    573, 131–2
    600, 122
    612–13, 118
    685, 130–1
    709, 131–2
    1056, 143
  Seven against Thebes
    681–2, 86
    734–41, 70–1
  Suppliants
    17–18, 194

37–9, 196
45, 188
146, 188–9
190, 190
223–8, 194–6
250–9, 189–90
260–70, 191–3
264, 199
267, 199
268, 199
287, 199
313, 188, 194, 196–7
338, 198
345, 191
356, 200–1
366, 199, 202
367, 199
372, 191
423–4, 196
609, 199, 201
618, 201
728, 194, 196–7
756, 194
905, 197
993, 199
1013, 194

Andocides
1.83–4, 79

Antiphon
5.82, 19–20

Aristophanes
Acharnians
44, 182
Clouds
308–13, 175–6
Lysistrata
1129–30, 177

Aristotle
[Ps.] *Constitution of the Athenians* 13.5, 184
Poetics
1449b24–1450a37, 7
1449b24–8, 3–4
1455b24–1456a2, 7
Politics 1275b25, 237

Demosthenes
20.158, 115, 177
23.72, 69
24.60, 177
25.21, 76
43.57, 91–2
43.57–8, 177
54.39, 182
57.3, 175
57.55, 184–5

Dinarchus
1.110, 110

Euripides
Electra
652–6, 142
792, 142
793–4, 142
1124–33, 142
Hecuba
16–17, 74
28–9, 74
Heracles
225–6, 173
1219–21, 209–10
1232–4, 209–10
Hippolytus
5–6, 46
21, 46
23, 46
29–32, 37–8
34–7, 37–8
100, 35
102, 33
121–69, 24
135–8, 33–4
148–50, 46
175, 40–1
181–5, 40–1
208–9, 40–1
214, 25
232, 35
241, 40–1
275, 40–1
296, 39–40, 42
316, 32–3
316–17, 26–7
317, 34–9, 43–4
337–43, 25–6
342, 35
401, 40–1, 42
447–8, 46
490–1, 42
616–50, 39
653–5, 34–5
767–71, 30–2
820, 26
831–3, 26
877, 36
935, 35
945, 36
946, 36
973, 36
1002–3, 36
1006, 36

270   *Index locorum*

Euripides (*cont.*)
   1297–8, 46
   1339–41, 46
   1379–83, 26, 27
   1422, 46
   1448, 36
Ion
   8–10, 215–16, 243
   10–11, 230–1
   20–1, 216, 243
   29–30, 216–17
   45, 222
   47–9, 223
   56, 233
   63, 216
   94–7, 222, 224
   102–3, 223, 232
   104–5, 222, 231
   106–8, 225
   109, 232
   109–11, 224
   136–40, 224–5
   150, 224
   184–218, 242–3
   228, 231
   230–2, 231
   290, 217, 237
   293, 217
   301, 243
   309–11, 224–5
   315, 222, 223
   321, 224–5
   323, 223
   338, 231
   414, 227–8, 234
   433–6, 226–7
   468–71, 238–9
   470–1, 222–3
   505, 233
   522, 226
   585–6, 240
   589–92, 217
   598–9, 234
   632, 234–5
   671–5, 219–20
   692–3, 219–20, 237
   719–20, 218
   1056–60, 218–19
   1058–9, 237
   1069–73, 218
   1070, 237
   1118, 229
   1132–65, 241–2
   1159–61, 236
   1333, 173, 228–9, 237–9
   1334, 228–9
   1416–35, 242
   1459, 233
   1471, 236
Iphigenia among the Taurians
   77–8, 155
   92, 154
   285–94, 148–9
   380–4, 158
   383, 170
   517, 165
   517–75, 164
   594, 166
   624, 150
   670–1, 165
   693–4, 150, 157
   704–5, 149–51
   760–1, 167
   933, 165
   943, 155
   979–80, 169
   994–5, 169
   1029–47, 168
   1031, 158, 168, 169–70
   1035–7, 158–9
   1047, 159
   1163, 159
   1178, 159
   1216, 150
   1223–4, 159
   1316, 159
   1337–8, 159–60
   1441, 154
   1459, 151
   1469–71, 155–6
Medea
   1268–70, 20
Orestes
   46–8, 178
   75–6, 144, 178
   259, 143
   314–15, 143
   396, 143
   400, 143
   517, 143–4
   597–8, 144
   1604, 144
Phoenissae
   815–16, 172
Trojan Women
   45–6, 74

Heraclitus
   fr. 44 Kahn, 123
   fr. 65 Kahn, 77, 91

Index locorum

Herodotus
  1.35, 137
  1.146–7, 183–4
  6.75–84, 22
  7.188–9, 18
Hippocrates
  On the diseases of women 1.2, 42
  On the diseases of young girls, 42
  On the sacred disease 1, 21–2
Homer
  Iliad
    18.504, 74–5
    21.447, 74
  Odyssey
    6.267, 74–5
    6.9–10, 178–9
    9.19–20, 56
Hyperides
  5 fr. 6, 110

IG
  II² 380, 244
  XI.2 203A.38, 244

Lex sacra Selinous (ed. Jameson, Jordan, Kotansky)
  B 10–11, 137–8, 177
Longinus
  On the sublime 33.5, 58
LSCG 56, 9
LSCG 97, 9
  A 25–9, 83
LSS 115, see *SEG* IX 72, 9, 138
Lycurgus
  1.77, 82

Philostratus
  Life of Apollonius 6.11, 140
Plato
  Menexenus 239a, 214
  Phaedo 58a–c, 29–30
Plutarch
  Lycurgus 27.1, 83–4

Scholia
  Aeschines 1.23, 181–2
  Aristophanes Acharnians 10, 140
SEG
  IX 72, 9, 138
    A §4, 9, 83
    B §20, 69, 137
  XIX 427, 18–19
Semonides
  7.46–9, 33

Solon
  fr. 36 West 18–20, 77, 91
  fr. 37 West 9–10, 77
Sophocles
  Antigone
    7–8, 88
    53, 88
    142, 88
    144–5, 88
    162–3, 90–1
    162–73, 98–100
    167, 91, 111
    172, 86, 106
    189–90, 91, 111
    191, 89
    205, 92
    206, 105, 112
    285–7, 89
    403, 91
    449, 88
    452, 89
    454–5, 93
    481, 88, 95–6
    484–5, 90
    604–5, 93
    608, 93
    661–80, 89–91
    663, 88–9
    675–6, 111–12
    712–13, 93
    746, 86, 100–1
    773–6, 86, 101–3
    792, 101
    794, 94, 101
    800–1, 94
    1016–18, 95–6, 107, 112–13
    1017, 112–13
    1039–44, 103–4
    1083, 113
    1101, 95–6
    1142, 86
    1197, 95
    1198, 112–13
    1238–40, 106
    1240, 106
    1284, 86, 107–8
    1291–2, 107–8
    1301, 107
    1315, 107
    1344–5, 108
  Oedipus at Colonus
    3, 207
    12, 207
    119, 207

Sophocles (*cont.*)
    123–5, 207
    155–6, 207
    208, 207
    226, 208
    233–6, 207–8
    470, 210
    548, 209
    637, 208
    833, 208
    1095–6, 208
    1132–4, 209–10
    1483, 210
  Oedipus Tyrannus
    4–5, 50, 54–5
    7–8, 47, 56, 57–8
    22, 53
    23–4, 52–3
    31–46, 50–1
    46, 53
    60, 53
    66–72, 51–2
    68, 53
    87, 53
    96–8, 52, 53, 60, 62–5, 66
    99–101, 54
    100, 70
    101, 53
    238–42, 177–8
    241–3, 59, 60–1, 62–4, 66
    307, 49
    312–13, 59, 60, 61–4, 66
    350–3, 59, 60, 62–4, 66
    367, 58
    397–8, 56
    413–15, 58
    912–13, 54–5
    921, 54–5
    1012, 60, 62–4, 66
    1036, 57
    1068, 57
    1193–5, 73
    1227–8, 69
    1276–81, 70–1
    1293, 49
    1360–84, 67–8
    1384–5, 68
    1388, 71
    1426–7, 67
    1451, 69–70
  Trachiniae
    1012, 172–3
    1060–1, 172–3
Stesichorus
  PMG 192, 162

Theophrastus
  Characters 16.9, 9, 82–3
Thucydides
  1.101, 20
  1.128, 20
  2.40.2, 235
  2.47, 21
  2.47–54, 22–3
TrGF, vol. 3, fr. 44, 204

Xenophon
  Hellenica
    1.7.22, 92
    2.4.20, 176

General index

abject, abjection, 97, 104
Aegyptus (sons of), transgressive, 194, 196–7
Aeschines, pure spaces in, 182
Aeschylus
   Erinyes in, 123–4, 129, 136, 138
   'father of tragedy', 140
   reperformance of, 140
Agamemnon
   and *dikē*, 117
   polluted, 121
agora, and purity, 180–1
agos, 20, 67, 102
anthropology (structural), 1, 6, 75, 87
   see Douglas, Mary
Aphrodite, 23, 44–5
   as literary construct, 46
Apis, purifying Argos, 191–3
Apollo
   authority of, 154–5
   oracle of, *see* oracle: Delphi, announcing pollution; oracle: Delphi, as place of knowledge
   purity of, 222–3, 229, 230–1
   responsible for matricide, 144
   temple of, *see* Delphi: temple of Apollo
   'transgressive', 230–1
appearance vs. reality, 35–6, 44, 127, 142
apragmosynē, of Ion, 234–5
archons, wearing crowns, 175
Arctinus of Miletus, 2
Areopagus, 118, 119, 130–1, 132–3, 137
Argos
   as defined space, 189–90
   purity of, 191–3, 203–4
Ariadne, 26
Aristophanes
   Athens and festivals in, 175–6
   socio-political community in, 177
Aristotle
   [Ps.], ethnic purity in, 184

catharsis, 3–4, 238
   on tragedy, 7
Artemis, 44–5
   and human sacrifice, 151, 158
   as literary construct, 46
Athena
   and *dikē*, 131–2
   and Orestes' purity, 137
   and stability, 130
   authority of, 154–6
   intervening in Orestes' favour, 132, 155–6, 170
Athens
   assimilation of ritual and legal status, 114–15
   and Athenian identity, 215–21, 240–1
   body politic, 110–11
   law and legal discourse, 79, 81–2
   and otherness, 236–7
   pure, 30, 219–20, 241
   pure spaces in, 180–2
      language used to refer to, 182
   purity of, problematic, 235–7
audience involvement, 57–8, 241
autochthony, 184, 216–17

blood, and pollution, 65, 125–7
body
   in Athens, 110–11
   and body politic, 109–10
   in S. *Ant.*, 111–13
   vs. mind, 44
body (female)
   as bounded space, 188–9
   in Hippocratic medicine, 41
   impure, 34
   as 'map of conflict', 40
   see also Danaids: purity of; Danaids: and transgression
boundaries
   and the body (politic), 109–10, 112–13
   and civic space, 88–90, 91, 93–4

273

boundaries (*Cont.*)
  (not) infringed, 85–6, 88–9, 196–7, 218–19, 226–7, 230–1
  demarcating space, 188–90
  and purity/pollution, 192–3, 195, 226–7
  relation to, of Ion, 226–7, 233–5
burial, Athens vs. S. *Ant.*, 91–2
Burkert, Walter, 55, 173

Cambridge ritualists, 5
categorisation, *see* anthropology (structural); Oedipus: beyond ritual categories; pollution: and categorisation
cathartic offerings, 54–5
causation
  and character, 32–9
  as fiction, 46
  and inherited evil, 25–8
  and medicine/the female body, 39–44
  polyphony of causation models, 45–6
  as provocation, 44–6
  rationalising accounts of, 21–3
  and ritual transgression, 28–32
Cecrops, otherness of, 236
chastity, *see hagnos*
circumambulation, 181–2, 244
citizenship
  and purity, 184–5
  in Eur. *Ion*, 219–20
  Periclean citizenship law, 184–5, 219, 237
Clytemnestra
  covered in blood, 126, 127
  and *dikē*, 117–18, 120
  Euripidean, resembling Aeschylean Agamemnon, 141
  polluted, as pollution, 62, 121, 122, 123
conscience, 143, 144
contagion, 34–5, 82–4
coping, with misfortune, 48, 54–5, 69, 71–2, 73
corpses, 'choreography' of, in S. *Ant.*, 105–8
Creon
  and boundaries, 88–90, 91, 96–7
  on gender differentiation, 90, 100, 101
  and law, 88–9
  naming pollution, significance of, 97
  and 'steadfast minds', 99–100, 101
  and 'straightness', 90–1, 98, 111–12
  and transgression, 88–9, 93, 96–7, 105
Creusa
  'in-born', 217
  rape of, 230–1
crisis
  as 'difficult situation', 9
  'embedded', and pollution, 9–10, 13
  'embedded', defined, 8

Danaids
  as *astoxenoi*, 200–1
  integration of, into Argos, 198–201
  purity of, 194–6, 197, 204
  shunning marriage, 193–4
  and transgression, 196–7
  see also virginity
defloration, 31
Delphi
  as place of knowledge, 52
  as setting in Eur. *Ion*, 240
  temple of Apollo, 221–2, 230, 240–1, 242–3
deme, purified, 92, 177, 244
Demosthenes
  burial in, 92
  ethnic purity in, 184–5
  exclusion of (polluted) murderer in, 177
  exile of homicide in, 69
  overlap of legal and ritual status in, 114–15
  religious identity in, 175
desire, and pollution, 37
deus ex machina, 154, 155
dikē, 129
  and evaluation, 117–21
  important in the *Oresteia*, 115–16
  and pollution, 122–5, 134–5
  between revenge justice and wider justice, 119–21, 124–5
  and stability, 129, 131–3
Dionysia, 1, 244
Dionysus, 86
disease, symptoms of, 40–1, 42, 53
Dodds, E. R., 122
Douglas, Mary, 6, 10–13, 75, 87, 245
  critique of, 11–13
Draco, 115

edict of excommunication, 59, 60–1, 177–8
ekdēmos, 37–8, 172
Electra
  and *dikē*, 118, 121
  feigning pollution, 142
  recognising Orestes, 141
ephebic oath, 82
Erinyes
  in Aeschylus, 123–4, 129, 136, 138
  in Euripides, 143, 148–9, 155
  outside of tragedy, 123
Eros, 94, 101
Eteocles, *see* fratricide, and category-confusion
ethnicity, 182–5, 200–1, *see also* autochthony; purity: ethnic; self and other
etymology
  Areopagus, 130
  see also wordplay

General index

Euripides
  Erinyes in, 143, 148–9, 155
  gods in, 44–5, 46, 154–6
  irony in, *see* irony: in Euripides
  myth in, 162–4, 213
  self-reference in, *see* self-reference
Eurydice, death of, 107–8
exclusion
  of outsiders from Athens, 217–19, 236–7
  of (polluted) murderer, 177–8
exile, 36, 37–8
  as (part of) purification, 69–70

festivals, 175–6
fratricide and category-confusion, 98–9

gender, differentiation, 90, 100, 101
Girard, René, 4–5, 12
gods
  in Euripides, 44–5, 154–6
  as literary constructs (in Eur.), 46
  in Sophocles, 93–4
  not reached by pollution, 103–4
Goldhill, Simon, 119, 125

hagnizō, 149, 150
hagnos
  anhagnos, 67, 117
  as chastity and/or virginity, 33, 194–6, 197
  between chastity/virginity and wider ritual purity, 33–5
  redefinition, from virginity to another *hagneia*, 204
  as (wider ritual) purity, 27, 136, 144
  see also virginity
Heracles, as 'purifier', 172–3
Herodotus
  and causation, 18, 22
  on ethnic purity, 183–4
Hippocratic medicine
  as diagnostic system, 53
  in Eur. *Hipp.*, 39–40, 41–3
  female physiology in, 41
  medical language/imagery in S. *OT*, 52–3
  vs. religious models of causation, 21–2
Hippolytus
  'excessive/uncivic', 38–9
  hagnos, 33, 34–5
  on inherited evil, 26, 27
  path towards doom, 35–6
historiography, causation in, 22–3
Homer
  silence on murder and death pollution, 2
  and spatial demarcation, 178–9
  stability of civic institutions in, 74–5

identity
  in A. *Supp*
    Argos, 190, 191–3, 203–4
    Danaids, 193–6, 198–201, 204
    civic, and ethnic purity, 182–5, *see also* identity: in Eur. *Ion*: Athens
    civic and religious, 176
    civic, and ritual purity, 180–2, *see also* identity: in A. *Supp*.: Argos
  in Eur. *Ion*
    Apollo, 230–1
    Athens, 214, 215–21, 240–1
    clarified identity, 238–9
    Ion, 223–8, 231–5
  in S. *OC*, 206
incest, 56, 63, 66, 88, 172, 206, 207
inherited evil
  in Eur. *Hipp.*, 25–8
  and pollution, 26–7
initiation (rites of), and space, 179–80
integration
  of Danaids into Argos, 198–201
  through purification, 71, 177
interpretation, *see* causation; understanding: of misfortune
Ion
  'apolitical', 234–5
  as male virgin, 233–4
  'non-identity', 232
  purity of, 223–8, 231–4, 236
  ethnic, 228–9
Iphigenia
  as actress, 168–9
  letter of, and its significance, 166–7
  mock-purification, 159–61, 168–70
  as playwright, 168–9, 170
  on pollution, 158–9
  ritual role in Eur. *IT*, 150
  sacrifice of, 117, 121
irony
  in Euripides, 35–7, 42, 44, 45, 152, 236–7
  in Sophocles, 57–62, 63–4, 66
Ismene, juxtaposing 'oneness' and 'twoness', 99

katharmos, 32, 54, 145
katharos, 159, 184–5, 209, 238–9
kēlis, 26, 67, 68, 209–10

law
  discourse about, 80–2
  monumentalised, significance of, 80
  physical appearance of, 78–9
  in S. *Ant.*, 85, 88–9
  and stability, 76–82

law (*Cont.*)
  written, first appearance of in archaeological record, 2, 78
  written, significance of, 79–80
legal and ritual status, overlap, 114–15, 122
liminal, liminality, 211–12
  see also margins, marginal, marginality
literature and religion, 5
lustral basins
  and civic space, 2, 181, 182
  in Eur. *Ion*, 226–8

madness
  of Cleomenes, 22
  of Orestes 143, 160
margins, marginal, marginality, 17, 97, 98, 104, 105, 106, 107, 174, 179–80, 187, 199, 200, 221, 223, 233
  see also liminal, liminality
matricide
  resulting in pollution, 121
  uncivic, 172
  (un)just, 118, 124–5, 132
metamythology, 163–4
  see self-reference
miaros, 101
miasma terminology
  absent and/or replaced by imprecise terminology, 105–8
  in S. *Ant.*, 96, 98–104
  in S. *OC*, imprecision of, 209–11
  in S. *OT*, 58–64, 66
    absent and/or replaced by imprecise terminology, 66–8
myth
  in Eur. *IT*, *see* metamythology
  innovations of, 54, 162, 213
  of foundation, 191–2

New Criticism, 5
Nietzsche, Friedrich, 5, 140

Oedipus
  asserting identity, 56
  beyond coping, 71–2
  beyond ritual categories, 209–11
  inside and outside, 208
  'Know-Foot', 56
  (not) known to the audience, 57–8
  (not) comprehended through concept of *miasma*, 63–5, 66–8
  'other', 207
  self-blinding, 70–1
  'Swollen-Foot', 57

oracle
  Delphi, announcing pollution, 52, 62–3
  Delphi, as place of knowledge, 51–2
  Dodona, and pollution, 18–19
  and pollution, 28
Orestes
  in Aeschylus
    and *dikē*, 118, 124–5
    polluted, 121, 134
    purified, 136
    purity in Athens, 136–7, 138
  in Euripides
    purified, 142
    ritual status of, 143–4, 156, 157, 158–9
    sick, mad, 143, 160
  see also release (of Orestes)
orthos, 53, 90–1, 98, 111–12
Osborne, Robin, 6, 12

Padel, Ruth, 34, 43
pagos, *pēgnumi*, 131
Parker, Robert, 3, 4, 5–6, 115, 245
parricide, 56, 63, 66, 88, 206, 207, 209
Parthenon, 240–1
Pasiphae, 26
Pelasgus, *see* Argos
performance, of identity, 225
peristiarchoi, 1, 244
Phaedra
  chastity of, 31
  disease, 40–1
  'excessive/uncivic', 37–8
  hagnos, 33–4
  miasma of the mind, 26–7, 34–5, 43–4
  passion as family curse/inherited evil, 25–6
  suicide, 30, 32
phrēn, 43
  see also pollution: of the mind
plague
  of Athens, 21
  of Thebes, 47, 52–3, 72–3
Plato, Delian embassy in, 29–30
Pnyx, and purity, 181–2
polis
  development of, and space, 178–9
  important in S. *Ant.*, 84–5
  rise of, and pollution, 2–3
  symbolic topography of, 179–82
pollution
  attaching meaning, 114, 121–2
  and categorisation, 10–12, 75, 87, 98–101, 104
  and desire, 37
  and *dikē*, 122–5, 134–5
  and 'embedded crises', 9–10, 13

'external', 65, 116, 125–7, 142
and the female body, 34
and guilt, 125
and inherited evil, 26–7
(in)visibility of, 64–5
limited, defined, 83–4, 101–2, 103–4
marking 'difficult situations', 9
miasma (not) providing understanding of Oedipus, 63–5, 66–8
of the mind, 26–7, 34–5, 43–4, 144
multifaceted, 245
named, 97
nameless, 96, 105–8
and otherness, 192–3, 199–200, 201
and person, distinction between, 62
in sacred laws, 9
and social exclusion, 177–8
as system of explanation, 19–20, 52–4
and tragedy, relation between, 3, 245–6
transgressive, 75, 82–4, 96, 105–8
ubiquitous in tragedy, 1–2
Polyneices
corpse of, 95–6, 108–9, 112–13
corpse of, differentiation friend vs. foe, 105
corpse of, location, significance of, 104–5
corpse, symbolic significance of, 109, 112–13
pollution emanating from corpse, 96
polyphony
of causation models in Eur. *Hipp.*, 45–6
of voices representing Athens (in Eur. *Ion*), 216
processions, and purity, 180
prophetic voices, important in S. *OT*, 62–3
purification
of the assembly, 181–2
by blood, 136
of the city, 30, 69
as 'civilising' act, 172–3, 191–3
corrupt, 32, 71
of the deme, 92, 177, 244
first recorded, 2
futile, 71–3
'illusionary', 159–61
as means of coping, 54–5
not enacted, 72–3
as precondition for release, 136–7, 138, 152
and social inclusion, 71, 177
of the theatre, 1, 244
through death, 133–4, 149–51
see also release (of Orestes)
purity
of Apollo, 222–3, 229, 230–1
of Argos, 191–3, 203–4
in Athens, Athenian, 180–2, 235–7, 241
of Danaids, 194–6, 197, 204
ethnic, 182–5, 214, 219–20

and intellectual clarity, 238–9
of Ion, 223–9, 231–4, 236
of space, and identity, 180–2, 191–3, 194–6, 202, 208
see also hagnos
Pythia, and Ion's identity, 225

rape, 230–1
release (of Orestes)
in Aeschylus
important topic, 135
purification rejected, 136–9
in Euripides
'illusionary', 160–1
rewritten in dialogue with Aeschylus, 169–71
scripted, 166–9
structure of, 151–2
uncertain, 154–6
religion
as 'system of explanation', 19

sacred and secular, 175–6
sacred laws
Cyrene cathartic law, 9, 69, 83, 137
Iulis (Keos), 9, 83
Kleonai, 9
Selinous, 137–8, 177
sacrifice
as part of purificatory process, 177
human, purificatory, 134, 149–51
self and other, 174, 186, 192–3, 199, 205–6, 207, 212, 236–7
self-reference, 161, 166–71, 241–3
see also metamythology
sexual purity, *see hagnos*
sexuality
and eating habits, 33
important in Eur. *Hipp.*, 33–4
'sharing lustral water', 176–7
sophia, poetic, 162
Sophocles
gods in, *see* gods: in Sophocles
irony in, *see* irony: in Sophocles
OT
comparable to fugue, 49
end of, 72, 73
space
in A. *Supp*
Argos, 189–90, 191–3
Danaids, 188–9, 194–6, 197, 198–9
overlaps, 190–1, 202
sacred, 190
in Athens
pure, 180–2
semantisation of, 179–82

space, *(cont.)*
  civic, defined, 75
  in Eur. *Ion*
    Athens, 218–19
    Ion, 225–7
    temple of Apollo, 221–2
  in S. *Ant*,
    civic, 88–91, 93–5
  in S. *OC*, 206
    purity of, and identity, 208
  see also boundaries; transgression
sphagion, sphagia, 107–8
stability
  as central theme in the *Oresteia*, 128–33
  in Homer, 74–5
  important for the civic community, 74–5
  and law, 76–82
  and pollution (general), 75, 82–4
  in S. *Ant.*, *see* boundaries; pollution: and categorisation; pollution: limited, defined; pollution: named; pollution: nameless; pollution: transgressive; transgression
strangulation
  as virginal death, 31
suicide
  and ritual disruption, 30
  as 'purification', 32, 107–8
suppliant drama, 186–7
supplication, 137–8
symptoms, *see* disease, symptoms of

theōria, *see* Theseus
Theseus
  ekdēmos, 37–8
  on inherited evil, 26
  not caring about pollution, 211
  theōria, 28–30
Thesmophoria, 33
Thucydides, and causation, 22–3
Tiresias
  naming pollution, 59, 63, 66
  not naming pollution, 96, 97
tithēmi, 81, 88, 128, 129
tragedy
  definitions of, 7–8
  Eur. *IT* as 'tragic', 145–7
  and pollution, relation between, 3, 245–6
  text and context, 13–15
transgression
  corpse of Polyneices, trangressive, 112–13

corpses transgressing, 105–8
  and Creon, 88–9, 93, 96–7, 105
  and Oedipus, 207
  pollution transgressive, 75, 82–4, 96
  (various) boundaries transgressed, 85–6, 88–9, 196–7, 218, 226, 230–1
  Zeus not impaired by, 93
transmission (of pollution), through words, 35
see also contagion

understanding of misfortune, 18–20
  characters struggling for, 23–4, 25–6, 45–6, 50–2
  provided by concept of pollution, 19–20, 52–4
  relating to Oedipus, 47, 56–8, 65–8

Valeri, Valerio, 11–12
virginity
  correlated to sacred space, 193–7, 198–9, 224–5
  and pollution, 199–200
  problematic, 187, 198, 233–4
  redefinition, from virginity to another *hagneia*, 204
  virginal body as 'walled' space, 188–9

walls, 74, 76–7, 179
wandering womb, 41
Whitman, Cedric, 238
women
  importance of, in *Ion*, 220–1
  'porous', 37
  see also gender, differentiation; body (female)
word play, 31–2, 51–2, 56, 57
Wright, Matthew, 147, 163
writing
  and law, 79–80
  and scripted performance, 166–7

Xenophon
  burial of traitor in, 92
  religious identity in, 176
Xuthus, as foreigner, 216, 217

Zeitlin, Froma, 40, 134, 228
Zeus
  and justice, 129
  and transgression, 93
  union with Io, 187, 188, 194, 196